Specification and Design of Embedded Systems

Daniel D. Gajski
Frank Vahid
Sanjiv Narayan
Jie Gong

University of California at Irvine

P T R Prentice Hall
Upper Saddle River, NJ 07458

Editorial/production supervision: *Harriet Tellem*
Cover design: *Wanda Lubelska Designs*
Manufacturing manager: *Alexis R. Heydt*
Acquisitions editor: *Paul W. Becker*
Editorial Assistant: *Maureen Diana*

Published by P T R Prentice Hall
Prentice-Hall, Inc.
A Pearson Education Company
Upper Saddle River, NJ 07458

Printed in the United States of America
10 9 8 7 6 5 4 3 2

ISBN 0-13-150731-1

Prentice-Hall International (UK) Limited,London
Prentice-Hall of Australia Pty. Limited, Sydney
Prentice-Hall Canada Inc., Toronto
Prentice-Hall Hispanoamericana, S.A., Mexico
Prentice-Hall of India Private Limited, New Delhi
Prentice-Hall of Japan, Inc., Tokyo
Pearson Education Asia Pte. Ltd., Singapore
Editora Prentice-Hall do Brasil, Ltda., Rio de Janeiro

CONTENTS

Preface

Rationale

In the last ten years, VLSI design technology, and the CAD industry in particular, have been very successful, enjoying an exceptional growth that has been paralleled only by the advances in IC fabrication. Since the design problems at the lower levels became humanly intractable and time consuming earlier than those at higher abstraction levels, researchers and the industry alike were forced to devote their attention first to problems such as circuit simulation, placement, routing and floorplanning. As these problems became more manageable, CAD tools for logic simulation and synthesis were developed successfully and introduced into the design process. As design complexities have grown and time-to-market requirements have shrunk drastically, both industry and academia have begun to focus on levels of design that are even higher than logic and layout. Since these higher levels of abstraction reduce by an order of magnitude the number of objects that a designer needs to consider, they have allowed industry to design and manufacture complex application specific integrated circuits (ASICs) in shorter periods of time.

Following in the footsteps of logic synthesis, behavioral synthesis has contributed to raising the abstraction levels in the design methodology. Behavioral synthesis, however, is used for the design of single ASICs. These ASICs, along with standard processors and memories, are used as components in systems whose design methodology requires even higher levels of abstraction. A system-level methodology focuses on the specification of systems in terms of computations to be executed on abstract data types, as well as the transformation or refinement of that specification into a set of connected components, including compiling software for standard processors and synthesizing hardware for custom components. To this point, however, in spite of the fact that systems have been manufactured for years, industry and academia have not been sufficiently focused on developing and formalizing a system-level methodology, even though there is a clear need for it. In order to manage complexity and shorten design cycles, industry has recently focused on developing a coherent system-level design methodology.

The main reason for emphasizing more abstract, system-level methodology is the fact that high-level abstractions are closer to a designer's usual way of thinking. It would be difficult to imagine, for example, how a designer could specify, document and communicate a system design by means of a circuit schematic with 100,000 gates, or a logic description with 100,000 Boolean expressions. The more complex the design, the more difficult it is for the designer to comprehend its functionality when it is specified with circuit, logic or register-level schematics. On the other hand, when a system is described as a series of complex computations that operate on abstract data types and communicate results through abstract channels, the designer will find it much easier to specify and verify proper functionality and to evaluate various implementations using different technologies.

It must be acknowledged that research on system design did start many years ago; at the time, however, it remained rather focused to specific domains and communities. For example, the computer architecture community has considered ways of mapping computations and algorithms to different architectures, such as systolic arrays, hypercubes, multiprocessors, and massively parallel processors. The software engineering community has been developing methods for specifying and engineering software code. The CAD community has focused on system issues such as interface synthesis, memory management, specification capture and design exploration. However, many problems still remain open, the most important of which are the lack of a universally accepted theoretical framework and the lack of CAD environments that support system design methodologies. In spite of these open problems, system design technology has matured to the point that a book summarizing the basic concepts and results developed so far will help students and practitioners in system design. In this book, we have tried to include ideas and results from a wide variety of research projects. However, due to the relative youth of this field, we may have overlooked certain interesting and useful projects; for this we apologize in advance, and hope to hear about those projects so they may be incorporated into future editions. Also, there are several important system-level topics that, for various reasons, we have not been able to cover in detail here, including formal verification, design for test, and cosimulation. Nevertheless, we believe that a book on system specification and design will help the electronic system design automation (ESDA) community to grow and prosper in the future.

Audience

This book is intended for three different groups within the computer science and engineering communities. First, it should appeal to system designers and engineering managers, who may be interested in ASIC and system design methodology, software-hardware codesign and design process management. Second, this book can also be used by CAD-tool developers, who may want to use some of its concepts in existing or future tools for specification capture, design exploration, and system modeling and refinement. Finally, since this book surveys the basic concepts in system design and presents the principles of system-design methodologies, including software and hardware, it could also be valuable for an advanced undergraduate or graduate course targeting students who want to specialize in computer architecture, design automation and/or software engineering.

Textbook Organization

This book has been organized into nine chapters that can be divided into four parts. Chapters 1 and 2 present the basic issues in system design and discuss various conceptual models that can be used in capturing system behavior and its implementation. Chapters 3, 4, and 5 deal with the languages used for specifying system functionality, as well as with the different issues involved in verifying a system's functionality through simulation. Chapters 6, 7, and 8 provide a survey of algorithms and techniques for system partitioning, estimation and model refinement, and Chapter 9 combines all of these topics into a consistent design methodology, including a discussion of the general environments for system design.

Given an understanding of the basic concepts defined in Chapters 1 and 2, each chapter should be self-contained and can be read independently. We have used the same writing style and organization in each chapter of the book. A typical chapter includes an introductory example, defines the basic concepts and describes the main problems to be solved. It contains a description of several well-known algorithms or solutions to the problems that have been posed, and explains the advantages and disadvantages of each approach. Each chapter also includes a short survey of other work in the field and some open problems.

At the end of each chapter we have included several exercises, which are divided into three categories: homework problems, project problems and thesis problems. The homework problems are designed to test the reader's understanding of the basic material in the chapter. To solve the project problems, indicated by an asterisk, the reader will need a more thorough understanding of the topic based on some literature research; these problems may require several weeks of student work. The thesis problems, indicated by a double asterisk, are open problems that could result in an M.S. or even a Ph.D. thesis if researched thoroughly.

This book could be used in two different courses. One course, for example, could concentrate on system specification, documentation, and verification, omitting the algorithms in Chapter 6, 7, and 8. A second course could emphasize design methodology and design-exploration techniques, omitting the material on languages and simulation. In which ever way it is used, though, we feel that this book will help to fill the vacuum in computer science and engineering curricula where we should be teaching system design techniques in addition to covering material on circuit and logic design, and computer architecture.

We hope that the material selection and the writing style will approach your expectations; we welcome your suggestions and comments.

Daniel Gajski, Frank Vahid, Sanjiv Narayan, Jie Gong
Irvine, California

Acknowledgements

We would like to thank all of our colleagues and students with whom we have discussed the basic problems in system design over the last six years. Without them, many issues would never have been clarified and many ideas would have gone unchallenged.

We would also like to thank those individuals who have helped us formulate the issues and focus the material to be presented in this book. In particular, we thank Peter Verhofstadt of the SRC and Bob Grafton of the NSF for encouraging research in this area, and Bob Larsen of the Rockwell International Corporation, who, over the years, helped us develop quality measures and objective methods for comparative analysis.

We would like to acknowledge Professors Nikil Dutt and Fadi Kurdahi of UC Irvine and Professor Sri Parameswaran of University of Queensland for their valuable insights during several meetings, and for pointing us to related works in system design. We would also like to thank Peter Fung of Matsushita Research and Development Laboratory for validating our design methodology. We extend our gratitude to the following members of the UC Irvine CADLAB for proof-reading and offering valuable suggestions to make this book more understandable: Smita Bakshi, Viraphol Chaiyakul, Tedd Hadley, Nancy Holmes, Pradip Jha, Erica Juan, Raghava Kondepudy, and Loganath Ramachandran. We would like to thank Sarah Wilde and Judy Olson for editing and patience in understanding difficult technical material. We are also grateful to Jon Kleinsmith for his assistance in coordinating authors and copy-editors.

This work was partially supported by the National Science Foundation (grants MIP-8922851) and by the Semiconductor Research Corporation (grant 93-DJ-146). The authors are grateful for their support.

Chapter 1

Introduction

In the past 20 years, there has been little substantial change in the actual sequence of steps we go through when designing a system. On the other hand, there has been a significant change in emphasis of the design steps: as the later phases have become more or less automated, designers have come to focus more and more on the earlier, more abstract phases of the system-design process. This shift in focus has enabled designers to create increasingly complex systems in shorter lengths of time. In designing such complex systems, achieving correct functionality is far more important and more difficult than minimizing silicon area or program-memory size. The system functionality, however, can best be understood during the earlier design steps, before a lot of implementation details have been added, and this is why these early phases of the process have become so crucial in system design.

In this chapter, we will explore this shift in emphasis from a number of angles, we will describe the steps involved in designing a system, taxonomize the types of design representations and abstraction levels at each step, provide a history of where design effort has been focused and how it has shifted, and describe the next shift to the system level that will likely occur, along with the tools and methodologies needed for that level.

1.1   Design Representation

For any particular product, the design process will always start with conceptualizing the product's functions, and will end only when we have produced a manufacturing blueprint. Before it is finished, many different people will have been involved in this process.

For example, the marketing department is needed to study market needs and to determine requirements for the new product. A chief architect is needed to convert those requirements into an architecture for the product. Technologists are involved in selecting the technology, the possible components and the suppliers, while computer-aided-design and computer-aided-software-engineering groups must either acquire or develop the tools necessary to support the design of the product, including each of its parts. A design team will develop the blueprint that indicates how to manufacture the product from the available components in the selected technology. The software engineers will write the code for the processors used in the product. The testing engineers are needed to develop test strategies and test vectors to determine the reliability of the product, while manufacturing engineers are needed to define the machine operations and to develop plant schedules for the actual manufacture of the product.

Each of these groups looks at the product from its own point of view, and requires specific information to support its particular work. Thus, each product, and consequently each design, must have several different representations or views, which differ in the type of information they emphasize. This is also true of single representations, which can acquire different levels of detail as the design cycle progresses.

The three most frequently used representations are those that emphasize the behavioral, structural and physical aspects of the product.

A **behavioral representation** views the design simply as a black box, while specifying its behavior as a function of its input values and expired time. In other words, a behavioral representation describes the system's functionality, but tells us nothing about its implementation; it defines how the black box would respond to any combination of input values, but omits any indications about how we would design that box.

A **structural representation**, by contrast, begins to answer some of these questions, as it serves to define the black box in terms of a set of components and their connections. In other words, this representation focuses on specifying the product's implementation, and even though the functionality of the black box can be derived from its interconnected components, the structural representation does not describe the functionality explicitly.

A **physical representation** carries the implementation of the design one step further, specifying the physical characteristics of the components described in the structural representation. For instance, a physical representation would provide the dimensions and location of each component, as well as the physical characteristics of the connections between them. Thus, while the structural representation provides the design's connectivity, the physical representation describes the spatial relationships among these interconnected components, describing the weight, size, heat dissipation, power consumption and position of each input or output pin in the manufactured design.

In general, the process of designing a system will proceed from a behavioral representation to a structural representation to a physical representation, gaining implementation details along the way. As mentioned above, however, while we need these details of the implementation in order to manufacture the product, they also tend to obscure the system's functionality, which can impede the designer in his or her attempt to ensure that the system functions properly. Consider, for example, a simple system which can add or multiply two 32-bit numbers. The behavioral representation would simply consist of two equations $a := a + b$ and $a := a \times b$. The structural representation, however, might consist of several interconnected registers, arithmetic units, and multiplexors, which could make the system's functionality difficult to discern, especially if the number of components is very large or if a particular component's functionality is only partially used. Thus, if we are to focus on the increasingly crucial problem of functional correctness, then we should recognize that designers will be more successful and create better products when working with behavioral representations as opposed to working with structural or physical representations.

Levels	Behavioral forms	Structural components	Physical objects
Transistor	Differential eq., current–voltage diagrams	Transistors, resistors, capacitors	Analog and digital cells
Gate	Boolean equations, finite–state machines	Gates, flip–flops	Modules, units
Register	Algorithms, flowcharts, instruction sets, generalized FSM	Adders, comparators, registers, counters, register files, queues	Microchips, ASICs
Processor	Executable spec., programs	Processors, controllers, memories, ASICs	PCBs, MCMs

Figure 1.1: Design representation and abstraction levels

1.2   Levels of abstraction

In the previous section, we described the most popular types of design representations: namely, the behavioral, the structural and the physical representations. At this point, then, we can move to the next stage, and note that in the design of electronic systems, each of these types of representation lends itself to several different levels of abstraction, or granularity. The different levels can be distinguished from each other on the basis of the types of objects they use, which fall into four categories: transistors, gates, registers and processor components. In Figure 1.1, these different levels of abstraction are summarized in relation to each type of representation.

According to the figure, the main components on the **transistor level** are **transistors, resistors** and **capacitors**. These objects can be combined to form analog and digital circuits that satisfy a given functionality. On this level, functionality is usually described by a set of **differential equations** or by some type of **current-voltage relationships**. Finally, a physical representation of such a circuit, called a **cell**, would consist of transistor-level components and the wires connecting them. Such cells often are defined in terms of their component layouts.

On the **gate level**, the main components are **logic gates** and **flip-**

flops. Logic gates are special circuits that perform Boolean operations, such as "or" and "and". Flip-flops are basic memory elements, each of which can store only one bit of information. These gates and flip-flops represent typical digital cells. These individual cells can be grouped and placed on a silicon surface in order to form arithmetic and storage modules, which can be described behaviorally by **logic equations and finite-state machine diagrams.**

The main components on the **register level** are arithmetic and storage units that are designed with gates and flip-flops, such as **adders, comparators, multipliers, counters, registers, register files, data buffers** and **queues.** Each of these register-level components is a physical object, having fixed dimensions, a fixed propagation time and fixed positions for its inputs and outputs on the boundary of the module. Register-level components are used in the design of microchips, which can be described by **flowcharts, instruction sets, generalized finite-state machines** or **state tables.**

Finally, the highest level of abstraction is called the **processor level,** since the basic components on this level are **processors, memories, controllers, interfaces** and custom microchips called **application-specific integrated circuits (ASICs).** One or more of these components can be placed on a **printed-circuit board (PCB),** where the microchips are soldered and connected by wires that are printed on the board. In order to reduce the dimensions of the board, a silicon substrate may be used to connect the microchips, instead of using the PCBs, in which case the package would be called a **multi-chip module (MCM).** The systems composed of processor-level components can be described behaviorally in several different ways, by using a natural language, by using an **executable specification** in a hardware description language, or, finally, as **algorithms** or **programs** in a programming language.

Now, it is important to keep in mind the fact that designers can only focus their efforts on the level at which the system is comprehensible to them, and that this level is largely determined by the need to keep the number of objects relatively small. For example, a designer might comprehend a system consisting of 10 Boolean equations, but certainly not one of 10,000 equations. In the latter case, he would have to keep moving to higher levels of abstraction until he reaches the point where the system can be represented by a manageable number of objects, such as by 10 algorithms. At the lower levels of abstraction, the system can be managed only when we divide it into small pieces and distribute it among a number of designers, or when we use automated tools to build it. Fortunately, as new design tools emerge at the lower levels, designers are free to focus on the higher levels, where decisions tend to impact quality much more heavily than at lower levels.

Inevitably, every electronic system will go through most of these levels of abstraction as it is taken through the design process, from conceptualization to manufacturing. The set of specific tasks in this design process, a particular order in which they are to be executed and a set of CAD tools to be used during the execution of each task is called a design methodology. In the next section, we will briefly discuss past and present design methodologies that have been predominant in industrial environments.

1.3   Current design methodologies

For the last 25 years, the majority of ASIC and system houses used a design process that was based on a **capture-and-simulate** design methodology. In this methodology, one starts with a specific set of requirements of the product, usually supplied by the marketing departments. Since these requirements would not contain any information about the implementation of the product, a small team of chief architects would then produce a rough block diagram of the chip architecture, that would serve as a preliminary, albeit incomplete, specification. In some cases, this initial block diagram would be refined further before given to a team of logic and layout designers whose task is to convert each functional block into a logic or circuit schematic that will finally be captured by schematic capture tools, and simulated to verify its functionality, timing and fault coverage. This captured schematic can also be used to drive the physical design tools for the placement and routing of gates in gate-array technologies, or it can be used in custom technologies to map gates into standard or custom cells before placement and routing.

It is only in the last few years that logic synthesis has come to be recognized as an integral part of the design process, and this recognition has led to an evolutionary change in design methodology, as the capture-and-simulate approach is steadily giving way to a **describe-and-synthesize** methodology. The advantage of this new methodology is that it allow us to describe a design in a purely behavioral form, void of any implementation details; specifically, we can describe the design using Boolean equations and finite-state machine diagrams. In this methodology, the design structure is generated by automatic synthesis using CAD tools, instead of by manual synthesis, since manual synthesis is very tedious for all but trivial circuits.

The describe-and-synthesize methodology can be applied on several levels of abstraction. On the gate level, functional and control units could be synthesized using **logic synthesis**. For example, functional units such as ALUs, comparators, and multipliers, can be described by Boolean equations, and then synthesized in two phases. In the first phase, called **logic minimization**, the number of "and" and "or" operators (or, equivalently, the number of literals) in the Boolean equations are minimized while simultaneously satisfying cost and time constraints. In the second phase, called **technology mapping**, these minimized Boolean equations are then implemented using the logic gates from the given gate library in a selected technology.

The control units, on the other hand, would be defined by finite-state machine diagrams, and then also synthesized in two phases. In the first phase, called **state minimization**, the number of states is minimized and a binary encoding assigned to each state so that the cost of implementing the next-state and output function will be reduced. In the second phase, the next-state and output functions defined by the Boolean equations are optimized through logic minimization and technology mapping, as described above.

On the register level, the microchips, which represent processors, memories and ASICs, can be synthesized using **behavioral (or high-level) synthesis** techniques. The structure of these microchips will consist of the functional, storage and control units that have been pre-designed and stored in a register-level library. The behavior of these microchips can be described by means of programs, algorithms, flowcharts, dataflow graphs, instruction sets or by generalized finite-state machines, in which each state can perform arbitrarily complex computations.

We transform such a behavioral description into a structural one by applying three major synthesis tasks: allocation, scheduling and binding.

The purpose of **allocation** is to determine the number of register-level components or resources that will be used in the microchip implementation. In other words, it determines the number of functional units, the operations executed by each unit, the number of pipeline stages, and the delay for each operation, as well as the cost and size of each unit. The allocation task must also determine the number of storage units, such as registers, register files, queues, and memories that will be needed, in addition to the size and cost of each unit and the number of ports it requires, and the access time needed for reading from and writing to each storage unit. Finally, allocation has to also determine the number, size, protocol, and delay of each bus in the system, and the various options for connecting the functional and storage units to these buses. In many cases, the task of allocation provides an opportunity to explore cost-performance trade-offs, which is an important consideration, since larger numbers of allocated resources such as functional, storage, and interconnect units, can improve performance, but also raise costs, in general.

Once resources have been allocated, the task of **scheduling** is intended to partition the behavioral description into time intervals, called control steps. During each control step, which is usually one clock-cycle long, data will be transferred from one register to another, and if necessary transformed by a functional unit during the transfer. All the register transfers in each control step are to be executed concurrently. Thus, the performance of the design is roughly proportional to the number of available resources in each control step.

It is important to note that the scheduling task may determine all the operations to be executed in each control step, but it does not assign them to particular register-level components. This job is performed by the **binding** task, which assigns variables to storage units and operations to functional units, as well as making sure that there is a particular communication path or bus assigned for each transfer of data from the storage units to the functional units and back again to the storage units.

By using logic and behavioral synthesis, the describe-and-synthesize methodology allows designers to describe a microchip's functionality with a behavioral description that is void of any timing, engineering or technological information, and then to synthesize automatically a structural description consisting of register-level components, which can later be synthesized themselves into gate-level components.

The significance of logic and behavioral synthesis is that, in the last ten years they have successfully converted the capture-and-simulate methodology into a describe-and-synthesize methodology. Logic synthesis was accepted by the design community first because designers found it easy to assimilate into the capture-and-simulate methodology, since this methodology was already focused on capturing and simulating gate-level schematics, or netlists, and thus, already had the requisite graphical capture tools, simulators, libraries and frameworks. In other words, it was clear that logic synthesis could add extra value to the capture-and-simulate methodology by optimizing its captured schematics. Once logic synthesis was established, designers began to use Boolean expressions to describe logic, instead of capturing the gates with graphic capture tools. Eventually, this new technique encouraged the practice of capturing a design through behavioral descriptions, instead of schematics, especially since the use of behavioral descriptions led to large increases in productivity.

The main reason it took longer to accept behavioral synthesis than logic synthesis was the lack of infrastructure available to support behavioral synthesis. In other words, there were no graphical capture tools on the register level, and designers were simply not used to capturing designs through hardware description languages, such as VHDL. The most fundamental problem, then, was that designers had been trained to think in terms of structure, not behavior, and this new approach would require them to address several new issues. For example, the first problem was that each design can be described in several ways, using different constructs in hardware description languages. Since the style of the description has a substantial impact on the quality of the synthesized design, behavioral synthesis would require an understanding of synthesis algorithms and the workings of CAD tools. Secondly, there were no component libraries with simulatable models for the register level of abstraction, so that each design team had to develop their own models. Finally, it was not until much later that exploration environments became available, in which a designer could make critical decisions and even partially specify the design before using behavioral synthesis tools for the rest of design. It was only gradually, as these issues were dealt with, that designers discovered large productivity gains by focusing on the specification of correct behavior, and then using automated tools to explore and compare the large number of possible solutions.

Now, after the successful introduction of logic and behavioral synthesis tools, system designers and the CAD community alike are questioning whether the describe-and-synthesize methodology might not be expanded to apply to complete systems, including software and hardware design. In other words, there is a possibility that productivity gains might be even higher if we continue this trend beyond chip-level design, and focus on even higher levels of abstraction. In the next section, we will describe the requirements and the essential issues for such a system-level methodology

1.4   System-level methodology

Design methodologies, in general, are not well established at the higher levels of abstractions. As we mentioned earlier, the marketing department usually defines market needs, while chief architects create informal block diagrams, from which a specification can be written after some preliminary design has been performed. The design decisions that lead to this block diagram, however, are usually based on a given designer's personal experience, rather than on a thorough exploration of all the possible architectural and technological alternatives. Furthermore, these block diagrams are usually created without a full understanding of the system's functionality. This kind of delay in defining the system's functionality oftens results in a design cycle which is longer than necessary, since inconsistencies that are discovered late in the process will require time-consuming design iterations.

Rather than approaching functionality in this ad-hoc manner, it would be preferable to devote more effort to specifying the system's functionality in the earliest stage of the process, before any design decisions have been made, since such early effort could lead to large overall savings. More specifically, there are great advantages to be derived from working with a specification, particularly an executable specification, since this would not only capture the product's functionality, but can also be used by marketing departments to study the competitiveness of the product in the market. In addition, an executable specification can serve as documentation during all steps of the design process, especially insofar as it fosters concurrent engineering, by clearly defining the functionality and the interface for the various subsystems assigned to various members of the design team. Furthermore, any change in any of these subsystems would be easy to incorporate, and its impact on other parts of the system could be rapidly evaluated. An executable specification is also amenable to the automatic verification of different design properties, as well as the functionality of the system. In addition, an executable specification has the advantage of allowing automation not just of functionality verification, but also of design exploration and design synthesis, once the proper technological decisions are made. Finally, an executable specification can also continue to serve as a starting point for all the product upgrades that occur during the life-time of the product, as well as supporting product maintenance.

Once we have adopted the concept of executable specification, the selection of a language for writing these specifications emerges as one of the main issues in a system methodology. Such a language must be easy to capture, to understand, and to use for interfacing with CAD tools. It must also be able to capture all the system's characteristics and allow the easy synthesis of their implementations. Finally, such a language should be able to model these systems and their implementations in a manner that is readable and complete, without being overbearing.

Language selection is not the only issue in defining a system design methodology. It is also necessary to assure that the selected system methodology allows an easy exploration of design alternatives once the system has been specified. In such a methodology designers must be first allowed to allocate architectural components and constraints. Architectural components are processors, memories and ASICs. Processors are defined by their instruction sets and the execution speed for each instruction; memories are defined by their sizes, read/write protocols and access times; ASICs are defined by their sizes in terms of gates (gate arrays) or number of transistors (custom design), propagation delays for gates or transistors, package size, and allowed power consumption, among other things.

The specification must then be partitioned into software and hardware parts. The software part will be implemented in software and executed on one or more of the allocated processors, whereas the hardware parts will be synthesized as one or more ASICs. The software part of the system can be further subdivided into two or more parts, each running on a separate processor. It is not difficult to imagine a host processor running the slower system functions and one or more coprocessors executing the faster data transformations. Similarly, the hardware part may not fit into one ASIC and might need to be implemented with several ASICs.

Since each different allocation of processor components and each different partition will produce one possible system implementation, evaluation of these various options will require designers to estimate quality metrics such as performance, cost, power consumption, testing and packaging costs for each implementation. Each set of estimated quality metrics is compared to the given requirements and the implementation that satisfies the requirements optimally is selected. Thus, this design exploration from the specification will allow designers to find the most cost-effective solutions.

Once the best solution has been found, the specification will need to be refined to reflect the allocation and partitioning decisions, such that the different pieces of the specification are moved to the appropriate components, and communication is maintained between the separated pieces.

After such refinement, the specification will reflect the product architecture, as did the block diagram created by the chief architect, with all the system components and the communications among them well defined, and with each component having its own specification, which can then be compiled by a standard compiler in the case of computations assigned to the processors, or synthesized with behavioral and logic synthesis tools in the case of computations assigned to custom ASICs. There are, of course, differences between the refined specification and the architect's block diagram: first, in that the refined specification has been obtained only after a thorough and organized exploration of a large number of solutions; and second, in that the refined specification, being derived formally from the original specifications, is far more likely to be consistent, eliminating the need for expensive, time-consuming design iterations.

1.5   System specification and design

In the previous section we have briefly described a system-level methodology that is based on the **specify-explore-refine** paradigm. The advantage of such a methodology is that it promises significant improvements in productivity, since precise specification, automatic exploration and refinement would help us to avoid long design cycles with many iterations. Such a methodology would only require designers to select technology, to allocate components and to specify requirements, before exploring automatically hundreds of design alternatives in a single day and then refining the specification by adding more structural detail as architectural and technological decisions are made. This process can be repeated until designers reach a completely structural description containing components at the proper level of abstraction, defined by the available component library.

We believe that in order to manage the increasing complexities of systems and the increasingly short time-to-market requirements, a clear and efficient system design methodology must be established and introduced into the design process. For this reason, this book surveys various techniques for specification, exploration and refinement of embedded systems. We begin with a brief survey of different models for capturing, analyzing and implementing software and hardware systems (Chapter 2). We follow this with a description of the basic characteristics of embedded systems, then survey several specification languages and compare them on the basis of how well they can support these characteristics (Chapter 3). To demonstrate the art of system specification, we develop a complete executable specification of a small embedded system — a telephone answering machine. We also demonstrate how the proper choice of a specification language can simplify the process of writing, understanding, and refining a specification (Chapter 4). In order to validate any executable specification, we need to verify it or simulate it in relation to predefined test vectors. In the latter case, the specification would need to be translated into some standard simulation language for which a simulator exists. For this reason, Chapter 5 surveys various translation techniques and demonstrates them using the IEEE standard VHDL language as an example.

The process of system exploration is covered by the discussion of specification partitioning and of the estimation of design quality metrics. In these areas, we survey various algorithms and techniques for specification partitioning (Chapter 6), as well as techniques for estimating quality metrics such as software performance, size of data and program memories, hardware performance, clock cycle duration, microchip area, and package cost (Chapter 7). After the system has been thoroughly explored, the specification will need to be refined to reflect those decisions that were made in the exploration phase. To this end, we survey various algorithms and techniques used for specification refinement (Chapter 8). In the final chapter (Chapter 9), we integrate the material in the first eight chapters into a consistent system level methodology and explain its role in the total design process.

We believe that this material will demystify the art of system design, and help readers to select the best system design methodology for their application and environment.

Chapter 2

Models and Architectures

The first step in designing a system is specifying its functionality, and, in turn, the first step of such specification would be figuring out exactly what that functionality should be. To help us understand and organize this functionality in a systematic manner, we can use a variety of conceptual models. In this chapter, we will survey the various conceptual models that are most commonly used for hardware and for software systems, as well as the various architectures that are used in implementing those systems.

2.1 Introduction

System design is the process of implementing a desired functionality using a set of physical components. Clearly, then, the whole process of system design must begin with specifying the desired functionality. This is not, however, an easy task. For example, consider the task of specifying an elevator controller. How do we describe its functionality in sufficient detail that we could predict with absolute precision what the elevator's position would be after any sequence of pressed buttons? The problem with natural-language specifications is that they are often ambiguous and incomplete, lacking the capacity for detail that is required by such a task. Therefore, we need a more precise approach to specify functionality.

The most common way to achieve the level of precision we need is to think of the system as a collection of simpler subsystems, or pieces. As the next section will show, there are at least five methods of decomposing functionality into these simpler pieces. Basically, what distinguishes these methods are the types of the pieces and the rules for composing these pieces to create system functionality. We call each particular method a **model**.

To be useful, a model should possess certain qualities. First, it should be formal so that it contains no ambiguity. It should also be complete, so that it can describe the entire system. In addition, it should be comprehensible to the designers who need to use it, as well as being easy to modify, since it is inevitable that, at some point, they will wish to change the system's functionality. Finally, a model should be natural enough to aid, rather than impede, the designer's understanding of the system.

It is important to note that a model is a formal system consisting of objects and composition rules, and is used for describing a system's characteristics. Typically, we would use a particular model to decompose a system into pieces, and then generate a specification by describing these pieces in a particular language. A language can capture many different models, and a model can be captured in many different languages.

The purpose of a model is to provide an abstracted view of a system. Figure 2.1, for example, shows two different models of an elevator controller, whose English description is in Figure 2.1(a). The difference between these two models is that Figure 2.1(b) represents the controller as a set of programming statements, whereas Figure 2.1(c) represents the controller as a state machine.

As you can see, each of these models represents a set of objects and the interactions among them. The state-machine model, for example, consists of a set of states and transitions between these states; the algorithmic model, in contrast, consists of a set of statements that are executed under a control sequence that uses branching and looping. The advantage to having these different models at our disposal is that they allow designers to represent different views of a system, thereby exposing its different characteristics. For example, the state-machine model is best suited to represent a system's temporal behavior, as it allows a designer to explicitly express the modes and mode-transitions caused by

"If the elevator is stationary and the floor requested is equal to the current floor, then the elevator remains idle.

If the elevator is stationary and the floor requested is less than the current floor, then lower the elevator to the requested floor.

If the elevator is stationary and the floor requested is greater than the current floor, then raise the elevator to the requested floor."

(a)

```
loop
    if (req_floor = curr_floor) then
        direction := idle;
    elsif (req_floor < curr_floor) then
        direction := down;
    elsif (req_floor > curr_floor) then
        direction := up;
    end if;
end loop;
```

(b)

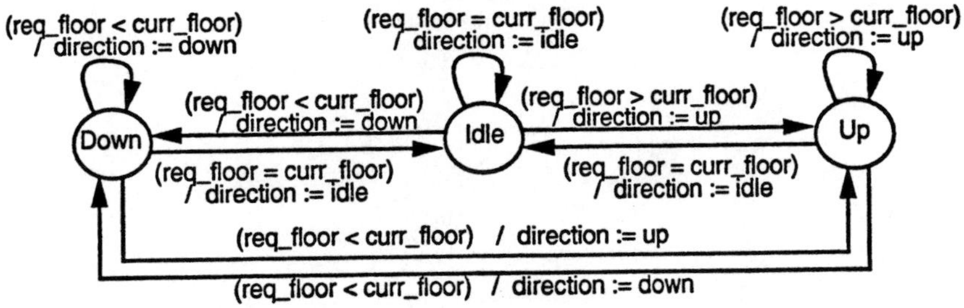

(c)

Figure 2.1: Conceptual views of an elevator controller: (a) desired functionality in English, (b) algorithmic model, (c) state-machine model.

external or internal events. The algorithmic model, on the other hand, has no explicit states. However, since it can specify a system's input-output relation in terms of a sequence of statements, it is well-suited to representing the procedural view of the system.

Designers choose different models in different phases of the design process, in order to emphasize those aspects of the system that are of interest to them at that particular time. For example, in the specification phase, the designer knows nothing beyond the functionality of the system, so he will tend to use a model that does not reflect any implementation information. In the implementation phase, however, when information about the system's components is available, the designer will switch to a model that can capture the system's structure.

Different models are also required for different application domains. For example, designers would model real-time systems and database sys-

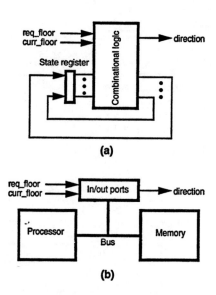

Figure 2.2: Architectures used in: (a) a register-level implementation, (b) a system-level implementation.

tems differently, since the former focus on temporal behavior, while the latter focus on data organization.

Once the designer has found an appropriate model to specify the functionality of a system, he can describe in detail exactly how that system will work. At that point, however, the design process is not complete, since such a model has still not described exactly how that system is to be manufactured. The next step, then, is to transform the model into an **architecture**, which serves to define the model's implementation by specifying the number and types of components as well as the connections between them. In Figure 2.2, for example, we see two different architectures, either of which could be used to implement the state-machine model of the elevator controller in Figure 2.1(c). The architecture in Figure 2.2(a) is a register-level implementation, which uses a state register to hold the current state and the combinational logic to implement state transitions and values of output signals. In Figure 2.2(b), we see a system-level implementation that maps the same state-machine model into software, using a variable in a program to represent the current state and statements in the program to calculate state transitions and values of output signals. In this architecture, the program is stored in the memory and executed by the processor.

Models and architectures are conceptual and implementation views on the highest level of abstraction. Models describe how a system works, while architectures describe how it will be manufactured. The **design process** is the set of design tasks that transforms a model into an architecture. At the beginning of this process, only the system's functionality is known. The designer's job, then, is to describe this functionality in some language which is based on the most appropriate models. As the design process proceeds, an architecture will begin to emerge, with more detail being added at each step in the process. Generally, designers will find that certain architectures are more efficient in implementing certain models. In addition, design and manufacturing technology will have a great influence on the choice of an architecture. Therefore, designers have to consider many different implementation alternatives before the design process is complete.

In the first part of this chapter, we will examine various models currently used in hardware or software design methodologies, showing how each model provides a view of the data, states, activities, and/or structure of a system. In the second part of this chapter, we will survey the various architectures that might be used in implementing these models.

2.2 Model taxonomy

System designers use many different models in their various hardware or software design methodologies. In general, though, these models fall into five distinct categories: (1) state-oriented; (2) activity-oriented; (3) structure-oriented; (4) data-oriented; and (5) heterogeneous. A **state-oriented model**, such as a finite-state machine, is one that represents the system as a set of states and a set of transitions between them, which are triggered by external events. A state-oriented model is most suitable for control systems, such as real-time reactive systems, where the system's temporal behavior is the most important aspect of the design. An **activity-oriented model**, such as a dataflow graph, is one that describes a system as a set of activities related by data or execution dependencies. This model is most applicable to transformational systems, such as digital signal processing systems, where data passes through a set of transformations at a fixed rate. Using a **structure-oriented model**, such as a block diagram, we would describe a system's physical modules and interconnections between them. Unlike state-oriented and activity-oriented models which primarily reflect a system's functionalities, the structure-oriented model focuses mainly on the system's physical composition. Alternatively, we would use a **data-oriented model**, such as an entity-relationship diagram, when we need to represent the system as a collection of data related by their attributes, class membership, etc. This model would be most suitable for information systems, such as databases, where the function of the system is less important than the data organization of the system. Finally, a designer could use a **heterogeneous model** – one that integrates many of the characteristics of the previous four models – whenever he needs to represent a variety of different views in a complex system.

It should also be noted that some methodologies use several different models together in order to represent different orthogonal views of the system. For example, the Statemate tool [HLN+88] incorporates three distinct models: (1) Activity charts for functional decomposition and information flow; (2) Statecharts for temporal behavior and control relations; and (3) Module charts for physical structure decomposition and information flow. Note that this kind of composite design model with separate views is not a heterogeneous model, since the information presented in the three different models can not be related to each other through a common data structure. In the case of a heterogeneous model, by contrast, we have a single tightly-integrated model in which different design views are derived from a single information model. Consider, for example, the control/data flow graph, which is considered a heterogeneous model since it accommodates two different views in one representation.

2.3   State-oriented models

2.3.1   Finite-state machine

A **finite-state machine** (FSM) is an example of a state-oriented model. It is the most popular model for describing control systems, since the

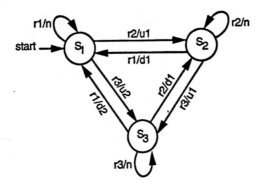

Figure 2.3: FSM model for the elevator controller.

temporal behavior of such systems is most naturally represented in the form of states and transitions between states.

Basically, the FSM model consists of a set of **states**, a set of **transitions** between states, and a set of **actions** associated with these states or transitions. More formally, a FSM is a quintuple

$$< S, I, O, f : S \times I \to S, h : S \times I \to O > \qquad (2.1)$$

where $S = \{s_1, s_2, \ldots, s_l\}$ is a set of states, $I = \{i_1, i_2, \ldots, i_m\}$ is a set of inputs, and $O = \{o_1, o_2, \ldots, o_n\}$ is a set of outputs; f is a next-state function, which determines the next state from the current state and input; and h is an output function, which determines the outputs, also from the current state and input. Note that each FSM has a state that is distinguished as the start state and a set of states distinguished as final states.

In Figure 2.3, we see an FSM that models an elevator controller in a building with three floors. In this model, the set of inputs $I = \{r1, r2, r3\}$ represents the floor requested. For example, $r2$ means that floor 2 is requested. The set of outputs $O = \{d2, d1, n, u1, u2\}$ represents the direction and number of floors the elevator should go. For example, $d2$ means that the elevator should go down 2 floors, $u2$ means that the elevator should go up 2 floors, and n means that the elevator should stay idle. In Figure 2.3, we can see that if the current floor is 2 (i.e., the current state is S_2), and floor 1 is requested, then the output will be $d1$.

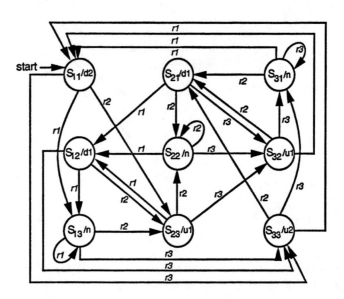

Figure 2.4: State-based FSM model for the elevator controller.

There are two types of FSMs that are specially well-known: namely, **transition-based** (Mealy) and **state-based** (Moore) FSMs, which differ primarily in the definition of the output function h. In a transition-based FSM, the output value depends on the state and input values ($h : S \times I \rightarrow O$); in a state-based FSM, however, the output value depends only on the state of the FSM ($h : S \rightarrow O$). In other words, the output will be associated with transitions in a transition-based FSM, whereas, in a state-based FSM, it will be associated with states. Note that the transition-based model was used in Figure 2.3 for modeling the elevator controller. By contrast, the state-based model for the same elevator controller is shown in Figure 2.4, in which the value of the output is indicated in each state.

In practical terms, the primary difference between these two models is that the state-based FSM may require quite a few more states than the transition-based model. This is because in a transition-based model, there may be multiple arcs pointing to a single state, each arc having a different output value; in the state-based model, however, each different output value would require its own state, as is the case in Figure 2.4.

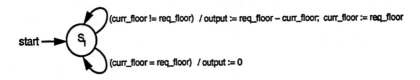

start → S_1

(curr_floor != req_floor) / output := req_floor − curr_floor; curr_floor := req_floor

(curr_floor = req_floor) / output := 0

Figure 2.5: FSMD model for the elevator controller.

In cases when an FSM must represent integer or floating-point numbers, we could encounter a state-explosion problem, since, if each possible value for a number requires its own state, then the FSM could require an enormous number of states. For example, a 16-bit integer can represent 2^{16} or 65536 different states. There is a fairly simple way to eliminate the state-explosion problem, however, as it is possible to extend an FSM with integer and floating-point variables, so that each variable replaces thousands of states. The introduction of a 16-bit variable, for example, would reduce the number of states in the FSM model by 65536.

This kind of extended FSM is called an **FSM with a datapath** (FSMD), to be specified as follows [GDWL91]: Define a set of storage variables VAR, a set of expressions $EXP = \{f(x, y, z, ...) \mid x, y, z, ... \in VAR\}$, and a set of storage assignments $A = \{X \Leftarrow e \mid X \in VAR, e \in EXP\}$. Further, define a set of status expressions as logic relations between two expressions from the set EXP, $STAT = \{Rel(a, b) \mid a, b \in EXP\}$. Given these definitions, an FSMD can be defined as the quintuple

$$< S, I \cup STAT, O \cup A, f, h > \qquad (2.2)$$

where, the set of input values has been extended to include status expressions, the output set has been extended to include storage assignments, and f and h are defined as mappings of $S \times (I \cup STAT) \rightarrow S$ and $S \times (I \cup STAT) \rightarrow (O \cup A)$ respectively. Using this kind of FSMD, we could model the elevator controller example in Figure 2.3 with only one state, as shown in Figure 2.5. This reduction in the number of states is possible because we have designated a variable $curr\_floor$ to store the value of the current floor, thus eliminating the need to allocate one state per floor.

In general, the FSM is suitable for modeling control-dominated systems, while the FSMD can be suitable for both control- and computation-dominated systems. However, it should be pointed out that neither the FSM nor the FSMD model is suitable for complex systems, since neither one explicitly supports concurrency and hierarchy. Without explicit support for concurrency, a complex system will precipitate an explosion in the number of states. Consider, for example, a system consisting of two concurrent subsystems, each with 100 possible states. If we try to represent this system as a single FSM or FSMD, we must represent all possible states of the system, of which there are $100 \times 100 = 10,000$. At the same time, the lack of hierarchy would cause an increase in the number of arcs. For example, if there are 100 states, each requiring its own arc to transition to a specific state for a particular input value, we would need 100 arcs, as opposed to the single arc required by a model that can hierarchically group those 100 states into one state. The problem with such models, of course, is that once they reach several hundred states or arcs, they become incomprehensible to humans.

2.3.2   Petri net

The **Petri net** model [Pet81, Rei92] is another type of state-oriented model, specifically defined to model systems that comprise interacting concurrent tasks. The Petri net model consists of a set of **places**, a set of **transitions**, and a set of **tokens**. Tokens reside in places, and circulate through the Petri net by being consumed and produced whenever a transition fires.

More formally, a Petri net is a quintuple

$$< P, T, I, O, u > \tag{2.3}$$

where $P = \{p_1, p_2, \ldots, p_m\}$ is a set of places, $T = \{t_1, t_2, \ldots, t_n\}$ is a set of transitions, and P and T are disjoint. Further, the input function, $I : T \rightarrow P^+$, defines all the places providing input to a transition, while the output function, $O : T \rightarrow P^+$, defines all the output places for each transition. In other words, the input and output functions specify the connectivity of places and transitions. Finally, the marking function $u : P \rightarrow N$ defines the number of tokens in each place, where N is the set of non-negative integers.

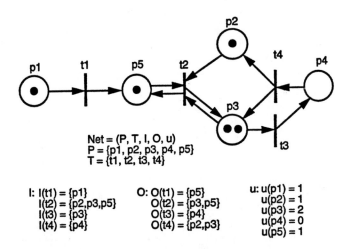

Figure 2.6: A Petri net example.

In Figure 2.6, we see a graphic and a textual representation of a Petri net. Note that there are five places (graphically represented as circles) and four transitions (graphically represented as solid bars) in this Petri net. In this instance, the places $p2$, $p3$, and $p5$ provide inputs to transition $t2$, and $p3$ and $p5$ are the output places of $t2$. The marking function u assigns one token to $p1$, $p2$ and $p5$ and two tokens to $p3$, as denoted by $u(p1, p2, p3, p4, p5) = (1, 1, 2, 0, 1)$.

As mentioned above, a Petri net executes by means of firing transitions. A transition can **fire** only if it is enabled – that is, if each of its input places has at least one token. A transition is said to have fired when it has removed all of its enabling tokens from its input places, and then deposited one token into each output place. In Figure 2.6, for example, after transition t_2 fires, the marking u will change to $(1, 0, 2, 0, 1)$.

Petri nets are useful because they can effectively model a variety of system characteristics. Figure 2.7(a), for example, shows the modeling of *sequencing*, in which transition $t1$ fires after transition $t2$. In Figure 2.7(b), we see the modeling of *non-deterministic branching*, in which two transitions are enabled but only one of them can fire. In Figure 2.7(c), we see the modeling of *synchronization*, in which a transition can fire only after both input places have tokens. Figure 2.7(d) shows how one would model *resource contention*, in which two transitions

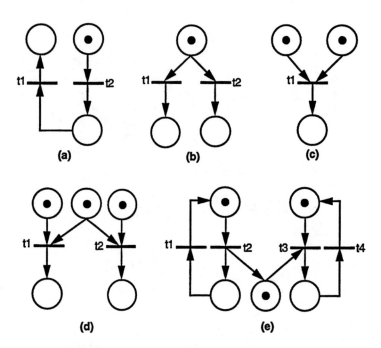

Figure 2.7: Petri net representing: (a) sequencing, (b) branching, (c) synchronization, (d) contention, (e) concurrency.

compete for the same token which resides in the place in the center. In Figure 2.7(e), we see how we could model *concurrency*, in which two transitions, $t2$ and $t3$, can fire simultaneously. More precisely, Figure 2.7(e) models two concurrent processes, a producer and a consumer; the token located in the place at the center is produced by $t2$ and consumed by $t3$.

Petri net models can be used to check and validate certain useful system properties such as safeness and liveness. **Safeness**, for example, is the property of Petri nets that guarantees that the number of tokens in the net will not grow indefinitely. In fact, we cannot construct a Petri net in which the number of tokens is unbounded. **Liveness**, on the other hand, is the property of Petri nets that guarantees a dead-lock free operation, by ensuring that there is always at least one transition that can fire.

Although a Petri net does have many advantages in modeling and analyzing concurrent systems, it also has limitations that are similar to those of an FSM: it can quickly become incomprehensible with any increase in system complexity.

2.3.3 Hierarchical concurrent finite-state machine

The **hierarchical concurrent finite-state machine** (HCFSM) is essentially an extension of the FSM model, which adds support for **hierarchy** and **concurrency**, thus eliminating the potential for state and arc explosion that occurred when describing hierarchical and concurrent systems with FSM models.

Like the FSM, the HCFSM model consists of a set of **states** and a set of **transitions**. Unlike the FSM, however, in the HCFSM each state can be further decomposed into a set of **substates**, thus modeling hierarchy. Furthermore, each state can also be decomposed into **concurrent substates**, which execute in parallel and communicate through global variables. The transitions in this model can be either structured or unstructured, with structured transitions allowed only between two states on the same level of hierarchy, while unstructured transitions may occur between any two states regardless of their hierarchical relationship.

One language that is particularly well-adapted to the HCFSM model is Statecharts [Har87], since it can easily support the notions of hierarchy, concurrency and communication between concurrent states. Statecharts uses unstructured transitions and a broadcast communication mechanism, in which events emitted by any given state can be detected by all other states.

The Statecharts language is a graphic language. Specifically, we use rounded rectangles to denote states at any level, and encapsulation to express a hierarchical relation between these states. Dashed lines between states represent concurrency, and arrows denote the transitions between states, each arrow being labeled with an event and, optionally, with a parenthesized condition and/or action.

Figure 2.8 shows an example of a system represented by means of Statecharts. In this figure, we can see that state Y is decomposed into two concurrent states, A and D; the former consisting of two further substates, B and C, while the latter comprises substates E, F, and G. The bold dots in the figure indicate the starting points of states.

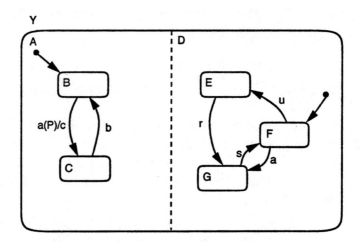

Figure 2.8: Statechart: hierarchical concurrent states.

According to the Statecharts language, when event *b* occurs while in state *C*, *A* will transfer to state *B*. If, on the other hand, event *a* occurs while in state *B*, *A* will transfer to state *C*, but only if condition *P* holds at the instant of occurrence. During the transfer from *B* to *C*, the action *c* associated with the transition will be performed.

Because of its hierarchy and concurrency constructs, the HCFSM model is well-suited to representing complex control systems. The problem with this model, however, is that, like any other state-oriented model, it concentrates exclusively on modeling control, which means that it can only associate very simple actions, such as assignments, with its transitions or states. As a result, the HCFSM is not suitable for modeling certain characteristics of complex systems, which may require complex data structures or may perform in each state an arbitrarily complex activity. For such systems, this model alone would probably not suffice.

2.4   Activity-oriented models

2.4.1   Dataflow graph

The state-oriented models we have been discussing are used mostly for reactive systems, in which the system's state changes in response to some external events. **Dataflow graphs** (DFG) [DeM79, Dav83, GDWL91], in contrast, are used mainly for transformational systems, in which the outputs are determined by a set of computations on the system's inputs. DFGs, then, have no states and no external events to trigger state changes. Rather, they simply consist of a set of **activities** (transformations) connected by a set of arcs that represent **data flow**.

More precisely, a DFG consists of a set of nodes and a set of edges. There are several types of nodes in the dataflow graph. One type of node includes **input** (also called source) and **output** (also called destination) nodes, which represent the input or output of data. A second type is the **activity** (also called process) nodes, which represent activities that transform or manipulate data. Such activities can be variously described by a program, a procedure, a function or one instruction, or even one arithmetic operation. The final type of node is the **data store** type, which represents different forms of data storage, such as records in a database, a file in an operating system, or a variable in a memory or a register. These various nodes in a DFG are interconnected by directed edges that are usually labeled in terms of the **data** being transmitted between the two nodes. This model supports **hierarchy**, since each activity node can be represented by another DFG.

A graphical representation of a DFG will generally use rectangles for input or output nodes, circles for activity nodes, and open-ended rectangles for data store nodes. Data flow is represented by arcs, labeled with the associated data. An example is shown in Figure 2.9(a). As we can see, this system consists of two activities, A_1 and A_2, the latter being further decomposed into activities $A_{2.1}$, $A_{2.2}$, and $A_{2.3}$. In this system, data X would flow from input to A_1, while data V would be computed by A_1 and stored in *File*. Data V' would then be taken from *File* and used as an input to A_2, in conjunction with data Y that was produced by A_1. Data Z and W are the output produced by A_2.

A dataflow model is valuable because it can be used in different application domains, or in different design phases of the same domain, simply by associating different objects with the nodes and edges in the graph. For example, in the digital signal processing domain, the nodes in the dataflow graph could represent **variables** and **arithmetic operations,** such as addition and multiplication, while the dataflow edges could indicate **data dependencies,** as in Figure 2.9(b). In this exam-

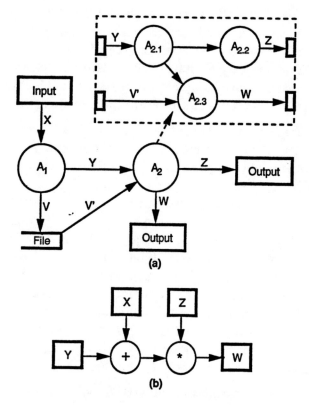

Figure 2.9: Dataflow diagram: (a) activity-level, (b) operation-level.

ple, operation '+' is dependent on data X and Y, and operation '*' is dependent on data Z and the output of operation '+'.

It should be noted that a DFG does not describe any other imposed sequencing beyond the problem-inherent data dependencies existing among its various activities. Furthermore, the DFG does not contain any information about its implementation. For these reasons, the DFG is often used during the system specification phase as a means of communication between designers and customers. We should also note that, since DFGs support hierarchical decomposition, this model is also suitable for specifying complex transformational systems. However, since this model does not express any of a system's temporal behaviors or control actions beyond its data dependencies, it is weak for modeling embedded systems.

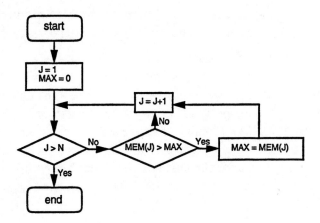

Figure 2.10: A flowchart representation of the max finding procedure.

2.4.2 Flowcharts

Flowcharts[Dav83, Sod90], also known as **control-flow graphs** (CFG), are activity-oriented models that are in many ways similar to DFGs, though they differ in their use of arcs. In a DFG, arcs are used to represent data flow, while a flowchart uses arcs to represent sequencing or **control flow**. Flowcharts also resemble FSMDs, in the sense that both emphasize the control aspect of a system, though they differ in the mechanisms that trigger their transitions: specifically, the transitions in an FSMD are triggered by the occurrence of external events, whereas the transitions in a flowchart are triggered whenever a particular activity is completed.

Basically, a flowchart consists of a set of nodes and a set of arcs. Among the several types of nodes are the **start** and **end** nodes, which indicate the beginning and end points of a flowchart. A second type is the **computation** nodes used to define data transformation through a sequence of assignment statements. Finally, there are the **decision** nodes, which are used for control branching. The various types of nodes in a flowchart are interconnected by means of directed edges, which indicate the order in which the nodes are to be executed. Graphically, a flowchart would use rounded rectangles to denote start and end nodes, rectangles for computation nodes, and diamond-shaped boxes for decision nodes. In Figure 2.10, there is an example of a flowchart, which computes the maximum of N numbers stored in the array MEM.

A flowchart is useful when we need to view a system as a set of sequenced activities, governed by a control flow. This model is suitable for those systems that have well-defined tasks that do not depend on external events. It can also be used to impose a specific order for executing the activities in a DFG when we need to supersede natural data dependencies. Since this kind of designer-imposed ordering would suggest a certain implementation of the system, flowcharts are used in this manner only when a system's implementation is well understood.

2.5   Structure-oriented models

2.5.1   Component-connectivity diagram

Component-connectivity diagrams (CCD) is a class of structure-oriented models which are used to describe a system's physical structure, as opposed to its functionality. Unlike DFGs or flowcharts, which represent a set of system activities connected by either data or control dependencies, a CCD represents a set of system components and their interconnections. In other words, it models a system's structural view.

A CCD consists of a set of nodes and a set of edges. The nodes represent various **components**, which are defined as structural objects with a defined set of inputs and outputs, such as gates, ALUs, processors or even sub-systems. The edges, then, would represent the various **connections** between these components, such as buses and wires.

Since this model allows us to associate different objects with its nodes and edges, a CCD can be incorporated in a variety of representation models. In Figure 2.11, for example, the CCD has been instantiated with three different levels of abstraction, producing a *system block diagram*, a *register-level schematic*, and a *gate-level schematic*. In the block diagram, the components are defined as system-level modules, such as processors, memories, or ASICs. Note that the connections between these components are only partially specified, since this diagram does not include detailed connection information, such as the width of the data bus and specific control signals. In the register-level schematic, the

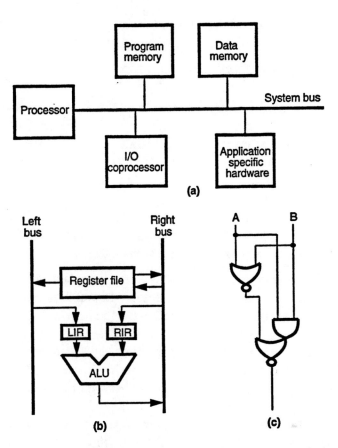

Figure 2.11: Structure-oriented modeling: (a) a system block diagram, (b) a RT-level schematic, (c) a gate-level schematic.

components are intended to represent register-level units, such as ALUs, registers, selectors or buses, and the connections define how data will be transferred between these arithmetic and memory elements. In this type of schematic, the control signals are usually not shown. Finally, the gate-level schematic uses gates as components, and in this case the connections between these components represent actual physical wires. In other words, data and control connections are completely specified.

Since the component-connectivity model is so well-suited to represent the system structure, it is often used in the later phases of the design process, when the designer wants to specify system implementation.

2.6   Data-oriented models

2.6.1   Entity-relationship diagram

A data-oriented model is very different from the state-oriented or activity-oriented models we have discussed so far, mainly because it focuses on representing data, as opposed to representing the activities manipulating the data. Data-oriented models are generally used in the design of information systems, since in this kind of system the organization of the data outweighs all other aspects of the design. An example of this kind of data-oriented model is the **entity-relationship diagram** (ERD) [Che77, Teo90], which defines the system in terms of a collection of entities and the various relations between them.

In an ERD, each entity is usually represented graphically by a rectangular box, while a relationship is represented by a diamond-shaped box. Suppose, for instance, we want to represent the information by means of which a department store orders different products for its customers. In an ERD model, we would need four entities: the *Customer*, the purchase *Order*, the *Product* and the *Supplier*, as shown in Figure 2.12. Next, we would need to represent the relationships between these entities, defined by the fact that customers request certain products, at which time the department store issues a purchase order to one of the suppliers who makes that product. In our diagram, these relationships are denoted as follows: *Availability* specifies all the suppliers and products they manufacture, *Requests* connect customers with the products they need, and *P.O. instance* connects a particular product with its particular supplier and customer order.

In this kind of diagram, each **entity** denotes a unique type of data that possesses one or more specific attributes. In the case of the department store, for example, the attributes of the entity *Customer* might be the name and address of each customer, while the attributes associated with the entity *Product* could be the name and price of each product. As a rule, each **relationship** reflects some "fact" relevant to its entities, as, for example, the relationship *P.O. instance* represents information about which customers want which products from which suppliers.

Since the ERD provides a good view of the data of the whole system, this model is particularly suitable when we need to organize the complex

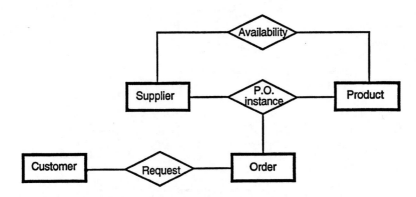

Figure 2.12: An example of entity-relationship diagram.

relations among various kinds of data. We must note, however, that the ERD model can not describe any of the functional or temporal behavior of a system.

2.6.2 Jackson's diagram

Another kind of data-oriented model is the **Jackson's diagram**[Sut88], which has its own particular advantages. Unlike an entity-relationship diagram, which tends to emphasize the attributes and interrelationships of the data it models, a Jackson's diagram models each individual data in terms of its **structure,** by decomposing that data into subdata. For example, a Jackson's diagram would be suitable for modeling a record that has several sub-fields. In fact, a Jackson's diagram is suitable for data that would need to be decomposed in a way that is much more complex than that appropriate for simple records.

The data in a Jackson's diagram is decomposed by means of a tree-type structure, in which the leaf nodes are the **basic** data types and the non-leaf nodes are the **composite** types of data that have been obtained through various operations like **composition** (AND), **selection** (OR), and **iteration** (*). Composition, for example, generates a type of data that incorporates two or more subtypes. Selection, on the other hand, generates its data by selecting only one of these subtypes. Finally, iteration generates data by replicating certain elements of its subtype.

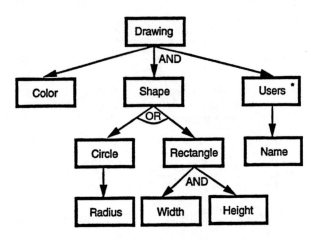

Figure 2.13: A Jackson's diagram.

Figure 2.13 shows an example of a Jackson's diagram, modeling a set of drawing objects. In this diagram, *Drawing* represents a composite type of data consisting of *Color*, *Shape*, and multiple *Users* indicated by the operation '*'. Further, each *User* type would consist of a *Name*, while each *Shape* type could be either a *Circle* or a *Rectangle*. Finally, the *Rectangle* type itself consists of two subtypes, *Width* and *Height*, whereas the *Circle* type has only one subtype, *Radius*.

A Jackson's diagram is most suitable for representing data that has a complex composite structure, as opposed to the ERD model, which is better suited to represent data that has complex interrelations. It should be noted, though, that the limitations of this model are similar to those of the ERD, in that it too would be unable to describe any functional or temporal behavior of the system.

2.7   Heterogeneous models

2.7.1   Control/data flow graph

The **control/data flow graph** (CDFG) [OG86, LG88] is a heterogeneous model, designed to combine the advantages of a flowchart (CFG) with those of DFG models. In other words, the CDFG incorporates

DFGs to represent data flow among activities, as well as a CFG, which can represent the sequencing of the DFGs. Thus, the CDFG model is able to explicitly show both the data dependence and the control sequence of a system in a single representation.

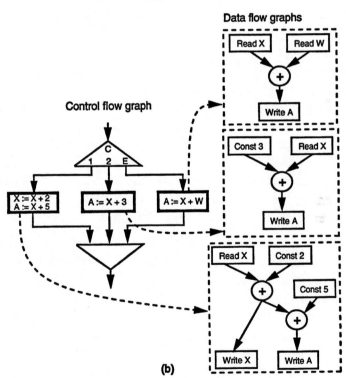

Figure 2.14: Control/data flow graph: (a) program code, (b) CDFG.

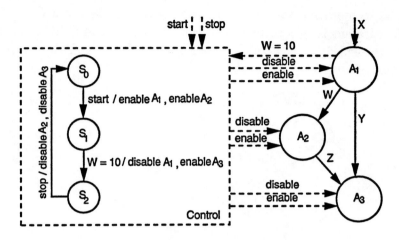

Figure 2.15: An activity-level CDFG.

In Figure 2.14(b), we see a CDFG representation of the program described in Figure 2.14(a). Note that the control constructs in the programming language, such as the *case* statement, have been mapped onto control-flow nodes, whereas the groups of assignment statements between these control-flow constructs have been represented by DFGs. Note also that the CFG and DFGs are connected by dashed lines, which indicate which activities in the DFGs are associated with which nodes in the CFG. Once the control enters a node, it will execute whatever activities have been associated with that node.

A CDFG is not, however, limited to represent the control constructs and assignment statements in a programming language. On the contrary, it can also be used to represent any complex activities and control actions required by a system, and it is frequently used in designing real-time systems. For example, the model presented in [WM85] consists of a DFG to which has been added a CFG, which is specified by a state-machine model. In this system, the CFG can respond to external and internal events, and can control the execution of the DFG by issuing control actions, such as *enable* to start an activity and *disable* to stop an activity.

In Figure 2.15, we see an example of an activity-level CDFG. According to this representation, when the CFG is in state S_0 and the event *start* occurs, activities A_1 and A_2 will be enabled and the system will then enter S_1. On the other hand, if it is in state S_1 and event $W = 10$ occurs, activity A_1 will be disabled, activity A_3 will be enabled, and the system's state will then change to S_2. Finally, if this system is in state S_2 and event *stop* occurs, activities A_2 and A_3 will be disabled and the system will return to state S_0. W, X, Y, and Z represent data flowing among the various activities specified in the DFG.

The primary advantages of the CDFG is that it corrects the inability of a DFG to represent the control of a system, as well as the inability of a CFG to represent data dependencies. Consequently, it appears complete and well-suited to many different design domains, such as real-time systems and the behavioral synthesis of ASICs [GDWL91].

2.7.2 Structure chart

The **structure chart** model [YC78], developed by Yourdon and Constantine, is another heterogeneous model, in this case designed to specify the data, activities and control accesses of a system in a single representation. With its comprehensive character, the structure chart is useful for designers who are working with programs.

Basically, the structure chart consists of a set of nodes, representing **activities**, and a set of edges, which represent the procedure or function **calls** in a programming language. The **data** passed between activities are indicated on the edges. The execution control of the activities themselves is described by means of a set of control structures, including **branch, iteration** and **subroutine call**.

Graphically, all the activities in the system would be represented by rectangles, and the data exchanged between these activities would be represented by labeled arrows. Structure charts further specify that the procedure calls between activities should be represented by arcs, a branch construct should be indicated by a diamond symbol, and an iteration construct should be shown by a self-looping arc.

In Figure 2.16, we see an example of a structure chart. In terms of the sequence of activities, we can see that the module $Main$ first calls the Get module to obtain data A and B. At that point, Get will call Get_A and Get_B in turn. The $Main$ module will then pass the data A and B to the $Transform$ module, which will either call $Change\_A$ to transform

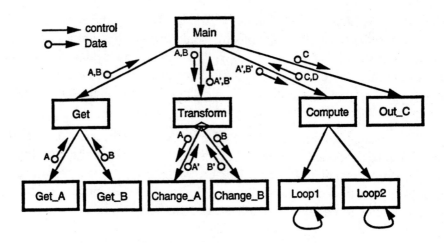

Figure 2.16: A structure-chart example.

A into *A'*, or it will call the *Change_B* module to transform *B* into *B'*, depending on values of certain conditions. After obtaining *A'* and *B'* from *Transform*, the *Main* module will pass this data to *Compute*, which will call two iterative modules, *Loop1* and *Loop2*. When these modules have completed their tasks, *Compute* will return data *C* and *D* to the *Main* module, which will then pass data *C* to *Out_C*.

As was the case with a CDFG, the structure chart can represent both control and data information. It should be noted, though, that the structure chart does not fully specify the sequence of execution. For example, we do not know the order in which *Get_A* and *Get_B* will be called, and the execution order of these modules is constrained by nothing more than the data dependencies. On the other hand, the structure chart model does provide constructs that can represent imposed control for branching, iteration, and procedural calls between modules. Because it can specify the order of execution to some extent, structure charts are used mainly in the preliminary stages of designing sequential programs.

2.7.3   Programming language paradigm

Like the structure chart, **programming languages** provide a heterogeneous model that can support data, activity and control modeling. Unlike the structure chart, programming languages are presented in a textual, rather than a graphic, form.

There are two major types of programming languages: imperative and declarative. The **imperative** class includes languages like C and Pascal, which use a control-driven model of execution, in which statements are executed in the order written in the program. LISP and PROLOG, by contrast, are examples of **declarative** languages, since they model execution through demand-driven or pattern-driven computation. The key difference here is that declarative languages specify no explicit order of execution, focusing instead on defining the target of the computation through a set of functions or logic rules.

In the aspect of data modeling, imperative programming languages resemble Jackson's diagrams, in the sense that they provide a variety of data structures. These data structures include, for example, **basic data types**, such as integers and reals, as well as **composite** types, like arrays and records. A programming language would model small activities by means of **statements**, and large activities by means of **functions or procedures**, which can also serve as a mechanism for supporting hierarchy within the system. These programming languages can also model control flow, by using control constructs that specify the order in which activities are to be performed. These control constructs can include **sequential** composition (often denoted by a semicolon), **branching** (*if* and *case* statements), **looping** (*while*, *for*, and *repeat*), as well as subroutine **calls**.

The advantage to using an imperative programming language is that this paradigm is well-suited to modeling computation-dominated behavior, in which some problem is solved by means of an algorithm, as, for example, in a case when we need to sort a set of numbers stored in an array.

A number of programming languages, such as communicating sequential processes (CSP)[Hoa78, Hoa85], ADA and VHDL, have been developed in order to support concurrent execution. These languages use different communication mechanisms. In CSP, for instance, communication between concurrent processes is accomplished by **message passing**, where data from one process is sent over channels to another process. In ADA, on the other hand, concurrent tasks communicate by means of a **rendezvous**, each task being required to wait at some synchronization point for data from the other tasks. Finally, in VHDL, concurrent processes communicate through a **shared memory**, wherein global signals can be read and written by the various processes.

The main problem with programming languages is that, although they are well-suited for modeling the data, activity, and control mechanism of a system, they do not explicitly model the system's states, which is a disadvantage in modeling embedded systems.

2.7.4   Object-oriented model

The **object-oriented model** [Boo91] evolved from the data-oriented model, and is characterized by its tendency to view a system as a set of **objects**. In terms of this model, each object would consist of a set of **data** and a set of **operations** for transforming that data. In certain respects, object-oriented models resemble real life systems consisting of entities, since each entity in systems usually has a set of well-defined operations through which it interacts with other entities and performs whatever services these other entities may require.

Object-oriented models have several features not found in other models. First, they are able to support **data abstraction** or **information hiding** by encapsulating data in each object and making it invisible to other objects. This capability means that when one object wants to change the data in another object, the former must request the service from the latter. Because of this requirement, the internal changes in one object will not affect other objects in the system. In addition, the object-oriented model is also able to represent **concurrency** in a natural manner, since any object that has been created as part of the system will continue to co-exist with the other objects through its life-time, executing its tasks independent of these other objects.

In Figure 2.17, we can see that, in addition to its objects, a system will also include a set of transformations, used to define the behavior of the system over time. As mentioned above, these transformations can not change data directly, but must rather request from each object the particular operations required for such changes.

Clearly, the object-oriented model has many advantages. Nonetheless, system designers sometimes find that, for systems in which sophisticated transformation functions are required, this model will not suffice,

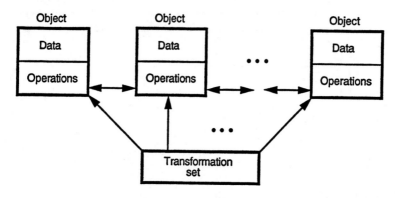

Figure 2.17: A system with objects and transformation functions.

unless it is supplemented by some other model that can adequately represent these transformations.

2.7.5   Program-state machine

A **program-state machine** (PSM) [GVN94, VNG91] is another instance of a heterogeneous model that integrates an HCFSM with a programming language paradigm. This model basically consists of a hierarchy of **program-states**, in which each program-state represents a distinct mode of computation. At any given time, only a subset of program-states will be active, i.e., actively carrying out their computations.

Within its hierarchy, the model would consist of both composite and leaf program-states. A **composite** program-state is one that can be further decomposed into either **concurrent** or **sequential** program-substates. If they are concurrent, all the program-substates will be active whenever the program-state is active, whereas if they are sequential, the program-substates are only active one at a time when the program-state is active. A sequentially decomposed program-state will contain a set of transition arcs, which represent the sequencing between the program-substates. There are two types of transition arcs. The first, a **transition-on-completion arc (TOC)**, will be traversed only when the source program-substate has completed its computation and the associated arc condition evaluates to true. The second, a **transition-**

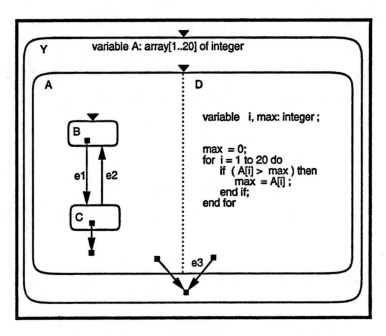

Figure 2.18: An example of program-state machine.

immediately arc (TI), will be traversed immediately whenever the arc condition becomes true, regardless of whether the source program-substate has completed its computation. Finally, at the bottom of the hierarchy, we have the **leaf** program-states whose computations are described through programming language statements.

When we are using the program-state machine as our model, the system as an entity will be graphically represented by a rectangular box, while the program-states within the entity will be represented by boxes with curved corners. A concurrent relation between program-substates is denoted by the dotted line between them. Transitions are represented with directed arrows. The starting state is indicated by a triangle, and the completion of individual program-states is indicated by a transition arc that points to the *completion point*, represented as a small square within the state. TOC arcs are those that originate from a square inside the source substate, while TI arcs originate from the perimeter of the source substate.

Figure 2.18 shows an example of a program-state machine, consisting of a root state Y, which itself comprises two concurrent substates, A and D. State A, in turn, contains two sequential substates, B and C. Note that states B, C, and D are leaf states, though the figure shows the program only for state D. According to the graphic symbols given above, we can see that the arcs labeled $e1$ and $e3$ are TOC arcs, while the arc labeled $e2$ is a TI arc. The configuration of arcs would mean that when state B finishes and condition $e1$ is true, control will transfer to state C. If, however, condition $e2$ is true while in state C, control will transfer to state B regardless of whether C finishes or not.

Since PSMs can represent a system's states, data, and activities in a single model, they are more suitable than HCFSMs for modeling systems which have complex data and activities associated with each state. A PSM can also overcome the primary limitation of programming languages, since it can model states explicitly. It allows a modeler to specify a system using hierarchical state-decomposition until he/she feels comfortable using program constructs. The programming language model and HCFSM model are just two extremes of the PSM model. A program can be viewed as a PSM with only one leaf state containing language constructs. A HCFSM can be viewed as a PSM with all its leaf states containing no language constructs.

2.7.6 Queueing model

The queueing model is somewhat different from the models described so far, in the sense that the latter are used mostly for system design, whereas the queueing model is used for analyzing a system, as, for example, when we need to find performance or resource bottlenecks in the system.

The distinctive feature of the **queueing model** [Gif78] is that it represents a system as a network of **queues** and **servers**. Arriving requests are stored in the queues while waiting to be processed by the servers. In Figure 2.19(a) and (b), we see examples of queueing models with single and multiple servers.

The value of queueing models is that they provide a basis for the kind of mathematical analysis often necessary to solve problems in a system. For instance, if we know certain characteristics of the system, such as number of servers, types of queues, interval between two consecutively arriving requests, and service time required by a request, the queueing

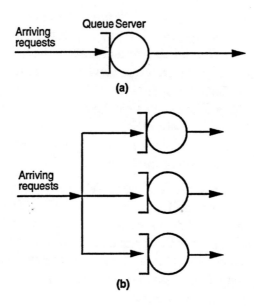

Figure 2.19: Queueing model: (a) a single server, (b) multiple servers.

model enables us to obtain further information about utilization (the proportion of time a server is busy), queueing length (the average number of requests waiting in a queue), and throughput (the rate at which requests pass through the server). Designers can then use this new information to locate any bottlenecks in the system.

It should be noted that different models can require different kinds of mathematical analyses. Some models, like those with a single server and a single queue, require relatively simple techniques, while others require more sophisticated techniques, and some are almost impossible to analyze quantitatively.

As an example, we analyze the model with a single server and a single queue. In order to perform the mathematical analyses to determine the system's behavior, we must know several of the model's parameters. For example, we must know the inter-arrival time between two successive requests, and we must also know the time required to serve each request. It is possible to model both of these times as random variables with well-defined distributions, as would be the case when we assume that the inter-arrival times and the service time are exponentially distributed. In such a case, if the mean interval between arrivals is λ and the mean service time is μ, then a stable queue can be achieved if $\lambda > \mu$, since this would prevent having too many requests waiting in the queue. If, however, $\lambda \leq \mu$, then the queue will be unstable, leading to infinite waiting times. The reader can refer to [Gif78, Laz84] for further analysis techniques used in queueing models.

2.8   Architecture taxonomy

To this point, we have demonstrated how various models can be used to describe a system's functionality, data, control and structure. An architecture is intended to supplement these descriptive models, specifying how the system will actually be implemented. The goal of an architecture, then, is to describe the number of components, the type of each component, and the type of each connection among these various components in a system.

Architectures can range from simple controllers to massively parallel processors. Despite this variety, however, architectures nonetheless fall into a few distinct classes, namely, (1) **application-specific architectures**, such as DSP systems, (2) **general-purpose processors**, such as RISCs, and (3) **parallel processors**, such as SIMD and MIMD machines.

2.9   Application-specific architectures

2.9.1   Controller architecture

The simplest of the application-specific architectures is the **controller** variety [GDWL91], which is a straight-forward implementation of the finite-state machine model presented in Section 2.3.1 and defined by the quintuple $< S, I, O, f, h >$. A controller consists of a register and two combinational blocks, as shown in Figure 2.20. The register, usually called the *State register*, is designed to store the states in S, while the two combinational blocks, referred to as the *Next-state function* and the *Output function*, implement functions f and h. *Inputs* and *Outputs* are

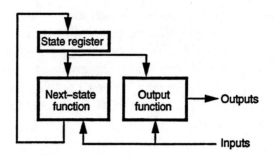

Figure 2.20: A generic FSM block diagram.

representations of Boolean signals that are defined by sets I and O.

As mentioned above, there are two distinct types of controllers, those that are transition-based and those that are state-based. These types of controllers differ in how they define the output function, h. For transition-based controllers, h is defined as a mapping $S \times I \to O$, which means that the *Output function* is dependent on two parameters, namely, *State register* and *Inputs*. For state-based controllers, on the other hand, h is defined as the mapping $S \to O$, which means the *Output function* depends on only one parameter, the *State register*. Since the inputs and outputs are Boolean signals, in either case, this architecture is well-suited to implementing controllers that do not require complex data manipulation. The controller synthesis consists of state minimization and encoding, Boolean minimization and technology mapping for the next-state and output functions.

2.9.2   Datapath architecture

Datapath architectures are used in many applications where a fixed computation must be performed repeatedly on different sets of data, as is the case in the digital signal processing (DSP) systems used for digital filtering, image processing, and video compression. A datapath architecture often consists of high-speed arithmetic units, connected in parallel, and heavily pipelined in order to achieve a high throughput.

In Figure 2.21, we can see two different datapaths, both of which are designed to implement a finite-impulse-response (FIR) filter, which

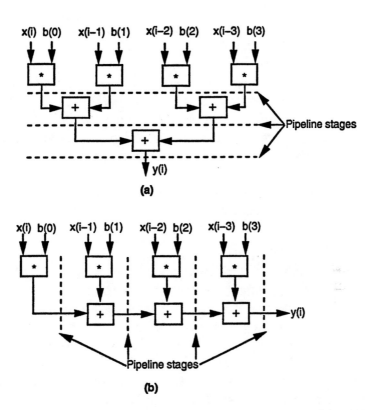

Figure 2.21: Two different datapaths for FIR filter: (a) with three pipeline stages, (b) with four pipeline stages.

is defined by the expression

$$y(i) = \sum_{k=0}^{N-1} x(i-k)b(k)$$

where N is 4. Note that the datapath in Figure 2.21(a) performs all its multiplications concurrently, and adds the products in parallel by means of a summation tree. The datapath in Figure 2.21(b) also performs its multiplications concurrently, but it will then add the products serially. Further, note that the datapath in Figure 2.21(a) has three pipeline stages, each indicated by a dashed line, whereas the datapath in Figure 2.21(b) has four similarly indicated pipeline stages. Although both datapaths use four multipliers and three adders, the datapath in Figure 2.21(b) is regular and easier to implement in ASIC technologies.

In this kind of architecture, as long as each operation in an algorithm is implemented by its own unit, as in Figure 2.21, we do not need a control for the system, since data simply flows from one unit to the next, and the clock is used to load pipeline registers. Sometimes, however, it may be necessary to use fewer units to save silicon area, in which case we would need a simple controller to steer the data among the units and registers, and to select the appropriate arithmetic function for those units that can perform different functions at different times. Another situation would be to implement more than one algorithm with the same datapath, with each algorithm executing at a different time. In this case, since each algorithm requires a unique flow of data through the datapath, we would need a controller to regulate the flow. Such controllers are usually simple and without conditional branches.

Normally, a datapath architecture would be implemented as an ASIC. A less costly solution would be to use one of the off-the-shelf DSP processors, whose datapath consists of a multiplier and an accumulator. This kind of DSP processor usually has an analog interface, with A/D and D/A converters on the same microchip. Also, it often has separate buses for instructions and data, so that instruction and data fetches can proceed concurrently, thus allowing a higher throughput. In some cases, it may have pre-programmed ROMs to perform standardized functions, such as Fourier transforms and digital filtering.

2.9.3   Finite-state machine with datapath

A **finite-state machine with datapath** (FSMD) is a kind of architecture that combines an FSM controller with a datapath, as shown in the block diagram in Figure 2.22. Note that the control unit contains a *State register* and two combinatorial blocks, representing the *Next-state function* and the *Output function*. The *datapath* itself contains functional units such as ALUs, multipliers and shifters, storage components such as registers and memories, as well as selectors and buses, designed to connect these various components. The *Control unit* inputs are the datapath's *Status* signals and outputs are the *Control* signals for controlling functional or storage components in the datapath. The datapath's *inputs* and *outputs* are connected to one or more memories that supply data for computation in the datapath and store the resulting data.

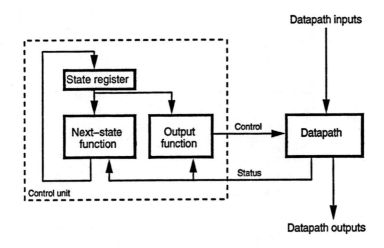

Figure 2.22: A generic FSMD block diagram.

As a general architecture, FSMDs are used for various ASIC designs. The FSM controller and DSP datapath mentioned above are two special cases of this kind of architecture. In addition, the FSMD is also the basic architecture for general-purpose processors, since each processor includes both a control unit and a datapath, in addition to data and program memories.

2.10 Processors

2.10.1 Complex instruction set computer

The primary motivation for developing an architecture of **complex-instruction-set computers** (CISC) was to reduce the number of instructions in compiled code, which would in turn minimize the number of memory accesses required for fetching instructions. The motivation was valid in the past, since memories were expensive and much slower than processors. The secondary motivation for CISC development was to simplify compiler construction, by including complex instructions that mimic programming language constructs in the processor instruction set. These complex instructions would reduce the semantic gap between programming and machine languages and simplify compiler construction.

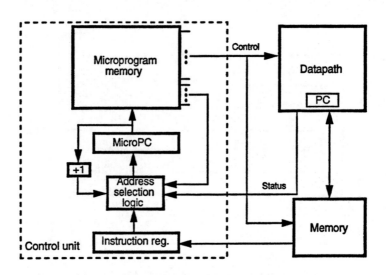

Figure 2.23: CISC with microprogrammed control.

In order to support a complex instruction set, a CISC usually has an equally complex datapath, as well as a controller that is microprogrammed, shown in Figure 2.23, which consists of a *Microprogram memory*, a *Microprogram counter (MicroPC)*, and the *Address selection logic*. Each word in the microprogram memory represents one control word, and contains the values of all the datapath control signals for one clock cycle. This means that each bit in the control word represents the value of one datapath control line, used for loading a register or selecting an operation in the ALU, for example. Furthermore, each processor instruction consists of a sequence of control words. When such an instruction is fetched from the *Memory*, it is stored first in the *Instruction register*, and then used by the *Address selection logic* to determine the starting address of the corresponding control-word sequence in the *Microprogram memory*. After this starting address has been loaded into the *MicroPC*, the corresponding control word will be fetched from the *Microprogram memory*, and used to transfer the data in the datapath from one register to another. Since the *MicroPC* is concurrently incremented to point to the next control word, this procedure will be repeated for each control word in the sequence. Finally, when the last control word is being executed, a new instruction will be fetched from the *Memory*, and the entire process will be repeated.

From this description, we can see that the number of control words, and thus the number of clock cycles can vary for each instruction. As a result, instruction pipelining can be difficult to implement in CISCs. In addition, relatively slow microprogram memory requires a clock cycle to be longer than necessary. Since instruction pipelines and short clock cycles are necessary for fast program execution, CISC architectures may not be well-suited for high-performance processors.

Although a variety of complex instructions could be executed by a CISC architectures, program-execution statistics have shown that the instructions used most frequently tend to be simple, with only a few addressing modes and data types. Statistics have also shown that the most complex instructions were seldom or never used. This low usage of complex instructions can be attributed to the slight semantic differences between programming language constructs and available complex instructions, as well as the difficulty in mapping language constructs into such complex instructions. Because of this difficulty, complex instructions are seldom used in optimizing compilers for CISC processors, thus reducing the usefulness of CISC architectures.

The steadily declining prices of memories and their increasing speeds have made compactly-coded programs and complex instruction sets unnecessary for high-performance computing. In addition, complex instruction sets have made construction of optimizing compilers for CISC architecture too costly. For these two reasons, the CISC architecture was displaced in favor of the RISC architecture which will be described in the next section.

2.10.2 Reduced instruction set computer

In contrast to the CISC architecture, the architecture of a **reduced-instruction-set computer** (RISC) is optimized to achieve short clock cycles, small numbers of cycles per instruction, and efficient pipelining of instruction streams. As shown in Figure 2.24, the datapath of an RISC processor generally consists of a large register file and an ALU. A large register file is necessary since it contains all the operands and the results for program computation. The data is brought to the register file by load instructions and returned to the memory by store instructions. The larger the register file is, the smaller the number of load and store

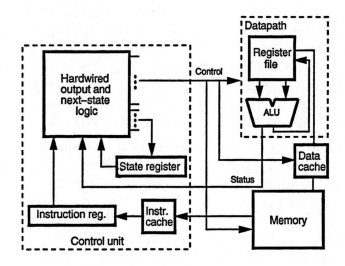

Figure 2.24: RISC with hardwired control.

instructions in the code. When the RISC executes an instruction, the instruction pipe begins by fetching an instruction into the *Instruction register*. The instruction is then decoded and the appropriate operands are fetched from the *Register file*. In the third stage, one of two things occurs: the RISC either executes the required operation in the *ALU*, or, alternatively, it transfers data to or from the *Data cache*. Note that the execution of each instruction takes only three clock cycles, approximately, which means that the instruction pipeline is short and efficient, losing very few cycles in the case of data or branch dependencies.

We should also note that, since all the operands are contained in the register file, and only simple addressing modes are used, we can simplify the design of the datapath as well. In addition, since each operation can be executed in one clock cycle and each instruction in three, the control unit remains simple and can be implemented with random logic, instead of microprogrammed control. Overall, this simplification of the control and datapath in the RISC results in a short clock cycle, and, ultimately, higher performance.

It should also be pointed out, however, that the greater simplicity of RISC architectures require a more sophisticated compiler. For example, a RISC design does not stop the instruction pipeline whenever instruction dependencies occur, which means that the compiler is responsible for generating a dependency-free code, either by delaying the issue of instructions or by reordering instructions. Furthermore, due to the fact that the number of instructions is reduced, the RISC compiler will need to use a sequence of RISC instructions in order to implement complex operations. At the same time, of course, although these features require more sophistication in the compiler, they also give the compiler a great deal of flexibility in performing aggressive optimization.

Finally, we should note that RISC programs tend to require 20% to 30% more program memory, due to the lack of complex instructions. However, since simpler instruction sets can make compiler design and running time much shorter, the efficiency of the compiled code is ultimately much higher. In addition, because of these simpler instruction sets, RISC processors tend to require less silicon area and a shorter design cycle than their CISC counterparts.

2.10.3 Vector machine

Vector machines were developed in the early 70s to satisfy a growing need for high-performance computing, which was obtained by reducing the clock to the minimum. Since the clock cycle was approximately one tenth of the duration of a memory access or arithmetic operation, designers used to implement memory and arithmetic units with many pipeline stages. In such a vector machine, memory is composed of many parallel blocks, and the data in all the blocks is accessed concurrently at the same address. In short, we could say that a vector of data is accessed in parallel. Each vector is transferred serially, to or from the *Vector registers* through the memory access pipeline (*Memory pipes*). Each vector instruction operates on two vector operands and generates one vector result. As shown in Figure 2.25, the vector machine also has *Scalar registers* and a *Scalar functional unit* for scalar operations.

The main advantage of vector machines is that they can be very fast, as long as there are enough vector operations in the code. We must note, however, that ordinary code was not written with vector machines in mind, which means that a vector machine will need a vectorizing compiler to optimize ordinary code for vector instructions. In general, such vectorizers work by decomposing the body of a loop into as many vector

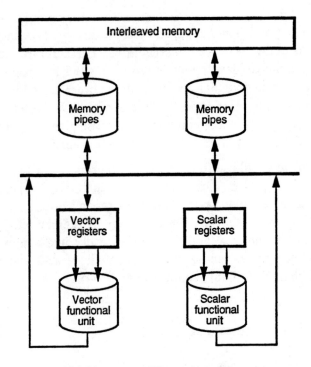

Figure 2.25: Vector machine.

operations as possible, each of which can be thought of as a loop with a single operation in its body. In addition, we should note that the performance of a vector machine tends to degrade during scalar operations and during access of arrays with non-linear indices.

2.10.4   Very long instruction word computer

A **very-long-instruction-word computer** (VLIW) exploits parallelism by using multiple functional units in its datapath, all of which execute in a lock step manner under one centralized control. A VLIW instruction contains one field for each functional unit, and each field of a VLIW instruction specifies the addresses of the source and destination operands, as well as the operation to be performed by the functional unit. As a result, a VLIW instruction is usually very wide, since it must contain approximately one standard instruction for each functional unit.

In Figure 2.26, we see an example of a VLIW datapath, consisting of

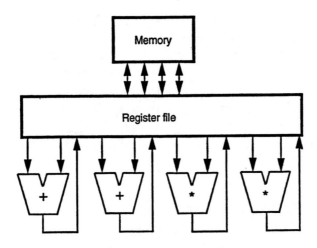

Figure 2.26: An example of VLIW datapath.

four functional units: namely, two ALUs and two multipliers, a register file and a memory. In order to utilize all the four functional units, the register file in this example has 16 ports: eight output ports, which supply operands to the functional units, four input ports, which store the results obtained from functional units, and four input/output ports, designed to allow communication with the memory. What is interesting to note here is that, ideally, the VLIW in Figure 2.26 would provide four times the performance we could get from a processor with a single functional unit, under the assumption that the code executing on the VLIW had four-way parallelism, which enables the VLIW to execute four independent instructions in each clock cycle. In reality, however, most code has a large amount of parallelism interleaved with code that is fundamentally serial. As a result, a VLIW with a large number of functional units might not be fully utilized. The ideal conditions would also require us to assume that all the operands were in the register file, with 8 operands being fetched and four results stored back on every clock cycle, in addition to four new operands being brought from the memory to be available for use in the next clock cycle. It must be noted, however, that this computation profile is not easy to achieve, since some results must be stored back to memory and some results may not be needed in the next clock cycle. Under these conditions, the efficiency of a VLIW datapath might be less than ideal.

Finally, we should point out that there are two technological limitation that can affect the implementation of a VLIW architecture. First, while register files with 8–16 ports can be built, the efficiency and performance of such register files tend to degrade quickly when we go beyond that number. Second, since VLIW program and data memories require a high communication bandwidth, these systems tend to require expensive high-pin packaging technology as well. Overall, these are the reasons why VLIW architectures are not as popular as RISC architectures.

2.11   Parallel processors

In the design of **parallel processors**, we can take advantage of spatial parallelism by using multiple processing elements (PEs) that work concurrently. In this type of architecture, each PE may contain its own datapath with registers and a local memory. Two typical types of parallel processors are the **SIMD** (single instruction multiple data) and the **MIMD** (multiple instruction multiple data) processors.

In SIMD processors, usually called **array processors**, all of the PEs execute the same instruction in a lock step manner. To broadcast the instructions to all the PEs and to control their execution, we generally use a single global controller. Usually, an array processor is attached to a host processor, which means that it can be thought of as a kind of hardware accelerator for tasks that are computationally intensive. In such cases, the host processor would load the data into each PE, and then collect the results after the computations are finished. When it is necessary, PEs can also communicate directly with their nearest neighbors.

The primary advantage of array processors is that they are very convenient for computations that can be naturally mapped on a rectangular grid, as in the case of image processing, where an image is decomposed into pixels on a rectangular grid, or in the case of weather forecasting, where the surface of the globe is decomposed into n-by-n-mile squares. Programming one grid point in the rectangular array processor is quite easy, since all the PEs execute the same instruction stream. However, programming any data routing through the array is very difficult, since the programmer would have to be aware of all the positions of each data for every clock cycle. For this reason, problems, like matrix triangula-

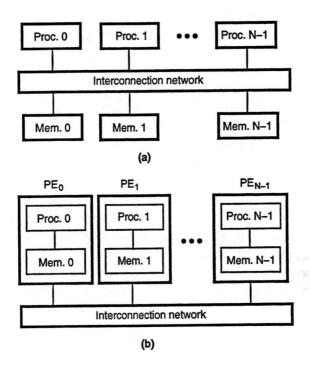

Figure 2.27: Multiprocessor communication using: (a) shared memory, (b) message passing.

tions or inversions, are difficult to program on an array processor.

Array processors, then, are easy to build and easy to program, but only when the natural structure of the problem matches the topology of the array processor. As a result, they can not be considered general purpose machines, because users have difficulty writing programs for general classes of problems.

An MIMD processor, usually called a **multiprocessor system**, differs from an SIMD in that each PE executes its own instruction stream. In this kind of architecture, the program can be loaded by a host processor, or each processor can load its own program from a shared memory. Each processor can communicate with every other processor within the multiprocessor system, using one of the two communication mechanisms shown in Figure 2.27. In a **shared-memory** multiprocessor, all the processors are connected to a shared memory through an N-port $\times$ N-port interconnection network, which means that each processor can access any data in the shared memory. In a **message-passing** multiprocessor, on the other hand, each processor tends to have a large local memory, and sends data to other processors in the form of messages through an interconnection network. The interconnection network for a shared memory must be fast, since it is very frequently used to communicate small amounts of data, like a single word. In contrast, the interconnection network used for message passing tends to be much slower, since it is used less frequently and communicates long messages, including many words of data. Because of their speed, the interconnection networks used for shared memory are much more difficult to design than message passing networks. Finally, it should be noted that multiprocessors are much easier to program, since they are task-oriented instead of instruction-oriented. Each task runs independently and can be synchronized after completion, if necessary. Thus, multiprocessors make program and data partitioning, code parallelization and compilation much simpler than array processors.

2.12 Conclusion

In this chapter we have discussed the various models that can be used to represent systems, as well as the various architectures that can be used to implement systems. Both models and architectures are crucial to the design process, since the whole aim of this process is to implement a desired functionality, as specified in the model, by means of a set of physical components, provided in the architecture. More importantly, this chapter has also shown how different models tend to focus on different aspects of a system, emphasizing its states, activities, data or control. Given this selective focus, it is crucial that the designer chooses a model that is appropriate to represent the most important features of the system under design. Furthermore, since a good language is measured by how directly it captures the desired model, it is equally crucial that the designer choose a language that is appropriate to this model. Interestingly enough, however, the languages most commonly used for specification often do not directly capture the best model for a given system. This problem, then, will be the subject of the next three chapters, in which we will consider the reasons, consequences and remedies for such situations.

2.13 Exercises

1. A system may be conceptualized using different models, such as a state machine, flowchart, algorithm, etc. Discuss the kind of conceptual models that are best suited for each of the following:

   (a) a modulo-10 counter,
   (b) a telephone answering machine,
   (c) an algorithm that finds the median of a set of numbers,
   (d) a temperature controller,
   (e) a communication protocol for accessing a memory, and
   (f) a microprocessor.

2. What are the advantages of hierarchical FSMs over traditional "flat" FSMs ?

3. How does an object-oriented model differ from a data-oriented model and an activity-oriented model?

4. List all the differences between a flowchart and a structure chart. Use a flowchart to represent the structure chart in Figure 2.16.

5. List the advantages and disadvantages of RISC and CISC architectures.

6. Define the most efficient architecture for implementing each of the conceptual models.

7. Specify each architecture as a subset or extension of the FSMD architecture.

8. Describe the differences between general-purpose and application-specific architectures.

9. What is the difference among operation pipeline, datapath pipeline, instruction pipeline, and control pipeline?

10. List the technological barriers for the scalability of each architecture.

11. What are the essential issues in design and manufacturing interconnection networks?

Chapter 3

Specification Languages

In the previous chapter, we saw how various conceptual models could be used to understand, organize and define a system's functionality. However, since a model is basically a theoretical concept, we need to use system specification languages to capture these models in a concrete form. In this chapter, we will describe some of the common characteristics of various models and consider how some of the more common specification languages can capture these characteristics. In particular, we will focus on the models and languages that work best for embedded systems.

3.1 Introduction

A system can be described at any one of several distinct levels of abstraction, each of which serves a particular purpose. By describing a system at the logic level, for example, designers can capture the structure of the system with schematic entry tools. Alternatively, at the system-component level, a hardware description language (HDL) would allow the designer to describe the functionality of each component without requiring the specification of any structural details. Such a system-component description might represent, for example, custom hardware, a memory or a processor executing a set of instructions. Finally, at the conceptual level, it is possible to describe the entire system's functionality without any notion of system components. Traditionally, we would describe a new product's functionality at the conceptual level, using a natural language such as

English. However, as today's systems become more complex, they tend to require a new approach to system conceptualization; Increasingly, designers need to describe the system's conceptual view in terms of an **executable specification** language, which is capable of capturing the functionality of the system in a machine-readable and simulatable form.

Such an approach has several advantages. First, simulating an executable specification allows the designer to verify the correctness of the system's intended functionality. In the traditional approach, which started with a natural-language specification, such verification would not be possible until enough of the design had been completed to obtain a simulatable system description (usually gate-level schematics). The second advantage of this new approach is that the specification can serve as an input to synthesis tools, which, in turn, can be used to obtain an implementation of the system, ultimately reducing design times by a significant amount. Third, such a specification can serve as comprehensive documentation, providing an unambiguous description of the system's intended functionality. Finally, it also serves as a good medium for the exchange of design information among various users and tools. As a result, some of the problems associated with system integration can be minimized, since this approach would emphasize well-defined system components that could be designed independently by different designers.

In Chapter 2, we introduced several models that are commonly used for conceptualizing various classes of systems. In relation to these conceptual models, it should be clear that the goal of any language is to capture the conceptual view of the system with a minimum of effort on the part of the designer. For example, the C++ programming language would be most useful when we want to capture an object-oriented conceptual model of the software, but the Statecharts [Har87] language would be more useful if the goal is to specify a hierarchical/concurrent finite-state machine model.

Since different conceptual models possess different characteristics, any given specification language can be well or poorly suited for that model, depending on whether it supports all or a few of the model's characteristics. To find the language that can capture a given conceptual model directly, we would need to establish a one-to-one correlation between the characteristics of the conceptual model and the constructs in the language.

In this chapter, we will begin by describing some of the characteristics commonly found in conceptual design models. We will then turn to the characteristics of one particular class of systems – **embedded systems**. At this point, we will analyze some of the common hardware description languages, such as VHDL, Verilog, HardwareC, Communicating Sequential Processes (CSP), Statecharts, Specification and Description Language (SDL), Silage and Esterel, focussing on how well they support the characteristics of embedded systems. Finally, we will introduce the SpecCharts language, which is based on the program-state machine model introduced in Chapter 2, and demonstrate how well it supports the specification of embedded systems.

3.2 Characteristics of conceptual models

In this section, we will present some of the characteristics most commonly found in conceptual models used by designers. In presenting these characteristics, part of our goal will be to assess how useful each characteristic is in conceptualizing one or more types of system behavior.

3.2.1 Concurrency

Any system can be decomposed into chunks of functionality called **behaviors**, each of which can be represented in several ways, such as a process, procedure or state machine. In many cases, the functionality of a system is most easily conceptualized as a set of concurrent behaviors, simply because representing such systems using only sequential constructs would result in complex descriptions that can be difficult to comprehend. If we can find a way to capture concurrency, however, we can usually obtain a more natural representation of such systems. For example, consider a system with only two concurrent behaviors that can be individually represented by the finite-state machines F_1 and F_2. A sequential representation of the system would be a cross product of the two finite-state machines, $F_1 \times F_2$, potentially resulting in a large number of states. A more elegant solution, then, would be to use a conceptual model that has two or more concurrent finite-state machines, as do the Statecharts [Har87] and PSM [GVN93] models.

The concept of concurrency can be applied at any one of several levels of abstraction [HB85]. **Job-level** concurrency, for instance, refers to the parallel execution of several jobs by means of mechanisms like multiprogramming, multiprocessing and time sharing. Concurrency at the **task-level**, in contrast, involves the simultaneous execution of the several tasks that comprise a job. Most systems are conceptualized at this level, with each task in the system being represented by a behavior. **Statement-level** concurrency refers to the parallel execution of the statements in a task. An example of statement-level concurrency would be the execution of the statements in a loop on a vector processor. Beyond this, there is **operation-level** concurrency, which involves the concurrent execution of several operations in the system. For example, an addition operation may be executed concurrently with a multiplication operation. Operation-level concurrency is usually found in processors, filters and digital signal processors. Finally, concurrency can also exist at a **bit-level** granularity, as in the case of the bit-wise computation performed inside an ALU.

Concurrency representations can be classified into two groups, data-driven or control-driven, depending on the ordering of actions in a behavior.

Data-driven concurrency

Some behaviors can be clearly described as sets of operations or statements without specifying any explicit ordering for their execution. In a case like this, the order of execution would be determined only by data dependencies between them. In other words, each operation will perform a computation on input data, and then output new data, which will, in turn, be input to other operations. Operation executions in such **dataflow** descriptions depend only upon the availability of data, rather than upon the physical location of the operation or statement in the specification. Dataflow representations are characterized by the **single assignment rule**, which means that each variable can appear exactly once on the left hand side of an assignment statement.

Consider, for example, the assignment statements in Figure 3.1(a). As in any other data-driven execution, it is of little consequence that the assignment to p follows the statement that uses the value of p to

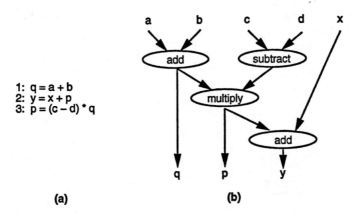

Figure 3.1: Data-driven concurrency: (a) dataflow statements, (b) dataflow graph for the execution of the operations.

compute the value of y. Regardless of the sequence of the statements, the operations will be executed solely as determined by availability of data, as shown in the dataflow graph of Figure 3.1(b). Following this principle, we can see that, since a, b, c and d are primary inputs, the add and subtract operations of statements 1 and 3 will be carried out first. Then the results of these two computations will provide the data required for the multiplication in statement 3. Finally, the addition in statement 2 will be performed to compute y.

An example of a system which exhibits data-driven concurrency is a digital signal processing system, which operates on continuous streams of data samples. It should be noted, however, that such systems may require additional storage, in case some data samples in the stream are required by future computations.

Control-driven concurrency

The key concept in control-driven concurrency is the control thread, which can be defined as a set of operations in the system that must be executed sequentially. As mentioned above, in data-driven concurrency, it is the dependencies between operations that determine the execution order. In control-driven concurrency, by contrast, it is the control thread or threads that determine the order of execution. In other words, control-

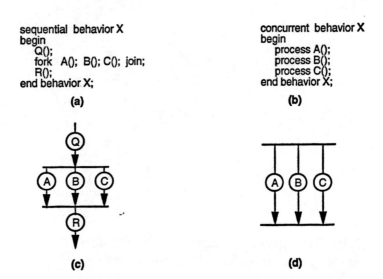

```
sequential behavior X              concurrent behavior X
begin                              begin
    Q();                               process A();
    fork  A(); B(); C(); join;         process B();
    R();                               process C();
end behavior X;                    end behavior X;

        (a)                                (b)
```

Figure 3.2: Control-driven concurrency: (a) fork-join statement, (b) process statement, (c) control threads for fork-join statements, (d) control threads for process statement.

driven concurrency is characterized by the use of explicit constructs that specify multiple threads of control, all of which execute in parallel.

Control-driven concurrency can be specified at the task level and the statement level. At the task level, constructs such as fork-joins and processes can be used to specify concurrent execution of operations. Specifically, a **fork** statement creates a set of concurrent control threads, while a **join** statement waits for the previously forked control threads to terminate. The fork statement in Figure 3.2(a), for example, spawns three control threads A, B and C, all of which execute concurrently. The corresponding join statement must wait until all three threads have terminated, after which the statements in R can be executed. In Figure 3.2(b), we can see how process statements are used to specify concurrency. Note that, while a fork-join statement starts from a single control thread and splits it into several concurrent threads as shown in Figure 3.2(c), a process statement represents the behavior as a set of concurrent threads, as shown in Figure 3.2(d). For example, the **process** statements of Figure 3.2(b) create three processes A, B and C, each representing a different control thread. Both fork-join and process statements may be nested, and both approaches are equivalent to each other in the sense that a fork-join can be implemented using nested processes and vice versa.

At the statement level, concurrency can be specified in one of two ways. In explicitly specified statement-level concurrency, special constructs are used to indicate that several statements are to be executed in parallel. For example, consider the *parallel compound* statement in HardwareC [KD88]:

```
<
  x = b + c;
  y = p -q;
>
```

This statement specifies that the computations associated with the assignments to x and y are to be performed simultaneously.

Statement-level concurrency can also be specified implicitly. For example, the updating of values scheduled to occur in the future would use implicit statement-level concurrency. An example is shown in the following assignments:

```
s <= b + c  after 20 ns;
wait for 20 ns;
v := 3;
```

These statements specify that the values of signal s and variable v are to be updated simultaneously after 20 ns.

3.2.2 State transitions

Systems are often best conceptualized as having various **modes**, or states, of behavior, as in the case of controllers and telecommunication systems. For example, a traffic-light controller [DH89] might incorporate different modes for day and night operation, for manual and automatic functioning, and for the status of the traffic light itself.

In systems with various modes, the transitions between these modes sometimes occur in an unstructured manner, as opposed to a linear sequencing through the modes. Such arbitrary transitions are akin to the use of *goto* statements in programming languages. For example, Fig-

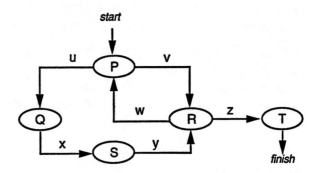

Figure 3.3: State transitions between arbitrarily complex behaviors.

ure 3.3 depicts a system that transitions between modes P, Q, R, S and T, the sequencing determined solely by certain conditions. Given a state machine with N states, there can be N^N possible transitions among them.

In systems like this, transitions between modes can be triggered by the detection of certain events or certain conditions. For example, in Figure 3.3, the transition from state P to state Q will occur whenever event u happens. In some systems, actions can be associated with each transition, and a particular mode or state can have an arbitrarily complex behavior or computation associated with it. In the case of the traffic-light controller, for example, in one state it may simply be sequencing between the red, yellow and green lights, while in another state it may be executing an algorithm to determine which lane of traffic has a higher priority based on the time of the day and the traffic density. In traditional and hierarchical finite-state machine conceptual models, simple assignment statements, such as $x = y + 1$, can be associated with a state. In the PSM [GVN93] model, any arbitrary algorithm with iteration and branching constructs can be associated with a state.

3.2.3   Hierarchy

One of the problems we encounter with large systems is that they can be too complex to be considered in their entirety. In such cases, we can see the advantage of hierarchical models. First, since hierarchical models allow a system to be conceptualized as a set of smaller subsystems, the system modeler is able to focus on one subsystem at a time. This kind of modular decomposition of the system greatly simplifies the development of a conceptual view of the system. Furthermore, once we arrive at an adequate conceptual view, the hierarchical model greatly facilitates our comprehension of the system's functionality. Finally, a hierarchical model provides a mechanism for scoping objects, such as declaration types, variables and subprogram names. Since a lack of hierarchy would make all such objects global, it would be difficult to relate them to their particular use in the model, and could hinder our efforts to reuse these names in different portions of the same model.

There are two distinct types of hierarchy – structural hierarchy and behavioral hierarchy – both of which are commonly found in conceptual views of systems.

Structural hierarchy

A structural hierarchy is one in which a system specification is represented as a set of interconnected components. Each of these components, in turn, can have its own internal structure, which is specified with a set of lower-level interconnected components, and so on. Each instance of an interconnection between components represents a set of wires connecting the components. The advantage of a model that can represent a structural hierarchy is that it can help the designer to conceptualize new components from a set of existing components.

This kind of structural hierarchy in systems can be specified at several different levels of abstraction. For example, a system can be decomposed into a set of chips/modules communicating over buses. Each of these chips may consist of several blocks, and each block, in turn, may consist of several RT components, such as registers, ALUs and multiplexers. Finally, each RT component can be further decomposed into a set of gates. In addition, we should note that different portions of the system can be conceptualized at different levels of abstraction, as in Figure 3.4, where the processor has been structurally decomposed into a datapath represented as a set of RT components, and into its corresponding control logic represented as a set of gates.

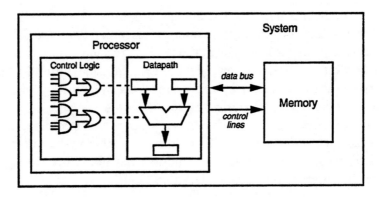

Figure 3.4: Structural hierarchy in a computer system.

Behavior hierarchy

The specification of a **behavior hierarchy** is defined as the process of decomposing a behavior into distinct subbehaviors, which can be either sequential or concurrent.

The **sequential decomposition** of a behavior may be represented as either a set of procedures or a state machine. In the first case, a **procedural sequential decomposition** of a behavior is defined as the process of representing the behavior as a sequence of procedure calls. Even in the case of a behavior that consists of a single set of sequential statements, we can still think of that behavior as comprising a procedure which encapsulates those statements. A procedural sequential decomposition of behavior P is shown in Figure 3.5(a), where behavior P consists of a sequential execution of the subbehaviors represented by procedures Q and R. Behavioral hierarchy would be represented here by nested procedure calls. Recursion in procedures allows us to specify a dynamic behavioral hierarchy, which means that the depth of the hierarchy will be determined only at run time.

Figure 3.5(b) shows a **state-machine sequential decomposition** of behavior P. In this diagram, P is decomposed into two sequential subbehaviors Q and R, each of which is represented as a state in a state-machine. This state-machine representation conveys hierarchy by allowing a subbehavior to be represented as another state-machine itself. Thus, Q and R are state-machines, so they are decomposed further

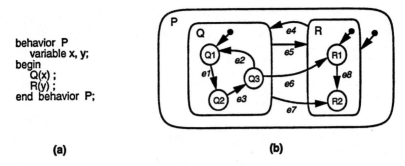

behavior P
  variable x, y;
begin
  Q(x) ;
  R(y) ;
end behavior P;

(a)

(b)

Figure 3.5: Sequential behavioral decomposition: (a) procedures, (b) state-machines.

into sequential subbehaviors. The behaviors at the bottom level of the hierarchy, including *Q1, ...R2*, are called **leaf behaviors.**

In a sequentially decomposed behavior, the subbehaviors can be related through several types of transitions: simple transitions, group transitions and hierarchical transitions. A **simple transition** is similar to that which connects states in an FSM model in that it causes control to be transferred between two states that both occupy the same level of the behavior hierarchy. In Figure 3.5(b), for example, the transition triggered by event *e1* transfers control from behavior *Q1* to *Q2*. **Group transitions** are those which can be specified for a group of states, as is the case when event *e5* causes a transition from *any* of the subbehaviors of *Q* to the behavior *R*. **Hierarchical transitions** are those (simple or group) transitions which span several levels of the behavior hierarchy. For example, the transition labeled *e6* transfers control from behavior *Q3* to behavior *R1*, which means that it must span two hierarchical levels. Similarly, the transition labeled *e7* transfers control from *Q* to state *R2*, which is at a lower hierarchical level.

For a sequentially decomposed behavior, we must explicitly specify the initial subbehavior that will be activated whenever the behavior is activated. In Figure 3.5(b), for example, *R* is the first subbehavior that is active whenever its parent behavior *P* is activated, since an arrow originating in a bold circle points to this first subbehavior. Similarly, *Q1* and *R1* would be the initial subbehaviors of behaviors *Q* and *R*, respectively.

The **concurrent decomposition** of behaviors can best be conceptualized by means of fork-join constructs or by modeling the system as a set of processes. These constructs were discussed in Section 3.2.1.

3.2.4   Programming constructs

Many behaviors can best be described as sequential algorithms. Consider, for example, the case of a system intended to sort a set of numbers stored in an array, or one designed to generate a set of random numbers. In such cases, if the system designer manages to decompose the behavior hierarchically into smaller and smaller subbehaviors, he will eventually reach a stage where the functionality of a subbehavior can be most directly specified by means of an algorithm.

The advantage of using such programming constructs to specify a behavior is that they allow the system modeler to specify an explicit sequencing for the computations in the system. Several notations exist for describing algorithms, but programming language constructs are most commonly used. These constructs include assignment statements, branching statements (if, case statements), iteration statements (while, for and repeat loops), and subroutines (functions and procedures). In addition, data types such as records, arrays and linked lists are usually helpful in modeling complex data structures.

Figure 3.6 shows how we would use programming constructs to specify a behavior that sorts a set of ten integers into descending order. Note that the procedure *Swap* exchanges the values of its two parameters.

```
type     buffer_type is array (1 to 10) of integer;
variable buf : buffer_type;
variable i, j : integer;

for i = 1 to 10
   for j = i to 10

      if (buf(i) > buf(j)) then
         Swap(buf(i), buf(j));
      end if;

   end for;
end for;
```

Figure 3.6: Sort behavior represented using programming constructs.

3.2.5 Behavioral completion

Behavioral completion refers to a behavior's ability to indicate that it has completed, as well as to the ability of other behaviors to detect this completion. A behavior is said to have completed when all the computations in the behavior have been performed, and all the variables that have to be updated have had their new values written into them.

In the finite-state machine model, we usually designate an explicitly defined set of states as **final states**. This means that, for a state machine, completion will have occurred when control flows to one of these final states, as shown in Figure 3.7(a).

In cases where we use programming language constructs, a behavior will be considered complete when the last statement in the program has been executed. For example, whenever control flows to a return statement, or when the last statement in the procedure is executed, a procedure is said to be complete.

The PSM model introduced in Chapter 2 denotes completion using a special predefined **completion point**. When control flows to this completion point, the program-state enclosing it is said to have completed, at which point the transition-on-completion (TOC) arc, which can be traversed only when the source program-state has completed, could now be traversed.

For example, consider the program-state machine in Figure 3.7(b). In this diagram, the behavior of leaf program-states such as *X1* have been described with programming constructs, which means that their completion will be defined in terms of their execution of the last statement. The completion point of the program-state machine for *X* has been represented as a bold square. When control flows to it from program-state *X2* (i.e., when the TI arc labeled by event *e2* is traversed), the program-state *X* will be said to have completed. Only then can event *e5* cause a TOC transition to program-state *Y*. Similarly, program-state *B* will be said to have completed whenever control flows along the TOC arc labeled *e4* from program-state *Y* to the completion point for *B*.

The specification of behavioral completion has two advantages. First, in hierarchical specifications, completion helps designers to conceptualize each hierarchical level, and to view it as an independent module, free

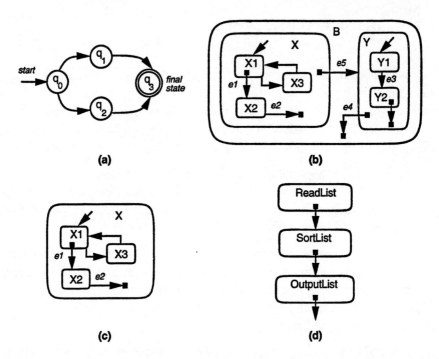

Figure 3.7: Behavioral completion: (a) finite-state machine, (b) program-state machine, (c) a single level view of the program-state X, (d) decomposition into sequential subbehaviors.

from interference from inter-level transitions. Figure 3.7(c), for example, shows how the program-state X in Figure 3.7(b) would look by itself in isolation from the larger system. Having decomposed the functionality of X into the program-substates $X1$, $X2$ and $X3$, the system modeler does not have to be concerned with the effects of the completion transition labeled by event $e5$. From this perspective, the designer can develop the program-state machine for X independently, with its own completion point (transition labeled $e2$ from $X2$). The second advantage of specifying behavioral completion is that the concept allows the natural decomposition of a behavior into subbehaviors which are then sequenced by the "completion" transition arcs. For example, Figure 3.7(d) shows how we can split an application which sorts a list of numbers into three distinct, yet meaningful subbehaviors: *ReadList*, *SortList* and *Output-List*. Since TOC arcs sequence these behaviors, the system requires no additional events to trigger the transitions between them.

3.2.6 Communication

Some systems consist of several concurrent behaviors or processes which need to communicate with each other. This kind of communication between portions of the system is usually conceptualized in terms of shared memory or message passing paradigms. We will discuss each of these individually.

Shared-memory communication model

In a shared memory model, each sending process writes to a shared medium, such as a global variable or port, which can then be read by all receiving processes. If synchronization is required between the communicating processes, it must be specified explicitly. For example, the sending process could incorporate a special "valid" flag to indicate that the shared memory has been updated with a new value, which can then be read by the receiving process. The shared memory model also includes the **broadcast** mechanism, which ensures that any value or event generated by one process or its environment will immediately be sensed by all the other processes.

Figure 3.8(a) shows how the communication between processes P and Q could occur through the use of a shared memory. To send data to process Q, process P simply updates the shared memory, which is then read by process Q.

The shared medium used for interprocess communication can be of the persistent or non-persistent variety. A **persistent** shared medium is one that retains the value written into it by one process until that value has been rewritten by another process. An example of a persistent shared medium would be a storage element, such as a register, latch or a memory, in which other processes can access the retained data at any time. In a **non-persistent** shared medium, by contrast, the data is available only at the instant when it is written by a process, since it is not retained by the medium between two successive writes. An example of a non-persistent shared memory would be a wire connecting the modules implementing two communicating processes.

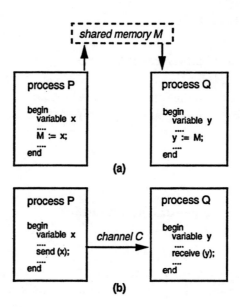

Figure 3.8: Inter-process communication paradigms: (a) shared memory, (b) message passing.

Message-passing communication model

In the message-passing model, the details of data transfer between processes are replaced by communication over an abstract medium called a **channel**, over which data or **messages** are sent. In each process, **send-receive** primitives would be used to transfer data over the channel.

Consider, for instance, Figure 3.8(b), which shows how the communication between processes P and Q could be achieved by using the message passing model. A channel C has been defined for the transfer of data from process P to process Q. The data, represented by the value of variable x in process P, is then transferred over the channel through the use of a "send" primitive. Finally, this data is received into the variable y in process Q by means of a "receive" primitive.

It must be emphasized that a channel is a virtual entity and therefore free of any implementation details. Only after synthesis would a channel be implemented, in the form of a bus consisting of a set of wires and a protocol to sequence the data transfered over these wires.

There are several variations among message passing models. First, the identity of the destination process of a "send" can be specified explicitly, or it can be left implicit in the interconnection specification for the channels. Further, a communication channel can be **uni-directional** or **bi-directional**, depending on whether data can be sent in only one direction or both directions. Finally, a channel can be a **point-to-point** channel, which connects exactly two processes, or a **multiway** channel, which enables more than two processes to communicate. In some cases, multiway channels might require that each process be assigned a unique address which would identify the sending/receiving processes involved with any data transfer.

A further distinction rests in whether the message-passing communication is blocking or non-blocking. A message-passing communication is said to be **blocking** if a process which communicates over a channel suspends or *blocks* itself until the other process is ready for the data transfer. In effect, blocking communication forces the two processes to synchronize before data transfer can be initiated. The advantage of blocking communication is that it requires no additional storage for implementing the communication. However, since one of the processes must be suspended until the other process is also ready to communicate, a blocking communication can result in performance deterioration. **Non-blocking** communication does not have this problem, since the processes do not have to synchronize with each other for data transfer to take place. In this case, however, external storage must be implicitly associated with the channel, usually in the form of a queue. The sending process writes the value to be sent across the channel to the queue, and then continues its normal execution, leaving the receiving process to receive the data from the queue whenever it is ready. Since the two processes operate independently of each other and only transfer data to/from the queue, non-blocking communication usually results in a better performance. This speed, however, is achieved only at the cost of the additional storage required to implement the queue. Furthermore, if the queue size is insufficient, the processes may still block at those points when the sender process is sending data to the queue at a faster rate than the receiver process is taking it off the queue, eventually causing the queue to fill and subsequent sends to block.

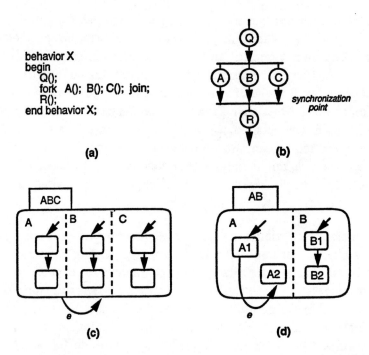

Figure 3.9: Control synchronization: (a) behavior X with a fork-join, (b) synchronization of execution streams by join statement, (c)&(d) synchronization by initialization in Statecharts.

3.2.7   Synchronization

In a system that is conceptualized as several concurrent processes, the processes are rarely completely independent of each other. Each process may generate data and events that need to be recognized by other processes. In cases like this, when the processes exchange data or when certain actions must be performed by different processes at the same time, we may need to synchronize the processes in such a way that one process is suspended until the other reaches a certain point in its execution. Common synchronization methods fall into two classifications, namely control-dependent and data-dependent schemes.

Control-dependent synchronization

In control-dependent synchronization techniques, it is the control structure of the behavior that is responsible for synchronizing two processes in the system. For example, the **fork-join** statement introduced in Section 3.2.3 is an instance of such a control construct. Figure 3.9(a) shows a behavior X which **forks** into three concurrent subprocesses, A, B and C. In Figure 3.9(b) we see how these distinct execution streams for the behavior X are synchronized by a **join** statement, which ensures that the three processes spawned by the fork statement are *all* complete before R can be executed. Another example of control-dependent synchronization is the technique of **initialization**, in which processes are synchronized to their initial states either the first time the system is initialized, as is the case with most HDLs, or during the execution of the processes. In the Statechart of Figure 3.9(c), we can see how the event e, associated with a transition arc that reenters the boundary of ABC, is designed to synchronize all the orthogonal states A, B and C into their default substates. Similarly, in Figure 3.9(d), event e causes B to initialize to its default substate $B1$ (since AB is exited and then reentered), at the same time transitioning A from $A1$ to $A2$.

Data-dependent synchronization

In addition to these techniques of control-dependent synchronization, processes may also be synchronized by means of one of the methods for interprocess communication: shared memory or message passing.

Shared-memory based synchronization works by making one of the processes suspend until the other process has updated the shared memory with an appropriate value. In such cases, the shared memory might represent an event, a data value or the status of another process in the system, as is illustrated in Figure 3.10 using the Statecharts language.

Synchronization by common event requires one process to wait for the occurrence of a specific event, which can be generated externally or by another process. In Figure 3.10(a), we can see how event e is responsible for synchronizing states A and B into substates $A2$ and $B2$, respectively. Another method is that of **synchronization by common**

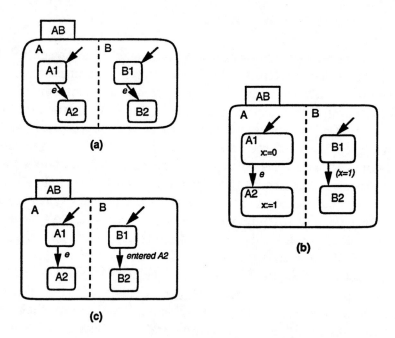

Figure 3.10: Data-dependent synchronization in Statecharts: (a) synchronization by common event, (b) synchronization by common data, (c) synchronization by status detection.

variable, which requires one of the processes to update the variable with a suitable value. In Figure 3.10(b), B is synchronized into state $B2$ when we assign the value "1" to variable x in state $A2$. Still another method is **synchronization by status detection**, in which a process checks the status of other processes before resuming execution. In a case like this, the transition from $A1$ to $A2$ precipitated by event e, would cause B to transition from $B1$ to $B2$, as shown in Figure 3.10(c). Such a method of synchronization can be useful when we must efficiently represent a complex situation like tristating the transmitter outputs when a universal asynchronous receiver-transmitter (UART) enters its receive mode.

Still another method is **synchronization by message-passing**, which uses blocking communication. In such a situation, the process that is ready to send or receive data first must wait until the other process is also ready for the communication. The CSP model, for example, would support this kind of synchronization mechanism.

3.2.8 Exception handling

Often, the occurrence of a certain event can require that a behavior or mode be terminated immediately, thus prohibiting the behavior from updating values further. Since the computations associated with any behavior can be complex, taking an indefinite amount of time, it is crucial that the occurrence of the event, or **exception**, should terminate the current behavior immediately rather than having to wait for the computation to complete. When such exceptions arise, the next behavior to which control will be transferred is indicated explicitly. Examples of such exceptions include resets and interrupts in a computer system.

The traditional finite-state machine has, in a trivial form, this kind of exception-handling. In such state machines, the actions associated with each state are assumed to execute in zero time, which means that the occurrence of an exception simply causes control to be transferred to the next appropriate state. The Statecharts and PSM models, on the other hand, support exception-handling by allowing transitions at higher levels of hierarchy to terminate all computations at lower levels.

3.2.9 Non-determinism

Occasionally, there is more than one way for a particular transition or computation to be performed in the system. In such cases, the system designer may not want to limit the system to any particular choice during the specification stage. This is the value of non-determinism in a conceptual model; it allows the designer to specify multiple options for any action or computation performed by the system. During simulation of the specification, one of the several choices would be selected arbitrarily.

There are two types of non-deterministic behavior in conceptual models. The first, **selection non-determinism**, refers to non-deterministic selection of exactly one of several choices. For example, consider the following specification, in which a and b are two distinct actions:

```
if (x) then
    do EITHER  a OR b
end if
```

The semantics of the above statements would allow any action a or b, but not both, to be performed indeterminately when x is true. Examples of such non-determinism can be found in the CSP conceptual model, each of which is specified by using the *guarded* statement.

The second type of non-determinism is **ordering non-determinism**, which involves a non-deterministic ordering of the several actions that have to be executed. For example, consider the following:

```
if (x) then
   do BOTH  a AND b
end if
```

While the above statement calls for executing both a and b whenever x is true, the order in which the two actions are executed will be is selected in a non-deterministic manner. By using this type of non-determinism, the system designer can avoid having to specify the exact order of actions during the system specification stage.

3.2.10   Timing

In system specifications, the notion of timing is important as a means to reflect real world implementations. In other words, by specifying timing, the information that the system designer gets from his simulations of the system will be more realistic. In general, the timing information that can be specified for a system falls into two classes: namely, functional timing and timing constraints.

Functional timing

In this first class belongs all timing information that will affect the simulation output of the system specification, thereby adding to the system's functionality. For example, in the Statechart model, timeout intervals can be specified to determine the maximum amount of time spent in a mode or state. Another example would be the timeouts in VHDL [IEE88] *wait* statements and the scheduling of signal values for future update by VHDL signal assignment statements. For example, consider the following VHDL statements:

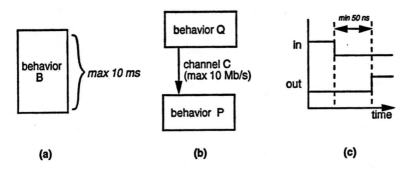

Figure 3.11: Timing constraints in system specifications: (a) execution time for behaviors, (b) data transfer bitrates, (c) inter-event.

```
a <= 30;
wait for 100 ns;
s <= a + 1 after 30 ns;
```

The statement that assigns s will be executed 100 ns after the assignment to a. However, due to the *after* clause in the assignment to s, the signal's value will only be updated 130 ns after the assignment to a.

Timing constraints

Timing constraints specified for a system are intended for use by synthesis and verification tools. A tight performance constraint, for example, will influence how resources are allocated to perform the computations in the system during synthesis. We can also check whether constraints can be satisfied by using verification tools. Such constraints ultimately would not affect the system functionality, in the sense that they will not influence the simulation of the specification.

Several types of timing constraints can be specified for a system. For instance, constraints on execution time can be specified for a behavior or a portion of it, as in Figure 3.11(a), where a constraint of 10 ms has been specified for behavior B. In other cases, a behavior could have constraints on its associated data transfer rate, specifying the rate at which the behavior must consume or generate data. In Figure 3.11(b), for example, behavior Q has been constrained to generate the data sent over channel C and processed by behavior P at a maximum rate of *10 Mb/s*. Finally, inter-event timing constraints can be used to specify the minimum/maximum time between the occurrences of two distinct events. In Figure 3.11(c), for example, the signal *out* can rise no sooner than 50 ns after *in* has fallen.

In the specification of timing constraints, it is important that the constraints be related to specific objects in the conceptual model. For example, if the designer wishes to constrain the execution time between two statements in a behavior, he might need to define statement labels in order to identify the particular pair of statements for which the constraint is to be specified. Similarly, the easiest way to specify constraints between two I/O events is to use timing diagrams.

3.3   Specification requirements for embedded systems

In the previous section, we have presented a range of characteristics that could be found in various conceptual models. It is important to note, however, that different classes of systems require specific subsets of these characteristics, and, this being the case, conceptualization of a particular system will require a conceptual model that possesses the appropriate set of characteristics. In this section, we will examine the particular set of characteristics appropriate for conceptualizing embedded systems.

An **embedded system** is one whose behavior is defined by its interaction with its environment, usually by sequencing between a set of **modes**, where each mode may represent a state of being or some computation. Such systems are constantly responding to external events and computing their outputs as a function of their inputs and their current state. Examples of embedded systems are controllers and telecommunication systems. In the list below, we examine several characteristics typical of embedded systems, some of which were briefly touched on in Section 3.2, but nonetheless require reexamination in this new context:

1. **State transitions:** Embedded systems are intrinsically state-based and constantly transition from one mode to another as determined by external events. In some cases, this transitioning between states

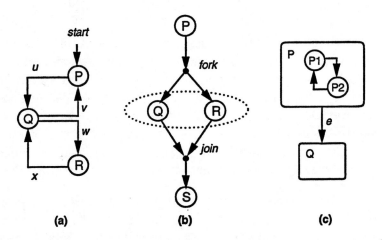

Figure 3.12: Embedded system characteristics: (a) state transitions, (b) sequential/concurrent behavior decomposition, (c) exceptions.

occurs in an unstructured manner, as illustrated by the relationship between modes P, Q and R in Figure 3.12(a).

2. **Behavioral hierarchy:** Embedded systems are more easily conceptualized when we regard their functionality as hierarchically decomposed into a set of sequential and concurrent behaviors. For example, consider the desired functionality of the embedded system shown in Figure 3.12(b). This system has been conceptualized as consisting of four distinct behaviors, P, Q, R and S. When P is executed, it will be followed by a concurrent execution of Q and R, which are then followed by S. It should be noted that any one of these four behaviors could be an (arbitrarily) complex computation, possibly even decomposed into additional levels of sequential/concurrent subbehaviors. Since an embedded system can consist of several such modes, each of which would respond differently to various external events, we can see that behavioral hierarchy is essential to manage the system's complexity in terms of specification size and readability.

3. **Concurrency:** Embedded systems often consist of concurrent behaviors which cooperate with each other in order to achieve the functionality intended by the system as a whole. Both task-level and statement-level concurrency are fundamental to such systems.

4. **Exceptions:** Certain events require an instantaneous response from the system. For this reason, embedded systems may be constantly interrupted, responding to such exceptions by terminating their current computations and transitioning to the next mode of computation. Figure 3.12(c) illustrates this concept of immediate termination. Upon the occurrence of event e, the computations encapsulated by P will be terminated, and control will be transferred to behavior Q, at which point its computations will be initiated.

5. **Programming constructs:** Certain computations performed by embedded systems can be represented more naturally by means of mathematical expressions, or as algorithms that rely on programming constructs such as branching and iteration.

6. **Behavioral completion:** Many of the activities in embedded systems neither repeat infinitely, nor are terminated by external events alone; instead, the execution of such activities will continue until it reaches a point when the behavior is complete. Because of this characteristic, it is important that we be able to specify completion of the behavior, since we may wish to initiate another activity on the basis of such completion.

3.4   Survey of specification languages

Keeping in mind these characteristics of embedded systems, we can now briefly consider some of the specification languages most commonly in use. The languages we have chosen to review encompass a broad range of description styles and application domains, and are fairly representative of current methods of design specification. In this section, we will pay particular attention to how well each language supports embedded system specification.

3.4.1   VHDL

The VHSIC Hardware Description Language (VHDL) [IEE88] was developed by the Department of Defense and standardized by the IEEE in

1987. This language was intended to assist in the development, documentation and exchange of designs. Since its development, VHDL has been widely accepted by the design community as a description language and has developed a wide range of tools for capture (using graphical front-ends), simulation, debugging, verification and synthesis.

The primary hardware abstraction in VHDL is a *design entity*, which is used to identify and represent a single portion of the larger design that performs a specific function and possesses well-defined inputs and outputs. The functionality of each entity can be described using programming statements, dataflow, structure, or a combination thereof.

In VHDL, **structural hierarchy** is supported by using nested *block* and *component instantiation* statements. In Figure 3.13(a), we can see the structural description of the modulo-10 counter. This counter is described as having two external ports: *clk* and *cnt*. The counter counts up at every rising edge of the clock signal, *clk*, resetting to 0 when the count reaches 9. In the architecture declaration portion, the components that are used are declared with their formal port parameters (*Reg_E, Add_E* and *Cmp_E*). Components are then instantiated in the architecture body (*Conreg, Adder,* and *Comparator*). The interconnection between the components is specified through association between component ports. For example, signal *cnt_out* is mapped to the formal ports *o* and *a* of the components *Conreg* and *Adder*, respectively, thus specifying that the output of *Conreg* is connected to one of the inputs of *Adder*.

VHDL supports a two-level **behavioral hierarchy**. At the top level, the specification can be decomposed into a set of concurrently-executing processes, thus supporting **task-level concurrency**. The second level consists of a sequential decomposition of these processes into procedures.

In addition to traditional programming variables, VHDL has signals, which differ from variables in that their value is defined over time. Thus, in addition to their current value, signals have a projected output waveform. VHDL signal assignment statements support **statement-level concurrency**, as shown explicitly in the following:

```
a  <= b ;
b  <= a ;
wait on a;
```

```
entity Counter_E is
    port (clk :  in bit ;  cnt : out integer);
end  Counter_E;

architecture  Counter_struct  of  Counter_E is

    component  Reg_E
        port (d : in integer ;  clk : bit ; o : out integer;
              clear:  in bit);
    end component ;

    component  Add_E
        port ( a, b : in integer ;  o : out integer ) ;
    end component ;

    component Cmp_E
        port ( i0, i1  : in integer ;  o : out bit )
    end  component ;
    ...........................
    signal  one : integer := 1 ;
    signal  nine : integer := 9 ;
    signal  cnt_in, cnt_out, add_out  : integer ;
    signal  clear : bit;
    ...........................
begin

    Conreg :  Reg_E
        port map ( cnt_in,  clk, cnt_out , clear) ;
    Adder :  Add_E
        port map ( cnt_out, one, add_out) ;
    Comparator : Cmp_E
        port map (nine, cnt_in,  clear);
    ...................

    cnt <= cnt_out ;

end Counter_struct ;
```

(a)

```
entity  Counter_E is
    port (clk :  in bit ;  cnt : out integer);
end  Counter_E;

architecture Counter beh of  Counter_E is
begin

    process
        variable convar : integer := 0;
    begin
        cnt <= convar;
        wait until (clk='1') and  not(clk'stable) ;
        if  (convar= 9) then
            convar := 0 ;
        else
            convar := convar + 1;
        end if;
    end process;

end Counter_beh ;
```

(b)

```
entity  Counter_E is
    port (clk :  in bit ;  cnt : out integer);
end  Counter_E;

architecture Counter dflow of  Counter_E is
    signal consig : integer := 0;
begin

    block ( (clk='1') and  not(clk'stable) )
    begin
        consig <=  guarded  0  when (consig=9)
                   else consig+ 1 ;
    end block ;
    cnt <= consig;

end Counter_dflow;
```

(c)

Figure 3.13: VHDL specification of a modulo-10 counter in three description styles: (a) structural, (b) behavioral and (c) dataflow.

These two assignments occur concurrently, swapping the values of signals *a* and *b*. Furthermore, the *after* clause in VHDL allows signal assignment statements to schedule future updates of a signal's value, thus supporting implicit statement-level concurrency, as discussed in Section 3.2.1.

VHDL also has full support for **programming constructs,** because a process consists of sequential statements similar to those found in the ADA programming language. Figure 3.13(b) shows a process description of a simple modulo-10 counter. VHDL also offers a wide variety of data types suitable for high-level modeling such as integer, real, enumeration, physical, array, record and pointer types.

The possibility of concurrent signal assignments in VHDL also allows the designer to express **dataflow** behavior, as in the dataflow description of the modulo-10 counter presented in Figure 3.13(c).

In addition, **communication** between processes can be achieved by adopting a shared memory model, which uses signals that can be assigned by any process and are visible to other processes.

In VHDL, **synchronization** can be achieved in one of two ways. The first method relies on a process's *sensitivity list*, which ensures that when an event occurs on any of the signals named in the sensitivity list, the process will begin to execute. For example, consider a process P, which has been defined as:

```
P : process (start, x)
   begin
      .....
   end process;
```

According to this definition, the process P will remain suspended until an event occurs on either of the signals *start* or x, thus enabling the designer to synchronize the execution of process P with other processes that incorporate the *start* or x signals.

A second method of synchronization would employ a *wait* statement, which will suspend the process until it detects either the occurrence of an event on one of the specified signals, or the presence of a specified condition. For example, the following wait statement ensures that the process execution will resume only when an event occurs on signals x or y, or when *start* = 1:

```
wait on x, y until (start = '1');
```

The specification of **timing** in VHDL is limited to the specification of functional timing, as, for example, when an *after* clause, such as a <= 2 after 20 ns, is used to specify the point in the future when the value of the signal is to be updated. Similarly, a *timeout* clause, such as wait on start for 100 ns, could be used to specify the maximum time to be spent at the wait statement. VHDL statements can also access the current value of the global time by means of the predefined expression *now*. The second type of timing characteristics, timing constraints, is not directly supported by VHDL, although such constraints can nonetheless be indirectly specified using attributes.

In relation to the characteristics of embedded systems, VHDL is lacking in some areas, too. For instance, VHDL has no constructs capable of terminating a process in response to an **exception**. Exceptions are only partially supported in VHDL through the use of guarded concurrent signal assignments. In this method of exception handling, a guard expression that is associated with a block statement will control the assignments to signals within the block.

Finally, it should be noted that VHDL does not support state transitions. Furthermore, a true behavioral hierarchy, in which concurrency can be specified at any level of the hierarchy, is not be supported by VHDL.

3.4.2   Verilog

Verilog [TM91, SST90] was originally developed as a proprietary HDL for specification and simulation of digital systems. In 1990, Verilog was transferred to the public domain, and it has since been widely used as a description language.

Verilog has a number of advantages for the designer, one of them being that it supports **structural hierarchy** by allowing a system to be specified as a hierarchy of interconnected *modules*. Each of these modules can then be described in one of two ways, either by using other lower level modules, or by specifying its behavior as a program.

Behavioral hierarchy is also supported in Verilog, in the sense that a process at any level of the hierarchy can spawn concurrent subprocesses by means of the fork-join statement, or can be decomposed into a set of procedures. These process descriptions can be specified by means of **programming constructs** with a C-like syntax. **Dataflow** behavior can also be captured, through the use of *continuous assignment* statements.

Communication would be implemented in Verilog by means of a shared memory model, using the wires connecting ports on modules, on registers and on memories to establish communication between processes. Verilog can also support **synchronization** in several ways, since control synchronization can be implemented by using the fork-join constructs, and event control statements that watch for a change in the value of an event can also be used to synchronize the computations in different processes. For example, the statement

```
@(negedge) clock #10  q = d;
```

ensures that *q* will be updated with the value of *d* 10 time units after the negative edge of *clock*. Alternatively, we could use the following *wait* statement in Verilog to achieve the same effect:

```
wait (clock=0);
    #10 q = d;
```

Timing specification is supported in Verilog by the modeling of delays of gates and nets. This means that for each rising, falling and turn-off delay, Verilog permits the designer to specify maximum, minimum and typical values. In addition, Verilog allows the designer to specify the delay that determines when the values in an assignment statement will be updated. In the assignment statement #10 q = d, for example, the value of *q* will be updated 10 time units after the negative edge on the clock.

Verilog can also handle **exceptions** by using the *disable* statement, which disables the named block of sequential statements and transfers control to the statement that follows that named block.

Finally, it remains only to point out that Verilog does not support the specification of state transitions.

3.4.3 HardwareC

HardwareC [KD88] was specifically designed to be a synthesis-oriented hardware description language. As a result, while HardwareC is based on the C programming language [KR78], it has additional well-defined semantics and constructs for hardware description. Because of these characteristics, this language was chosen as the most effective way to specify input for the Hercules behavioral synthesis system [DK88].

In HardwareC, a specification of a system would consist of a single level of concurrent processes which communicate with each other. These processes can be enclosed within a hierarchy of blocks, in which case these blocks and their interconnections can specify a **structural hierarchy**.

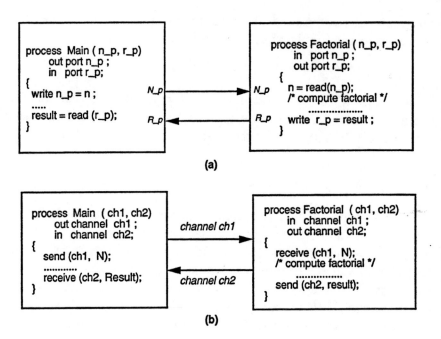

Figure 3.14: Interprocess communication in HardwareC: (a) port passing, (b) message passing.

In HardwareC, we can specify **task-level concurrency** by means of processes, each of which specifies an algorithm as a set of sequential operations, which would themselves be described by using a subset of programming constructs of the C language. Each process restarts itself upon completion. **Statement-level concurrency** can also be specified, using the *parallel compound statement* presented in Section 3.2.1.

Communication between processes can be specified in HardwareC using either the shared memory or message passing models. *Port passing*, for example, would assume the existence of a shared medium, such as wires or a memory, connecting the declared ports. The designer would define these ports on the boundaries of the communicating processes or their enclosing blocks, and would use explicit HardwareC commands to read, write, and tristate a global port. The protocol which governs the communication could then be specified as part of the process description, as, for example, in Figure 3.14(a), where process *Main* provides the value n to process *Factorial* over port n_p, and receives the result over port *r_p*. *Message passing*, on the other hand, would use explicit send-receive constructs for data transfer and synchronization, by declaring communication channels between the communicating processes/blocks. Communication over these channels can be synchronous and blocking. Using these constructs, the designer need only specify the data to be transferred across the channel – the handshaking protocol and the corresponding hardware will be synthesized automatically by the synthesis tools. In Figure 3.14(b), for example, we can see that process *Main* uses channel *ch1* to send the value *n*, and receives the result over channel *ch2*.

To **synchronize** two processes in HardwareC, the designer would use blocking message passing. The language possesses a *msgwait* construct, which detects pending messages that are already waiting in the channels. By using this construct, the designer can make a process wait until an appropriate signal, represented as a single bit message, has been received from another process.

An interesting feature of HardwareC is its ability to specify parameterized descriptions, or *templates*, for various models (e.g., blocks, processes, procedures and functions). These templates can be instantiated by providing integer values for their formal parameters, at which point we can use them to describe library components such as adders and multipliers with formal parameters that may relate to bit width, number of inputs, and so on. The designer could also instantiate a template and invoke a specific instance of it, as a means of specifying binding information that can be used by synthesis tools. For example, a particular add operation could be bound to a specific instance of an adder template, enabling the system designer to specify resource sharing at the description level.

In HardwareC, we can specify **timing constraints** between pairs of statements by associating *tags* or labels with each statement and then using the tags to specify the constraints. In addition, resource constraints can be specified, determining how many instances of a given model will be used to synthesize the design (similar to the allocation task in high-level synthesis [GDWL91]).

Finally, we need to note that HardwareC does not support the specification of dataflow behavior, state transitions or exceptions.

3.4.4   CSP

The Communicating Sequential Processes [Hoa78] language (CSP) was proposed by C.A.R. Hoare in 1978 to overcome those limitations of traditional programming languages having to do with programs that run on multi-processor machines. As the name implies, CSP allows the designer to specify a program as a set of concurrent processes, using constructs that simplify the specification of communication and synchronization between these processes. In addition to its use as a programming language, CSP has also been used to specify hardware systems [Aul91].

A CSP program consists of a list of *commands*. By using the *parallel* command, a process can spawn subprocesses (task-level concurrency) at any level of the hierarchy, thus providing support for **behavioral hierarchy**. All processes in the parallel command will be executed concurrently, and the parallel command is complete only when all its processes have terminated. In addition, each process is itself a list of commands which could potentially contain its own parallel commands.

In CSP, each process can be described with **programming constructs**. Subroutines are implemented as coroutines, which means that the subroutine is implemented as a process that executes concurrently with the calling process. Recursive subroutines can also be simulated by using an array of processes, each element of which represents one level of recursion.

Control constructs in CSP are implemented using the *guarded* command, which consists of a list of guards or conditions, and a command list that will be executed only when all the conditions in the guard list evaluate as true. To specify the execution of exactly one of the constituent guarded commands, we would use *alternative* commands. Thus, the C language "if" statement –

```
if ( a > b )  max = a;
   else       max = b;
```

– can be represented by using the following alternative command in CSP:

$$[a > b \rightarrow max := a [] a \leq b \rightarrow max := b]$$

It is possible that, while using the alternative command, we might encounter a situation where several of the constituent guarded commands are successful. Under such circumstances, an arbitrary guard would be selected and executed, resulting in **non-deterministic** behavior.

There are no global variables in CSP. For this reason, **communication** between concurrent processes can be achieved only by means of message-passing, with explicit *input* and *output* commands specified. Communication occurs between two processes only when all of the following criteria are met:

1. The output command of the first process specifies the second process as the destination of the data to be sent.

2. The input command of the second process specifies the first process as the source of the data to be received.

3. The type of the target (into which the data is received) in the input command matches the expression of the output command.

This type of communication through the use of input/output commands in two processes is a form of blocking, and constitutes the only mechanism for synchronization in CSP.

It must be recognized that CSP has a number of limitations, having no constructs for specifying structure, state transitions, timing, dataflow behavior, or exception handling.

3.4.5 Statecharts

The Statecharts [Har87, DH89] language was designed primarily for specifying *reactive systems*, which are essentially event-driven, control-dominated systems, such as those used in avionics and communication networks. Statecharts can provide elegant representations, because it extends traditional FSM's to include three additional elements: hierarchy, concurrency and communication.

By way of introduction of the Statecharts language, consider Figure 3.15, which represents a universal asynchronous receiver transmitter (UART). The basic object in Statecharts is a *state*. and transitions between states are determined by a combination of events and conditions.

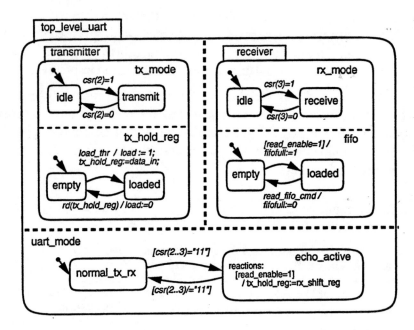

Figure 3.15: Statecharts: partial specification of the UART.

Statecharts supports **behavioral hierarchy** by allowing any specification to be decomposed into a hierarchy of states. This can be accomplished in one of two ways:

1. **OR (sequential) decomposition :** A state could be composed of a state machine comprising sequential substates and transition arcs. In Figure 3.15, for example, state *tx_mode* consists of two sequential substates, *idle* and *transmit.*

2. **AND (concurrent) decomposition :** A state could also be composed of orthogonal substates, in which all the substates are active whenever the parent state is active. In Figure 3.15, the orthogonal or concurrent states are those separated by dotted lines, which means that state *top_level_uart* consists of three concurrent states: *transmitter, receiver* and *uart_mode.* AND decomposition in Statecharts specifies task-level concurrency.

Because it allows the decomposition of a state into sequential and concurrent substates, Statecharts allows us to avoid the exponential blowup of states that can occur in conventional FSM's, which are inherently flat and sequential. Actions can be associated with both transition arcs and states, and are assumed to represent zero-delay computations. The actions associated with a state may be specified either to execute continuously as long as the system is in that state, or to execute whenever that state is entered or exited. Statecharts also allows **state transitions** across multiple levels in the hierarchy.

To specify **functional timing** in a Statechart, we would use a special timeout transition arc that defines the maximum and minimum amounts of time the system can spend in the desired state.

Communication in Statecharts is implemented through a broadcast mechanism, by means of which any event generation, variable update or transition that takes place in any portion of the Statechart will immediately be sensed by the rest of the Statechart. An interesting feature of this language is its versatility in supporting several **synchronization** mechanisms: Statecharts can synchronize by initialization, common event, common data and status detection, all of which were discussed in detail in Section 3.2.7.

Statecharts also supports the concept of a system's **history** as a way of determining the starting substate of a group of substates. In 'Enterby-history,' for example, control enters a group of substates by revisiting the substate that was visited most recently.

In addition, Statecharts can specify non-deterministic behavior, by since when there are two arcs from a state that simultaneously could be transitioned, one of those arcs is chosen non-deterministically.

The disadvantages of Statecharts are that it does not support programming constructs and has no constructs for specifying structure, behavioral completion, or dataflow behavior.

Argos

Argos [Mar91, Hal93] is a graphical synchronous language used for specifying reactive systems. The basic processes in Argos are finite automata which receive and emit signals. The graphic conventions adopted by Argos are identical to those of Statecharts, but this language differs from Statecharts in several ways. First, Argos allows a more modular

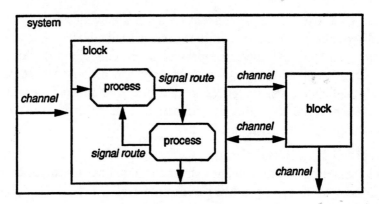

Figure 3.16: Hierarchical decomposition of an SDL specification into system, blocks and processes.

decomposition of a system into subsystems, since it restricts transitions between states to a single-level of the hierarchy. Also, unlike Statecharts, in which all events are broadcast to the entire system, Argos introduces a *local event* operator which can be used to reduce the scope of certain events, confining them to specific subsystems or modules in the specification. Finally, Argos also allows us to specify **behavioral completion** through its *self termination* mechanism.

The disadvantages of Argos are that it does not support programming constructs and has no constructs for specifying structure or dataflow behavior.

3.4.6 SDL

The Specification and Description Language [BHS91] (SDL) was standardized by the CCITT, and has been used mainly in the telecommunication field for protocol specifications.

SDL specifications basically consist of hierarchical dataflow diagrams with a state machine at the leaf level. SDL can specify a **structural hierarchy**. The target object for specification in SDL is a *system*, which can be specified in terms of a hierarchy of *blocks*, the main structuring concept in SDL. Each system contains one or more blocks which are connected with each other and with the boundary of the system by *channels*, as shown in Figure 3.16. These channels are essentially the pathways over which the signals associated with them are conveyed. Repeated decomposition of blocks into other blocks will allow us to specify a structural hierarchy consisting of a block tree structure with the system at the root. A *leaf* block may have one or more *processes*.

In SDL, **behavioral hierarchy** has only limited support, in that its specifications have only a single level of processes, contained within leaf blocks. On the other hand, SDL does support a state-machine sequential decomposition of its processes, which can be activated either at the time of system initialization or at some other point in the lifetime of the system by another process. Once created, a process is terminated only when its *stop* construct is reached, which means that SDL does support **behavioral completion.**

State transitions are also supported in SDL, since each process consists of a state machine. Variables can be declared and assigned within the processes, and the processes themselves can either be in a state or perform transitions between states. During a transition, a process can manipulate variables, make decisions, create new process instances, send signals to other processes and activate or reset timers used to generate timing signals.

Process **communication** is achieved by using signals that are conveyed over *signal routes*, which connect processes with each other and to the block boundary. In addition, SDL has an input queue associated with each process, which serves to buffer each incoming signal. The signals are removed from the queue when they are consumed by the process. **Synchronization** in SDL is achieved by allowing a process to check and wait for an appropriate value on a signal. **Timing specification** in SDL is supported by allowing a process to declare a *timer* object, which generates a *timer signal* upon expiration of a preset time interval.

Finally, SDL does not support dataflow descriptions, programming constructs or exception handling.

3.4.7 Silage

The Silage language [HR92, Hil85] was developed to address issues related to the specification of digital signal processing (DSP) systems. A

DSP system is best conceptualized as a set of operations performed on continuous streams of input data values. To support such systems, Silage is an *applicative* language, in that it only specifies application of functions to manipulate data values, without any variables or variable assignments.

The main advantage of Silage is that it excels in specifying **dataflow** descriptions, such as data-driven concurrency. Silage expressions represent *streams of values*, which means that, in the expression $a + b$, a and b represent a stream of numbers rather than the variables or array elements found in conventional programming languages. A Silage program receives the set of input values arriving in a synchronized manner. Results of Silage expressions also yield streams of data values. A Silage program consists of a set of *definitions*, which define new values as a function of other values. The order of definitions is not significant since they do not represent assignments to variables (which would introduce dependencies between statements).

The recurrences in Silage, in which any element of a stream depends on previous values of the stream, allow for a limited specification of **functional timing**. The delay operator "@" is used to denote previous values in a stream, as in the following statement:

```
d =  d@1 + 1 ;
```

Here, each value in the stream represented by d would be one higher than the previous value.

Silage has *array constructors* which can represent specific elements of a vector concisely. In addition, reduction operators like *sum* and *max* can be used to operate on entire arrays, and conditional expressions allow us to select one of the expressions from a set of expressions, based on the condition of a guard. Silage also has stream manipulation operators such as *decimate* and *interpolate*, which can be used to reduce and increase respectively a signal's sampling rate. A function in Silage represents a grouping of definitions and is implemented as a macro expansion. Silage does not permit recursion or iterations with non-static bounds.

Since Silage was developed as an applicative language, it does not support programming language constructs. Furthermore, as mentioned above, it has no variables or assignment operators, and state-transitions, behavioral hierarchy and exception handling are not supported.

3.4.8 Esterel

Esterel [Ber91, Hal93] is a synchronous programming language that was developed for the specification of reactive systems. To date, it has been used for the specification of controllers, communication protocols, man-machine interfaces and system drivers.

The Esterel language is based on the **perfect synchrony hypothesis**, which states that control, communication and computation in a program take no time. **Programming constructs** are fully supported in Esterel, and **structural hierarchy** can be specified using a hierarchy of *modules*, where each module has a well defined interface and can instantiate other modules. Support for **behavioral hierarchy** in Esterel is comprised of procedural sequential decomposition and concurrent decomposition achieved using a parallel statement, which has semantics similar to a fork-join statement.

Communication in Esterel is achieved through signal broadcasting, meaning that signals emitted by one process are sensed by all other processes. **Exceptions** in Esterel can be handled in several ways. For example, we can use the *watching* statement, as in

```
do
    <statements>
watching s
```

the *do-upto* statement, as in

```
do
    <statements>
upto s
```

or the *trap* statement, as in

```
trap t in
    <statements>; exit T
|| await s; exit T
end
```

since all these statements are identical insofar as they will terminate the enclosed statement block upon the occurrence of an event involving signal *s*.

Synchronization can also be specified in several ways in Esterel. For example, an *await* statement ensures that the process will wait for the occurrence of the specified signal, as in "await s." Alternatively, the watchdog and do-upto statements could be used for synchronization if we specify the halt statement as the only statement in the enclosed statement block.

Esterel is not, however, fully adequate to specification of embedded systems because it does not possess constructs for the specification of state transitions, timing or dataflow behavior.

3.5   SpecCharts

As we have shown, none of the languages presented so far can capture all the characteristics for embedded system specification, as outlined in Section 3.3. In the next section, we will present the SpecCharts language, which was specifically developed to capture directly a conceptual model possessing these particular characteristics.

3.5.1   Language description

SpecCharts [NVG91a, NVG92, GVN93] is based on the program-state machine (PSM) model introduced in Chapter 2, and is defined as an extension of VHDL. As is apparent in Figure 3.17, the basic object in SpecCharts is a **behavior**, which corresponds directly to a program-state in the PSM model.

SpecCharts supports **behavioral hierarchy** in the sense that it captures a system as a hierarchy of behaviors. Each behavior is either a composite behavior or a leaf behavior.

Composite behaviors are decomposed hierarchically into either a set of concurrent subbehaviors or a set of sequential subbehaviors. In the first case, all subbehaviors are active whenever the behavior is active, but in the second case, the subbehaviors are only active one at a time. In Figure 3.17, behaviors *B* and *X* are composite behaviors. Note that while *B* consists of concurrent subbehaviors *X*, *Y* and *Z*, *X* consists of sequential subbehaviors *X1* and *X2*. In a sequentially decomposed composite behavior, the first in the list of subbehaviors would be the **initial** subbehavior, to which control is transferred when the parent behavior is activated. Thus, in the SpecCharts specification of Figure 3.17, behavior X will be initialized into subbehavior $X1$ upon activation. For a behavior with concurrent subbehaviors, on the other hand, the order in which subbehaviors are listed is irrelevant.

Leaf behaviors are those that exist at the bottom of the behavioral hierarchy and their functionality is specified with **programming constructs** using VHDL sequential statements. In Figure 3.17, for example, $X1$, $X2$, Y and Z are leaf behaviors.

In SpecCharts, subbehavior descriptions are nested within the parent behavior, just as the descriptions of $X1$ and $X2$ are enclosed within that of X in Figure 3.17. Similarly, the descriptions of subbehaviors X, Y and Z are enclosed within that of behavior B.

SpecCharts also supports **state transitions**, in the sense that we can represent the sequencing between subbehaviors by means a set of transition arcs. In this language, an arc is represented as the 3-tuple $< T, C, NB >$, where T represents the type of transition, C represents the event or condition triggering the transition, and NB represents the next behavior to which control is transferred by the transition. If no condition is associated with the transition, it is assumed to be "true" by default.

As does the PSM model, SpecCharts has two types of transition arcs. A **transition-on-completion arc (TOC)** is traversed whenever the source behavior has completed its computation and the associated arc condition evaluates as true. A leaf behavior can be said to have completed when the last VHDL statement has been executed, and all variables and signals have been updated with their final values. A sequentially decomposed behavior is said to be complete only when it makes a transition to a special predefined completion point, indicated by the name *complete* in the next-behavior field of a transition arc. In Figure 3.17, for example, we can see that behavior X completes only when subbehavior $X2$ completes and control flows from $X2$ to the *complete* point upon occurrence of event $e2$ (as specified by the arc $X2:< TOC, e2, complete >$). Finally, a concurrently decomposed behavior can be said to be complete when all (or a selected subset) of its subbehaviors have completed. In Figure 3.17, for example, behavior

B completes when both the concurrent subbehaviors *X* and *Y* have completed and control has flowed to the completion point (as specified by the arcs $X : <TOC,\ true,\ complete>$ and $Y : <TOC,\ e3,\ complete>$). Note that the completion of behavior *B* is not affected by the execution status of subbehavior *Z*. However, subbehavior *Z* is affected by behavior *B*, in the sense that when *B* completes due to the transitions from *X* and *Y* to the completion point, *Z* is terminated too.

```
entity E is
    port ( P : in integer;  Q : out integer );
end E

architecture A of E is
begin
        behavior B type concurrent subbehaviors is
            type int_array is array (natural range <>) of integer;
            signal M : int_array(15 downto 0);
        begin

            X: (TOC, true, complete);
            Y: (TOC, e3, complete);
            Z: ;

            behavior X type sequential subbehaviors is
            begin
                X1: (TI, e1, X2);
                X2: (TOC, e2, complete);

                behavior X1   type code is .........
                behavior X2   type code is .........
            end X;

            behavior Y  type code is
                variable max : integer;
            begin
                max := 0;
                for J in 0 to 15 loop
                    if (M(J) > max) then
                        max := M(J);
                    end if;
                end loop;
            end Y;

            behavior Z   type code is ........

        end B;

    end A ;
```

Figure 3.17: A sample SpecCharts specification.

Unlike the TOC, a **transition-immediately arc (TI)** is traversed instantaneously whenever the associated arc condition becomes true, regardless of whether the source behavior has or has not completed its computation. For example, in Figure 3.17, the arc $X1 :< TI, e1, X2 >$ terminates $X1$ whenever event $e1$ occurs and transfers control to behavior $X2$. In other words, a TI arc effectively terminates all lower level subbehaviors of the source behavior. The *timeout arc* is a special kind of TI arc which is traversed whenever its associated time interval expires, determined with respect to the time at which the behavior was activated.

In SpecCharts, only a subset of the program-states are actively carrying out their computations at any given time. Only the single root program-state, representing the entire system, is always active. Note that the execution semantics of SpecCharts are similar to those of VHDL, and the active behaviors in SpecCharts are identical to VHDL processes, except there is no implicit loop enclosing the behavior. In other words, behaviors execute until suspended at wait statements, there is no delay between two successive wait statements, and all signals are updated in delta-time. Inactive behaviors are ignored and treated as suspended VHDL processes, with all signal drivers shut off.

In cases when a sequential subbehavior completes but no TOC arc condition is true, there is an implicit wait until a condition becomes true. SpecCharts descriptions are deterministic, in the sense that the transitions leaving a subbehavior are prioritized in the order in which they are listed in the description. As a rule, TI arcs have priority over TOC arcs, and the TI arcs highest in the hierarchy have the highest priority.

In SpecCharts, a behavior can contain VHDL declarations, such as types, signals, variables, and procedures, whose scope extends to all subbehaviors.

SpecCharts supports **synchronization** in two ways. In the first method, wait statements can be used to check for events and conditions, as in VHDL. Thus, the following statement in a behavior –

```
wait until (start='0') and (not start'stable);
```

– will suspend the behavior until it detects a falling transition on *start*. In the second method, we could use a TI transition arc from behavior B

back to itself in order to synchronize all the concurrent subbehaviors of
B to their initial states.

SpecCharts also supports a **structural hierarchy** similar to that
found in VHDL, insofar as the system or portions thereof can be encapsulated as an *entity*. Ports can be declared for each entity, as well
as being connected to ports of other entities, by means of signals. In
Figure 3.17, for example, the hierarchy of behaviors is encapsulated as
an entity, E, with port declarations specifying the entity's interface.

Communication in SpecCharts is achieved through the use of variables and signals. Sequential behaviors are allowed to read and write the
same variable, whereas communication between concurrent behaviors is
implemented with signals. Message-passing communication can also be
specified in SpecCharts, by defining appropriate send-receive procedures.
Since VHDL allows subprogram name overloading, we can define send-
receive procedures for each data type sent across channels.

Timing specification in SpecCharts is supported by *wait* statements and *after* clauses in signal assignments, and is therefore identical
to that in VHDL. An additional timing specification is the *timeout* TI
arc, which specifies the maximum amount of time that can be spent in
a behavior.

3.5.2   Embedded system specification in SpecCharts

Having established a basic familiarity to SpecCharts, we are now in a
position to demonstrate that this language satisfies all the requirements
of embedded systems outlined in Section 3.3. SpecCharts, in other words,
can accomplish a direct mapping between its language constructs and the
conceptual model for embedded systems.

Figures 3.18, 3.19, and 3.20 show how SpecCharts can capture **state
transitions, behavioral hierarchy** and **exceptions**, respectively. The
state transitions are handled by the TOC and TI arcs, which sequence
behaviors. Behavioral hierarchy is also directly supported, in that a behavior can consist of sequential or concurrent subbehaviors. Exceptions
can be captured directly by a TI arc. Note the direct correspondence
in these figures between the conceptual model on the left and the Spec-
Charts description on the right.

In addition, it should be clear that, since SpecCharts is built on top of the VHDL language, it supports **programming constructs** directly by using VHDL sequential statements. Finally, **behavioral completion** can easily be handled by TOC arcs and completion points.

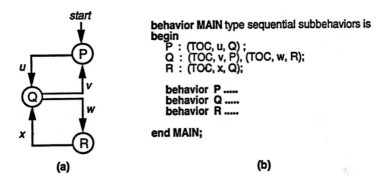

behavior MAIN type sequential subbehaviors is
begin
    P : (TOC, u, Q) ;
    Q : (TOC, v, P), (TOC, w, R);
    R : (TOC, x, Q);

    behavior P .....
    behavior Q .....
    behavior R .....

end MAIN;

(a)   (b)

Figure 3.18: Specifying state transitions: (a) desired functionality, (b) SpecCharts description.

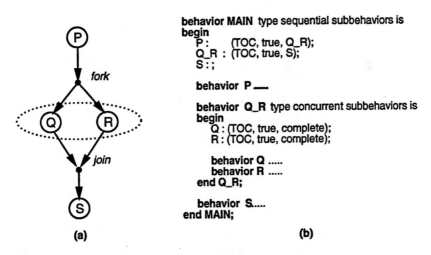

behavior MAIN type sequential subbehaviors is
begin
    P :   (TOC, true, Q_R);
    Q_R : (TOC, true, S);
    S :;

    behavior P .....

    behavior Q_R type concurrent subbehaviors is
    begin
        Q : (TOC, true, complete);
        R : (TOC, true, complete);

        behavior Q .....
        behavior R .....
    end Q_R;

        behavior S.....
end MAIN;

(a)   (b)

Figure 3.19: Capturing sequential/concurrent behavior decomposition: (a) desired functionality, (b) SpecCharts description.

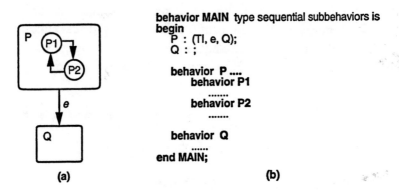

behavior **MAIN** type sequential subbehaviors is
begin
    P : (TI, e, Q);
    Q : ;

    behavior P ....
        behavior P1
        ....
        behavior P2
        ....

    behavior Q
        ......
end MAIN;

(a)   (b)

Figure 3.20: Capturing exceptions: (a) desired functionality, (b) Spec-
Charts description.

3.5.3 Equivalent graphical version

In Figure 3.17, we introduced the SpecCharts language as a textual representation. State transitions, however, are often easier to conceptualize
graphically, in the form of state transition diagrams. In recognition of
this fact, the SpecCharts language has an equivalent graphical version
which can be used to capture state-transition constructs in visual form.
In Figure 3.21, we present the equivalent graphical version of the textual
SpecCharts specification of Figure 3.17. In some cases, the graphical
conventions for SpecCharts are similar to those presented in [Har87].

In Figure 3.21, we can see that an entity is represented by a rectangular box, and behaviors within an entity are represented by boxes with
curved corners. Concurrent subbehaviors are separated by a dotted line
between them. Transitions are represented with directed arrows. In the
case of a sequentially-decomposed behavior, an inverted bold triangle
points to the first subbehavior. An example of such an initial subbehavior is *X1* of behavior *X*. The completion of sequentially decomposed
behaviors is indicated by a transition arc pointing to the completion
point, represented as a bold square within the behavior. Such a completion point is found in behavior *X* (transition from *X2* labeled *e2*).

TOC and TI transition arcs have different graphical representations.
TOC arcs originate from a bold square inside the source subbehavior, as
do the arcs labeled *e2* and *e3*. TI arcs, in contrast, originate from the

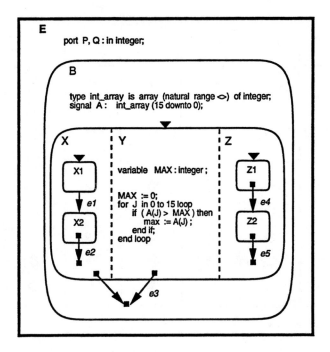

Figure 3.21: Equivalent SpecCharts graphical representation

perimeter of the source subbehavior, as does the arc labeled *e1*.

Ultimately, however, it is not important whether a system is captured graphically or textually – on the contrary, it is the constructs that provide the language's expressive power. For example, a state machine can be represented textually with a state table, or it can be captured graphically using state transition diagrams. While both the textual and graphical descriptions have certain advantages, it is the concept of state transitions itself that is of greatest value. The choice between a textual or graphical approach is beyond the scope of this chapter.

3.5.4 Possible language extensions

The SpecCharts language could be extended in several ways. First, designers often need to decompose a behavior that has been specified as a set of sequential statements into a set of concurrent subbehaviors. In such cases, it would be useful to have a fork-join capability that could

Language	Embedded System Features					
	State Transitions	Behavioral Hierarchy	Concurrency	Program Constructs	Exceptions	Behavioral Completion
VHDL	○	◉	●	●	○	●
Verilog	○	●	●	●	●	●
HardwareC	○	◉	●	●	○	●
CSP	○	●	●	●	○	●
Statecharts	●	●	●	○	●	○
SDL	●	◉	●	○	○	●
Silage	–	–	●	–	–	–
Esterel	○	●	●	●	●	●
SpecCharts	●	●	●	●	●	●

● Feature fully supported   ◉ Feature partially supported   ○ Feature not supported   – Not applicable

Figure 3.22: Language support for conceptual model characteristics of embedded systems.

be applied to leaf behaviors. Second, a system designer might wish to describe a behavior that continually performs a set of concurrent assignments. An example of such a behavior would be to define a signal *enabled* as high whenever the power is "on" (i.e., *power = 1*) and the external reset pin is low (i.e. *reset= 0*). It would be useful to have the capability to define *enable* in terms of *power* and *reset* throughout the life of the system, as in the following VHDL concurrent signal assignment:

```
block
begin
    enable <= power and (not reset);
end block;
```

Another useful extension would be the ability to parameterize behaviors. We could then specify large, regular systems consisting of a many near-identical behaviors, differing in only a few parameters, simply by instantiating the required number of behaviors with the appropriate parameters. Currently, even if there are N identical behaviors in a system, all N of them have to be entirely specified in the SpecCharts description.

3.6 Conclusion and future directions

The purpose of this chapter was to demonstrate the need for a direct mapping between the conceptual model characteristics and the language constructs we use to capture those characteristics. In the absence of such a one-to-one correspondence, the task of system specification can become cumbersome and the likelihood of error or incompleteness in the specification is increased. We presented various characteristics of common conceptual models, and then surveyed eight languages with respect to how well they support these characteristics (summarized in Figure 3.22). For the particular case of embedded systems, we have shown that the ease with which the constructs in the SpecCharts language are able to capture the PSM model's characteristics makes the language well-suited for embedded system specification. When there is a good match between a language and a model, we can expect shorter specification times and fewer errors, in addition to enhancing the comprehensibility and adaptability of the specifications themselves.

It is important to realize, however, that as languages move to higher levels of specification, the expressive power of the language often increases only at the expense of ease of design implementation. Even with widely used languages like VHDL, for example, synthesis tools can handle only a limited subset of the language's constructs. If languages are to be useful as more than mere documentation, their future development will have to address the issue of synthesizability. Specifically, if certain language features do not have hardware equivalents, they should not be used during system modeling unless we are willing to dispense with a direct synthesis. Furthermore, the increasing complexities of system tend to make "verification by simulation" infeasible, since the large number of signals and events in the specification and the correspondingly large number of cases to be simulated can become unmanageable. Consequently, we need to develop languages that lend themselves to formal verification techniques, so that it will be possible to verify properties of the system automatically.

3.7   Exercises

1. Which of the conceptual model characteristics presented in Section 3.2 are supported by the C programming language?

2. List the conceptual model characteristics that would be required to conceptualize the following:

   (a) digital signal processing systems,
   (b) communication protocols,
   (c) database systems,
   (d) instruction set processors.

3. Compare VHDL, HardwareC, Statecharts, CSP, SDL and Spec-Charts with respect to their ability to support the following conceptual model characteristics, listing the constructs relevant to each language: (Hint: refer to [NG93]):

   (a) synchronization,
   (b) communication,
   (c) timing.

4. Generate a flat FSM from the hierarchical FSM of Figure 3.5. What are the advantages of hierarchical FSMs over traditional, flat FSMs?

5. The Statecharts conceptual model possesses the following characteristics: state transitions and hierarchy. Consider a Statechart which has H levels of hierarchy. At each hierarchical level, a state is OR-decomposed into S sequential substates. Each substate has a single transition arc emerging from it (i.e., each level has S transition arcs). Assume that there are no inter-level transitions. Formulate equations for the following:

   (a) total number of states,
   (b) total number of transitions.

6. If the Statechart in the previous exercise were flattened to one finite-state machine, how many states and transitions would there be in the flattened representation?

7. Consider the following set of VHDL sequential statements, designed to compute the maximum values of a, b and c:

```
process(a, b, c)
begin
  if (a > b)
    then max <= a;
    else max <= b;
  end if;
  wait on max;
  if (c > max)
    then max <= c;
  end if;
end process;
```

Rewrite the above as dataflow statements using VHDL concurrent signal assignments.

8. Contrast the semantics of the VHDL signal and variable assignment statements. Specifically, if *a* and *b* have values *10* and *20*, what are their final values after the execution of each of the following?

    (a) the signal assignments:

```
a <= b;
b <= a;
wait for 1 ns;
```

    (b) the variable assignments:

```
a := b;
b := a;
```

9. Rewrite the description of the modulo-10 counter of Figure 3.13 in the following languages:

    (a) Verilog,
    (b) HardwareC,
    (c) CSP,
    (d) Esterel,
    (c) SpecCharts.

10. Consider the following set of statements:

```
a = 1;
x = 3;
y = x + b;
b = a + 1;
```

On execution, what will be the value of b and y if the above represents a set of sequential statements? Dataflow statements? (Assume that the previous value of both b and x is 2.)

Chapter 4

A Specification Example

In the previous chapter, we saw that the best specification language for a given system is the one that can most easily capture the characteristics of a natural model for that system. In this chapter, we will present an actual specification of a small but complete embedded system, in order to show the benefits to be gained when there is a good match between the conceptual model and the language in which the specification is written.

4.1 Introduction

In this chapter, we use a telephone answering machine to demonstrate system conceptualization and executable-specification development. We start with a natural-language description of an embedded system's desired functionality, and step through the development of a PSM model in the SpecCharts language. We shall see several advantages to using an executable language for specification over the traditional approach of using a natural language such as English.

We also describe several experiments that demonstrate the reduction in capture time, comprehension time, and functional errors that can be achieved by specifying embedded systems with SpecCharts rather than VHDL. The reductions result directly from the SpecCharts language's support of the PSM model. We discuss an experiment that quantifies differences among SpecCharts, VHDL, and Statecharts specifications. Finally, we describe an experiment demonstrating that top-down design with an executable specification does not degrade design quality.

117

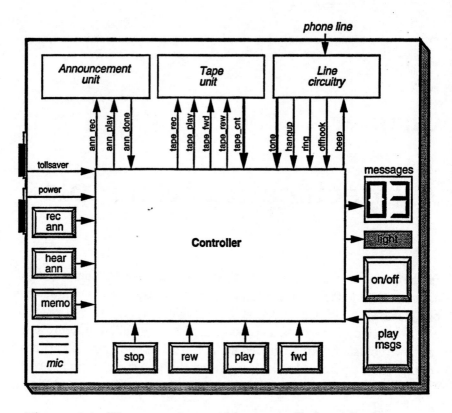

Figure 4.1: The answering machine controller's environment.

4.2   Telephone answering machine

The example system is a controller for a telephone answering machine currently available on the market. The controller's environment is shown in Figure 4.1. We will describe this environment and the controller's interface to it.

An **Announcement unit** records and plays a short outgoing announcement. The interface consists of three ports:

ann_rec:	directs the unit to record the machine owner's announcement from the microphone.
ann_play:	directs the unit to play the announcement.
ann_done:	indicates to the controller that the end of the announcement has been reached.

A **Tape unit** records messages on a tape and plays them back. The interface consists of five ports:

tape_rec:	directs the unit to record input from the phone line onto the tape.
tape_play:	plays the tape.
tape_fwd:	forwards the tape.
tape_rew:	rewinds the tape.
tape_count:	indicates the current tape position as an integer, with 0 representing the start of the tape.

Standard **Line circuitry** answers a call, detects a ring, detects a hangup, decodes a button tone, and produces a beep. The controller interfaces with this circuitry through five ports:

tone:	represents a 4-bit binary encoding of the button tone detected over the line.
hangup:	detects a hangup over the line.
ring:	detects a ring over the line.
offhook:	instructs the line circuitry to answer the line.
beep:	instructs the line circuitry to produce a beep over the line.

A **display** shows the current number of messages and the on/off state of the machine. The interface consists of two parts:

| *messages:* | denotes the number of received messages in 5 bits, appearing on the machine's display. |
| *light:* | turns on the light indicating the machine is on, i.e., set up to answer the phone. |

Nine touch-sensitive **buttons** allow the machine's user to edit the announcement and hear messages. The corresponding ports are the following:

on_off:	toggles the machine's answering state from on to off or vice-versa. When on, the machine answers after four rings, unless configured to answer after two rings.
play_msgs:	plays the messages tape from the beginning.
fwd:	forwards the messages tape.
play:	plays the messages tape from the current position.
rew:	rewinds the messages tape.
stop:	stops the messages tape from rewinding, forwarding, playing or recording.
memo:	records a message from the microphone rather than the phone line.
hear_ann:	plays the announcement.
rec_ann:	records an announcement from the microphone.

These ports differ from the earlier ports of the *Announcement unit* and the *Tape unit* in that they merely indicate user requests. Only after the controller sets the proper values on the announcement or tape unit's ports will the actions actually occur.

The machine also has two **switches**.

power:	provides power to the machine. When the switch is "off," the machine ignores the phone line and all buttons, and turns off the number-of-messages display and the machine light. This port differs from the *on/off* port, which affects only whether the machine should answer the line when the power is "on."
tollsaver:	indicates that when the machine's answering state is "on," the machine should answer after only two rings (as opposed to four rings) when at least one message has been recorded.

```
entity Controller_E is
(
        — Interface to Announcement unit
        ann_rec        : out bit;          — 1 causes unit to record
        ann_play       : out bit;          — 1 causes unit to play
        ann_done       : in bit;           — 1 indicates end of announcement

        — Interface to Tape unit
        tape_rec       : out bit;          — 1 causes unit to record
        tape_play      : out bit;          — 1 causes unit to play
        tape_fwd       : out bit;          — 1 causes unit to forward
        :
        :
);
end entity;

architecture Controller_A of Controller_E is
        ...
```

Figure 4.2: The answering machine controller's interface.

4.3 Specification capture with SpecCharts

We shall now capture an executable specification of the answering machine controller's functionality using SpecCharts. The graphical constructs introduced in the previous chapter are used in the figures to represent composite behaviors. The controller's functionality is described in English in Appendix A; portions are reproduced below.

First we specify the system's interface. Figure 4.2 shows a subset of the interface specification. This specification is easily derived from the English description of the interface ports in Section 4.2.

Next we describe the controller's behavior by decomposing it into simpler behaviors. These behaviors are successively decomposed into smaller and smaller behaviors, until the stage is reached at which each behavior can be described using sequential statements.

Controller behavior: The English description states, "When the 'power' switch is in the 'off' position, the machine ignores the phone line and all buttons." Thus, at the highest level of abstraction, the controller is always in one of two modes: "on" or "off." We decompose Controller into two sequential subbehaviors, **SystemOn** and **SystemOff**, as shown in Figure 4.3. If *power* becomes 1 while in SystemOff, the controller enters SystemOn. A TI arc is used to achieve this transition. A similar

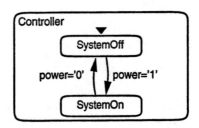

Figure 4.3: Highest-level view of the controller

arc immediately returns the controller to SystemOff when *power* becomes '0.' An identical on/off decomposition is common in many systems.

SystemOff behavior: When the system is "off," it is completely idle. Thus SystemOff possesses no functionality. We specify it as a leaf behavior containing the single VHDL statement "null;."

SystemOn behavior: The English description of the system's "on" functionality is divided into two sections: "Responding to external buttons and switches" and "Responding to the phone line." We thus decompose SystemOn into two subbehaviors, **RespondToMachineButton** and **RespondToLine**, as in Figure 4.4. To determine their transitions, we note that the description states, "Machine buttons have priority over the machine answering the phone; hence pressing any external button will also terminate any current activity." This statement implies that a machine button causes an immediate reaction. We thus add a TI arc from RespondToLine to RespondToMachineButton, which transitions if any button is pressed. For readability we create a new signal, *any_button_pushed*, which is a logical OR of all machine button signals.

There is a possibility that another machine button can be pressed while the controller is still responding to the first button. For example, if the "rewind" button is pressed, the response is to rewind the tape to its beginning. However, the user can press "stop" before the beginning is reached. We therefore add another TI arc pointing from RespondToMachineButton back to itself in order to respond to the newly pressed button. To prevent the undesirable behavior of exiting and reentering the RespondToMachineButton multiple times during a single pressing of a machine button, we specify that the transition should only occur on the rising edge of the *any_button_pushed* signal.

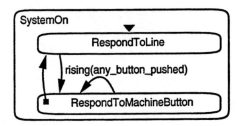

Figure 4.4: The SystemOn behavior

Nothing in the English description explicitly states the condition for transitioning back to RespondToLine. Since there are no exceptions that could cause this transition, we assume it occurs only after the response to the button is completed. Hence we add a TOC arc from Respond-ToMachineButton to RespondToLine with a default "true" condition. The "true" condition signifies that as soon as RespondToMachineButton completes, we enter RespondToLine.

RespondToMachineButton behavior: Each button obviously requires a different response (details of the responses are in the appendix). We capture each response in a procedure, and use an if-then-else statement to call the appropriate procedure for the particular button pressed, as shown in Figure 4.5(a). Note that, when the end of the code is reached, RespondToMachineButton is complete, causing the transition to RespondToLine mentioned in the previous paragraph.

Equivalently, we can decompose RespondToMachineButton into sequential subbehaviors. A subbehavior is created for each particular response, and arcs are used to determine which subbehavior to activate, as shown in Figure 4.5(b). TOC arcs point from each subbehavior to the special completion point of RespondToMachineButton. Both specifications are functionally equivalent, so the system modeler is free to choose that which is most convenient and readable.

RespondToLine behavior: The English description indicates that, when the machine is responding to the line, it performs one of three tasks: "Monitoring the line for rings," where rings are counted until the required number are detected; "Normal answering activity," where the announcement is played and the message is recorded; and "Remote-operation answering activity," where the caller (assumed to be

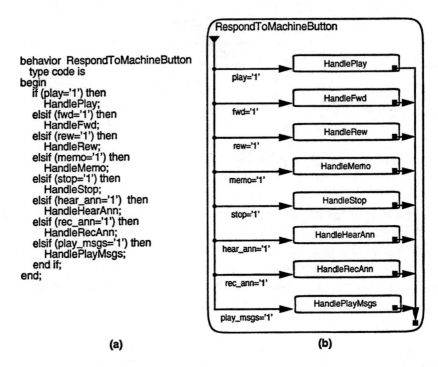

```
behavior RespondToMachineButton
  type code is
begin
  if (play='1') then
    HandlePlay;
  elsif (fwd='1') then
    HandleFwd;
  elsif (rew='1') then
    HandleRew;
  elsif (memo='1') then
    HandleMemo;
  elsif (stop='1') then
    HandleStop;
  elsif (hear_ann='1') then
    HandleHearAnn;
  elsif (rec_ann='1') then
    HandleRecAnn;
  elsif (play_msgs='1') then
    HandlePlayMsgs;
  end if;
end;
```

(a)   (b)

Figure 4.5: The RespondToMachineButton behavior: (a) sequential statements, (b) equivalent subbehavior decomposition.

the machine's owner) can listen to the saved messages by pressing a sequence of buttons. We decide that RespondToLine is best understood by decomposing it into two major subbehaviors called **Monitor** and **Answer**, as shown in Figure 4.6. The normal versus remote-operation distinction will be specified later in the Answer behavior.

When the appropriate number of rings is detected, Monitor completes and Answer is activated. Thus we add a TOC arc from Monitor to Answer. The English description states that after the message is recorded, "The machine hangs up and again monitors for rings." Thus we add a TOC arc from Answer to Monitor. We also find the following: "If 'on/off' is pressed after the machine has answered, any current activity is terminated and the machine monitors the phone line. Such functionality is useful for screening calls, since one can listen to a message and then pick up the phone and press 'on/off' to turn the machine 'off' and begin speaking with the caller." This functionality is captured as a

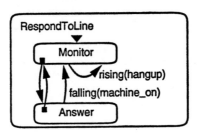

Figure 4.6: The RespondToLine behavior.

TI arc from Answer to Monitor with the condition *falling(machine_on)*. The *machine_on* signal introduced into the specification is "true" if the current state of the machine is "on."

The English description does not explicitly mention that, if the phone begins ringing but the caller hangs up before the call is answered, Monitor should start over again. We capture this behavior as a TI arc from Monitor pointing back to itself, which is transitioned if a hangup is detected, causing Monitor to start again. Equivalently, we could have specified this hangup behavior as part of Monitor itself. The TI arc solution results in a simpler Monitor behavior.

Monitor behavior: Monitor counts rings until the required number of rings is detected. The English description specifies three different possibilities based on several conditions: "When 'on,' the machine usually answers after *four* rings. However, if 'tollsaver' is 'on' and at least one message is recorded, the machine answers after *two* rings. Tollsaver allows the machine owner to determine over the phone whether any messages have been recorded. If the phone rings three times, then there are no messages and the owner can hang up, avoiding long-distance charges. Sometimes the owner will forget to turn on the machine before leaving home. Therefore, even when 'off' the machine answers after *fifteen* rings."

Although the English description does not explicitly say so, these conditions can change while the phone is ringing. For example, suppose the required number of rings to answer is fifteen, and five rings have already occurred. Suppose *machine_on* then becomes '1,' changing the required number of rings to four; the call should then be answered immediately.

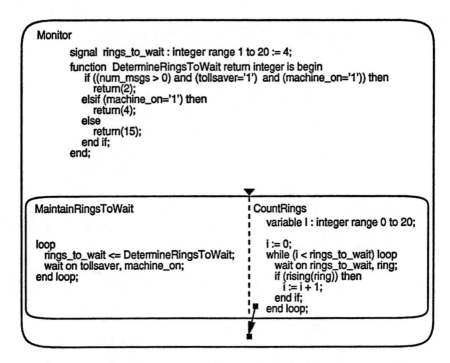

Figure 4.7: The Monitor behavior.

Monitor can be described as two concurrent subbehaviors: one computes the number of rings to wait for before answering, and the other counts the rings and answers when the required number is detected. We decompose Monitor into subbehaviors **MaintainRingsToWait** and **CountRings**, as shown in Figure 4.7. The signal *rings_to_wait* is declared, which is written by MaintainRingsToWait and read by CountRings. Monitor is considered complete when the required number of rings is detected, so a TOC arc points from CountRings to the completion point of Monitor.

Monitor can also be described as a single algorithm using sequential statements. The system modeler is free to describe the functionality in the most convenient and readable manner.

Answer behavior: The functionality of the answering activity is described as follows: "Once the machine has answered the line, it plays the announcement. When the announcement is complete, a beep is

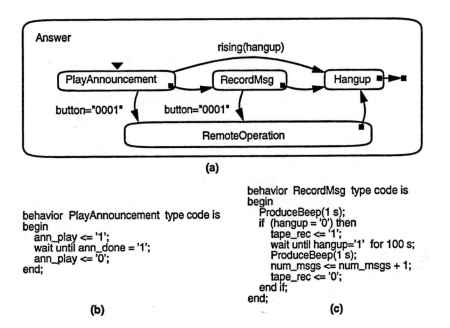

(a)

behavior PlayAnnouncement type code is
begin
    ann_play <= '1';
    wait until ann_done = '1';
    ann_play <= '0';
end;

(b)

behavior RecordMsg type code is
begin
    ProduceBeep(1 s);
    if (hangup = '0') then
        tape_rec <= '1';
        wait until hangup='1' for 100 s;
        ProduceBeep(1 s);
        num_msgs <= num_msgs + 1;
        tape_rec <= '0';
    end if;
end;

(c)

Figure 4.8: The Answer behavior: (a) decomposition into subbehaviors, (b) statements for PlayAnnouncement, (c) statements for RecordMsg.

produced and the message on the phone line is recorded until a hangup is detected, or until a maximum message time expires. The machine hangs up and again monitors for rings. If a hangup is detected while playing the announcement, the machine immediately hangs up, and does not proceed to record a message. If button-tone 1 is detected, either while playing the announcement or while recording a message, the machine immediately enters remote-operation mode."

We thus decompose Answer into four subbehaviors: **PlayAnnouncement**, **RecordMsg**, **Hangup** and **RemoteOperation**, as shown in Figure 4.8(a). As long as no exceptions occur, we perform the first three in order, transitioning on completion using TOC arcs. One exception that can occur is a hangup during PlayAnnouncement. In such a case, we transition immediately to Hangup using a TI arc. A hangup occurring during RecordMsg is not considered an exception, but a normal completion. Another exception is the occurrence of *tone = "0001"* during PlayAnnouncement or RecordMsg. Such an occurrence requires an immediate transition to RemoteOperation, as indicated by TI arcs from each of PlayAnnouncement and RecordMsg. After RemoteOperation is complete, we transition to Hangup. Completion of Hangup is always followed by transition to Answer's completion point.

PlayAnnouncement behavior: Playing the announcement consists of three simple steps, which are captured as the three sequential statements shown in Figure 4.8(b).

RecordMsg behavior: Recording a message is also very simple. The steps required are captured as sequential statements as shown in Figure 4.8(c). After a one-second beep, the message is recorded until a hangup occurs or until 100 seconds pass. A second beep is produced to indicate the end of the message and the number of messages is incremented.

Note that the description accounts for the possibility that the caller may hang up during the one second beep. If the caller does hang up, then *hangup* will be '0,' so the behavior completes without executing the statements that record and increment the number of messages.

RemoteOperation behavior: The description of remote operation begins as follows: "The first step in the remote-operation mode is to check a user-identification number. The next four button-tone numbers that are pushed are compared to four numbers stored internally. If they do not match, the machine hangs up the phone. If they do match, the machine enters the *basic-commands mode*, in which it can be instructed to perform any of several basic commands."

We thus decompose RemoteOperation into two sequential subbehaviors, **CheckCode** and **RespondToCmds**, as shown in Figure 4.9(a). After checking the entered four-digit code with the stored user identification number, we transition to RespondToCmds only if the code was correct. We introduce a boolean signal *code_ok*, which CheckCode will set to "true" only if the code was correct. Two TOC arcs are used. One causes transition from CheckCode to RespondToUserCommands only if *code_ok* is "true." The other causes transition from CheckCode to RemoteOperation's completion point if *code_ok* is "false." If a hangup occurs during CheckCode, a TI arc transitions to RemoteOperation's completion point.

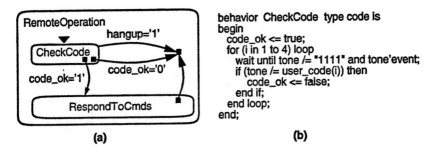

behavior CheckCode type code is
begin
  code_ok <= true;
  for (i in 1 to 4) loop
    wait until tone /= "1111" and tone'event;
    if (tone /= user_code(i)) then
      code_ok <= false;
    end if;
  end loop;
end;

(a) **(b)**

Figure 4.9: The RemoteOperation behavior: (a) decomposition into subbehaviors, (b) statements for CheckCode.

CheckCode behavior: The behavior for CheckCode can be described using the statements in Figure 4.9(b). From the program we see that, if the next four button tones match those stored in *user_code*, *code_ok* will be "true," otherwise it will be "false." Note that even if an incorrect tone is detected, the algorithm continues until all four tones sound. This continuation prevents the machine from hanging up immediately after an incorrect button is pressed, which would inform an invalid user which button tone was incorrect.

Specification of RespondToCmds continues in a similar manner. We have omitted the discussion of its specification for brevity. Figure 4.10 summarizes the decompositions of Controller into subbehaviors and transitions. Declarations and leaf statements are omitted; see Appendix B for the complete answering machine controller specification in SpecCharts.

4.4 Sample testbench

To verify the controller's functionality through simulation, we create a testbench. A testbench instantiates the component under test, drives its inputs with values to imitate real use, and ensures that correct values appear at its outputs. In Figure 4.11, we first set *power* to '1.' Then we turn on the machine by "pressing" the on/off button, achieved by setting *on_off* = '1' for a short time. We generate four "rings" and determine whether the call has been answered by ensuring *offhook* = '1'. If the call has not been answered, an error message is printed during simulation. Testbenches of this sort may contain several thousand lines of code.

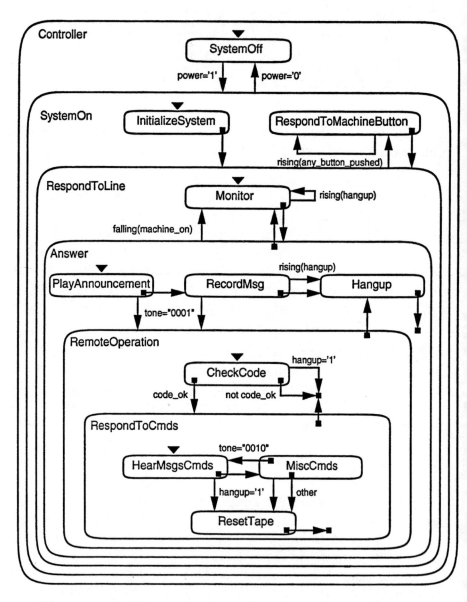

Figure 4.10: The answering machine controller specification.

```
entity testbench_E is
...
end entity;

architecture testbench_A is
begin

   component  Controller_E
      port
        ( tone : in bit_vector(0 to 3);
          hangup : in bit;
          ring: in bit;
          ...
        );
   end component;

   -- instantiate component, add global signals for ports
   ...

   process

      procedure PressButton(but: out bit) is
      begin
         but <= '1';
         wait for button_hold_time;
         but <= '0';
      end;

      procedure Ring is
      begin
         ring <= '1';
         wait for ring_hold_time;
         ring <= '0';
         wait for ring_hold_time;
      end;

   begin
      -- turn on the machine
      power <= '1';
      tollsaver <= '0';
      PressButton(on_off);

      -- place a call
      Ring; Ring; Ring; Ring;
      wait for 1 s;
      assert (offhook='1') report "ERROR1: did not answer";
      ...
```

Figure 4.11: Sample testbench for the answering machine.

4.5   Advantages of executable specification

Before examining the strengths of SpecCharts and its underlying PSM model, consider the advantages of specifying a system in an executable language, as the above example demonstrates, rather than using a natural language. The main advantage is the reduction of functional errors in the derived design. Fewer functional errors occur mainly because a natural-language specification is usually written in such a way that it is easily readable, but such readability is gained at the expense of lower precision. A readable natural-language specification is usually organized as a list of scenarios, whereas an executable specification of the same function is organized as an algorithm handling all scenarios. For example, consider the following natural-language description from above:

> The "on/off" button is used to toggle the machine from "on" to "off," and vice-versa. When "on," the machine usually answers after *four* rings. However, if "tollsaver" is "on" and at least one message has been recorded, the machine answers after *two* rings.

Each of the last two sentences describes a reaction to a particular scenario. Suppose we were to explicitly describe behavior for all possible scenarios. We would then have to add sentences such as the following:

> During the process of counting rings, *machine_on* or *tollsaver* may change. In this case we must recompute the required number of rings the machine must wait for, and then continue counting rings until this number is reached.

If we try to list explicitly all possible scenarios in this manner, the natural-language description would become very large and difficult to read, perhaps looking more like a legal code than an easily comprehended document. To cover all scenarios in a more concise manner, we might reorganize the description to look like an algorithm, as follows:

> First the required number of rings to wait for is determined. Second, the following is repeated until the required number of rings has been detected:

> We wait for a ring or for a change on *on_off* or *toll-saver*. If a ring is detected, we increment the current number of rings. If *on_off* or *tollsaver* changed, we redetermine the required number of rings the machine must wait for.

Such a description is unnatural to write and difficult to comprehend.

Unlike natural languages, executable languages excel at describing algorithms such as the above example. Hence, we see that the natural-language description and the executable specification serve different but complementary purposes. The natural-language description highlights the general behavior as a set of scenarios, with much left for the reader to infer, whereas the executable specification describes the detailed behavior with no room for varying interpretations. A well-documented executable specification can serve *both* purposes.

By creating an executable specification, one is forced to consider the system's detailed functionality before implementation. In addition, after capturing the specification, one can mentally pose scenarios and determine whether the functionality is correct. For example, we can pose this question: "What happens if *machine_on* becomes 0 after five rings have already occurred?" The code for Monitor answers this question precisely: the call is answered. The natural-language description does not answer the question directly.

Yet another benefit of executable specification is the use of simulation to verify the functionality further. All of this up-front effort greatly reduces the number of functional errors in the eventual design, meaning that time-consuming design modifications are rare, thereby reducing the overall time spent on the design.

4.6 Strengths of the PSM model

Th answering machine controller example demonstrates that the Spec-Charts language, with its underlying PSM model, easily captures all six of the embedded system characteristics outlined in Section 3.3.

4.6.1   Hierarchy

The system was decomposed hierarchically in a top-down manner. For example, at the topmost level, the system was viewed as having two modes of behavior, SystemOff and SystemOn. SystemOn was then hierarchically decomposed into several subbehaviors. Since people tend to think hierarchically to manage complexity, natural-language descriptions also tend to be hierarchical. SpecCharts' support of hierarchy enabled a simple mapping of this conceptual hierarchy in the natural-language description to SpecCharts constructs.

4.6.2   State transitions

Many behaviors in the system were sequential to one another, but transitioning occurred in a unstructured manner. For example, the Answer behavior contained four subbehaviors and six possible transitions between them. Such unstructured transitioning was easily mapped to the state-transition constructs in SpecCharts, because from any behavior we can go directly to any other behavior. Such transitions are difficult to describe using sequential statements alone as required in most programming or hardware-description languages. Describing unstructured transitioning using sequential statements requires a goto statement, but in order to enforce readability and modularity of programs, most languages do not allow such statements.

4.6.3   Programming constructs

The simplest manner to specify certain behaviors was by using an algorithm. For example, the CheckCode behavior was described as a seven-line algorithm with a loop and a conditional branch. The algorithms in the example were written as a sequence of operations, as are most algorithms, so they mapped easily to sequential programming constructs in SpecCharts.

4.6.4 Concurrency

We saw that the Monitor behavior was decomposed into two concurrent subbehaviors, MaintainRingsToWait and CountRings. If concurrency were not supported, the concurrent behaviors would have to be described sequentially. While in this case, the behaviors are small enough that a sequential description is feasible, sequentializing larger behaviors often results in very complex, unreadable descriptions. Since any behavior in SpecCharts can be decomposed either sequentially or concurrently at any level of hierarchy, the concurrency in the example was easily mapped to a concurrently decomposed behavior in SpecCharts.

4.6.5 Exception handling

There were numerous exceptions that had to be handled in this system at almost all levels of hierarchy. A hangup required special and immediate handling in RemoteOperation, Answer, and RespondToLine. A button tone sounding over the line required immediate handling in Answer. A change on *machine_on* required immediate action in RespondToLine. A depressed machine button required immediate action in SystemOn. Finally, a change on *power* required immediate action in Controller.

Exceptions were easily handled using the TI arc construct. With so many possible exceptions that could occur at any time, it would seem that specifying the priorities among the exceptions would be very difficult to do. However, hierarchy makes such prioritizing simple. If multiple events occur, the TI arc highest in the SpecCharts hierarchy has priority.

4.6.6 Completion

Since the system was decomposed hierarchically, in many instances we developed transitions between subbehaviors based on a subbehavior's completion *before* specifying that subbehavior. For example, in RespondToLine, we created a transition from Monitor to Answer upon completion of Monitor. As we later saw, Monitor could be specified as sequential statements or as concurrent subbehaviors. Completion is defined for Monitor regardless of whether it is specified as sequential statements or as subbehaviors, making hierarchical decomposition simple.

4.6.7　Equivalence of state decomposition and code

As noted earlier, a behavior can be specified as subbehaviors or as program code. From a hierarchical perspective, both methods are functionally equivalent. The system modeler is free to choose the method that seems best. In the example, we had the option to write Respond-ToMachineButton and Monitor either as programs or as sequential or concurrent compositions of subbehaviors. With an abundance of such choices, writing good specifications is as much an art as it is a science, just as is software engineering.

4.7　Experiments

The above example should have provided some intuitive sense of the benefits of using SpecCharts to capture embedded system specifications. Without it, capture time may be longer, comprehension of the system's functionality may be reduced, and functional errors may be more abundant. We have performed several experiments to demonstrate these issues quantitatively. The experiments compare the use of SpecCharts to VHDL for specification of embedded systems.

4.7.1　Specification capture

The goal of this experiment was to demonstrate that using SpecCharts for specification capture reduces the specification time and the number of errors in the specification. Two groups of modelers were given an English description of an example system. One group was asked to specify the system in VHDL, and the other in SpecCharts. The specification time required and the number of errors in the specifications of these two groups were then compared.

The example was an aircraft traffic-alert and collision-avoidance system [LHHR92]. This system was chosen since it represents an existing embedded system, and secondly because its documentation was available from an outside source, thus reducing the possibility of experimenter bias. Because of time limitations, only a subset of the system's functionality was selected for specification. Three modelers specified the selected subset in VHDL, and three in SpecCharts.

	VHDL	SpecCharts
Average specification–time in minutes	40	16
Number of modelers	3	3
Number of incorrect specifications first time	2	0
Number of incorrect specifications second time	1	0

Figure 4.12: Specification capture statistics.

The results of specification capture by the two groups of modelers are summarized in Figure 4.12. The VHDL modelers required an average of 2.5 times as long to capture the specification of the system. In addition, two of the VHDL specifications possessed a major control error, resulting in very slow system reactions to external events. This problem was pointed out to the VHDL modelers, who then attempted to fix their specifications. Only one modeler was able to remedy the problem in the allotted time. SpecCharts proved to be more effective because of its support of state transitions and exceptions.

4.7.2 Specification comprehension

The goal of this experiment was to show that a SpecCharts specification is easier to comprehend than a corresponding VHDL specification. One group of modelers was given the VHDL specification of a system and another the SpecCharts specification; each group was asked several questions about the system's functionality. The number of correct answers and the time required by each group to understand the system functionality were then compared.

The example chosen was a portion of an Ethernet coprocessor [GD92], for which an HDL specification was available from an outside source. We manually created a functionally equivalent SpecCharts specification. Three modelers were given the VHDL description, and three were given the SpecCharts specification. The time each person took to understand the specification was measured. After the specification was understood, fourteen questions were asked about the system, such as "What happens when the Enable signal goes low?" "How many preamble bytes are transmitted for any given data?" "What is the purpose of variable v?"

The modelers who were given the VHDL specification took three times as long to understand the general behavior. In addition, they averaged two incorrect answers to the questions, whereas the persons given the SpecCharts description answered all questions correctly.

4.7.3   Specification quantification

To quantify the several differences between SpecCharts, VHDL and Statecharts specifications, a single system was specified in all three languages. Several different characteristics of each specification were then measured.

The example chosen was the telephone answering machine presented in this chapter. An English description was captured in SpecCharts, VHDL, and Statecharts. Two VHDL versions were created. One maintained the hierarchy by using nested blocks and processes communicating via control signals, as will be discussed in Section 5.6. The other flattened the hierarchy into a single program-state machine, which was then described as a single process.

Figure 4.13 shows the results of this experiment. The flat VHDL has fewer program states since only leaf program-states exist. This reduction is achieved at the expense of almost four times as many arcs, an increase required for the following reasons. In the hierarchical model, one arc high in the hierarchy can demonstrate concisely that a true arc condition requires a transition to another state, regardless of which leaf state the system is in. In the flattened model, such an arc must be replicated to point explicitly from *each* leaf state to the correct next state. Immediate transitions, moreover, require polling throughout the code, as described earlier. Furthermore, arcs are represented using sequential statements. These three reasons result in over four times as many words in the flat VHDL as in SpecCharts.

The hierarchical VHDL does not require any additional program states or arcs, but does require adding 84 control signals, two per program state, for control among the many processes. Writing and reading these signals, along with the polling required for immediate transitions and the representation of arcs with sequential statements, result in almost four times as many words as in a SpecChart. Clearly, the higher the number of lines and words in a specification, the greater the specifi-

	Conceptual model	SpecCharts	VHDL (hierarch.)	VHDL (flat)	Statecharts
Specification attributes Program–states	42	42	42	32	80
Arcs	40	40	40	152	135
Control signals	—	0	84	1	0
Lines/leaf	—	7	27	29	—
Lines	—	446	1592	963	—
Words	—	1733	6740	8088	—
Shortcomings No sequential program constructs					X
No hierarchy			X	X	
No exception constructs			X	X	
No hierarchical events				X	
No state–transition constructs			X	X	

Figure 4.13: Comparison of SpecCharts, VHDL and Statecharts.

cation time, comprehension time, and occurrence of errors. With regard to leaf program-states, both VHDL versions require about four times as many statements per leaf program-state as SpecCharts. The increase is significant because it impairs the readability of the leaf program-state, defeating the leaf's purpose of modularizing the functionality into easily understood portions.

The consequence of the lack of programming constructs in Statecharts can be clearly seen in this example. Because the programming constructs in the leaf behaviors must be described using states and arcs, the Statecharts description contains almost twice the number of states and three times as many arcs as the SpecCharts description. Using states and arcs to describe the programming constructs can be quite tedious and unnatural, compared to using sequential program constructs. For example, a simple *for loop* must be described using several states and arcs. Note that, since Statecharts is only defined graphically, lines and words are undefined.

4.7.4   Design quality

The goal of this experiment was to demonstrate that designing from SpecCharts does not produce a lower design quality than designing from English. We compared the number of transistors in a design derived from an English specification with the number derived from a SpecCharts specification.

The example chosen was the answering machine described in this chapter. An English specification was given to two designers. One designer generated a datapath and controller directly from this specification. The other designer first specified the system with SpecCharts, flattened the hierarchy automatically, and then generated a datapath and controller from the flattened SpecCharts specification. In both cases, the KISS tool from UC Berkeley was used to synthesize controller logic from an FSM description of the controller.

Results are shown in Figure 4.14. Design time for each person was roughly the same, about 30 person-hours. Note that the number of transistors in the final design obtained from SpecCharts is not greater than that obtained from English. In this case, the number is actually smaller, since fewer control states are used in the design. The reason for the reduction in states is as follows. The English-specification designer captured the functionality using an FSM. The FSM served as the only precise specification of functionality. The designer had to keep this FSM readable in order to mentally verify the correctness of the machine's functionality. This readability requirement prevented him from grouping many states into a single state, since such a grouping would have made mental verification more difficult. On the other hand, the SpecCharts designer verified the functionality using the SpecCharts specification. When translating to an FSM, readability of the FSM was thus not an issue. States were grouped during this translation, resulting in less control logic.

4.8   Conclusion

Use of an executable specification yields many advantages over a natural-language description of system functionality. It forces explicit considera-

Design attribute	Designed from English	Designed from SpecCharts
Control transistors	3130	2630
Datapath transistors	2277	2251
Total transistors	5407	4881
Total pins	38	38

Figure 4.14: Design quality comparison.

tion of precise functional details early in the design process, when changes to such details are easy to make. The executable specification can be input to simulators for verification, and to synthesis tools for automated design. The specification also serves as excellent documentation for future use. These advantages yield shorter design time and hence shorter time to market.

In order to create an executable specification of a system's functionality, one must first determine the conceptual model that can be used to organize the system in the most concise and comprehensible manner. One must then choose a language that supports capture of this model. This chapter demonstrated the appropriateness of the PSM model and the SpecCharts language for specifying the functionality of embedded systems.

A strong analogy can be made between the role of executable specifications in system design and the role of structured programming languages in software design. In the past, software was developed at the level of assembly language. As programs became more complex, development efforts shifted to the more abstract level of structured programming languages such as C. Such languages are much more comprehensible to humans, resulting in fewer functional errors and faster development times. In system design, design effort is presently at the level of FSM's and datapath components. Efforts are now shifting to executable-specification languages such as VHDL and Verilog, again because of drastically improved human comprehension of complex systems. In software, advanced languages have evolved to handle new conceptual models, such as C++ for supporting an object-oriented model. In system design, advanced languages will also evolve, such as SpecCharts for supporting a PSM model.

4.9   Exercises

1. Rewrite CheckCode of Figure 4.9(b) as a finite-state machine. Which version do you feel is easier to comprehend?

2. Assume the current behavior of the answering machine is RecordMsg as specified in Figure 4.8(d), and *tape_rec* = *'1'*. Suppose *power* becomes '0'; how can we return *tape_rec* to '0' to terminate recording of the message? (Hint: see the SystemOff behavior in the Appendix B.)

3. Specify the Monitor behavior with Statecharts.

4. Specify a simple CPU with fetch and execute stages, and any instructions you choose, using VHDL, SpecCharts, and Statecharts. Modify each specification to incorporate an asynchronous reset.

5. Describe the major differences between a functional specification of a system and its structural implementation. What are the useful aspects of each?

6. *Use SpecCharts to specify the functionality of a commercial answering machine different from the machine presented in this chapter. Compare this specification with an English description of the functionality.

7. *Specify a traffic-light controller with SpecCharts and with Statecharts.

8. *Both an executable specification and its structural implementation can be simulated to verify correct functionality. Devise a technique that compares the simulation output of each in a manner that ensures that the same outputs are generated for the same set of inputs, even though the times at which the outputs appear may be different.

9. **Formulate a methodology for converting an English description of functionality into an executable specification.

10. **Devise a subset of English which enables a specification of functionality to be written in a precise yet naturally-reading form.

11. **High-level synthesis is the task of converting an executable specification to a register-transfer structure. However, an executable specification is often written for readability and not necessarily for synthesis. Describe the differences between readable and synthesizable specifications, and define a set of transformations that can be used to convert one into the other.

Chapter 5

Translation to VHDL

In the previous two chapters, we discussed the benefits to be derived from finding the specification language that best supports a good model for a given system. Unfortunately, though, the best language will not always be the one that has the best supporting tools. In this chapter, we will show how to overcome this problem by translating the desired language into another language that does have good supporting tools.

5.1 Introduction

Several purposes are served by specifying a system's desired functionality in terms of an executable language. First, such a language can serve as a medium for **conceptualizing** the system, facilitating the actual mental process of defining the system's desired functionality by providing a concrete form that can be continually changed and refined, by more than one person if necessary, until it is complete. Second, when we capture this functionality in a language, we provide ourselves with a concrete form of specification. In this sense, a specification captured in an executable language serves as **documentation** that can be revisited in the future. Finally, an executable language can serve as **input to tools**, such as simulation, debugging, synthesis and verification tools. The ideal language, then, would be one that fulfills all three purposes equally, although this is not often the case. The third purpose, for instance, is best served by a *standard* language, because it has a large base of tools already in existence. The first two purposes, however, will be served only if the language supports a conceptual model that can easily and concisely organize the given system's functionality, as discussed in Chapter 3.

Consider the case of a system modeler who has chosen a suitable conceptual model for a given system. Ideally, he would then capture the system model in a standard language that supports this model. Unfortunately, quite often there exists no standard language that fully supports every characteristic of the chosen conceptual model. For example, the best conceptual model for an embedded system may be program-state machines, whereas most standard languages such as VHDL support the concurrent tasks model. Since the system modeler cannot wait for a new standard language to be developed for his conceptual model, such a situation would require him to adopt one of three alternatives:

1. Standard language – This choice is the most common in practice. When using an existing standard language, one must work around its deficiencies, finding a way to describe each unsupported characteristic of the conceptual model through an often complex combination of the constructs available in the standard language. This approach has several advantages. First, even though the language does not fully support the chosen model, we can still exploit the language's existing base of tools and expertise, thus allowing the model to be integrated easily into a new or existing framework. Further, the language itself will be easy to learn, either because it is already familiar, or because good documentation is readily available. The tools may also be easy to learn for the same reasons. In addition, no new tools will need to be implemented, and the existing tools are likely to be of high quality. This approach also has disadvantages, however, primarily because the conceptual model's unsupported characteristics must be forced into existing language constructs. The model must therefore be described implicitly, resulting in a specification that is difficult to read and maintain, and therefore less useful for conceptualization and less readable as documentation. In this sense, choosing a standard language contradicts two of the three purposes of using a formal language.

2. Application-specific language – In this option, one chooses a language that directly corresponds to the desired conceptual model, even though such a language might lack a large base of supporting tools

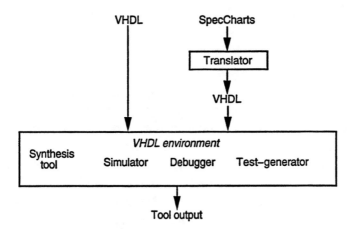

Figure 5.1: The role of SpecCharts as a front-end language in the VHDL environment.

or expertise. We refer to such a language as *application specific*. The advantage of this option is that it ensures a good match between the model and the language, and therefore fulfills the first two purposes of using an executable language, aiding in conceptualization and documentation. This option does, however, have disadvantages, in that new tools must be implemented and learned. Further, these new tools, along with any existing tools, may not be very efficient or reliable. Finally, learning the language may take time, especially if good documentation is not available.

3. Front-end language – Basically, this option combines the advantages of both the above options. A **front-end** language is a language that is intended for a particular conceptual model and that is translatable to a standard language. In this approach, one would choose a language that matches the desired conceptual model, so that the language serves the purposes of conceptualization and documentation. One would then translate to a standard language in order to take advantage of existing tools. This option does require that we implement a translator, but this is still much simpler than implementing a simulator or synthesis tool for an application-specific language. The primary disadvantage of this option is that some time is needed to learn the front-end language. However, this time can be shortened if the front-end language is an extension of a standard language. For example, SpecCharts is an extension of VHDL, which means that anyone familiar with VHDL needs only a few hours to learn SpecCharts. Figure 5.1 illustrates how SpecCharts could be used as a front-end language in a VHDL environment.

On a more general level, the above discussion should demonstrate the importance of language-to-language translation in any practical system specification and design environment. More specifically, it should be apparent that the key issue in language-to-language translation is actually model-to-model translation. Model-to-model translation is the translation of one conceptual model of a system onto another model. For example, if we wish to translate an FSM captured in the KISS language onto the C language, we must first translate the FSM model to a sequential program model; the constructs of the KISS and C languages are largely irrelevant to this translation. As another example, suppose we wish to translate an FSM captured in the C language to SpecCharts. If we merely perform language-to-language translation, then each C construct will be translated to a compatible SpecCharts construct, and the resulting SpecCharts description will consist of a single sequential program similar to the C program. If instead we perform model-to-model translation, we would first abstract the FSM model from the C, and then translate the FSM to a PSM. The resulting SpecCharts description would consist of several behaviors (states) and arcs, which means that the state-transitioning functionality is more easily recognizable by humans and by tools than it would be from a sequential program.

Note that, when capturing a specification in a standard language that does not support the desired model, model-to-model translation techniques often must be applied manually. For example, if one must capture an FSM in C, one has to manually perform the translation of an FSM to a sequential program.

There are several issues that we must consider when defining translation techniques. First, we have to ensure that the input and output specifications are functionally equivalent. Second, the output should be readable and correlatable to the input. These two qualities are important, since one may have to examine the output when applying other tools, and also because many companies require a standard-language specification as design documentation. Third, we must ensure that the output specification will simulate efficiently, and finally, that the output will be amenable to synthesis.

In the remainder of this chapter, we shall discuss common techniques for translating one model's characteristics into another model. Of course, there are too many possible combinations of characteristics and models to discuss in their entirety, so we shall focus only on techniques that might be used to translate several common characteristics into a concurrent-tasks model. We have chosen concurrent tasks as the destination model because this model is supported by the IEEE standard language VHDL, as well as by Verilog, another commonly used standard language. After discussing the translation of individual characteristics into the concurrent-tasks model, we shall describe the translation of program-state machines into the concurrent-tasks model.

5.2   State-transitions

State-transitions allow the decomposition of functionality into a set of modes with a set of arc transitions among them, as discussed in Section 3.2.2. State-transitions are usually mapped to sequential statements of a single task [DCH91, AWC90, Hal93], so that translation would involve creating a state variable, a block of statements for each state's actions, and a series of branches to execute the appropriate block. The translation technique is best described by an example.

Figure 5.2(a) shows a set of state transitions between states P, Q and R. These transitions can be translated into the equivalent set of sequential statements shown in Figure 5.2(b). In this translation, we have declared *state* to be a variable that can hold one of three values, P, Q or R, with an initial value of P. We have created an infinite loop to describe the never-ending transitioning between states. Within this loop, we have added a case statement to execute actions for either P, Q or R, depending on *state*'s value. We have followed these actions with statements that set *state* to the next appropriate state based on the arc conditions.

To see how these statements describe the state-transitions, consider their execution. Initially, *state* equals P. We thus execute the first branch of the case statement, corresponding to P's actions. Following this execution, we check the arc condition u. If *true*, we set *state* to Q; otherwise, we set it to R. We then reach the end of the case statement, bringing us

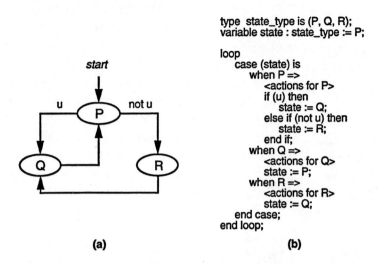

(a)

```
type state_type is (P, Q, R);
variable state : state_type := P;

loop
    case (state) is
        when P =>
            <actions for P>
            if (u) then
                state := Q;
            else if (not u) then
                state := R;
            end if;
        when Q =>
            <actions for Q>
            state := P;
        when R =>
            <actions for R>
            state := Q;
    end case;
end loop;
```

(b)

Figure 5.2: State machine translation: (a) original state-machine, (b) VHDL sequential statements.

back to the beginning of the loop. If *state* were set to Q, then we would execute the second branch of the case statement, corresponding to Q's actions. We would then set *state* to P, and repeat the entire sequence.

The above translation technique is adequate for one state-machine. However, conceptual models often describe concurrently-executing **communicating state-machines**. We can easily handle these communicating state-machines by mapping each state-machine to its own task, and allowing communication to take place through global variables (e.g., signals in VHDL).

Other conceptual models describe **hierarchical state-machines**, which can be translated using several approaches. For example, one technique for translating hierarchical state-machines to sequential statements maintains the hierarchy, whereas another technique other flattens the hierarchy. In the former, hierarchy-maintaining technique, we would modify the above translation technique as follows. Recall that a case-statement branch usually describes the actions of a state. For a hierarchical state, however, the branch would describe yet another state-machine, including a new state variable, loop, and case statement. For example, consider Figure 5.3(a), which is identical to Figure 5.2(a) ex-

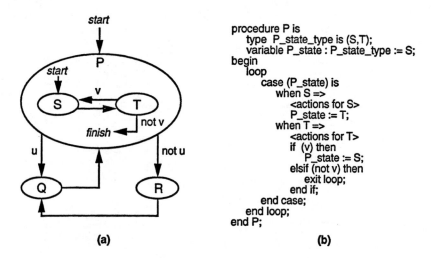

(a)   **(b)**

Figure 5.3: Hierarchy-maintaining state-machine translation: (a) original hierarchical state-machine, (b) procedure for hierarchical state P.

cept that *P* is now a hierarchical state containing another state-machine. The translation to sequential statements is done as previously shown in Figure 5.2(b), except that the actions for *P* have been replaced by a call to a procedure that executes another state-machine. Figure 5.3(b) shows such a procedure for *P*. Note that, when control flows to the *finish* point of *P*, the procedure returns, meaning that the actions for *P* of Figure 5.2(b) are complete.

Alternatively, in the hierarchy-flattening technique, we can flatten the hierarchical state-machine so that only leaf states remain. We then translate the flattened state machine to sequential statements as illustrated in Figure 5.2. For example, we can flatten the state machine of Figure 5.3(a) to obtain the new state machine of Figure 5.4(a). We could then translate this state machine to the statements of Figure 5.4(b).

Each of these techniques has its own advantages. The advantage of the hierarchy-maintaining technique is that one can easily correlate the sequential statements with the original state-machine, since the hierarchy is the same and the number of arcs does not change. On the other hand, the advantage of the hierarchy-flattening technique is that hardware synthesized from the sequential statements is simpler.

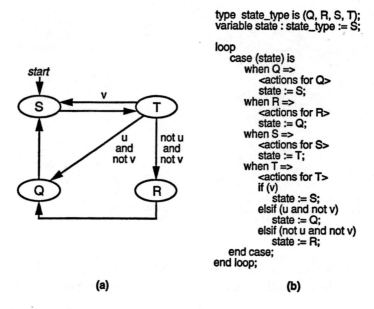

```
type state_type is (Q, R, S, T);
variable state : state_type := S;

loop
    case (state) is
        when Q =>
            <actions for Q>
            state := S;
        when R =>
            <actions for R>
            state := Q;
        when S =>
            <actions for S>
            state := T;
        when T =>
            <actions for T>
            if (v)
                state := S;
            elsif (u and not v)
                state := Q;
            elsif (not u and not v)
                state := R;
    end case;
end loop;
```

(a)   (b)

Figure 5.4: Hierarchy-flattening state-machine translation: (a) flattened state-machine, (b) VHDL sequential statements.

5.3   Message-passing communication

The purpose of message-passing constructs is to keep communication between concurrent behaviors abstract and comprehensible, as discussed in Section 3.2.6. In message-passing communication, data is sent and received over abstract communication channels. Such message-passing constructs can be mapped to a language without such constructs, such as VHDL, in which case we would replace the channels with shared variables, and "sends" and "receives" with explicit actions that transfer the data by means of these variables.

5.3.1   Blocking message passing

In blocking message passing, a message's sender must wait until the message is received before proceeding. In Figure 5.5(a), for example, we illustrate the translation of such message-passing. A channel *chan* is declared for transmission of integer data. A process *P1* sends integer data

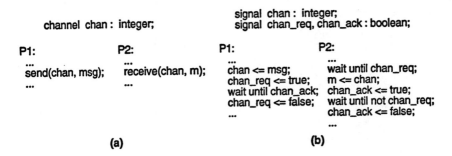

Figure 5.5: Blocking message-passing translation: (a) original message transfer, (b) transfer via shared variables.

from variable *msg* over this channel, and process *P2* receives this data into a variable *m*. In Figure 5.5(b) we show the statements obtained after translation. We have replaced the declaration of *chan* with a global variable, or signal in VHDL, and added two new global signals: *chan_req*, which indicates that a message is available in chan, and *chan_ack*, which indicates that the message has been read from *chan*. We have also replaced the send in *P1* with a write of *chan* along with an assertion of *chan_req*. Finally, we have replaced the receive in *P2* with a wait until *chan_req* is asserted, which would then be followed by a read of *chan*. Therefore, *P1* sends data by writing it to *chan* and initiating a handshake with *P2*. When the handshake is complete, *P1* knows the data has been received, and so continues its execution.

Note that, in the previous example, the sender initiated the data transfer. In transfers in which the receiver initiates, the transfer is translated in a similar fashion, except the receiver would assert a request, and then wait for an acknowledge from the sender, indicating that a message is available. The receiver would then read the message and remove the request.

The difficulty with the above translation technique is that, while it results in functionally correct code, the code is often unreadable because the processes can become cluttered with all the detailed statements necessary for sending and receiving. We can, however, easily hide such send and receive details by encapsulating them in procedures, thus improving the readability of the code. The readability can be further improved by grouping all signals related to a particular channel into a single record

```
type integer_channel is record
    msg : integer;
    req,ack  : boolean;
end record;

procedure send                          signal  chan : integer_channel;
    (chan : inout integer_channel;
    msg  : in integer) is        P1:                P2:
begin                            ...                ...
    chan.msg <= msg;             send(chan, msg);   receive(chan, m);
    chan.req  <= true;           ...                ...
    wait until chan.ack;
    chan.req  <= false;
end;

procedure receive
    ...
```

              (a)   **(b)**

Figure 5.6: Message-passing translation: (a) detail-hiding declarations, (b) transfer with details hidden.

construct, as in Figure 5.6(a). In this example, we have declared a record type called *integer_channel* with three fields: an integer representing a message, and two booleans for the request and acknowledge. Further, we have declared a procedure *send* with two parameters, one the channel and the other the message. A *receive* procedure would be declared similarly. Given such procedures and records, we need only declare a channel of the correct record type and use the send/receive procedures, as shown in Figure 5.6(b). Note that communication has been specified in a manner nearly as abstract as it would be in a language that had explicit message-passing constructs. (Compare Figure 5.5(a) and Figure 5.6(b)).

In cases where the destination language allows procedure-name overloading, as VHDL does, we could declare multiple procedures named *send* or *receive*, each with a different channel and message type. Otherwise, we could give each send/receive procedure a name uniquely identifying the type of data being transferred, such as *send_integer* and *send_character*.

5.3.2   Non-blocking message passing

Non-blocking message passing differs from blocking message passing in that the sender does not wait (block) until the message is received before continuing execution. As a result, at a given time the channel may con-

```
process
  variable msg_queue : integer_queue_type(queue_size);
begin

  wait until chan.send_req or chan.rec_req;

  if (chan.send_req) then
    QueueAdd(msg_queue, chan.send_msg);
    chan.send_ack <= true;
    ... — finish handshake
  end if;

  if (chan.rec_req) then
    QueueDelete(msg_queue, chan.rec_msg);
    chan.rec_ack <= true;
    ... — finish handshake
  end if;

end;
```

Figure 5.7: Queue process for a non-blocking channel.

tain more than one message that has been sent but not yet received. In this case, the channel acts as an implicit queue: Each send adds a message to the queue, while each receive deletes a message from the queue. To translate non-blocking message passing, we will need to modify our translation technique to describe the queue explicitly.

For each channel, we can model the queue using the process shown in Figure 5.7, by declaring a variable to describe the queue itself. A queue data type and access routines (e.g., add, delete) are assumed to be already defined. A non-blocking send of data between behaviors *P1* and *P2* can be replaced by a blocking send between *P1* and the queue process, and a blocking receive between the queue process and *P2*. When a send is requested by *P1*, the queue process will receive the message and add it to the queue. When a receive is requested by *P2*, the queue process will delete a message from the queue and send it. Although the sends and receives are converted to blocking, the blocking does not delay the transfer. There is no delay because the response by the queue process to send/receive requests is immediate, since it does nothing else but respond to such requests. In contrast, such an immediate response does not occur in the blocking transfer of Figure 5.5, because *P2* performs many other actions and therefore may not be ready to respond immediately to a send request. Communication with a queue process requires only a small delay for handshaking, which is negligible, meaning that the overall effect with regard to the sender is the same as nonblocking.

Note that each channel requires two sets of message, request, and acknowledge signals, one set between the sender and the queue process, and the other between the queue process and the receiver.

As a side note, the queue may use either static or dynamic allocation. If static allocation is used, the queue size must be large enough to handle the maximum number of messages that could potentially appear in the queue. Although the implicit queue is infinitely large, techniques are described in [AB91] to determine a maximum queue size for certain systems. This is important because, if the queue has a fixed size, it may become full, so any send requests must be blocked until data is popped from the queue by a receive operation.

A similar approach to modeling nonblocking message passing is provided in [LGR92], except that the queuing of sent and received messages is handled by creating one process for each existing process, rather than one process per channel.

In summary, it is possible to keep communication abstract even when we translate blocking and non-blocking message passing constructs to a language that does not support such constructs, as we can easily hide the details by encapsulating them within the procedures.

5.4   Concurrency

There are many models that are capable of describing concurrent behaviors. Among such models are those that permit dataflow descriptions, where each operation transforms data in parallel with other operations. Other models allow a sequential thread of control to fork into several threads, which later recombine into a single thread. We shall now describe how to translate these two different types of concurrency to a concurrent tasks model.

5.4.1   Dataflow

In a dataflow description, a set of operations transforms a stream of input data into a stream of output data, as discussed in Section 3.1. Dataflow graphs can be translated to sequential statements using two techniques,

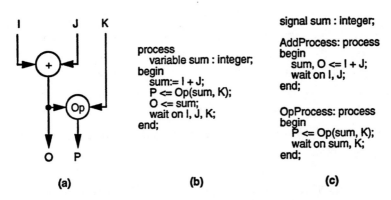

Figure 5.8: Dataflow translation: (a) original dataflow graph, (b) one process per dataflow graph, (c) one process per dataflow operation.

one of which uses one process per dataflow graph, while the other uses one process per dataflow operation.

In the **one-process-per-graph** technique, each output is specified as a function of the inputs by means of an arithmetic expression. All of the outputs are computed in the same process, which waits for a change on any of the inputs, and then recomputes all outputs. For example, consider the dataflow graph of Figure 5.8(a). Inputs I and J are added to produce an output O. This sum also serves as input along with input K to an operation Op, producing an output P. Figure 5.8(b) shows this dataflow graph translated to a single process, which computes the intermediate value *sum* and sets O to its value, then sets P to the result of $Op(sum,K)$, where Op is described as a function. Whenever I, J or K changes, the process repeats its computations.

Alternatively, one could use the **one-process-per-operation** technique, in which each operation would be described as a process, and data between operations would be represented as global signals. Each process would monitor its input data for a change, and when it detected a change, would recompute new output data. We provide an example of this technique in Figure 5.8(c). The process *AddProcess* computes $I+J$ and sets the global signal *sum* and the output O to the result. When I or J changes, the process repeats. At the same time, another process, *OpProcess*, computes $Op(sum, K)$ and sets the output P to the result. When *sum* or K changes, the process repeats.

These two techniques can also be combined, in the sense that, given a dataflow graph, any subgraph can be represented as a process. Such a process waits for a change on the subgraph's inputs, and then generates the subgraph's outputs. The one-process-per-operation technique is actually an extreme case of the one-process-per-graph technique, in which each operation is treated as a subgraph.

These translation techniques can also be extended to handle **hierarchical dataflow graphs**, in which any given operation may be defined as another dataflow graph. Just as with hierarchical state machines, we can either maintain the hierarchy or flatten it when translating. In the one-process-per-graph technique, we maintain the hierarchy by describing each hierarchical operation as a function specifying the operation's subgraph. In the one-process-per-operation technique, each hierarchical operation would be described as a process that forks off the processes corresponding to the operations in the subgraph. As with state machines, the advantage of maintaining the hierarchy is that it permits easy correlation of the dataflow graph with the generated processes. It does not, however, lend itself to efficient hardware.

Another technique for handling hierarchy is described in [TLK90]. This technique is virtually identical to the one-process-per-operation technique, with the extension that each process is encapsulated as a structural component. Such encapsulation elegantly supports hierarchical dataflow graphs, since each operation can be described as a component, with hierarchical operations being described as a set of interconnected components.

These dataflow translation techniques can also be extended to handle **uninterpreted operations**, which have no specified functionality. In such cases, the operation generates output whenever input is available, but the value of that output is unknown. Such output is referred to as a token. The translation technique for such operations is similar to the one-process-per-operation technique described above: Global signals would be declared for data between operations, as before, but these signals would simply be booleans, indicating the presence or absence of a token. Each process would wait until each of its inputs has a token, and then generate a token on each of its outputs. This technique for handling uninterpreted operations is described in [HAWW88].

Finally, we can also extend this translation technique in order to handle dataflow models that allow **queueing** of data (either real data or tokens). During translation, such queuing would be explicitly represented by means of the techniques described in Section 5.3.2.

5.4.2 Fork

A fork is that point in a thread of control that activates several threads concurrently. In some cases, these activated threads will be simple statements; in others, they will be complex tasks. We will now describe how to handle each of these two types of forks.

Statement-level

A statement-level fork occurs when a single thread of control executes several statements in parallel. Upon completion of these statements, the thread will then execute subsequent statements. A statement-level fork can be translated to sequential statements by inserting temporary variables, whose function is to ensure that any variables written in the parallel statements will not be updated in the generated sequential statements until all the original parallel statements have executed.

For example, Figure 5.9(a) shows a statement-level fork. After *statement1* executes, the two statements $x := y$ and $y := x$ execute in parallel, implementing a swap of x and y. After the swap, *statement2* will execute. Figure 5.9(b) shows the same fork after it has been translated to a language without a parallel statements construct. In the process of translation, we have replaced each write to a variable in the parallel statements by a write to a temporary version of that variable. Thus, the write to x is replaced by a write to x_temp. At the end of all the statements, we add statements that update each variable with the value of its temporary version. Thus, x is set to x_temp at the end of the statements. Note that, if a variable, such as y, is not read after it is written in the parallel statements, there is no need to introduce a temporary version since updating the variable immediately will not affect the end results.

The process of mapping parallel statements to sequential statements is especially useful when translating to a standard sequential programming language for the purposes of software compilation.

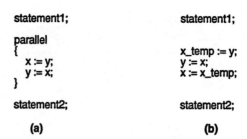

Figure 5.9: Concurrent assignments translation: (a) original concurrent assignments, (b) sequential statements.

Task-level

A task-level fork occurs when a single thread of control activates several tasks concurrently. Upon completion of one or more of those tasks, the single thread continues. Task-level forking would be translated to a set of concurrent tasks by introducing a set of global signals, which are used to activate the tasks of the fork and to indicate completion of those tasks.

For example, Figure 5.10(a) shows a task-level fork. After *statement1* executes, procedures *P1* and *P2* will execute in parallel. Then, when both procedures complete, *statement2* will execute. Note that the only difference between this example and the previous one is the granularity of the behaviors executing in parallel. Figure 5.10(b) shows the fork after translation to a set of concurrent processes, when a process has been added for each forked procedure: *P1_process* waits until a global signal *fork* is asserted, then executes *P1* and asserts *P1_done*. *P2_process* is defined similarly. We replace the fork with a statement that asserts *fork*, and a statement that waits until *P1_done* and *P2_done* are asserted.

To see how these changes implement a fork, consider executing this behavior. First *statement1* executes. Then *fork* is asserted, activating *P1_process* and *P2_process*. *P1_process* calls procedure *P1*. When *P1* returns, the process asserts *P1_done*. *P2_process* executes similarly. After some time, both *P1_done* and *P2_done* will be asserted, so *statement2* will execute. The other processes wait for *fork* to be asserted again.

Similar techniques for handling forking are described in [NVG91b, JPA91, MW90], differing mainly in the number of control signals used.

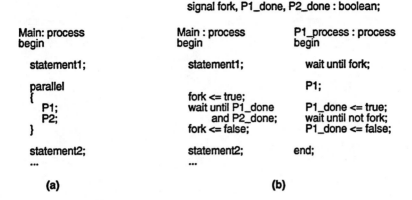

Figure 5.10: Fork translation: (a) original fork, (b) concurrent tasks.

5.5 Exception handling

Often, an exception caused by an external event will require immediate termination of the execution of a set of statements. A construct that specifies such an exception can be translated to a set of sequential statements by inserting checks for the event, with a jump to the end of the statements if the event is detected. Such repeated checking for an event is called *polling*.

For example, Figure 5.11(a) shows a set of statements labeled *T*, which terminate immediately upon occurrence of event *e*. After such termination, the statements labeled *S* execute. In Figure 5.11(b) we see the handling of the exception after it has been translated to a language without an exception construct. Each statement in *T* is followed with an *if* statement that checks for the event. If event *e* occurs, a goto statement will jump to the first statement in *S*, ignoring any remaining statements in *T*. If the event does not occur, each statement in *T* will execute as normal.

It must be noted that the above solution is based on the assumption that the target language supports goto statements. However, to encourage modular program development, most programming languages do not support such statements. At the same time, though, most of these languages do support a statement that exits a loop from anywhere

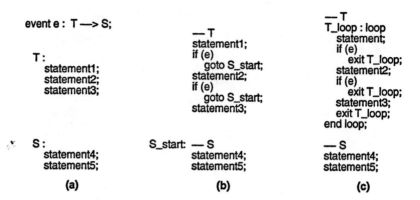

Figure 5.11: Exception translation: (a) original exception, (b) statements with goto's, (c) statements with loop exits.

within the loop. Such a statement is adequate for exception handling. Figure 5.11(c) provides an example of how exceptions can be handled by using loop exit statements instead of goto statements. We have enclosed T's statements in a loop. If event e is detected, we will exit the loop, after which S's statements execute as desired. If the event is not detected, we will eventually exit the loop anyway, but only after executing T's statements. In other words, we never actually loop back to the beginning of T.

This translation technique can also be adjusted for languages that incorporate timing models. In such languages, only specific statements advance time, such as the wait statement in VHDL. Since events can only occur when time passes, the checks for an event need only follow time-advancing statements.

While the above translation technique yields correct functionality, it can have disadvantages, as the resulting statements can become cluttered with repeated checks for events, which can make the original functionality difficult to comprehend. There is, however, a common technique that reduces this clutter, making the resulting statements easier to read. In this technique, the original set of statements is divided into subsets, each subset being treated as a state, with an arc pointing from each state to the next state, corresponding to the next set of statements to execute. In this manner, an exception can be handled by adding an arc from every

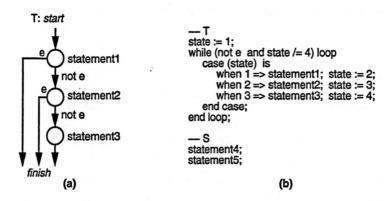

Figure 5.12: Exception translation: (a) translation to an FSM model, (b) statements for the FSM.

state to the final state of the state machine, such that the arc will be transitioned only if the exception occurs. The state machine would then be translated as described in Section 5.2. For example, Figure 5.12(a) shows *T's* statements translated to an FSM, with arcs added for handling the exception. We would translate this FSM back to sequential statements as shown in Figure 5.12(b). Because event *e* will be checked for after every state, we can simply check it in the enclosing loop's condition. This way, if *e* occurs at any time, then we will not transition to the next state, but will instead proceed to execute *S*'s statements. Note that there is now only one statement that checks for event *e*, as opposed to there being many statements that performed such checks, as was the situation in Figure 5.11(c).

The above example should have made clear the important distinction between language-to-language translation and model-to-model translation. The exception-handling characteristic in a sequential program model was first translated to constructs in a FSM model, and then back to a sequential program model. The resulting sequential program of Figure 5.12(b) is more structured and readable than the program of Figure 5.11(c), which was obtained by translating directly from the original sequential program.

5.6   Program-state machines to tasks

5.6.1   Overview

The previous sections of this chapter defined a set of techniques for translating individual model characteristics. With these techniques at our disposal, we are now ready to consider translating the entire PSM conceptual model to the concurrent tasks model. Such translation can be used to convert a language such as SpecCharts to VHDL.

The PSM model supports three characteristics that the concurrent tasks model does not: state-transitions, task-level forking, and exceptions. A straightforward translation scheme would use the techniques described in this chapter to translate each characteristic. However, while the concurrent tasks generated would be functionally equivalent to the original PSM, we could greatly enhance readability and correlatability of the generated description by slightly modifying the techniques of the previous sections.

First, we could map every program-state to its own process, rather than mapping sequential program-substates to actions in a case branch. Since there would be one process per program-state, the PSM could easily be correlated with the processes. Second, we could use a signal to indicate that a given program-state's process should terminate, rather than explicitly polling for all exceptions in the process' statements. The new signal would be a boolean, which would be true when any of the relevant exceptions occurs. Using such a signal would yield simpler expressions in the generated processes, making it more readable.

With these modified techniques, we can now present a new scheme for translating PSM's to concurrent tasks. Granted, several translation schemes already address the translation of some PSM characteristics to concurrent tasks [DCH91, AWC90, JPA91, MW90], but none addresses all PSM characteristics in a unified manner, which is our goal.

In this translation scheme, each program-state will always be considered *inactive, executing,* or *complete.* Each program-state in the PSM model can be mapped to its own process with these three distinct sections. A process representing a composite program-state, when *executing,* asserts and deasserts control signals in order to activate or deactivate the processes of its program-substates. If the target language possesses block constructs for declaration scoping, then nested blocks will be used to maintain the hierarchy of the PSM.

5.6.2 Algorithm

Algorithm 5.6.1 shows a recursive algorithm for translating a SpecCharts description to an equivalent VHDL description, using the concepts described above. For a more detailed algorithm, refer to [NVG91b]. Recall that in SpecCharts, a program-state is called a behavior, and in VHDL, a task is described as a process. The input to the algorithm is the SpecCharts behavior, and the output is a VHDL description. The algorithm uses a procedure *CreateCompletionHandshake(B)* to create a set of statements that, first, indicates completion of behavior B to its parent behavior by asserting the *B_complete* signal, then waits until the parent deactivates B through deassertion of the *B_active* signal, and finally deasserts *B_complete*. Procedure *CreateWaitOnArcs(arcs)* creates a wait statement, which determines whether an arc transition should occur. An arc transition should occur either if a subbehavior S has completed and a transition-on-completion arc condition from S is true, or if a subbehavior S is active and a transition-immediately arc condition from S is true. Procedure *CreateArcsIf(arcs)* creates an if-then-else statement with a branch for each arc. The statements in each branch deactivate the current subbehavior and activate the arc's destination subbehavior. Procedure *InsertPolling(stmts, active_sig)* inserts polling code into statements *stmts*, causing a jump to the end of the statements if *active_sig* is deasserted, as discussed in Section 5.5. Procedure *CreateSignalShutoffs(stmts)* creates statements that shut off the drivers for all signals written in *stmts*. This action is necessary because processes for inactive behaviors must be completely ignored, and thus should not drive a value for a signal. See [IEE88] for more information on VHDL signal drivers. Finally, procedure *Append(l,m)* appends list m to the end of list l.

Starting with the topmost (root) behavior in the hierarchy, the algorithm traverses the behaviors in depth-first order, outputting VHDL as each behavior is visited. The VHDL code for each behavior is enclosed in a block, so that the nested blocks maintain the hierarchy of the SpecCharts and the correct scoping of declarations.

Algorithm 5.6.1 : BehaviorToVhdl(B)

>   **output** start of block labeled *B_block*, with *B.declarations*
>   **if** IsCompositeBehavior(*B*) **then**
>   **for each** *S* in *B.subbehaviors* **loop**
>   **output** boolean signal declarations *S_active*, *S_complete*
>   BehaviorToVhdl(S) /* recursive call */
>   **end loop**
>   **end if**
>
>   /* The INACTIVE section */
>   *stmts = NULL*
>   Append(*stmts*, "wait until *B_active*;")
>
>   /* The EXECUTING section */
>   **if** IsCompositeBehavior(*B*) **then**
>   Append(*stmts*, "loop")
>   Append(*stmts*, CreateWaitOnArcs(*B.arcs*))
>
>   Append(*stmts*, CreateArcsIf(*B.arcs*))
>
>   Append(*stmts*, "end loop;")
>   **elsif** IsLeafBehavior(*B*)
>   Append(*stmts*, *B.statements*)
>   **end if**
>
>   /* The COMPLETE section */
>   Append(*stmts*, CreateCompletionHandshake(*B*))
>
>   InsertPolling(*stmts*, *B_active*)
>   Append(*stmts*, CreateSignalShutoffs(*stmts*))
>   **output** process with label *B* and statements *stmts*
>   **output** end of *B_block*

A VHDL process is included in the VHDL block corresponding to each behavior, containing three sections:

1. *Inactive*: In this section, the behavior is waiting to be activated via assertion of a control signal by the process corresponding to the parent behavior.

2. *Executing*: Composite behaviors in this section are activating or deactivating appropriate subbehaviors via control signals, while leaf behaviors are executing their VHDL code.

3. *Complete*: After indicating completion via a control signal, the behavior is waiting to be deactivated by its parent via deassertion of a control signal.

Note that the algorithm can handle deactivation via the B_active control signal, since it modifies a process' statements to jump to their end in such a case, thus causing the process to reenter the inactive section.

The translation algorithm presented in this section has several advantages. First, the VHDL is functionally equivalent to the SpecCharts for all cases, not just for a subset, as in previous schemes. Second, the algorithm maintains the behavioral hierarchy of the SpecCharts in the output VHDL, and there is a one-to-one mapping between SpecCharts behaviors and VHDL processes, making correlation between the Spec-Charts and VHDL easy. Finally, the algorithm's recursive aspect makes it easy to implement.

5.6.3 Time-shift

The translation scheme we have presented does have one problem, however, which may lead to incorrect simulations. SpecCharts allows signals to be updated after an infinitely small unit of time, called a *delta*, has passed. Such signals are translated to VHDL signals. At the same time, though, the translation scheme is introducing new signals for process control. Now, suppose a particular behavior B is to be deactivated due to some event. B's parent behavior will detect the event and deassert a control signal, causing B to terminate its actions. However, the control signal will be updated only after a delta, during which time a SpecCharts signal may be updated when it shouldn't have been. In more general terms, the delta-time required for process-control signals to be updated may interfere with the delta-time updates of signals in the SpecCharts.

The simple solution is to shift the time in which SpecCharts signals are updated to a larger unit than the time in which the control signals are updated. For example, we can shift the updates for SpecCharts signals to the femtosecond time scale; likewise, we can shift each other time scale to the next higher level. In this case, an inverse time shift of the simulation output would also be required. Details of this approach are described in [VG91].

It should be noted that the same signal-interference problem can occur in *any* translation scheme that introduces control signals during translation, as do most of the above-referenced schemes. This time-shift solution can be applied to any of those schemes.

5.6.4   Synthesis

The VHDL generated by the translation scheme has another potential problem, in that it may result in inefficient hardware when VHDL synthesis tools are used, primarily because current synthesis tools assume that one controller and one datapath are required to implement each VHDL process. Since the generated VHDL contains one process per behavior, synthesis from the VHDL may result in an excessive number of controllers and inefficiently used datapaths. The simple solution to this problem, though, is to flatten the hierarchical behaviors into sequential statements of one leaf behavior before translation. Such flattening is easily automated.

5.7   Conclusion and future directions

Front-end languages are an essential part of any system-specification environment, since they enable us to specify various classes of functionality in a natural and comprehensible manner. To be truly practical, however, a front-end language must be translated to a standard language in order to utilize existing tools and expertise.

In this chapter, we described techniques for translating a number of common front-end language characteristics to the standard language of VHDL. Similar techniques can be applied to translating other front-end languages to a variety of standard languages. A translator is nothing more than of a combination of these techniques, making a translator far simpler to implement than a language-support tool such as a simulator. Using such translators to support a front-end language can substantially reduce specification capture time and functional errors, as illustrated in the previous chapter.

There still remains work for the future, which will include developing new front-end languages and translation schemes for various classes of systems. Also needed are tools to support front-end language development, such as debuggers, which leverage off existing standard-language support tools.

5.8 Exercises

1. Consider a VHDL process with the following sequential statements:

```
process P
begin
    wait on start for 100 ns;
    for I in 1 to n loop
        wait on input;
        sum := sum + input;
    end loop;
    wait;
end process;
```

Assume we want to suspend the process instantaneously by transferring control to the last wait statement, whenever the condition *interrupt* = '1') becomes true. What modifications will have to be made in the above process to handle this exception?

2. Represent the computations in process P above, using a finite-state machine where actions are associated only with the transitions between the states.

3. Consider the following set of statements with a fork-join:

```
P();
fork
    Q();
    R();
join
S();
```

Assume $P(), Q(), R()$ and $S()$ represent a set of sequential statements. Model the above fork-join in a language (like VHDL) that has only a single level of processes.

4. Describe five different ways to specify a finite-state machine using sequential statements.

5. Write an algorithm to translate a finite-state machine to a set of sequential program statements.

6. Write an algorithm to flatten a hierarchical finite-state machine to one with leaf states only. Such flattening is usually necessary before implementing a hierarchical FSM. Ignore the possibility of concurrent substates.

7. Write an algorithm to flatten a hierarchical program-state machine to one with leaf states only. You must handle both TI and TOC arcs. Ignore the possibility of concurrent program-substates.

8. *Formulate a method for translating a set of sequential statements into a set of equivalent dataflow statements. (Hint: refer to the Assignment Decision Diagrams in [CG93].)

9. *Formulate an algorithm to translate an arbitrarily complex VHDL wait statement to a set of statements in which the only wait statement is a trivial one, e.g., *wait until CLK='1'*. Such an algorithm is an essential part of a VHDL to C translator.

10. **Formulate a method to extract a finite-state machine that has been described using sequential statements. Your method should handle the various ways that an FSM can be described.

Chapter 6

System Partitioning

In the last four chapters, we have discussed the key issues in developing a functional system specification: models, languages, and translation. Once we have obtained this functional specification, though, we must turn our efforts to system design itself. In this area, one of the most challenging and most important tasks is finding a way to partition the system's functionality among various system components so that all of the design constraints will be satisfied. In this chapter, we will describe the basic issues and techniques for the task of system partitioning.

6.1 Introduction

The functionality of a system is implemented with a set of interconnected system components. Examples of system components include standard processors or microcontrollers, custom or ASIC chips, memories, and buses. In order to obtain such an implementation, the system designer must solve two problems: selecting a set of system components, and partitioning the system's functionality among those components. The selected set of components is called an **allocation**, and the partitioned functionality is called a **partition**. The allocation and partition must be chosen such that they will lead to an implementation that satisfies a set of design constraints, such as monetary cost, performance, size and power consumption.

In this chapter we discuss system partitioning. After differentiating between structural and functional partitioning, we focus on functional partitioning of an executable specification. We define the major partitioning issues and survey basic algorithms. We highlight published techniques for partitioning functionality among hardware components. We then describe algorithms and techniques for partitioning functionality among both hardware and software components, where hardware components are implemented by designing structure and software components by compiling software. Finally, we demonstrate with an example one of the most useful applications of partitioning from executable specifications: rapid design exploration.

6.2   Structural versus functional partitioning

There are two very different approaches to system partitioning. In the structural partitioning approach, the system is implemented with structure first and then partitioned. In the functional partitioning approach, the system is partitioned first and then implemented. We now describe the features and advantages of each partitioning approach in more detail. We assume that the system components are allocated manually before applying partitioning.

6.2.1   Structural partitioning

In this approach, we first implement the system with structure. Structure is an interconnection of hardware objects, where each object may be a boolean gate or a flip-flop, an RT-level unit such as a counter or register, or even a complex computational unit such as a floating-point multiplier or a Fourier transform. Second, we partition the structure. Partitioning separates the objects into groups, where each group represents a system component.

The structural partitioning approach is very popular, partly because of its straightforward method for obtaining size and pin estimations. A group's size is estimated as the sum of the sizes of the group's objects, and its number of pins is estimated as the number of wires which cross from the group to another. Also contributing to its popularity is the ease with which it allows the structural partitioning problem to be mapped to a graph partitioning problem, for which an extensive body of formal theory, sophisticated algorithms, and tools assist partitioning. To demonstrate this mapping, we define a graph as a set of vertices and a set of edges, where each edge connects a subset of vertices. Each vertex and each edge has an associated value called a weight. A cluster p is a subset of vertices, which has a total weight equal to the sum of the weights of its vertices, and a cutsize equal to the sum of the weights of the edges that connect any of p's vertices with at least one vertex that is outside p. We map each hardware object in a structure to a vertex with a weight equal to the object's size, and we map each interconnection in a structure to an edge with a weight equal to the number of interconnecting wires. We can then estimate the size of a structural group as the weight of the corresponding graph cluster, and the external pin count of a structural group as the cutsize of the corresponding graph cluster.

Another reason structural partitioning is popular is that it has produced good results for many systems. Those results were dependent on the fact that, in the past, system component capacities were not tremendously larger than the sizes of the hardware objects being partitioned, and that the number of hardware objects was not extraordinarily large. Note, however, that the ability to obtain such results may be affected as system-component capacities continue to increase along with the number of hardware objects that implement a system.

There are three main drawbacks to the structural partitioning approach:

1. Size/performance tradeoffs are difficult — When implementing the structure, it is difficult to make decisions trading off size and performance, since subsequent partitioning steps may nullify those decisions. The result may be excessive interchip communication or hardware. For example, consider the following common situation: a designer wants to create the smallest design that meets performance constraints. He may choose to share an adder between two behaviors, knowing that such sharing reduces size without affecting performance. However, partitioning may not place all objects implementing those two behaviors on the same chip. In order to get data to the adder's inputs, interchip transfers must occur, which decrease system performance. Thus the shared adder was a poor choice. On the other hand, suppose the designer used one adder for each behavior, but then partitioning placed all objects for both behaviors on the same chip. One adder would have been sufficient. Now consider the fact that the act of designing structure requires hundreds, even thousands, of decisions similar to the above cost/performance decisions made just for that one adder. The examples described above show that attempting to make such decisions before obtaining a partition may yield poor results.

One possible solution is to modify the structure after partitioning. Unfortunately, major modifications of structure are difficult to make, because a single behavior has been mapped to several objects and several behaviors share a single object. Thus, changing one object may affect many parts of many behaviors, the ramifications of which are difficult to determine. Changes made to structure are usually relatively minor, such as introducing redundant gates or moving gates from one side of a latch to another. An analogy to software can be drawn: once assembly code has been generated, only minor performance optimizations can be made, such as eliminating a memory access by using a register. Sweeping changes, such as converting the code to run on a multiprocessor system, are difficult. In the design of hardware as well as in the design of software, substantial changes require knowledge of the high-level functional and timing information, which cannot be easily discerned from structure or assembly code.

2. Large numbers of objects — Systems are increasing in size and therefore being implemented with increasingly greater numbers of objects. Greater numbers of objects lead to poor results from partitioning algorithms. Such large numbers of objects also make it more difficult for the designer to interact during the partitioning process and to comprehend the resulting partition.

3. Hardware-only solutions — A third drawback of the structural partitioning approach is that it is limited to hardware designs. When processors or microcontrollers are allocated as system components, parts of the functionality are compiled to software. Since in structural partitioning the entire functionality is first converted to structure, such software solutions are neglected.

As systems become more complex and system components become larger, the drawbacks of relying solely on structural partitioning become more prominent.

6.2.2 Functional partitioning

In the functional partitioning approach, we first decompose the system's functionality into non-divisible pieces called **functional objects**. We then partition those objects among system components, after which we implement each component's functionality either as hardware or as software. There are several advantages of functional partitioning over structural partitioning:

1. Size/performance tradeoffs — A key advantage of functional partitioning is that, during the subsequent structural implementation step, size/performance tradeoffs can be made with full knowledge of the partition. Such knowledge enables components to be shared extensively within a system component. Also, performance estimates during structural implementation are accurate since all data transfers between system components are known.

2. Small numbers of objects — A second advantage is the reduction in the number of objects to be partitioned, since there are fewer functional objects than RT-level structural objects. With fewer objects, algorithm performance is better and it is easier for the designer to interact.

3. Hardware/software solutions — The most important advantage of functional partitioning is that it allows hardware/software partitioning, because the partitioned objects are functional. Functional objects mapped to a processor can be compiled into an instruction set, while objects mapped to hardware can be implemented with structure. Since many systems contain both hardware and software parts, the ability to partition between hardware and software is a crucial requirement of any system partitioning approach.

The traditional approach to functional partitioning, which starts from an informal natural-language description, is not adequate for several reasons. First, since natural-language descriptions are not machine readable, we cannot automate estimation and partitioning. The quality of a partition is thus heavily influenced by the designer's experience. Second, we cannot perform early verification using the natural language, so functional errors are not detected until late in the design cycle. Third, since natural-language descriptions are usually ambiguous (as discussed in Section 4.5), it is difficult to integrate system components. The integration problem arises when a different designer implements each system component. Each designer will likely interpret the description differently. Such different interpretations manifest themselves as errors when we integrate and test the components.

Executable-specification partitioning has evolved to address the above limitations. In this specific approach to functional partitioning, we first capture the system's functionality with an executable specification-language. We derive the functional objects from this specification, and then partition them. The approach possesses many advantages common to most executable-language-based design approaches. First, because the specification is machine readable, we can develop tools to automate estimation and partitioning, thereby reducing our reliance on highly-experienced designers. Second, verifying the specification through simulation eliminates errors early, preventing costly changes late in the design cycle. Third, because the functional objects mapped to each system component are formally defined, the specification of each component is precise. Thus, fewer problems arise during integration of implemented components, since there is no room for different interpretations of functionality.

Many techniques have been proposed for executable-specification partitioning. Because this area is relatively new, most techniques have focused on a small subset of the general functional-partitioning problem. In the rest of this chapter, we will define several key issues of functional partitioning, will provide a brief survey of basic algorithms, and will then describe the various partitioning techniques that have been published in recent years.

6.3   Partitioning issues

The various partitioning techniques are better understood and compared if we separate the entire partitioning problem into eight essential issues: specification abstraction-level, granularity, system-component allocation, metrics and estimations, objective and closeness functions, partitioning algorithms, output, and flow of control and designer interaction. Figure 6.1 illustrates the separation of the problem into these issues. Note that the set of issues is not intended to serve as a formal taxonomy.

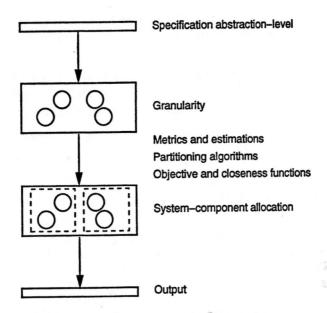

Figure 6.1: Basic issues of a partitioning system

6.3.1 Specification abstraction-level

The various partitioning techniques usually define their input form by the specification language used. However, the language alone is an insufficient input definition, since the same language can be used to represent many different conceptual models, each of which requires different partitioning approaches. For example, VHDL can be used to describe a Fourier transform as an algorithm, as a set of register-transfers, or even as a gate-level netlist.

It is therefore more relevant to define the input by the level of abstraction of the conceptual model. We loosely define abstraction level as a measure of the number of low-complexity structural objects in the specification. A low level of abstraction indicates a high number of low-complexity objects. For example, a specification consisting of an interconnection of gates has a very low level of abstraction.

There are several specification abstraction levels considered by various partitioning techniques. We describe each level of abstraction beginning with the highest:

1. Task-level dataflow graph — The input represents a dataflow graph, where each operation represents a task (see Section 2.4.1). A task is any computation more complex than a basic arithmetic operation. Such a model does not define the actual computations of each task, but instead defines the data transfers between the tasks, and various characteristics of each task such as delay or size.

2. Tasks — The input represents a set of tasks, where each task is described as a sequential program, as discussed in Section 2.7.3. This abstraction level is often called the behavioral level.

3. Arithmetic-level dataflow graph — The input is a dataflow graph of arithmetic operations such as addition or subtraction, possibly along with some control operations, as described in Section 2.7.1. This is the most common model used in the partitioning techniques, probably because it is used in most high-level synthesis research and tools. It is often called a control/dataflow graph, or **CDFG**.

4. FSM with datapath — The input represents a finite-state machine with possibly complex expressions being computed in a state or during a transition, such as $a = b + c \times d$, as described in Section 2.3.1. Of course traditional finite-state machines can also be used, in which only boolean expressions are allowed.

5. Register transfers — The input represents a set of register transfers, where, for each machine state, the transfers between registers is provided.

6. Structure — The input represents a structural interconnection of physical components, often called a netlist. As noted earlier, the components themselves can be at any of various levels of abstraction.

Of course, a single input specification may be comprised of multiple portions at various abstraction levels. For example, one portion of the input may be described as tasks, while another already-designed portion is described as an interconnection of gates.

The various abstraction levels represent the various intermediate implementations during design. Design usually begins with higher abstraction levels since humans initially conceptualize at those levels. Adding structural detail to the system results in a lower abstraction level. Thus the various levels of input to partitioning techniques represent varying amounts of design already performed before applying partitioning.

6.3.2 Granularity

The second partitioning issue is the granularity of the functional objects into which the input is decomposed. As mentioned earlier, the specification is decomposed into functional objects which are then partitioned among system components. The granularity of the decomposition is a measure of the size of the specification in each object. Coarse-granularity means that each object contains a large amount of the specification. Fine-granularity means that each object contains only a small amount of the specification, so there will be many more objects.

For certain input abstraction levels, there is only one reasonable granularity of decomposition. For example, the task-level dataflow graph is usually decomposed to the level of tasks, while the arithmetic-level dataflow graph is decomposed to the level of arithmetic-operations.

The input abstraction level of tasks has the most flexibility for decomposition. One may consider only the tasks themselves, or further decompose tasks into procedures, or further decompose tasks and procedures into statement blocks, such as if-then-else or loop bodies. One may even consider each statement independently.

Clearly, the more finely one decomposes the input, the higher the number of possible partitions that can be obtained, and therefore the better the optimization that can be achieved. However, fine granularity has several drawbacks. First, since there are more objects to partition, partitioning must use more computation time or it will yield poor results. Second, manual interaction is more difficult to support because designers cannot recognize fine-grained objects. Third, the partitioning output is less comprehensible to humans and thus more difficult to design or modify manually. Fourth, estimation is more difficult.

To understand why estimation is more difficult for lower levels of granularity, consider the estimation of hardware size during partitioning. Suppose that an accurate size estimator is available, with a computational complexity of $O(n^2)$, where n is the number of arithmetic operations. If partitioning is done at the low level of operations and there are 10,000 operations, the number of computations required for size estimation is 100,000,000 computations per partition, which is clearly impractical if a large number of partitions are to be examined. Instead, if we consider partitioning at the higher level of tasks, then we can use the size estimator to obtain an estimate for each task before partitioning. While this estimation is computationally complex, it is only done once. The result is that each task now has a size estimate, or perhaps more complex associated size information, as will be discussed in Section 7.5.4. Estimating size for a given task-level partition requires only that we combine the estimates of the tasks. Combining such estimates for each partition is far simpler than performing an operation-level estimation for each partition.

6.3.3   System-component allocation

A partitioning technique must designate the types of system components to which functional objects can be mapped. Some common component types include processors, ASICs, memories, register files, datapaths, and buses.

System-component allocation is the process of choosing system component types from among those that are allowed, and selecting a number of each to use in a given design. The set of selected components is called an **allocation**. Various allocations can be used to implement a given specification, each differing primarily in monetary cost and performance. Other issues to consider when choosing an allocation include power consumption, design time, and vendor reliability. Allocating is typically either done manually, or performed in conjunction with a partitioning algorithm.

6.3.4   Metrics and estimations

A technique must define the attributes of a partition that determine the partition's "goodness." Such attributes are called **metrics**. Common metrics include monetary cost, execution time, communication bitrates, power consumption, area, pins, testability, reliability, program size, data size, and memory size.

Some techniques group objects one at a time, before a complete partition exists. Since the above metrics are only defined for a complete partition, we need a new type of metric that predicts the benefit of grouping any two objects. Such metrics are called **closeness** metrics. For example, a structural object is close to a particular group of structural objects if there are many wires interconnecting them. A task is close to a group of tasks if many variables are shared among them. Discussions of closeness metrics appear in Section 6.5.2, Section 6.5.3, and Section 6.7.3.

There must be methods for computing a metric's value. A difficulty arises because all metrics are defined in terms of the structure (or software) that implements the functional objects, whereas, during partitioning, no such implementation exists. We are faced with two options for computing metrics. The first is actually to create an implementation. While this approach produces accurate metric values, it is impractical, because it requires too much time. Implementation may require days or months to create. Even if only a few minutes were required to create an implementation, such time would still be excessive if non-trivial partitioning algorithms were used, since such algorithms can generate thousands of partitions for which metrics must be computed.

The second option is to create a rough implementation quickly, from which metrics are then computed. A rough implementation contains the major RT components of a design, but does not include many details, such as precise routing or optimized logic, that require much design time. Determining metric values from a rough implementation is called **estimation**. Estimation is the subject of the next chapter.

Speed and accuracy are competing goals of estimation. Speed results from the omission of detail in the rough implementation, whereas accuracy results from the inclusion of detail. Hence, there are various implementation models for each metric which trade off speed and accuracy.

Inaccuracy can sometimes be tolerated as long as the relative goodness of any two partitions is determined correctly from the estimations. Estimations that enable us to predict the relative goodness of any two partitions are said to have high **fidelity**.

Note that, the lower the abstraction level of the input to the partitioning process, the more accurate will be the estimates, because estimation attempts to predict the results of subsequent design steps, and a lower abstraction level with fewer design steps that need to be predicted will obviously yield fewer erroneous predictions.

6.3.5   Objective functions and closeness functions

Partitions are not usually evaluated based on a single metric. Instead, multiple metrics, such as monetary cost, performance and power, are weighed against one another. An expression combining multiple metric values into a single value that defines a partition's "goodness" is called an **objective function**. The value returned by such a function is called the **cost**.

Since there may be many metrics of varying importance, combining these metrics into a single value is not a trivial issue. Most approaches use a weighted-sum objective function, which adds all the products of metrics and their weights, where weights indicate each metric's relative importance. For example, the following objective function is a weighted sum function in which three metric values, *area*, *delay*, and *power* are weighted by constants k_1, k_2 and k_3 respectively, and then summed:

$$Objfct = k_1 \cdot area + k_2 \cdot delay + k_3 \cdot power \qquad (6.1)$$

Giving k_1 a larger value than k_2 and k_3 makes area the most important metric.

Since most design decisions are driven by constraints, simple functions such as Equation 6.1 are rarely used. Constraints must be incorporated into the function so that partitions that meet constraints are considered better than those that don't. For example, we can extend the above objective function as follows:

$$
\begin{aligned}
Objfct \;=\;\; & k_1 \cdot F(area, area\_constr) \\
+\;\; & k_2 \cdot F(delay, delay\_constr) \\
+\;\; & k_3 \cdot F(power, power\_constr) \qquad (6.2)
\end{aligned}
$$

where F is a function indicating how close the metric's estimate is to the given constraint. A common form of F returns the amount by which the metric's estimate violates the constraint, returning zero when there is no violation. Thus, if two partitions meet the power constraint, power plays no role in comparing them, even if one partition's power is much less than the other's. This form of F causes the objective function to return zero when a partition meets all constraints, making the goal of partitioning to obtain a cost of zero.

Another issue in combining various metrics into a single value is normalization of the metrics' units. For example, the area estimate may be 10,000 area-units with a constraint of 9,000 area-units, whereas delay may be ten time-units with a constraint of one time-unit. Assuming equal k's in the objective function, we should be more concerned about reducing the delay than the area, since delay is ten times greater than its constraint. Specifically, the function should favor a five delay-unit reduction over a five area-unit reduction, since the former represents a 50% delay reduction, while the latter represents only a 1% area reduction. One approach to favor the former reduction is to normalize each F value by dividing it by the metric constraint.

While an objective function combines metrics to evaluate a partition, a **closeness function** combines closeness metrics to indicate the desirability of grouping objects, before a complete partition exists. The discussion of weighing and normalizing objective functions also applies to closeness functions.

6.3.6 Partitioning algorithms

Given a set of functional objects and a set of system components, a partitioning algorithm searches for the best partition. The best partition is the one with the lowest cost, as computed by an objective function.

The best partition can obviously be found through exhaustive search, which generates all possible partitions, evaluates each, and chooses the best. Unfortunately, such an algorithm is impractical because of the amount of computation required. If there are n objects and m system components, then there are m^n possible mappings. A relatively small problem, for instance, in which $n = 20$ and $m = 4$, would have over one trillion possible mappings. It follows that the essence of a partitioning algorithm is the manner in which it chooses the subset of all possible partitions to examine.

There are two general classes of partitioning algorithms: constructive and iterative. Constructive algorithms group objects into a complete partition. Such algorithms use closeness metrics to group objects in the hope that such indirect metrics will lead to a good partition. The computation time in a constructive algorithm is spent constructing a small number of partitions.

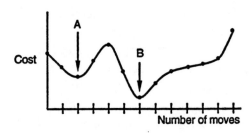

Figure 6.2: Escaping local minimums in iterative partitioning

Iterative algorithms modify a complete partition, in the hope that some modifications will improve the partition. Such algorithms use an objective function to evaluate each partition, which yields more accurate evaluations than closeness functions used by constructive algorithms. The computation time in an iterative algorithm is spent evaluating large numbers of partitions. Iterative algorithms differ from one another primarily in the ways in which they modify the partition and in which they accept or reject bad modifications. The goal is to escape local minimums while performing as little computation as possible. The concept of a local minimum is demonstrated in Figure 6.2, which shows a sequence of moves and the cost after each move. A move is a partition modification that remaps an object from one group to another. The leftmost point represents the cost of an initial partition. The first two moves decrease the cost to A. The next two moves increase the cost, but subsequent moves decrease the cost to B, which is lower than A. A is referred to as a **local minimum**, whereas B is a global minimum. An algorithm that accepts only moves that decrease cost is called a **greedy algorithm**. Such algorithms cannot escape local minimums. An algorithm that can escape a local minimum is often called a **hill-climbing algorithm**.

In practice, a combination of constructive and iterative algorithms is employed. Basic partitioning algorithms are described in Section 6.4.

6.3.7 Output

Any partitioning technique must define the representation format and potential use of its output. The format may, for example, be a list indicating which functional object is mapped to which system component.

It may instead be a new version of the input specification that contains structural objects for the system components and defines a component's functionality using the functional objects mapped to it. The potential use of the output describes the role that the output plays in subsequent design tasks. For example, the output may serve as a functional specification for humans who must implement each component. It may be used as input for a synthesis tool. It may even provide hints to a synthesis tool that can choose to use some or all of the partition output to guide its own decisions.

6.3.8 Flow of control and designer interaction

The above discussion demonstrates that the act of partitioning a specification among system components requires several decisions, such as selecting an object granularity, allocating system components, selecting quality metrics, selecting the objective or closeness functions, and choosing a partitioning algorithm. These decisions can be made in the order listed or in any other order, and some decisions must be remade several times. For example, we may select granularity, select closeness metrics, select a closeness function, allocate components, apply a constructive partitioning algorithm, reselect another closeness function, reapply the constructive algorithm, select an objective function, apply an iterative partitioning algorithm, reallocate system components, and reapply the iterative partitioning algorithm. Thus the flow of control through the entire process can vary. A partitioning technique must specify the possible sequences of decisions. Since different sequences yield different results, the technique may specify sequences that yield good results for a particular design goal, such as maximizing performance.

To be of practical use, a partitioning system must allow designer interaction. There are two classes of possible interactions. The first class, called directives, describes the possible actions the designer can perform manually, such as allocation, moving specific objects to specific components, and overriding an estimation when he has a better estimate. The second class, called feedback, describes the current design information available to the designer. For example, a graph may represent the number of wires between objects, or a histogram may represent the degree to which constraints are being violated.

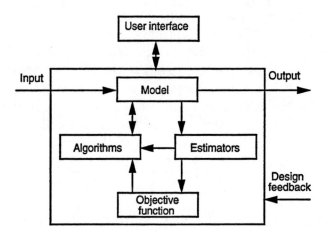

Figure 6.3: Typical configuration of a partitioning system

6.3.9   Typical system configuration

Figure 6.3 illustrates a typical configuration of an executable-specification partitioning system. The *Input* specification is converted to a functionally-equivalent internal *Model* to which various partitioning *Algorithms* are applied. The algorithms require *Estimators* which operate from the model, and an *Objective function*, which uses the estimates. The partitioned model is converted to an *Output* form suitable for further design or analysis. Metrics which are obtained from a subsequent implementation, called *Design feedback*, can be used to improve the partition further. A designer can usually interact with the various parts of the system through a *User interface*.

6.4   Basic partitioning algorithms

A partitioning algorithm maps each functional object to exactly one group, where each group represents a system component. Ideally, the partition that is produced by the algorithm is the one which yields the minimal cost, as computed by the selected objective function. We define the partitioning problem formally as follows:

Definition 6.4.1: The partitioning problem

Given a set of objects $O = \{o_1, o_2, ...o_n\}$, determine a **partition** $P = \{p_1, p_2, ...p_m\}$ such that $p_1 \cup p_2 \cup ...p_m = O$, $p_i \cap p_j = \phi$ for all $i, j, i \neq j$, and the cost determined by an objective function $Objfct(P)$ is minimal.

We now describe several partitioning algorithms: random mapping, hierarchical clustering, multi-stage clustering, group migration, ratio cut, simulated annealing, genetic evolution, and integer linear programming.

6.4.1 Random mapping

A commonly used constructive algorithm is random mapping, where each object is randomly assigned to one of the given components. The algorithm is usually used to create an initial partition for an iterative algorithm. The computational complexity of the algorithm is $O(n)$, where n is the number of objects.

6.4.2 Hierarchical clustering

Hierarchical clustering is a commonly used class of constructive partitioning algorithms [Joh67, LT91, MK90, CB87, GDWL91]. It uses closeness metrics to group objects, since other metrics cannot be determined without a complete partition. Closeness metrics are intended to yield a partition with good global metric values. The approach groups the closest objects, recomputes closenesses after the grouping, and repeats until some termination condition is met.

Algorithm 6.4.1 details such an algorithm, using the notation of Definition 6.4.1. The algorithm uses a procedure, *ComputeCloseness*, which computes a closeness value between two objects o_i and o_j, with the resulting closeness stored in a variable $c_{i,j}$ belonging to a set C. For the initial objects, *ComputeCloseness* uses a closeness function to determine the closenesses, as described in Section 6.3.5. However, for a hierarchical object formed after a merge, there are several ways to determine the closenesses. One way again uses the closeness function, but such repeated use of the function requires much computation. Another way is to approximate the closeness between a hierarchical object o_{ij} and another object o_k as the minimum, maximum, average, or sum of the closeness values $c_{i,k}$ and $c_{j,k}$.

A procedure *FindClosestObjects* finds the pair of objects with the highest closeness value. Another procedure, *Terminate*, returns true when the algorithm should stop. One common form of *Terminate* returns true once the objects have been merged into a certain number of groups. Another form returns true if all closeness values are less than a certain number; such a number is called a **closeness threshold**.

Algorithm 6.4.1 : Hierarchical clustering

```
/* Initialize each object as a group */
for each oᵢ loop
    pᵢ = oᵢ
    P = P∪pᵢ
end loop

/* Compute closenesses between objects */
for each pᵢ loop
    for each pⱼ loop
        cᵢ,ⱼ = ComputeCloseness(pᵢ, pⱼ)
        C = C∪cᵢ,ⱼ
    end loop
end loop

/* Merge closest objects and recompute closenesses */
while not Terminate(P) loop
    pᵢ, pⱼ = FindClosestObjects(P, C)
    P = P − pᵢ − pⱼ∪pᵢⱼ
    for each pₖ loop
        cᵢⱼ,ₖ = ComputeCloseness(pᵢⱼ, pₖ)
    end loop
end loop

return P
```

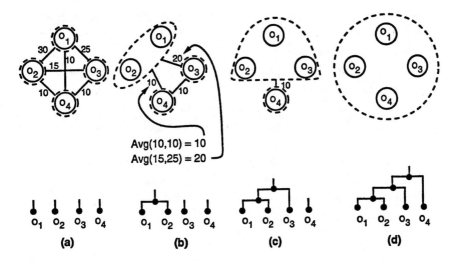

Figure 6.4: Hierarchical clustering

The algorithm begins by initializing each object as a group, and then computing closenesses between every pair of objects. The main portion of the algorithm merges the closest objects into a new object (actually a group) and then recomputes the closeness between this new object and every other object. The main portion repeats until the termination condition is met. The complexity of the algorithm is dominated by the computation of closeness between all object pairs, which is $O(n^2)$.

For example, Figure 6.4(a) shows four objects – o_1, o_2, o_3 and o_4 – and their closeness values. The two closest objects are o_1 and o_2, with a closeness value of 30. In Figure 6.4(b), we merge o_1 and o_2, and approximate the closeness values between the new object and o_3 and o_4 as the average of the previous closeness values. In Figure 6.4(c), we again merge the closest objects and compute a new closeness value. Assuming that the algorithm terminates when no closeness exceeds a threshold of 15, the final partition is o_1, o_2, o_3 in one group and o_4 in another group.

We can modify the algorithm to create a **cluster tree** to maintain a history of the order in which the objects are merged, and continue merging until only one group exists. We can use such a history to generate a variety of possible partitions. Creation and use of such a tree is best described with an example. In Figure 6.4(a), objects o_1, o_2, o_3 and o_4

serve as leaves of a tree. When we merge o_1 and o_2 into a new object in Figure 6.4(b), we add a new node to the tree as a parent of the two merged nodes. When we merge the new object with o_3 in Figure 6.4(c), we add yet another node to the tree. When we merge with the final object o_4, the node we add is the tree root. Figure 6.4(d) shows the cluster tree we obtain. A horizontal line drawn across the tree generates a partition. For example, drawing a line above the second level of nodes, as in Figure 6.5(a), defines a partition consisting of o_1, o_2 in one group, o_3 in another, and o_4 in another. Such a line is called a **cutline**. The line can be drawn at any level of the tree, and can actually be drawn at an angle. Drawing such lines generates numerous possible partitions, where each partition consists of groups whose objects are close to one another.

6.4.3   Multi-stage clustering

We have seen that, in hierarchical clustering, multiple closeness metrics are combined into a single closeness value. When there are many possible closeness metrics, it may be beneficial to start hierarchical clustering with one metric, and then continue with another metric. Each clustering with a particular metric is a stage. Any number of stages can be used. The overall approach was introduced in [LT91] and is called multi-stage clustering.

Figure 6.5 illustrates a two-stage clustering. Figure 6.5(a) shows the cluster tree of the previous example. The cutline defines three groups, which serve as new objects in the next stage of clustering of Figure 6.5(b). We recompute the closeness values between these objects using different metrics from those of the previous stage. We then repeat hierarchical clustering in Figure 6.5(c) and generate a new cluster tree.

Each stage introduces a new hierarchical clustering of $O(n^2)$ complexity. A small number of stages thus multiplies the complexity of hierarchical clustering by a small constant number, leaving the theoretical complexity at $O(n^2)$.

Clustering and random mapping can construct an initial partition for use by an iterative improvement algorithm, so we must choose one of these constructive algorithms. When the iterative algorithm is powerful,

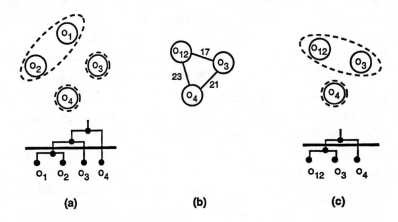

Figure 6.5: Multi-stage hierarchical clustering

the final results do not depend heavily upon our choice of constructive algorithm. In such a case, we prefer random mapping, since it requires less computation than clustering does. In fact, some experiments show that clustering can lead to worse results than random mapping because the partition it constructs is a local minimum, which the iterative algorithm cannot escape. Other experiments, however, show that when the numbers of objects is large, clustering substantially improves the final results.

6.4.4 Group migration

This iterative improvement algorithm, often referred to as the min-cut or Kernighan/Lin algorithm, was designed to improve two-way partitions [KL70], and has been modified to require less computation [FM82] and to obtain better results [Kri84]. The original version of the algorithm minimized the number of wires, or cut, between groups; hence the name "min-cut." The algorithm has since been used with many metrics other than the cut. The algorithm's control strategy has yielded excellent results for structural partitioning, and it can be applied just as successfully to functional partitioning.

We shall introduce the control strategy by extending a simple two-way partitioning algorithm which repeats the following: for each object, determine the decrease in cost if the object were moved to the other group, and then move the object that produces the greatest decrease. This algorithm cannot detect a case in which no single move decreases the cost, but a sequence of two or more moves does decrease the cost. In other words, the algorithm cannot escape a local minimum.

Group migration extends the algorithm to overcome some local minimums. The algorithm is modified to move the object that produces the greatest decrease *or the smallest increase* in cost. To prevent an infinite loop in the algorithm, created by moving the same object back and forth between groups, each object can only be moved once. After all the objects have been moved once, we select the lowest-cost partition we have encountered.

The entire algorithm is iterated using the new partition as the initial partition, until we no longer encounter a lower-cost partition. It has been observed experimentally that the number of times the process repeats is usually less than five [KL70].

Algorithm 6.4.2 details a group migration algorithm for improving a two-way partition $P\_in = \{p_1, p_2\}$. A procedure $Move(P, o_i)$ returns a new partition obtained by moving the given object to the opposite group. Each object o_i is extended with a flag, *moved*, which indicates whether the object has been moved. Once moved, the object should not be moved again. Variables $prev\_P$ and $prev\_cost$ represent the partition and cost previous to making any moves during an iteration of the algorithm. The variable $bestmove\_obj$ is the object that, when moved, yields the best cost improvement, and $bestmove\_cost$ is the resulting cost. The variable $bestpart\_P$ represents the partition with the smallest cost encountered during the moves, and $bestpart\_cost$ represents that partition's cost.

The outermost loop iterates the algorithm until the generated sequence of moves does not improve the cost. During each iteration we create a sequence of n moves, where n is the number of objects. Each move is created by tentatively moving every object to see which object move results in the best cost, and then moving that object and marking it to prevent it from being moved again. If the cost is the best one encountered while creating the sequence, the partition is saved. After all n moves have been made, we check to see whether the best partition saved is better than the partition we had at the start of this iteration. If it is better, we iterate again. Otherwise, we return the previous partition.

Algorithm 6.4.2 : Group migration

$P = P\_in$
loop
   /* Initialize */
   $prev\_P = P$
   $prev\_cost = \text{Objfct}(P)$
   $bestpart\_cost = \infty$
   for each o_i **loop**
      $o_i.moved = \text{false}$
   end loop

   /* Create a sequence of n moves */
   for i **in** 1 **to** n **loop**
      $bestmove\_cost = \infty$
      for each o_i, **not** $o_i.moved$ **loop**
         $cost = \text{Objfct}(\text{Move}(P, o_i))$
         if $cost < bestmove\_cost$ **then**
            $bestmove\_cost = cost$
            $bestmove\_obj = o_i$
         end if
      end loop
      $P = \text{Move}(P, bestmove\_obj)$
      $bestmove\_obj.moved = \text{true}$
      /* Save the best partition during the sequence */
      if $bestmove\_cost < bestpart\_cost$ **then**
         $bestpart\_P = P$
         $bestpart\_cost = bestmove\_cost$
      end if
   end loop

   /* Update P if a better cost was found, else exit */
   if $bestpart\_cost < prev\_cost$ **then**
      $P = bestpart\_P$
   else return $prev\_P$
   end if
end loop

The complexity of the algorithm is dominated by the creation of a sequence of n moves. Selecting the best object for each move requires checking an average of $n/2$ objects. Assuming the objective function also requires order of n computation, the complexity of the algorithm is $O(n \times n/2 \times n)$, or $O(n^3)$. In Section 7.5.4, we describe techniques to decrease the complexity of the objective function to a constant. The decrease is obtainable since group migration moves only one object at a time, permitting the use of incremental estimation techniques. The complexity of the algorithm is thus reduced to $O(n^2)$. In [FM82], the algorithm is modified specially for structural partitioning in such a way that the complexity is reduced to $O(n)$.

The algorithm is easily extended for multiway partitioning. In two-way partitioning, we tentatively moved every object to its opposite group to see which object move produced the lowest cost. In multiway partitioning, we tentatively moved every object to every other group. A new variable, *bestmove_group*, indicates the destination group for the best move. The complexity of the algorithm is multiplied by the number of groups. Assuming the two-way form of the algorithm is of complexity $O(n^2)$, this multiway modification yields a complexity of $O(mn^2)$, where m is the number of groups.

In an alternative extension for multiway partitioning, we first create two groups using two-way partitioning, and then repeatedly partition each group into two groups, again using two-way partitioning. We continue partitioning groups until we obtain the desired number of groups. The complexity is also $O(mn^2)$ since m partitionings are required.

6.4.5   Ratio cut

Ratio cut partitioning is a constructive algorithm that was originally developed for structural partitioning, and has proven very effective for large numbers of objects. We shall introduce it in a general form suitable for functional partitioning. The algorithm groups objects until a termination condition has been met, meaning that no objects are considered close enough to be merged. The termination condition is defined such that the algorithm terminates when "natural" groups have been formed, without specifying a fixed number of groups or a closeness threshold, as was necessary in Section 6.4.2.

The new termination condition relies upon the definition of a new partition metric. We shall introduce this metric by extending the known metric of cutsize, which is the total edge weight crossing a group's boundary. A partition can be evaluated by the cutsizes of its groups, since small cutsizes indicate that close objects have been grouped, as desired. However, if cutsize is the only metric, then the best cutsize is reached by merging all objects into one group, even if the objects are not considered close. To avoid ending up with a single group we could impose a constraint on the number of objects or the size of a group, but such a constraint would prevent us from finding good partitions consisting of unbalanced group sizes. Based on the above considerations, the goal of ratio cut partitioning is to group objects to reduce the cutsizes without grouping objects that are not close, and without constraining the size of a group.

This goal is achieved by replacing the cutsize metric with a new metric called **ratio**. Given a partition $P = \{p_1, p_2\}$, let $cut(P)$ be the sum of the weights of the edges that cross between p_1 and p_2. Let $size(p_1), size(p_2)$ be the size of p_1, p_2 respectively. A partition's ratio is defined as the following, where a small ratio is considered better than a large one:

$$ratio = \frac{cut(P)}{size(p_1) \times size(p_2)} \tag{6.3}$$

The ratio metric balances the competing goals of grouping objects to reduce the cutsize without grouping distant objects. The numerator encourages grouping objects, especially those groupings resulting in only small-weight edges between groups, since in that case $cut(P)$ will be small. The denominator encourages maintaining multiple groups with balanced sizes, since in that case $size(p_1) \times size(p_2)$ will be large.

Given this new ratio metric, we wish to find the partition that produces the minimal ratio. Such a partition is called the Ratio Cut. A heuristic algorithm is proposed in [KC91] using ratio as the objective function. The algorithm creates an initial partition and applies group migration several times.

6.4.6   Simulated annealing

We have seen in Section 6.4.4 that group migration escapes local minimums by accepting cost-increasing moves if they are part of a sequence of moves that leads to a lower-cost partition. The computational complexity is limited by moving each object only once in the sequence. The simulated annealing algorithm [KGV83] also accepts cost-increasing moves. In contrast to group migration, simulated annealing may move each object more than once, limiting the complexity by decreasing over time the tolerance for accepting cost-increasing moves. The algorithm is intended to model the annealing process in physics, where a material is melted and its minimal energy state is achieved by lowering the temperature slowly enough that equilibrium is reached at each temperature.

The algorithm starts with an initial partition and an initial simulated temperature, and then the temperature is slowly decreased. For each temperature, random moves are generated. The algorithm accepts any move that improves the cost. Otherwise, it may still accept the move, but such acceptance becomes less likely at lower temperatures.

Algorithm 6.4.3 details a simulated annealing algorithm. A variable *temp* maintains the current simulated temperature. A procedure *RandomMove* creates a new partition *P_tentative* by randomly selecting an object in the current partition *P*, and moving that object from one group to another. Variables *cost* and *cost_tentative* hold the costs of the current and tentative partitions, respectively. A variable $\Delta cost$ stores the (possibly negative) cost improvement between a tentative partition and the current partition. The procedure *Accept* determines whether to accept a move based on the cost improvement and current temperature, and is defined in [KGV83] as:

$$Accept(\Delta cost, temp) = min(1, e^{-\frac{\Delta cost}{temp}}). \qquad (6.4)$$

When $\Delta cost$ is negative, meaning that the tentative partition is better than the current one, *Accept* returns 1. Otherwise, it returns a value in the range of [0,1]. The procedure *Random(0,1)* returns a random value in the range of [0,1]. The procedure *Equilibrium* determines whether the partitioning process for the current *temp* has reached equilibrium, which can be approximated as no improvement for some number of iterations. The procedure *DecreaseTemp* decreases the temperature after equilibrium has been reached, and is often defined as follows, where $0 < \alpha < 1$:

$temp\_new = \alpha \times temp\_old$. The procedure *Frozen* determines whether the smallest value of *temp*, usually near zero, has been reached, which means the algorithm should terminate.

Algorithm 6.4.3 : Simulated annealing

    $temp$ = initial temperature
    $cost = \mathrm{Objfct}(P)$
    while not Frozen **loop**
        while not Equilibrium **loop**
            $P\_tentative = \mathrm{RandomMove}(P)$
            $cost\_tentative = \mathrm{Objfct}(P\_tentative)$
            $\Delta cost = cost\_tentative - cost$
            if $(\mathrm{Accept}(\Delta cost, temp) > \mathrm{Random}(0,1))$ **then**
                $P = P\_tentative$
                $cost = cost\_tentative$
            end if
        end loop
        $temp = \mathrm{DecreaseTemp}(temp)$
    end loop

For a particular temperature, we attempt to improve the partition by generating and possibly accepting random moves, until equilibrium is reached. A move is accepted if the value of *Accept* is greater than a random number between 0 and 1. Since *Accept* returns 1 if a move improves the cost, such moves are always accepted. After equilibrium is reached, we decrease the temperature and attempt improvement again, until the lowest temperature is reached.

Theoretical studies [RSV85, Len90] have shown that the simulated-annealing algorithm can climb out of a local minimum and find the globally optimal solution if the process reaches an equilibrium state at each temperature, and if the temperature is lowered infinitely slowly. The above conditions require an infinite number of iterations at an infinite number of temperatures, which is clearly impractical, so several heuristic approaches [OvG84, HRSV86] have been developed to control the simulated-annealing process. These heuristics define the equilibrium state and describe how to lower the temperature. The complexity of the algorithm is therefore dependent on the form of the *Accept, Equilibrium, DecreaseTemp* and *Frozen* procedures used. Thus, the complexity can range anywhere from exponential to constant, though the procedures are usually chosen in such a way that the complexity is polynomial [Len90]. In general, simulated annealing usually produces good results but suffers from long run times.

6.4.7   Genetic evolution

The group migration and simulated annealing algorithms improve a current partition by moving a number of objects, saving the best partition encountered, and iterating the process with this best partition. However, we need not restrict ourselves to save only one partition from one iteration to the next.

One class of algorithms that saves a set of partitions between iterations is modeled after the genetic evolution process. In such algorithms, a set of partitions is referred to as a generation. Genetic algorithms create a new generation from a current one by imitating three evolution methods found in nature. One method is **selection**, which randomly selects a low-cost partition P and copies it to the next generation. In other words, some "strong" members of the generation survive to the next generation. A second method is **crossover**, which randomly selects two strong partitions P_a, P_b and replicates a trait of one, such as the group p_i in P_a, in the other. In other words, some strong members will intermix and survive to the next generation. A third method is **mutation**, which randomly selects a partition and modifies it by moving some randomly selected objects between groups.

Algorithm 6.4.4 details a genetic partitioning algorithm, which is a variation of the algorithm in [KV93]. A procedure *CreateRandomPart(O)* returns a random partition of the given set of objects O. The procedure *Select(G,num_sel)* returns *num_sel* partitions created by applying selection on generation G. The procedure *Cross(G,num_cross)* returns *num_cross* partitions created by applying crossover on generation G. The procedure *Mutate(G,num_mutate)* mutates *num_mutate* partitions in generation G; *num_sel*, *num_cross* and *num_mutate* are algorithm inputs. The procedure *BestPart(G)* returns the lowest-cost partition in G. The procedure *Terminate* returns true when a termination condition is met, meaning the algorithm should stop, a common condition being that the best partition has survived for some fixed number of generations. The variable *P_best* represents the lowest-cost partition encountered at any time. The input *gen_size* specifies the number of partitions to appear in the first generation.

Algorithm 6.4.4 : Genetic evolution

```
/* Create first generation with gen_size random partitions */
G = φ
for i in 1 to gen_size loop
    G = G ∪ CreateRandomPart(O)
end loop
P_best = BestPart(G)

/* Evolve generation */
while not Terminate loop
    G = Select(G, num_sel) ∪ Cross(G, num_cross)
    Mutate(G, num_mutate)
    if Objfct(BestPart(G)) < Objfct(P_best) then
        P_best = BestPart(G)
    end if
end loop

/* Return best partition in final generation */
return P_best
```

We first create *gen_size* random partitions to form the first generation. We then create a new generation by using selection, crossover, and mutation, and repeat until the termination condition is met. We return the best partition encountered throughout the entire process.

Genetic algorithm complexity is heavily influenced by the *Terminate* procedure's form. Like simulated annealing, genetic algorithms usually produce good results but suffer from long run times. Also, since genetic algorithms maintain multiple partitions, they require more memory.

6.4.8   Integer linear programming

The partitioning problem can also be solved using a linear program formulation. A linear program formulation consists of a set of variables, a set of linear inequalities that constrain the values of the variables, and a single linear function of the variables which serves as an objective function. The goal is to choose values for the variables to satisfy all inequalities and minimize the objective function.

Formally, linear programming can be defined as follows. Determine positive values for a set of variables $v_1, v_2, ..., v_n$ that minimize the objective function $\sum_{j=1}^{n} k_j v_j$, where each k_j is a constant. The variables are subject to m inequalities of the form $\sum_{j=1}^{n} a_{ij} v_j \leq b_i$, a_{ij} and b_i are constants, and $1 \leq i \leq m$. Note that the objective function and the left-hand side of the inequalities are simply linear functions of the variables, where each variable is multiplied by a constant.

In a linear program formulation of partitioning, we use the variables to represent partitioning decisions or metric estimations. For example, the mapping of an object o_i to a group p_j can be described by setting an integer variable $map_i = j$. One map variable per object thus enables description of a complete partition. We can also define a variable $area_j$ to represent the estimated area of group p_j. We use the linear inequalities to represent constraints. For example, a maximum area constraint A for the group p_j is added as the linear inequality $area_j < A$. The objective function may then be defined as in Section 6.3.5, where the goal is to satisfy all constraints.

A linear program in which the variables can only hold integer values, rather than real values, is called an integer linear program, or ILP. A partitioning problem can be formulated as an ILP. Once formulated, an ILP can be solved using any of a variety of techniques, such as branch-and-bound and Lagrangian relaxation, which are beyond the scope of this book. Since solving an ILP is an NP-hard problem [GJ79], the algorithms used are heuristics. As with simulated annealing, these algorithms can range in complexity [Len90]. Although using ILP formulations can yield good partitioning results, solving an ILP often requires more computation time than the constructive and iterative partitioning algorithms described above.

6.5 Functional partitioning for hardware

We now provide a brief survey of published techniques for partitioning a system's functionality among hardware components. We describe the motivation for each technique, and the relevant issues from Section 6.3.

6.5.1 Yorktown Silicon Compiler

Motivation

The Yorktown Silicon Compiler, or YSC [CvE87, CB87], generates logic-level expressions from a functional specification. Logic synthesis is then applied to optimize the logic expressions and map the logic operators to gates in a target technology. The number of operations is often so large that long runtime or large memory requirements can be expected. To alleviate these problems, the logic operators are partitioned, and each group of operators is synthesized independently.

Overview

YSC converts a functional specification, such as the example in Figure 6.6(a), into a set of expressions containing arithmetic operations such as addition, subtraction and shifting, as well as boolean operations such as AND and OR. The partitioner's input is thus the set of expressions. An example is shown in Figure 6.6(b) in the form of a dataflow graph.

The objects to be partitioned are the operations in a given set of expressions. These objects are mapped to modules, which represent a block of combinational logic; logic synthesis will be applied to each block independently. The number of modules is determined by the partitioning algorithm.

YSC uses a hierarchical clustering algorithm, in which a closeness threshold serves as the termination condition, as was described in Section 6.4.2. The closeness function used in the algorithm incorporates several metrics, which include the number of interconnect wires between two operations, the number of common interconnections of two operations with other operations, the sharability of logic by two operations, and the number of transistors in a cluster of operations. The closeness function attempts to merge highly connected pieces of logic while maintaining balanced partition areas. The function is as follows:

$$Closeness(p_i, p_j) = \left(\frac{Conn_{i,j}}{MaxConn(P)}\right)^{k_2} \times \left(\frac{size\_max}{Min(size_i, size_j)}\right)^{k_3}$$

$$\times \left(\frac{size\_max}{size_i + size_j}\right) \tag{6.5}$$

$Conn_{i,j}$	$= k_1 \times inputs_{i,j} + wires_{i,j},$
$inputs_{i,j}$	equals the number of common inputs shared by groups p_i and p_j,
$wires_{i,j}$	equals the number of output to input and input to output connections between p_i and p_j,
$MaxConn(P)$	equals the maximum $Conn$ over all pairs of groups p_x, p_y in partition P,
$size_i$	equals the estimated size of group p_i in transistors,
$size\_max$	equals the maximum group size allowed, and
k_1, k_2, k_3	are constants.

The first term of the equation favors merging clusters that share common data, i.e., clusters that are highly connected. The second term favors merges that involve a small cluster, which aid in creating balanced partitions by making all final partitions large. The third term attempts to prevent any single cluster from greatly exceeding a given limit.

As an example, consider Figure 6.6. We compute closeness values between the operations of Figure 6.6(b) as follows. We see from the figure that $wires_{-,<} = 4$ because of the four-bit connection between $-$ and $<$. Since no other operations are connected, all other $wires$ values are 0. Also, $inputs_{+,=} = 4 + 4 = 8$, and 0 for all other pairs. Thus $MaxConnectivity(P) = 8$. Assuming the $+, =, -, <$ operations require 120, 140, 160, and 180 transistors, respectively, we obtain the following closeness values:

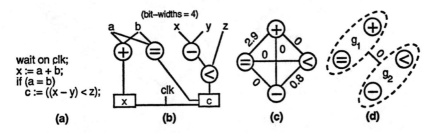

Figure 6.6: YSC partitioning example: (a) input, (b) operations, (c) operation closeness values, (d) clusters formed with 0.5 threshold.

$$Closeness(+, =) = \frac{8 + 0}{8} \times \frac{300}{120} \times \frac{300}{120 + 140} = 2.9$$

$$Closeness(-, <) = \frac{0 + 4}{8} \times \frac{300}{160} \times \frac{300}{160 + 180} = 0.8$$

All other operation pairs have a closeness value of 0. The closeness values between all operations are shown in Figure 6.6(c).

Figure 6.6(d) shows the results of hierarchical clustering with a closeness threshold of 0.5. The $+$ and $=$ operations form one cluster, and the $<$ and $-$ operations form a second cluster.

The partitioning results can be improved by considering the potential results of logic optimization. Some pairs of operations are more amenable to logic optimization than others, meaning they can share logic. Such operations should be given a higher closeness value to encourage their merging during clustering. For example, the equality and addition operation can share logic. An equality operation can be implemented by performing a bitwise exclusive-OR and ANDing the complement of all the outputs. An addition operation can be implemented using an exclusive-OR to generate the sum value for each bit pair. If the two operations have the same inputs, then logic optimization can share the exclusive-OR gates of these two operations, reducing the required logic.

In order to incorporate the potential for logic optimization into partitioning, a new closeness metric is defined. The **similarity** of two atomic operations is a measure of the amenability of an operation pair to successful logic optimization. Similarity is computed by attempting logic

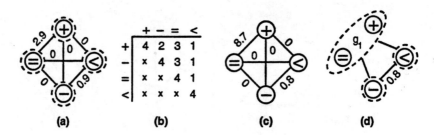

Figure 6.7: YSC partitioning with similarities: (a) clusters formed with 3.0 closeness threshold, (b) operation similarity table, (c) closeness values with similarities, (d) clusters formed.

synthesis for various configurations of each pair before partitioning. If synthesis of the operations results in shared logic, the pair is given a high similarity. During partitioning, the closeness value between an operation pair is multiplied by the pair's similarity, as follows, so that similar operations will be given an even higher closeness value:

$$Closeness(p_i, p_j)' = similarity_{i,j} \times Closeness(p_i, p_j) \qquad (6.6)$$

Figure 6.7 provides an example using similarity. Figure 6.7(a) shows the results of clustering the previous example with a threshold of 3.0 instead of 0.5. Note that no operations are grouped with such a threshold. However, we know that + and = are excellent candidates for merging, because logic optimization results in shared logic. This knowledge is incorporated into clustering by using similarity. Figure 6.6(b) provides the similarities between the operations (details of determining the similarities are omitted). In Figure 6.6(c), each closeness value is multiplied by the corresponding similarity. Such multiplication causes the closeness value between + and = to exceed the threshold of 3.0. Figure 6.6(d) shows the results of clustering with the similarity-enhanced closeness values. The + and = operations have been grouped, as desired, due to incorporation of similarity into the closeness function.

Manual partitioning in this partitioning technique is not very practical, since the abstraction-level of the objects is very low. Designer interaction is limited to selection of the constant values in the closeness function, and selection of a maximum size constraint.

6.5.2 BUD

Motivation

BUD [MK90, McF86] was developed because physical design characteristics such as placement and routing have a strong impact on area and delay metrics. Since system designers make heavy use of such "bottom-up" information when making high-level design decisions, so should synthesis tools. Hence, accurate estimates of area and delay must be available throughout high-level synthesis.

Estimating at every step of high-level synthesis requires too much computation, so a technique must be developed to reduce the time spent estimating. BUD reduces estimation by generating a small number of partitions of CDFG operations, and then performing estimation for each partition. Given a partition, simple scheduling and allocation algorithms are applied, so a partition essentially corresponds to a scheduling and allocation. Area and delay are estimated from a design created from this scheduling and allocation.

Overview

BUD converts a single input task to a CDFG, and then decomposes the CDFG into operations for partitioning. The operations are partitioned among datapath modules, where the number of modules is not fixed beforehand. The resulting partition defines an allocation and binding, and heavily impacts the scheduling in high-level synthesis.

BUD uses a hierarchical clustering algorithm to partition the operations. BUD uses closeness metrics between two operations, including the number of connecting wires, the number of wires in common with other operations, the potential for parallel execution, and the functional-unit area and delay. The following closeness function is used:

$$Closeness(o_i, o_j) = \left(\frac{FU\_cost(o_i) + FU\_cost(o_j) - FU\_cost(o_i, o_j)}{FU\_cost(o_i, o_j)} \right)$$
$$+ \left(\frac{Conn(o_i, o_j)}{Total\_conn(o_i, o_j)} \right)$$
$$- N \times (Par(o_i, o_j)) \qquad (6.7)$$

o_i	is the i'th operation,
$FU\_cost(o_i, o_j)$	is the cost, based on delay and area, of the minimal number of functional units needed to perform the given operations,
$Conn(o_i, o_j)$	is the number of wires shared by o_i and o_j,
$Total\_conn(o_i, o_j)$	is the total number of wires to either o_i or o_j, and
$Par(o_i, o_j)$	is 1 if o_i and o_j can be executed in parallel, 0 otherwise.

The first term in the equation favors merging operations with implementations that parts of the implementations can be shared, thus reducing hardware size. For example, addition and subtraction have similar implementations, since a subtractor is just an adder with one input complemented. The second term favors merging operations which use common data, thus reducing routing area. The third term discourages the merging of operations that can be executed concurrently, thus improving performance, since merging two operations results in sequential execution and hence worse performance.

The equation can be improved by weighing each term with its significance to the overall design. The first term is multiplied by the area of the functional unit needed to perform operations o_i and o_j, divided by the total area of the design, so that large-scale merges are more likely than small ones. For example, a merge which results in a $1000mm^2$ functional unit has more effect on the overall area than a merge which results in a $10mm^2$ unit. The third term of the equation is multiplied by the probability that either o_i or o_j will be executed in one start-to-finish execution cycle of the input behavior, divided by the average number of steps in the cycle. The result is that seldomly-used operations are more likely to be merged, and hence executed sequentially, even if they could have been executed concurrently. Such merging reduces hardware size with almost no degradation of performance, because the seldom-used operations do not contribute significantly to overall performance.

BUD builds a hierarchical cluster tree using the above closeness function, and then evaluates the partitions defined by each tree level, using an objective function that is a weighted sum of area and execution time.

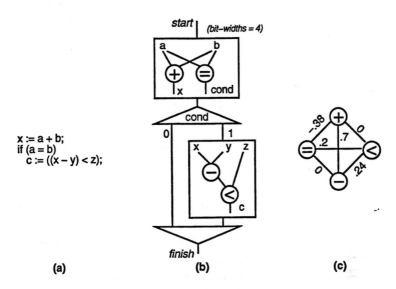

Figure 6.8: BUD example: (a) input, (b) CDFG, (c) operation closeness values.

The flow of control is as follows: first, compute the closeness between every pair of operations. Second, build a cluster tree, using *Average* to compute closenesses between a new hierarchical object and other objects. Third, estimate area and time for each partition determined by a cut of the tree. Fourth, choose the lowest-cost partition and generate the output structure through high-level synthesis.

Example

Figure 6.8 demonstrates the BUD technique using an example. BUD converts the input behavior of Figure 6.8(a) to the CDFG of Figure 6.8(b). (Actually, the CDFG is a different form, but the differences are not relevant here.) Execution starts at the top box, which sets x to $a + b$ and sets a new signal *cond* to '1' if $a = b$, and to '0' otherwise. If *cond* is '1' the second box executes, otherwise execution finishes. The second box sets C to the result of the comparison $x - y < z$.

Figure 6.8(c) provides closeness values between all operations, which are computed as follows. Assume the following FU_cost values are given:

Operations	Functional unit	Cost
+	adder	20
−	subtractor	25
+, −	adder/subtractor	30
<	less-than comparator	20
=	equality comparator	10
<, =, >	comparator	25
other comb.	−	sum of costs

Thus, the functional unit cost is 20 for the addition operation and 25 for subtraction. The cost for putting both addition and subtraction in a single cluster is only 30, which is less than the sum of the individual operation costs, because addition and subtraction can share hardware. Costs are given for less-than and equal operations, as well as for less-than, equal, and greater-than operations in a single cluster. Finally, it is specified that the cost for all other combinations of operations is determined by summing the operation costs.

Given the *FU_cost* table, and assuming that all data is 4-bits, we obtain the following closeness values between + and the other operations:

$$Closeness_{+,=} = \frac{20+10-30}{30} + \frac{4+4}{4+4+4+1} - 1 = -0.38$$

$$Closeness_{+,-} = \frac{20+25-30}{30} + \frac{4}{12+8} - 0 = 0.70$$

$$Closeness_{+,<} = \frac{20+20-40}{40} + \frac{0}{12+9} - 0 = 0.00$$

Closeness values between the remaining operations are computed in a similar manner.

Figure 6.9(a) shows a cluster tree, which was formed as described in Section 6.4.2. Four partitions obtained from the four possible cuts of the tree appear in the table of Figure 6.9(b), along with area and time estimates of each partition. These estimates are provided to one of BUD's objective functions, *Objfct = Area × Time*, resulting in the costs shown. The lowest-cost partition is the third cut. This partition is input to a high-level synthesis tool, which creates a controller and three datapath modules. Each module corresponds to a partition, as shown in Figure 6.9(c).

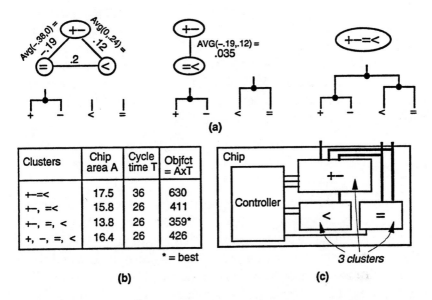

(a)

Clusters	Chip area A	Cycle time T	Objfct = AxT
+−=<	17.5	36	630
+−, =<	15.8	26	411
+−, =, <	13.8	26	359*
+, −, =, <	16.4	26	426

* = best

(b)

(c)

Figure 6.9: BUD partitioning example (continued): (a) cluster tree creation, (b) cutline evaluations, (c) output.

Regarding designer interactions, manual partitioning is difficult because of the low level of abstraction of the operations. Hence, designer interaction is limited mainly to selecting the constants in the objective and closeness functions, and specifying area and execution-time constraints.

6.5.3 Aparty

Aparty [LT91, LT89] seeks to overcome two apparent limitations in the BUD technique. The first is that, as a cluster tree is built, the closeness of two clusters will contain some error, since it is not actually recomputed, but is instead taken as an average of the weights between the cluster members. The second is that the closeness metrics of interconnect, functional-unit sharability, and potential parallelism are all incorporated as terms of a single closeness function, and it may be difficult or impossible to balance the relative weights of these terms to achieve the desired design. There may also be other useful metrics, as larger problems are addressed.

The first limitation is solved by using multi-stage clustering. Such clustering requires that closeness be defined between groups of operations rather than just pairs. The second limitation is addressed by providing a variety of closeness functions, each of which concentrates on specific metrics. Since clustering is now done in stages, each stage can use any one of these functions. In addition, different objective functions can be used to evaluate the partitions of each stage.

Overview

The input to Aparty is a single task. This task is converted to an arithmetic-level dataflow graph, as in BUD. The operations in the graph are partitioned into a set of modules, where each module may represent a datapath module or a custom processor (i.e., a controller and datapath). Each such module may represent a chip or a block on a chip. The number of modules is determined by the partitioning algorithm. The output partition defines a scheduling, allocation, and binding, so it serves as input to high-level synthesis.

A multi-stage clustering algorithm is used for partitioning. The metrics considered in the closeness functions focus on one of three goals. **Control transfer reduction** seeks to reduce the number of times that control is passed between clusters, thus improving performance if communication between clusters is slow. This assumes that multiple controllers can be generated for the partitions. **Data transfer reduction** seeks to reduce the wires required for data transfer between clusters, which may also indirectly improve performance. **Hardware sharing** seeks to reduce the overall hardware size by sharing functional units. These three types of metrics are combined to form five closeness functions. We shall now describe each function.

Control closeness of operations: The goal of this function is control transfer reduction. The closeness function is as follows:

$$Closeness(o_i, o_j) = Prob(o_j | o_i) \qquad (6.8)$$

$Prob(o_i | o_j)$ is the probability that operation j is executed given that operation i is executed, and both operations belong to the same acyclic CDFG. For example, in Figure 6.8, $Prob(o_+, o_=) = 1$, while we might determine through simulations that $Prob(o_+, o_-) = .8$. This function favors merging operations that are likely both to be executed in a single pass through an acyclic behavior.

Data closeness of clusters: The goal of this function is data transfer reduction. The closeness function is as follows:

$$Closeness(p_i, p_j) = \frac{Conn(p_i, p_j)}{Total\_conn(p_i) + Total\_conn(p_j)} \qquad (6.9)$$

Conn and *Total_conn* are defined as in Section 6.5.2, extended for a pair of operation groups, rather than just a pair of operations. Note that the function is $Closeness(p_i, p_j)$, and not $Closeness(o_i, o_j)$, since we are dealing with clusters, not operations. See Figure 6.8 for an example. This function favors merging clusters that would otherwise require many data lines between them for passing data.

Control closeness of clusters: The goal of this function is control transfer reduction. The closeness function is as follows:

$$Closeness(p_i, p_j) = Prob(p_i \cap p_j) = Prob(p_i) \times Prob(p_j|p_i) \qquad (6.10)$$

$Prob(p_i)$ is the probability that an operation in cluster p_i is activated, where each operation may belong to any of the acyclic CDFG's. This function favors merging clusters (as opposed to operations) that are likely both to be executed in a single pass of the sequential behavior. Notes: (1) This function considers cluster pairs rather than just operation pairs. (2) There may be cyclic relationships between any acyclic CDFG's. Thus, the additional $Prob(p_i)$ factor produces a higher closeness value between operations that are commonly executed than between operations that are rarely executed. Commonly executed operations have a greater effect on performance so making them more likely to be merged should produce favorable results. (3) $Prob(p_i \cap p_j)$ also equals $Prob(p_j) \times Prob(p_i|p_j)$. This value may differ from that given above, since calls between procedures are not necessarily symmetric. Aparty uses the maximum of the two possible values.

Parameter data closeness of clusters: The goal of this function is data transfer reduction. The closeness function is as follows:

$$Closeness(p_i, p_j) = \frac{CommCalls(p_i, p_j)}{\sum_k ExternCalls(p_i, p_k) + \sum_k ExternCalls(p_j, p_k)} \qquad (6.11)$$

$CommCalls(p_i, p_j)$ is the number of procedures called by both p_i and p_j, p_k is a procedure, and $ExternCalls(p_i, p_k)$ is the total number of calls, made from anywhere, to the procedure p_k, if p_k is called in p_i (otherwise it is zero). This function favors merging clusters which would otherwise require many data lines for passing procedure parameters between themselves or to another cluster. Notes: the denominator terms decrease the closeness value if a common procedure is also called from many other clusters. Conversely stated, the closeness of two clusters is increased if some procedure is called only by those two clusters.

Functional unit sharability of operations: The goal of this function is hardware sharing. The closeness function is as follows:

$$Closeness(p_i, p_j) = \frac{\sum_{o_k \in p_i} Y(o_k, o_l)size(p_i) + \sum_{o_k \in p_j} Y(o_k, o_l)size(p_j)}{size(p_i) + size(p_j)}$$

(6.12)

$Y(o_k, o_l)$ $\qquad \bigvee_{o_l \in p_i} f(o_k, o_l) \wedge g(o_k, o_l)$

$f(o_k, o_l)$ $\qquad$ 1 if o_k, o_l are scheduled into different control steps, 0 otherwise

$g(o_k, o_l)$ $\qquad$ 1 if o_k, o_l can share a functional unit, 0 otherwise

This function favors merging operators that can share the same functional unit. It discourages merging operations that are scheduled concurrently, since otherwise the operations would have to be rescheduled sequentially to execute on the same functional unit, thus negatively affecting performance. Notes: The CDFG must have been preliminarily scheduled.

Several possible objective functions can be used to select the best cutline. There are three classes of objective functions described in Aparty, but the actual objective function details must be specified by the designer. The first class of functions seeks to minimize area. Area estimates are made by using the minimum number of functional units per cluster, and adding the areas of such functional units and multiplexors. The second seeks to minimize the number of wires between clusters. The wires are estimated as the average number and size of external data values accessed by each cluster. The third seeks to minimize the schedule length.

For Aparty's built-in objective function, if more than one cutline is valid for area or schedule length evaluation, then the highest one is chosen. It is assumed that higher cuts encourage shared functional units, which in turn are assumed to yield lower overall area.

The flow of control is as follows: first, choose a closeness function $Closeness(o_i, o_j)$. For every object pair, compute $Closeness(o_i, o_j)$. Second, build a cluster tree, using *Minimum* or *Maximum* to compute closenesses to a new object after a merge. Third, select an objective function and apply it to each partition determined by a cut of the tree. If constraints are violated, go to the next level. Fourth, choose the lowest-cost partition. Repeat the first step using the new partition, unless instructed by the designer to finish. The resulting partition is input to high-level synthesis tools.

The main interactions for the designer are selecting the closeness functions, selecting the objective functions, and specifying area and execution-time constraints.

6.5.4 Other techniques

Given an arithmetic-level dataflow graph, the technique described in [Geb92a] uses an ILP formulation to perform the high-level synthesis tasks of scheduling, allocation, and binding. In [Geb92b], the formulation is extended to include multiple chips, in such a way that each operation in the graph is mapped to a functional unit on a specific chip. Special techniques are used to solve the ILP efficiently, but they are beyond the scope of this book.

A technique described in [KP91], called CHOP, can be used to evaluate a dataflow-graph partition. This technique first generates a set of RT-level implementations for each group in the given partition, such that each group's design satisfies size, pin, and timing constraints for that group. After this first step, there may be tens or hundreds of possible implementations for each group, so there may be thousands of possible implementations for the entire system. In the second step of this technique, then, the thousands of possible system implementations are narrowed down to a small number of them that satisfy global performance and bitrate constraints. Thus, this technique can be used by a partitioning tool to rapidly evaluate dataflow-graph partitions.

6.6   Hardware/software partitioning algorithms

Combined hardware/software implementations are common in embedded systems. Software running on an existing processor is less expensive, more easily modifiable, and more quickly designable than an equivalent application-specific hardware implementation. However, hardware may provide better performance. A system designer's goal is to implement a system using a minimal amount of application-specific hardware, if any at all, to satisfy required performance. In other words, the designer attempts to implement as much functionality as possible in software.

The hardware/software partitioning problem is a specialized form of the general partitioning problem of Definition 6.4.1. One of its special features is that it is two-way partitioning, involving hardware and software. More importantly, there are two key metrics, one of which (performance) is improved by moving objects to a specific group (hardware), while the other (hardware size) is improved by moving objects out of that same group. These special features have led to the creation of specialized algorithms for hardware/software partitioning. In this section we shall describe three algorithms that have been suggested specifically for the hardware/software partitioning problem.

6.6.1   Greedy algorithms

One simple and fast algorithm starts with an initial partition, and moves objects to the opposite group as long as improvement occurs. Such an algorithm is shown below. It uses a procedure, $Move(P, o_i)$, which returns a new partitioning P', obtained by moving o_i to software if it is currently in hardware, or vice-versa.

Algorithm 6.6.1 Greedy move
  repeat
    $P\_orig = P$
    for i **in** 1 **to** n **loop**
      if $\text{Objfct}(\text{Move}(P, o_i)) < \text{Objfct}(P)$ **then**
        $P = \text{Move}(P, o_i)$
      end if
    end loop
  until $P = P\_orig$

Algorithm 6.6.2 shows the greedy algorithm of [GD92], similar to the above algorithm with an extension to ensure that performance constraints are met. The algorithm uses a procedure, *Successors(o_i)*, which returns a set of objects that succeed o_i in the internal model of the system's functionality. The procedure *SatisfiesPerformance(P)* returns true if partition P satisfies all performance constraints.

Algorithm 6.6.2 Vulcan II algorithm

$P = \{O, \phi\}$ /* all-hardware initial partition */
repeat
  $P\_orig = P$
  for each $o_i \in$ hardware **loop**
    $\text{AttemptMove}(P, o_i)$
  end loop
until $P = P\_orig$

procedure $\text{AttemptMove}(P, o_i)$
  if $\text{SatisfiesPerformance}(\text{Move}(P, o_i))$
      and $\text{Objfct}(\text{Move}(P, o_i)) < \text{Objfct}(P)$ **then**
    $P = \text{Move}(P, o_i)$
    for each $o_j \in \text{Successors}(o_i)$ **loop**
      $\text{AttemptMove}(P, o_j)$
    end loop
  end if

The algorithm begins by creating an all-hardware partitioning, thus guaranteeing that a performance-satisfying partition is found if it exists (actually, certain behaviors considered unconstrainable are initially placed in software). A performance-satisfying partition is one in which all performance constraints are satisfied. To move an object in the algorithm requires not only that cost be improved, but also that all performance constraints still be satisfied (actually they require that maximum interfacing constraints between groups be satisfied). Once a behavior is moved, the algorithm tries to move closely related objects first.

While greedy algorithms are fast, their chief drawback is that they cannot escape a local minimum.

6.6.2   Hill-climbing algorithms

To overcome the limitation of greedy algorithms, others have proposed using an existing hill-climbing algorithm such as simulated annealing. Such an algorithm accepts some negative moves to overcome many local minimums. One simply creates an initial partition and applies the algorithm.

In [EHB94], an approach is described that uses an all-software solution for the initial partition. A hill-climbing partitioning algorithm is then used to extract objects from software to hardware in order to meet performance constraints. Such an extraction may result in less hardware than the previous approach, where objects are extracted in the other direction, from hardware to software.

Cost function

We now consider devising a cost function to be used by the hill-climbing partitioning algorithm. A problem lies in trying to balance in the same cost function the goals of satisfying performance constraints and of minimizing hardware. Algorithm 6.6.2 avoids this problem by removing performance constraints from the cost function; the algorithm simply rejects all partitions that are not performance-satisfying. We saw that this approach is easily trapped in a local minimum. Some hill-climbing approaches avoid the problem by removing hardware size from the cost function, fixing it beforehand. This approach has the limitation of requiring the designer to try numerous hardware sizes manually, reapplying partitioning for each, to try to find the smallest hardware size that yields a performance-satisfying partition.

A third solution is to use a cost function with two terms, one indicating the sum of all performance violations, the other the hardware size. The performance term is weighed very heavily to ensure that a performance-satisfying solution is found; i.e., minimizing hardware is a secondary consideration. The cost function is as follows:

$$Objfct(P) = k_{perf} \times \sum_{i=1}^{m} Violation(C_i) + k_{area} \times Size(hardware) \quad (6.13)$$

$Violation(C_i) = Performance(G_i) - V_i$ if the difference is greater than 0; otherwise, $Violation(C_i) = 0$. Also, $k_{perf} >> k_{area}$, but k_{perf} should *not* be infinity, since then the algorithm could not distinguish a partition that almost meets constraints from one that greatly violates those constraints.

We refer to this solution as the PWHC (performance-weighted hill-climbing) algorithm. It produces excellent results as compared to Algorithm 6.6.2.

6.6.3 A binary constraint-search algorithm

While incorporating performance and hardware-size considerations in the same cost function, as in PWHC, tends to yield much better results than previous approaches, a third approach may yield even less hardware. This approach involves decoupling, to a degree, the problem of satisfying performance from the problem of minimizing hardware. The hardware/software partitioning problem is viewed as the task of determining the smallest hardware-size constraint for which a given partitioning algorithm can find a zero-cost solution. In other words, we must search for the first zero-cost solution in the sequence of hardware-size constraints between zero and the hardware size for an all-hardware implementation (*AllHwSize*). The first zero-cost solution found in the search should be near the minimal hardware size. It is well-known that problem of searching a sequence of items can be solved very efficiently through the use of binary search.

We now describe the hardware-minimizing partitioning algorithm based on a binary search of the sequence of costs for the range of possible hardware constraints, which we refer to as the BCS (binary constraint-search) algorithm. The algorithm uses the variables *low* and *high* to indicate the current window of possible constraints in which a zero-cost constraint lies, and the variable *mid* to represent the middle of that window. Another variable, *P_zero*, stores the zero-cost partitioning that has the smallest hardware constraint encountered so far. The procedure *PartAlg* represents an iterative partitioning algorithm, such as simulated annealing.

Algorithm 6.6.3 Binary constraint-search (BCS) hw/sw partitioning

$low = 0, high = AllHwSize$
while $low < high$ **loop**
    $mid = \frac{low+high+1}{2}$
    $P' = \text{PartAlg}(P, C, mid, \text{Cost}())$
    if $\text{Cost}(P', C, mid) = 0$ **then**
        $high = mid - 1$
        $P\_zero = P'$
    else
        $low = mid$
    end if
end loop
return P_zero

The algorithm performs a binary search through the range of possible constraints, applying partitioning and then the cost function as each constraint is "visited." The algorithm looks very much like a standard binary-search algorithm, with two modifications. First, *mid* is used as a hardware constraint for partitioning, whose result is then used to determine a cost, in contrast to using *mid* as an index to an array item. Second, the cost is compared to 0, in contrast to an array item compared to a key.

Algorithms form just a part of the hardware/software partitioning problem. Research into the general problem is at an early stage. In

[TAS93] and [KL93], overviews of the problem are provided. Issues such as granularity, estimation, and simulation of interacting hardware and software components (cosimulation) are discussed. In [EHB94] and [GD93], hardware/software partitioning systems are described along with the algorithms used and cosimulation techniques. In [YEBH93], a fast software performance estimation technique is described, which can be used to evaluate partitions rapidly.

6.7 Functional partitioning for systems

We now provide a brief survey of published techniques for partitioning a system's functionality among hardware and software components. We describe the motivation for each technique and discuss the relevant issues from Section 6.3.

6.7.1 Vulcan

Motivation

Vulcan is comprised of two different pieces. Vulcan I partitions functionality among multiple ASICs when just one ASIC is too small [GD90], while Vulcan II partitions functionality among hardware and software in order to reduce ASIC costs by using software [GD93].

Vulcan I overview

The input to Vulcan I is a set of tasks and a set of chips. Granularity for partitioning can vary from the tasks themselves, to statement blocks, to arithmetic operations. Vulcan I converts the set of tasks into a hierarchical CDFG.

Vulcan I first attempts to partition at the coarsest granularity. If a constraint-satisfying partition is not found, a CDFG node is decomposed to a finer granularity, and partitioning is repeated.

Vulcan I supports the group migration and simulated annealing algorithms. It uses the following objective function, where *avgcut* is the average cutsize of all p_i, T is the schedule length, *maxschedule* is the maximum allowed schedule length, and k_1, k_2 are constants:

$$Objfct = k_1(avgcut) + k_2(T - maxschedule)$$

Partitions that do not meet area, pin, or execution-time constraints are considered invalid.

Vulcan I outputs a CDFG and a set of mappings of each node to a chip. The CDFG and mappings are input to a high-level synthesis tool which synthesizes hardware for each chip.

The flow of control is as follows: first, merge operations that will be implemented with the same hardware, so they cannot be separated during partitioning. Second, estimate the area of each operation, the wire width of each interconnection, and the schedule length of the dataflow graph. Third, apply a two-way partitioning algorithm. If area constraints cannot be met, decompose the subgraph of the largest operation and then partition that subgraph. Create multi-way partitions by repeated two-way partitioning. Fourth, synthesize structure for each chip.

Vulcan II overview

Vulcan II decomposes an input set of tasks into statement blocks for partitioning. It assumes a target architecture of one processor, one hardware component that can later be divided into chips, one system bus, and one global memory through which all hardware/software communication takes place.

A key aspect of the technique is the separation of operations into three classes. Operations with unbounded delays are called nondeterministic operations. If the nondeterminism results from waiting for an external event, the operation is an external nondeterministic operation. Otherwise, if the nondeterminism results from internal data-dependence, such as conditionals or data-dependent loops, the operation is an internal nondeterministic operation. All other operations are deterministic, since their delays are bounded. An assumption is that internal nondeterministic operations cannot be performance-constrained, so all such operations are placed in software. A second assumption is that all external nondeterministic operations must reside in hardware. Hence, only deterministic operations remain to be partitioned.

Vulcan II uses an objective function which incorporates the metrics of hardware size, program/data storage, bus bandwidth, data rates, synchronization overhead, and time between certain operations. Vulcan II uses the custom hardware/software partitioning algorithm described in Section 6.6.1. Starting with all (deterministic) operations in hardware, the algorithm moves operations to software to reduce hardware cost while still satisfying performance constraints. The resulting partition serves as input to high-level synthesis and compilation tools.

6.7.2 Cosyma

Motivation

Cosyma [EHB94] automatically partitions a set of tasks among a simple hardware/software architecture, as in Vulcan II. The technique is software-oriented in that (1) the input executable-specification may contain constructs such as pointers that can be implemented only in software, and (2) the partitioning algorithm attempts to place as much functionality in software as possible while still meeting performance constraints.

Overview

Cosyma decomposes an input set of tasks into statement blocks for partitioning. It uses a target architecture similar to that of Vulcan II, consisting of one processor, one hardware component, one global memory and one system bus, over which all hardware/software communication takes place.

Cosyma uses an objective function that incorporates the metrics of statement-block execution time and of communication time. Cosyma uses a simulated-annealing partitioning algorithm, although different algorithms can be added. Starting with an all-software solution, the algorithm moves objects to hardware until performance constraints are satisfied.

A key aspect of the technique is the focus on iteration between partitioning and implementation. After partitioning, the designer implements the hardware and software parts using C compilers and high-level synthesis tools, and simulates the design to evaluate the partitioning. The designer then repartitions based on this evaluation. Future plans include incorporation of the evaluation results directly into the objective function in order to guide repartitioning automatically.

6.7.3 SpecSyn

Motivation

We saw in Section 6.1 that there are two major problems in system design: allocating physical system components, and partitioning behavior among those components. The techniques described above have focused primarily on partitioning functions among logic blocks, functional units, chips, or processors. SpecSyn [GVN94, VG92] extends the scope of the problem in three key ways. First, it includes two additional system component types, memories and buses, which are essential in system design but have been neglected. Second, it includes two aspects of functionality, variables and communication channels, which, together with behaviors, comprise an executable specification, but which have also been neglected. Third, it treats allocation of varying numbers and types of physical system components as an integral part of system design.

There are thus three distinct partitioning problems in SpecSyn. The first is the mapping of behaviors to system components such as custom or standard processors, the second is the mapping of variables to memories, and the third is the mapping of communications to buses. The latter two problems are mostly ignored in other techniques.

In addition to performing the partitioning tasks, SpecSyn was developed with the goal of providing for extensive designer interaction. Such interaction is considered to be a crucial part of a system design tool. Designer interaction in other techniques is quite limited, mainly because the objects being partitioned are foreign to the designer. SpecSyn outputs a readable, modifiable refined specification, rather than a complete implementation. Such a specification encourages concurrent design while supporting both manual and automated component-design techniques.

Overview

The SpecSyn partitioner decomposes an input set of tasks to one of three levels of granularity. The first level consists of the tasks themselves, the second consists of the tasks and subroutines, and the third consists of statement blocks. The designer chooses the granularity, which can vary for different portions of the input. SpecSyn supports several system components, including chips, blocks on a chip, off-the-shelf processors, memories (for variables), and buses (for communications). It supports the metrics of chip area, block area, task execution time in hardware or software, software instruction and data size, memory size, bus width, bitrates, and monetary cost. The objective function is a weighted sum of violations, but other cost functions can be added by the designer.

As mentioned above, there are actually three different partitioning problems the designer must solve. Since there is no optimal order in which to solve these problems, the designer can choose any order, and he can repeat finding solutions to any problem. Any basic partitioning algorithm can solve each partitioning problem. Each problem requires different closeness metrics and objective functions, but the algorithm control strategies stay the same. SpecSyn uses special hardware/software partitioning algorithms, namely PWHC and BCS (see Section 6.6). We now describe the various **closeness metrics** supported in SpecSyn.

Behaviors to custom/standard processors

There are four closeness metrics that can be used to group behaviors for execution on a custom or standard processor. **Interconnection** is the estimated number of wires shared between the behaviors. Grouping heavily interconnected behaviors results in fewer pins. **Communication** is the estimated number of bits of data transferred between the behaviors, independent of the number of wires used to transfer the data. Grouping heavily communicating behaviors results in better performance, due to decreased communication time. **Sequential execution** is a boolean value, which is true if the behaviors must execute sequentially for correct functionality. Mapping sequential behaviors to the same controller does not decrease performance, whereas mapping concurrent behaviors to the same controller does. **Hardware sharing** is the estimated percentage of hardware that can be shared between the behaviors. Grouping behaviors that can share hardware results in lower overall hardware size.

Variables to memories

There are three closeness metrics that can be used to group variables for implementation in a memory. **Sequential access** is a boolean value which is true if the variables are only accessed sequentially. Mapping sequentially-accessed variables to the same memory does not decrease performance, whereas mapping concurrently-accessed variables to the same memory does due to access conflicts. **Common accessors** is the number of behaviors which access all the given variables. Grouping such variables results in fewer overall wires. **Width similarity** is the similarity in bitwidths of the variables. Grouping variables with similar bitwidths results in fewer wasted memory bits.

Channels to buses

There are three closeness metrics that can be used to group channels for implementation on a bus. **Sequential access** is a boolean value which is true if the channels are only accessed sequentially. Mapping sequentially-accessed channels to the same bus does not decrease performance, whereas mapping concurrently-accessed channels to the same bus does due to access conflict. The merging of sequentially-accessed channels is also discussed in [FKCD93]. **Common accessors** is the number of behaviors which access all of the given channels. Grouping such channels results in fewer overall wires. **Width similarity** is the similarity in bitwidths of the channels. Grouping channels with similar bitwidths results in fewer wasted bus wires during transfers.

The output of the SpecSyn partitioner is a set of mappings that serves as input to a refinement tool. The refinement tool generates a new specification, with the functional objects partitioned among newly introduced system components. The tool also adds communication details and arbiters, if required.

The flow of control and designer interaction in SpecSyn are discussed in detail in Chapter 9. We include only a brief summary of directives and feedback here. The main directive is the manual partitioning of functional objects among system components. Such manual interaction is possible because most of the functional objects are recognizable to the designer. The designer can also manually allocate system components. A second directive is the customization of the objective function by the designer. Finally, the designer can choose to apply automated algorithms in any order. The main feedback information to the designer is the estimated values of the various design metrics, along with a comparison of those values with imposed constraints. In addition, closeness information between functional objects can be displayed as an ordered list.

6.7.4 Other techniques

Given a set of tasks and a set of interconnected processors, a common problem is to schedule each task for execution on a specific processor in such a way that performance constraints are satisfied. A technique outlined in [SP91] extends the problem to select the processors as well, rather than providing the interconnected processors as input. The input to the technique is a set of tasks whose internal functionality need not be specified, and the data communications between those tasks. In addition, available processor types and their costs are provided, as well as the execution time of each task on each processor type. The processor allocation and task scheduling problems are formulated as an ILP. Designer interaction consists of adding constraints to the ILP formulation.

6.8 Exploring tradeoffs

Functional partitioning from an executable specification permits rapid exploration of the design space. To demonstrate this, consider the problem of allocating system components. Given several system-component types, we must select the types and numbers of system-components to use. Such selection is difficult since we can obtain values for quality metrics for an allocation only after the time-consuming tasks of partitioning and implementation. We can obtain quality metric values more quickly by using estimation rather than design. Since partitioning and estimation can be automated in the executable-specification approach, metric values are obtained rapidly.

We shall use an example to demonstrate one use of quickly obtainable metric values in making tradeoffs. The example is a real-time medical system used to measure the volume of a bladder. A monitoring device external to the system inputs sonic data. The system then performs

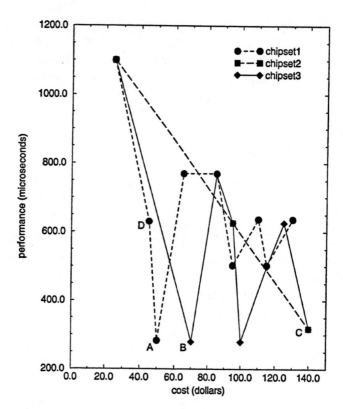

Figure 6.10: Cost vs. performance tradeoffs of various allocations of three chipsets for the volume measurement system

several computations with this data to detect the walls of the bladder and its volume, dynamically repositioning the monitoring device as needed.

Assume that three vendors each provide a chip set, i.e., system-component types with varying cost and performance characteristics. We must choose a chip set, and then choose an allocation from that chip set. Assume, too, that a processor can be used with each chip set.

We automatically generate all possible allocations for each chip set, with a monetary cost under $145. For each allocation, we automatically partition the system's functionality, considering performance and package size/pin constraints. If size and pin constraints are not satisfied, the allocation is rejected. For the remaining allocations, we estimate system performance. The entire process is automated and requires 2.5 hours running on a Sparc 2 for the example system.

Results are shown in Figure 6.10. The first point for each curve corresponds to an all-software design running on the processor. The remaining points correspond to allocations with one or more of each chip set's package types, with or without the processor. If we want the best performance solution with the lowest cost, we note that chipset 1 provides such a solution at Point *A*. That point corresponds to a single 20,000 gate chip. Chipset 2 also provides similar performance for slightly higher cost at Point *B*, in which a 20,000 gate chip is also used. Obtaining similar performance with chipset 3 is much more expensive, as shown with Point *C*. If we don't need best performance, but instead are satisfied with a performance below 650 microseconds, then chipset 1 provides the cheapest solution, as shown with Point *D*. This solution consists of the processor and a 10,000-gate chip.

There are several factors to consider in choosing an allocation, in addition to monetary cost and system performance. These factors include non-recurring engineering costs (NRE), power dissipation, package size, development time, yield, vendor reliability, and vendor support. Balancing these factors in comparing different allocations is a complex task, for which tradeoff curves can be extremely useful.

6.9 Conclusion and future directions

Functional partitioning is a crucial part of system design with a substantial effect on the quality of the final design. Functional partitioning is best performed starting from an executable specification, since such specifications are machine readable and thus enable application of automated estimation and partitioning tools. Such tools permit rapid exploration of design alternatives, and therefore result in good overall designs. As an added benefit, the executable specification and the specific steps applied with the tool can be combined to form excellent design documentation, which in turn can greatly reduce design and redesign time.

There are several topics for future research. After a design is implemented, it is sometimes found that estimates during partitioning were inaccurate, resulting in a design that can be improved. It would be useful if metrics obtained from the implementation could be fed back to the partitioning task, and partitioning reapplied with consideration of these more accurate metrics. In other words, the more accurate metric values obtained from the implementation would be used to guide the partitioning algorithm to find an even better solution.

A comparative analysis of various partitioning algorithms would prove helpful. Previous algorithm comparisons for circuit partitioning are not necessarily valid for functional partitioning. Of additional interest are the quality of results obtained through the many possible selections and orderings of closeness metrics.

The effect of granularity on quality could be better understood. Approaches which partition at multiple levels of granularity may also prove beneficial.

Many systems exhibit a high degree of regularity. By regularity we mean that many of the behaviors in the system are identical to one another, differing only in the data on which they operate. Such systems are often designed with multiple chips that are identical to one another; hence, only one chip design need be implemented. Future algorithms should incorporate techniques to partition regular and semi-regular behaviors.

In summary, since partitioning is a fairly mature field, the majority of future tasks involve adaptation of existing techniques for applicability at the functional level.

6.10   Exercises

1. Determine the computational complexity for each algorithm described in this chapter.

2. (a) Create an expression indicating the number of possible mappings of N objects among M partitions. (b) How many possible mappings are there of 100 objects among 3 partitions? (c) If a particular partitioning algorithm examines N^2 partitions, what fraction of the total number of possible partitions has been examined?

3. Decompose the *Answer* behavior from the answering machine of Chapter 4 to the granularity of: (1) tasks, (2) statement blocks, and

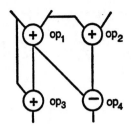

Figure 6.11: A sample data-flow graph.

(3) statements, by listing the functional objects for each. Ignore the *RemoteOperation* behavior, for the sake of simplicity. (a) How many objects exist for each? (b) Which granularities would you be able to partition manually?

4. Assume an executable specification can be decomposed into 50 behaviors, 250 statement blocks, 1750 statements, or 2000 control/dataflow graph operations. If a partitioning algorithm examines n^2 partitions and requires five milliseconds to evaluate each, what is the approximate runtime for the algorithm for each of the four decomposition granularities?

5. Address the differences between hierarchical clustering and multistage clustering, and the advantages and disadvantages of each.

6. Determine the closeness between all pairs of objects for the graph in Figure 6.11, using the closeness function described for **BUD**, where adder cost = 1 and subtractor cost = 1.

7. Manually perform a structural and a functional two-way partitioning for just the *Answer* behavior of the answering machine of Chapter 4 (*or the entire system if time permits), with the goal of obtaining roughly equally-sized partitions with a minimal number of pins. Compare the final implemented structure for each approach in terms of estimated size and pins.

8. Show how group migration would improve the graph partitioning of Figure 6.12. Each vertex has a size of one and each edge a weight of one. Assume the objective function is $5 * SizeViolations +$

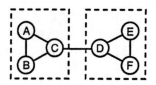

Figure 6.12: Example partitioning

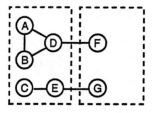

Figure 6.13: Example partitioning

Edges_crossing, where the size constraint of a partition is 4. Perform moves in alphabetical order and if several moves yield equal costs, choose the first. Note that negative moves are accepted before an overall lower cost is found.

9. Extend group migration to be able to detect that moving E in Figure 6.13 is better than moving D, because a subsequent move of C results in one less edge crossing. (Hint: see [Kri84].)

10. Develop an ILP formulation for partitioning a graph into M partitions, given constraints on the total size and cutsize of each partition. Discuss how to extend this formulation for functional partitioning.

11. Suppose hardware/software partitioning is done at the level of CDFG operations. A portion of the CDFG will thus be mapped to software. (a) Develop an algorithm to convert a CDFG as in Figure 6.8(b) to equivalent software. (b) Convert the CDFG of Figure 6.8(b) to software using your algorithm.

12. Consider the CDFG of Figure 6.8(b). Assume that the + and − operations are mapped to hardware, with the rest of the CDFG mapped to software. Provide a VHDL functional specification of

the hardware and software parts, making sure to specify precisely the interfaces of the two components and the details of the manner in which communication is achieved.

13. *Implement a weighted-graph partitioning tool incorporating the algorithms described in this chapter.

14. *Using the tool of the previous problem, perform a comparative analysis of the various algorithms for a set of examples. Compare the runtime and the design quality as measured by an objective function of your choice.

15. **Develop a method for incorporating implementation quality metrics into partitioning to encourage iterations between the step of partitioning with estimations and the step of implementation.

16. **Develop a method for combining functional partitioning with high-level synthesis.

Chapter 7

Design Quality Estimation

In the previous chapter, we described some of the basic issues and techniques for partitioning a system's functionality among various system components, such that constraints on various design metrics, such as performance and area, would be satisfied. In order to determine if these constraints have actually been satisfied, however, we must be able to obtain metric estimates as rapidly as possible. In this chapter, then, we will describe some of the techniques that can be used for such rapid estimation of both hardware and software quality metrics.

7.1 Introduction

Estimation of design quality at the system level is essential for two reasons. First, it enables the designer to evaluate the design quality by comparing the estimates of any design metric with the constraints specified for that metric. For example, if the design's estimated area is greater than the allowed die size, then one or more array variables in the specification may need to be implemented as an off-chip memory to satisfy the die-size constraint. Second, estimates enable the system designer to explore design alternatives by providing quick feedback for any design decision. This way a designer can explore a greater number of alternatives instead of synthesizing a complete implementation and measuring the particular design quality metric for each design alternative.

Design model		Additional tasks	Accuracy	Fidelity	Speed
			low	low	fast
a)	Mem	Mem allocation			
b)	Mem + FUs	FU allocation			
c)	Mem + FUs + Reg	Lifetime analysis			
d)	Mem + FUs + Reg + Muxes	FU binding			
e)	Mem + FUs + Reg + Muxes + Wiring	Floorplanning			
			high	high	slow

Mem: memories   FUs: functional units   Reg: registers   Muxes: multiplexers

Figure 7.1: Typical estimation models and associated accuracy, fidelity and speed of estimation.

We can define a **design model** used for estimating each quality metric. Any estimate's effectiveness and usefulness depends upon the accuracy with which the design model represents the real design.

To demonstrate the impact of design models on estimation, we list in Figure 7.1 typical design models that may be used for estimating a system's area from its functional specification. The various types of design models in the figure represent a **progression of detail** that needs to be estimated in order to improve the accuracy of the area estimate. For each model in the figure, we also list additional tasks that an estimator must perform in order to achieve a more accurate estimate in comparison to the previous model.

For example, if only the size of the memories in the system is used as a model, as shown in Figure 7.1(a), *Memory allocation* will be required to determine the type and size of the memories and thus the area of the design. If functional units are added to the model, as shown in Figure 7.1(b), in addition to memory allocation, *Functional unit allocation* is required to determine the types and numbers of functional units in the design. Similarly, incorporating registers and latches in the model, as shown in Figure 7.1(c), requires variable *Lifetime analysis* in order to determine the number of variables that need to be stored at any time. Further addition of multiplexers to the design model, as in Figure 7.1(d), requires *Functional-unit binding* in order to determine the number of connections from storage units to the functional units, which in turn determines the size of the multiplexers. Finally, in Figure 7.1(e), incorporating the wiring area in the design model requires *Floorplanning* in order to determine the physical locations and orientations of components, and thus the approximate position and length of the wires that connect them.

7.1.1 Accuracy versus speed

The preceding discussion makes clear that an important issue in selecting a design model is the tradeoff between the accuracy and the speed of computing an estimate. The **accuracy** of an estimate is a measure of how close the estimate is to the actual value of the metric measured after design implementation. Let $E(D)$ and $M(D)$ represent the estimated and the actual measured values, respectively, of a quality metric for a design implementation D. The accuracy of the estimate, $\mathcal{A}$, is defined as the following:

$$\mathcal{A} = 1 - \frac{|E(D) - M(D)|}{M(D)} \qquad (7.1)$$

Hence, a perfect estimate has an accuracy $\mathcal{A} = 1$, and others have an accuracy less than 1. The accuracy depends upon the degree of detail in the design model. For example, the model of Figure 7.1(a) approximates design area as the sum of the memory areas. Estimators based on such simple models execute rapidly and are very easy to develop, since only a few design characteristics are included in the computation of the estimated metric. However, simple models do not have the accuracy that would be required to guide the system designer in selecting proper design alternatives.

On the other hand, a design model may incorporate several aspects of the design. For example, a detailed area estimate would require determining the number and size of the memories, functional units, registers and multiplexers in addition to the wiring area. These calculations would in turn involve performing tasks such as functional-unit allocation, variable lifetime analysis, functional-unit binding and floorplanning, as shown in the example of Figure 7.1(e). Estimators based on such detailed design models require longer computation times, but also produce more accurate estimates, and therefore allow a better selection of design alternatives.

In general, simplified estimation models yield fast estimators but result in greater estimation error and less accuracy. On the other hand, a high level of accuracy may not always be required as long as the estimated value of the quality metric allows the system designer to make proper tradeoff decisions between any pair of design alternatives. In this case, we would need to select an estimation model that will yield estimates that have high fidelity.

7.1.2   Fidelity of estimation

The **fidelity** [KGRC93] of an estimation method is defined as the percentage of correctly predicted comparisons between design implementations. If the estimated values of a design metric for two different implementations bear the same comparative relationship to each other as do the measured values of the metric, then the estimate correctly compares the two implementations. In other words, the estimated metric can be used for selecting the best implementation from a set of several possible implementations. The higher the fidelity of the estimation, the more likely that correct design decisions will be made based on comparing the estimates of two implementations.

To define fidelity formally, consider an arbitrary functional specification. Let $\mathcal{D} = \{D_1, D_2...D_n\}$ be the set of implementations of this specification. Let's define μ_{ij}, for all i, j such that $1 \leq i, j \leq n$ and $i \neq j$, as follows:

$$\mu_{ij} = \begin{cases} 1 & \text{if} & \begin{aligned} E(D_i) &> E(D_j) \quad \text{and} \quad M(D_i) > M(D_j), \text{or} \\ E(D_i) &< E(D_j) \quad \text{and} \quad M(D_i) < M(D_j), \text{or} \\ E(D_i) &= E(D_j) \quad \text{and} \quad M(D_i) = M(D_j) \end{aligned} \\ 0 & \text{otherwise} \end{cases}$$

$$(7.2)$$

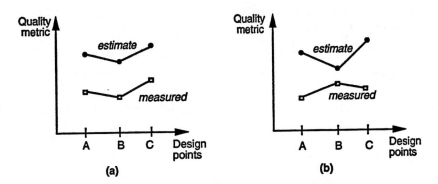

Figure 7.2: Two examples of estimation fidelity: (a) 100%, (b) 33%.

The fidelity, F, of an estimation method can then be defined as a percentage of correct predictions, by the following equation:

$$\mathcal{F} = 100 \times \frac{2}{n(n-1)} \sum_{i=1}^{n} \sum_{j=i+1}^{n} \mu_{ij} \qquad (7.3)$$

Figure 7.2 illustrates the computation of fidelity for estimates of some quality metric based on three design points A, B and C. Consider the estimates of the quality metric produced by an estimator and the actual values of the metric obtained from the design implementations shown in Figure 7.2(a). Both the estimated and actual values of the metric are higher for design implementation A than for design implementation B. The same holds true for design implementation pairs (B, C) and (A, C). The fidelity of such an estimator is 100%.

Now, consider the pair of design points (A, B) in Figure 7.2(b). Looking at the figure, we can see that $E(A) > E(B)$, while $M(A) < M(B)$. The same is true for design point pair (B, C). Of the three design point pairs, only (A, C) has a non-zero value for μ_{ij}, as computed in Equation 7.2. Therefore, the estimator fidelity in Figure 7.2(b) is only 33%.

During the selection of one of several design implementations, predictions of design quality based on estimates with high fidelity will result, on average, in better designs. Fidelity depends upon the design model used to estimate the design parameter. In general, the more accurate the model, the higher the fidelity of estimation.

7.2   Quality metrics

In this section, we describe some of the quality metrics commonly used to characterize a design. The two most important metrics are the cost and performance of hardware and software implementations. Although other metrics play a significant role, many high-level decisions are based entirely on these two metrics.

7.2.1   Hardware cost metrics

Hardware cost metrics include the cost of manufacturing the chips, packaging cost, testing cost, and prorated engineering and design cost.

The manufacturing cost depends on the size of the design implementation. The most common size metric is the design **area**, which is a measure of the silicon area required by an implementation. For a given design, an area estimate may include the area required for the storage elements (registers and memories), functional units (ALUs), interconnect units (multiplexers and buses), control logic and the wiring area required to connect these components.

Area estimates are useful at the system level when deciding whether certain portions of the design can fit into a given chip area predicted to produce the maximum yield during fabrication. For example, if a design is estimated to have an area of 80,000 square microns, it cannot be implemented on a chip with maximum allowed chip area of 50,000 square microns. The design will have to be partitioned and implemented as two or more chips.

Occasionally, the size of an implementation is approximated not by the area of the design, but by related measures such as the number of transistors, gates, register-level components, the size of the PC board, or the cabinet space required by the system. For example, for semicustom (gate array) and programmable (FPGA) technologies, the number of gates or the number of combinational logic blocks on any one chip are limited. Estimates of these metrics will enable the system designer to determine how many gate arrays or FPGAs will be required for implementing the design. Such size metrics offer very high fidelity, since the size of each transistor, gate or register-level component is well known and the area can be approximated as a summation of these component sizes multiplied by an appropriate constant to account for wiring and I/O. In addition, the number of components is available much earlier in the design cycle than the design area is.

The packaging cost is often approximated as the number of **pins** in the design. The ability to estimate pins is important: the designer always attempts to minimize the number of pins in the design, since the number of pins on a chip affects not only the packaging cost, but also the board area resulting from interconnecting all the chips on the board.

7.2.2 Software cost metrics

While a hardware implementation has the advantage of enhanced performance, portions of the design are often implemented as software executing on a specific microprocessor. Several advantages are associated with a software implementation. First, the cost of such an implementation is very low, since programmable components such as processors and micro-controllers are usually manufactured on a large scale. Second, the development time required for software implementations could be significantly shorter. Given an executable specification, a software implementation mainly requires compilation, whereas a hardware implementation requires several design tasks, including testing and fabrication. Finally, software implementations lend themselves to specification changes at a late stage in the design cycle. Such changes in a hardware implementation will often require a great deal of redesign.

A specification implemented in software will be compiled into the selected processor's instruction set. The two cost metrics associated with a software implementation are the program memory size and data memory size. **Program memory size** is a measure of the memory required to store the compiled specification's instructions. **Data memory size** represents the amount of memory required to store all the data values (variables and arrays) created or manipulated during the computations performed by the system. For example, for a program that computes the standard deviation of a set of data values stored in an array, the designer might want to know how many instructions are needed on a specific processor and how much memory is required for storing the arrays and all intermediate values.

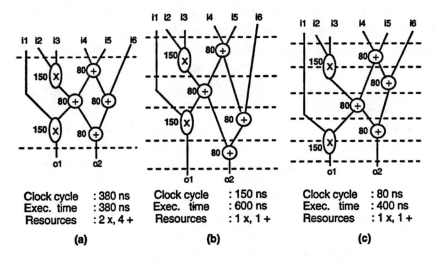

Figure 7.3: Clock cycle effect on execution time and resources required.

Estimation of program and data size metrics is important to determine design cost and to indirectly determine performance. Specifically, we may want to determine if a program will fit in a processor's built-in program memory. If not, we must add an external program-memory chip, which raises the design's cost. In addition, we may want to know the data size since it determines how many data memories we need, which in turn fixes the data memory cost. We might also want to determine if the data size is small enough to be mapped to on-chip registers or cache, in which case we would expect better performance.

7.2.3   Performance metrics

Performance metrics can be divided into computation and communication metrics. Computation metrics measure the time required to perform the computations within a behavior. These metrics can be classified according to the type of the time units used in the computation of the metric. Generally, three types of units are used: clock cycles, control steps and execution times. Communication metrics are related to the time spent by a behavior in interacting with the other behaviors in the system.

Clock Cycle

An important decision in system design is the choice of the clock cycle which will be used for implementing the design. Selecting a clock cycle before performing synthesis tasks is important, since the choice of a clock cycle could affect the execution time and the resources required to implement the design.

For example, consider using three different clock cycles (380 ns, 150 ns and 80 ns) for implementing the dataflow graph in Figure 7.3. In Figure 7.3(a), a clock cycle of 380 ns allows the fastest possible execution time but requires 2 multipliers and 4 adders to implement the design, where the multiplier and adder have a delay of 150 ns and 80 ns, respectively. On the other hand, the clock cycle of 150 ns in Figure 7.3(b) requires only one adder and one multiplier, but results in a total execution time of 600 ns. The most efficient implementation, in terms of performance per resource, is obtained with an 80 ns clock cycle, as shown in Figure 7.3(c). Its execution time is comparable to that of the first implementation, and it requires the same number of resources as the second implementation.

The clock cycle also determines the technology that can be used for implementing the design. Certain technology libraries specify a maximum frequency at which certain components in the library can operate. For example, the VDP100 library [VTI88] specifies 75 Mhz as the maximum frequency at which the clock input of a bistable circuit may be driven such that stable transitions of logic levels are maintained. Any clock frequency higher than the specified maximum, will remove such libraries from consideration during design implementation.

Control steps

The control unit of the FSMD architecture introduced in Section 2.9.3 sequences the operations in the system through a series of **control steps**. A control step corresponds to a single state of the control unit state machine. Operations in the functional specification are assigned to these control steps during synthesis. The number of control steps required to implement a behavior affects the complexity of the control logic in the implementation. If a design is scheduled into N control steps, the

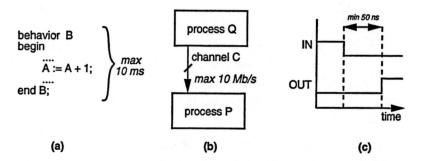

Figure 7.4: System-level performance metrics: (a) behavior execution time, (b) data transfer rate, and (c) inter-event timing.

number of bits in the state register will be $log_2 N$. In addition, if a behavior is specified as straight-line code, then the behavior's execution time is directly proportional to the number of control steps. Even if a behavior has branching and iteration constructs, the number of control steps affects the execution time. For example, if a loop body has a larger number of control steps, the loop as a whole will have a longer execution time.

Execution time

The execution time of a behavior in the design is defined as the average time required by the behavior from start to finish. The execution time is directly proportional to the number of control steps required to execute the behavior.

Estimating the execution time is important for two reasons. First, a performance constraint may have been specified for certain behaviors, such as behavior B in Figure 7.4(a) which has a maximum execution time constraint of 10 ms. This constraint may be derived from some real-time requirements, such as reading data from a rotating disk that fetches data at a fixed rate. The designer must be able to evaluate the impact of any design decision on the execution time of constrained behaviors to determine whether any time constraints are being violated. For example, the designer might want to know if an allocation of two adders to implement behavior B will cause a performance constraint violation. Second, execution time constraints will influence the technology or component libraries that can be used for design implementation. Estimates of execution time, for example, will enable the designer to select between a low-cost standard processor with compiled software and a more costly custom ASIC implementation.

Often, design implementations may be **pipelined**. The input to a pipeline is a stream of data samples arriving at a constant rate. The pipeline performs computations on the data and generates a stream of results at the same rate. The main motivation behind pipelining is to increase the rate at which results can be computed by the design, and to increase the utilization of the functional units in the design. The first goal is achieved by dividing the set of computations in the behavior into stages, with the partial results latched after each stage. The second goal is achieved by splitting functional units with large delays into two or more pipelined stages. Pipelined functional units allow concurrent operation on several pairs of operands, each getting partially computed in one stage of the same pipelined unit. The clock period can then be shortened to equal the delay of the longest stage.

Two metrics commonly associated with pipelined designs are the stage delay and the execution time.

The **stage delay** of a pipeline is the length of time required by any stage to perform its computations. Since all the stages in the pipeline start processing data at the same time, the stage delay also represents the minimum time interval during which two successive samples of data can be applied to the inputs of the pipeline. The **throughput** of a pipeline measures how often results are generated by the pipeline. In other words, if *stage_delay* represents the delay of the longest stage in the pipeline, then the throughput and the stage delay of a pipeline are related to each other as follows:

$$throughput = \frac{1}{stage\_delay} \tag{7.4}$$

The **execution time** for a pipeline is the total elapsed time between the arrival of data to the pipeline and the generation of its corresponding results. The pipeline's execution time is often referred to as its **latency** [HP90]. If the number of pipeline stages is represented by *num_stages*, the pipeline execution time is computed as follows:

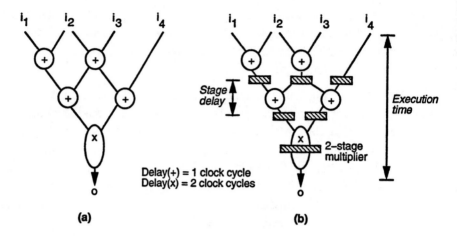

Figure 7.5: Pipelining: (a) non-pipelined design, (b) 4-stage pipeline.

$$execution\_time \;=\; num\_stages \times stage\_delay \qquad (7.5)$$

The differences between nonpipelined and pipelined designs are illustrated in Figure 7.5. The dataflow graph of a behavior is shown in Figure 7.5(a). It can be divided into a four-stage pipeline by using a 2-stage multiplier and latches, which are indicated by the shaded rectangles in Figure 7.5(b). The stage delay and execution time of the pipeline are indicated in the figure. Assuming that each stage has a delay equal to one clock cycle, the results corresponding to a set of inputs will be available after a time equal to four clock cycles in both cases. However, in the non-pipelined design of Figure 7.5(a) that has a stage delay of 4 clock cycles, the throughput will be one result every four clock cycles. On the other hand, in the pipelined design of Figure 7.5(b) that has a stage delay of of one clock cycle, the throughput will be one result per clock cycle, i.e., four times higher than that of the non-pipelined design.

Communication metrics

Communication between concurrent behaviors (or processes) is usually represented as messages sent over an abstract **channel**. Each channel transfers a fixed-size message between two behaviors – the message is

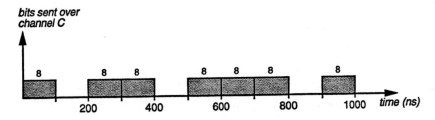

Figure 7.6: Computing average and peak channel rates.

generated by one behavior, called the **producer**, and received by the other behavior, called the **consumer**. Over its lifetime, the producer behavior will initiate several data transfers over the channel. The data transfer rate, or **bitrate**, measures how fast a message can be sent over a communication channel. For example, process P in Figure 7.4(b) receives data from process Q over channel C at a maximum rate of 10Mb/s.

For each communication channel, two types of data transfer rates can be defined: average and peak channel rates. The **average rate** of a channel C, *avgrate(C)*, is defined as the rate at which data is sent during the entire lifetime of the two communicating behaviors. The average data transfer rate for a channel can be computed by dividing the total number of bits transferred over the channel by the execution time of the behavior that sends data over it. As an example, Figure 7.6 shows data transfers of 8-bit messages over channel C. Each message occupies the channel for 100 ns. Since the channel sends 56 bits of data over a period of 1000 ns, the average rate of channel C is computed as

$$avgrate(C) = \frac{56\ bits}{1000\ ns} = 56\ Mb/s$$

The **peak rate** of a channel C, *peakrate(C)*, is defined as the rate at which data is sent in a single message transfer across the channel. The peak rate is computed by dividing the number of bits sent in a single message by the time required for message transfer. For channel C in Figure 7.6, each message transfer requires 100 ns. Since the size of each message is 8 bits, the peak rate is computed as

$$peakrate(C) = \frac{8\ bits}{100\ ns} = 80\ Mb/s$$

Estimating the data transfer rates is essential at the system level for several reasons. First, since each channel will be implemented by a bus, which will consist of a set of wires and a protocol that controls data transfers over the wires, the data transfer rates of the communication channel will directly affect the buswidth. Thus, an implementation of a channel with higher average and peak rates will require a wider bus.

Second, the channel rates directly affect the execution times of the two behaviors communicating over the channel. Slower data transfer rates over the channel will require the consumer and producer behaviors to spend more time during communication, which will lead to much longer execution times for these behaviors.

Finally, the communication rates play an important role when behaviors are partitioned into chips, and channels into buses. Behaviors that communicate with each other over channels with high bitrates are more likely to be assigned to the same chip to minimize off-chip access delays. Also, channels with very high bitrates are less likely to be grouped together in the same bus to minimize the performance degradation that will result if several behaviors attempt to send data over the same bus simultaneously.

Inter-event timing

Often, the designer may specify inter-event timing for pairs of events in the specification. Such timing relationships represent the elapsed time between the occurrence of the two events. For example, in Figure 7.4(c), the designer has specified that the signal *OUT* must be asserted no earlier than 50 ns after the signal *IN* is deasserted. Inter-event timing can represent constraints between events and is commonly used in timing diagrams that represent interfaces between components of the system. Constraints specified between two events translate directly into constraints on computations that need to be performed between the occurrence of the two events.

7.2.4   Other metrics

We now present several quality metrics which are also applicable to system design.

Power dissipation

Power dissipation in system components refers to the dissipation of energy caused by the charging and discharging of load capacitances during the switching of CMOS circuits. The power dissipation is dependent on the clock frequency and the number of gates which are actually active (i.e., undergo a change in their value) in each clock cycle. The higher the clock frequency and number of active gates in a component, the greater the power dissipation by the component.

Estimation of power dissipation is useful for several reasons. In battery-operated systems, the increased demand for power requires larger batteries, which can substantially increase the cost and weight of the product. Since large amounts of power dissipation by a component is likely to cause component failure, portions of the design that are likely to dissipate more power are less likely to be assigned to the same package to avoid a component failure at a later stage. Finally, attempts to improve the design performance by increasing the clock frequency must take into account the increased power dissipation resulting from a smaller clock cycle.

Design for testability

Design for testability produces a design with a minimal test cost. Test cost is essentially a tradeoff between built-in test hardware and the cost of testing after the design has been implemented. Built-in test hardware in the component enhances the controllability and observability of the internal states of the design, thus reducing the time required for testing once the component has been implemented. **Controllability** defines the ability to initialize the internal logic of the design into specific controlled states for the purpose of testing. **Observability** refers to the ability to measure the internal states of the design externally.

Testability affects a number of system level parameters. Extra test pins may be required in order to enhance controllability and observability, resulting in increased packaging cost and package assembly times. In addition, the extra pins will require more area and power dissipation due to increased test circuitry, and more I/O drivers for the pins. Also, as circuit complexity increases due to built-in test hardware, yields may be reduced significantly. Thus, while design for testability may reduce the testing overhead, it may increase the cost of production.

Design time

Design time is defined as the time required to obtain an implementation from the functional specification. The design time is dependent upon the design methodology adopted. For example, given an English specification document for the system, the abstraction level at which design automation is introduced in the methodology will profoundly impact the design time. Capturing the system using a high-level language and using high-level synthesis, logic synthesis and physical design tools will require significantly less time than manually converting a functional specification to transistor schematics. Design time can also be reduced by using more programmable and off-the-shelf components and fewer custom components, since the latter requires significant design and testing overheads.

Time to market

Time to market is perhaps the single most important factor driving system design, especially since the profit potential of any design is directly proportional to how early it is made available to the end user. Time to market can be defined as the total time elapsed from design conceptualization to the actual delivery of the product to the customer. In addition to the design time, this includes the time required for performing a market study, specification definition from user requirements, fabrication, testing, distribution and development of supporting hardware and software to make the design usable.

Manufacturing cost

The manufacturing cost is a measure of the financial implications associated with realizing an implementation for the design. The manufacturing cost includes the cost of manpower, raw material, fabrication, packaging, testing and maintaining facilities.

7.3 Hardware estimation

7.3.1 Hardware estimation model

In this section we will discuss a general design model for estimating quality metrics for a hardware implementation.

Given the specification of a system for which estimates have to be computed, the corresponding design is assumed to be implemented as an FSMD. As explained in Chapter 2, the FSMD architecture consists of a control unit and a datapath, as shown in Figure 7.7.

The datapath consists of registers, register files, functional units and multiplexers. A typical datapath may have a two-level multiplexer structure, as shown in Figure 7.7. A typical operation in the *Datapath* reads the operands from the *Registers* or *Register file*, computes the result in the *Functional units*, and finally writes the result into a destination register. All memory accesses are routed through registers by load and store operations that load data values into registers before their use in the datapath, and store the results of computations into registers before they are written to the memory.

The *Control unit* consists of the *State register*, the *Control logic* to drive the control lines for the datapath components, and the *Next-state logic* to compute the next state to be stored in the state register. Status lines from the datapath carry the results of comparison operations to the next-state logic.

To see how the control logic and datapath delays affect the system clock cycle, consider the various paths in the design model of Figure 7.7. Each path in the design defines a flow of data from one register to another that must be completed in one clock cycle. Path p_1, associated with reading the memory, starts from the address register, AR, through the *Memory* and finally terminates at the data register, DR, to which data fetched from the memory is written. The delays associated with this path include the delay associated with reading the address register, the access time of the memory, the set-up time for the data register and the delays of the nets connecting these components. Another register-to-register path in the design, labeled p_2, reads data from the *Registers*, routes it to the *Functional units* through the *Multiplexers*, and routes

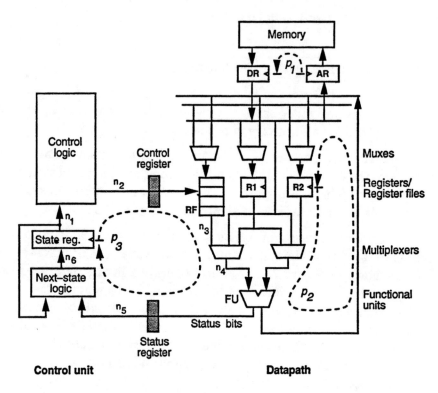

Figure 7.7: Control unit/datapath model for estimation.

the results of the computation back into the registers through another multiplexer. Another path, labeled p_3, starts from the *State register* through the *Control logic, Register file, Multiplexer, Functional unit,* and finally through the *Next-state logic* back to the *State register.*

In order to accomplish the data transfer associated with each path in the design, the clock cycle, *clk*, should be greater than the delay of the longest path in the design. Typically, path p_3 through the control logic has the largest delay. Consequently, the minimal clock cycle is equal to or greater than the sum of all the delays associated with the components and the nets in path p_3. Thus, ignoring the control and status register for the time being, we observe the following:

$$clk \geq delay(SR) + delay(CL) + delay(RF) + delay(Mux) +$$
$$delay(FU) + delay(NS) + setup(SR) + \sum_{1 \leq i \leq 6} delay(n_i) \quad (7.6)$$

where:

> $delay(SR)$ is the delay for reading the *State register*,
> $delay(CL)$ is the delay of the *Control logic*,
> $delay(RF)$ is the delay for reading the *Register file*,
> $delay(Mux)$ is the delay of the *Multiplexer*,
> $delay(FU)$ is the delay of the *Functional unit*,
> $delay(NS)$ is the delay of the *Next-state logic*,
> $setup(SR)$ is the setup time for the *State register*, and
> $delay(n_i)$ is the delay associated with net n_i.

Clearly, the clock period calculated above may be too long, leading to a significantly reduced performance for the design. The clock period can be reduced by **control pipelining** [GDWL91, RG93], i.e., inserting registers at appropriate points between the datapath and the control unit. Figure 7.7 shows how a control and status register may be inserted to reduce the clock period. For example, if both these registers are inserted between the datapath and the control unit, the clock cycle will now be the maximum delay of three paths: one from the state register to the control register, another from the control register to the status register through the datapath, and the third from the status register to the state register.

Having presented a design model for a hardware implementation of a system, we will describe in the next sections methods for computing the following quality metrics: system clock cycle, number of control steps, execution time, communication rates, design area, and pins.

7.3.2 Clock cycle estimation

In Section 7.2.3, we showed how the choice of a clock cycle can affect the execution time and the number of resources required by the design. Thus, it is important that clock cycle be estimated prior to performing system design.

In most synthesis tools [WC91, PK89a, PKG86, BM89, MK90], the clock cycle must be specified by the designer before synthesis. Either the clock cycle is specified explicitly or the delays of components are expressed in multiples of a clock cycle. Designer-specified clock cycles are applicable in situations where the design being developed is part of a larger system. In this case, the clock cycle used for some of the standard components in the system is known and can be used for the remainder of the design.

In case the clock cycle is not specified by the designer, we need to estimate one. In this section, we present methods for estimating the system clock cycle.

Maximum-operator-delay method

Some synthesis tools [PPM86, PP85, JMP88] equate the clock cycle with the delay of the slowest operation in the design. Let $delay(t_i)$ be the delay of the functional unit implementing an operation of type t_i. Then the clock cycle, $clk(MOD)$, estimated by the maximum-operator delay method is computed as

$$clk(MOD) = \text{Max}_{\text{all } t_i} (\ delay(t_i)\ ) \qquad (7.7)$$

For example, consider the second-order differential equation example [PKG86], which has add, subtract and multiplication operations. Assume that

$$delay(+) = 49 \text{ ns}, \ delay(-) = 56 \text{ ns}, \ delay(\times) = 163 \text{ ns}$$

From Equation 7.7, the clock period is estimated to be the maximum delay amongst the above functional units, i.e., $clk(MOD) = 163$ ns.

The advantage of the maximum-operator-delay method is that the clock cycle estimation is extremely fast and easy to implement. However, the maximum-operator-delay clock leads to underutilization of the faster functional units. The reason for low utilization of faster units is that in the presence of a slower functional unit such as a multiplier, which has a large delay, the clock period will be at least as long as the multiplier delay, and faster functional units implementing other operations will be idle for a significant portion of the clock cycle. Hence, longer execution times can be expected for a design using the maximum-operator-delay clock.

Clock slack

In order to improve the performance of the design, we need to minimize the idle time of functional units. The **clock slack** associated with a functional unit represents the portion of the clock cycle for which this functional unit is idle. **Slack** is defined as the difference between the functional unit delay and the next higher multiple of the clock cycle. As before, let $delay(t_i)$ represent the delay associated with a functional unit implementing an operation of type t_i. For a given clock cycle clk and operation type t_i, the slack $slack(clk, t_i)$ associated with the corresponding functional unit is computed by the following equation:

$$slack(clk, t_i) \; = \; (\; \lceil delay(t_i) \div clk \rceil \times clk \;) - delay(t_i) \qquad (7.8)$$

In general, we may postulate that a smaller slack associated with a functional unit will result in a higher utilization of that functional unit, and in shorter execution times for the same number of resources.

Figure 7.8 graphically depicts the slack associated with the different operations for the differential equation example. Assume that the maximum operator delay method was used to determine the clock period. Since the multiplier has the largest delay, the clock cycle $clk(MOD) =$ 163 ns. Using Equation 7.8, we get the following slacks:

$$slack(163, \times) = (\lceil 163 \div 163 \rceil \times 163) - 163 = 0 \text{ ns}$$
$$slack(163, -) = (\lceil 56 \div 163 \rceil \times 163) - 56 = 107 \text{ ns}$$
$$slack(163, +) = (\lceil 49 \div 163 \rceil \times 163) - 49 = 114 \text{ ns}$$

The lightly shaded regions in Figure 7.8 represent the delays of the adder, subtractor and multiplier that will be used to implement the operations in the design. For a clock period of 163 ns, the adder and subtractor have large slacks, shown as the dark region in the figure. A long clock cycle, together with the fact that some functional units are idle for significant portions of the clock period, will lead to longer execution times if the 163 ns clock is used in the design.

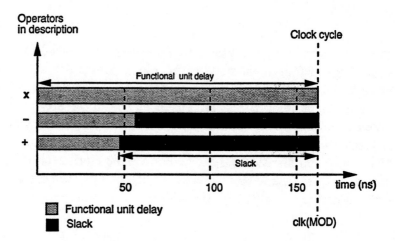

Figure 7.8: Functional-unit slack associated with clock cycle of 163 ns.

Slack-minimization method

The main motivation behind the slack-minimization method [NG92] is to minimize the slack in each clock cycle under the assumption that a smaller slack will increase the functional-unit utilization, and in turn decrease the execution time for the behavior.

The slack computation associated with a functional unit was given by Equation 7.8. For a given clock cycle *clk*, the **average slack**, denoted as *ave_slack(clk)*, is defined as the portion of the clock cycle during which each unit in the design is idle on average. If $occur(t_i)$ represents the number of occurrences of operation of type t_i in a behavior, and T represents the number of distinct operation types (such as addition, subtraction and multiplication), then the average slack is computed as:

$$ave\_slack(clk) = \frac{\sum_{i=1}^{T} (\ occur(t_i) \times slack(clk, t_i)\ )}{\sum_{i=1}^{T} occur(t_i)} \tag{7.9}$$

Clock utilization is defined as the percentage of the clock cycle utilized for useful computation by all the functional units in the design.

In other words:

$$utilization(clk) = 1 - \frac{ave\_slack(clk)}{clk} \qquad (7.10)$$

The slack-minimization method examines a range of potential clock cycles, computing the utilization for each clock cycle. The clock cycle that maximizes the utilization for a behavior B is returned as the slack minimal clock.

Algorithm 7.3.1 : Slack minimization

/* Determine number of occurrences for each operation type */
ComputeRange(T, $clkmax$, $clkmin$)
for each $t_i \in T$ **loop**
    $occur(t_i)$ =FindOccurrences(B, t_i)
end loop

/* Compute utilization for each possible clock */
$max\_utilization = 0$
for $clkmin \le clk \le clkmax$ **loop**
    for each $t_i \in T$ **loop**
        $slack(clk, t_i) = (\lceil delay(t_i) \div clk \rceil \times clk) - delay(t_i)$
    end loop
    $ave\_slack(clk) = \dfrac{\sum_{i=1}^{T} [\ occur(t_i) \times slack(clk, t_i)\ ]}{\sum_{i=1}^{T} occur(t_i)}$
    $utilization(clk) = 1 - \dfrac{ave\_slack(clk)}{clk}$
    if $utilization(clk) > max\_utilization$ **then**
        $max\_utilization = utilization(clk)$
        $max\_utilization\_clk = clk$
    end if
end loop
return($max\_utilization\_clk$)

Algorithm 7.3.1 describes clock estimation by the slack-minimization method. The number of distinct operation types is denoted by T. The procedure *ComputeRange* determines the range of clock cycles that will

operation	occur(t_i)	delay(t_i)
add	2	48 ns
subtract	2	56 ns
multiply	6	163 ns

Figure 7.9: Occurrences and delays of operations in the differential equation example.

be examined by the algorithm by examining the delays of the functional units that will implement each of the T distinct operation types in the behavior. The range of clock cycles is represented by ($clkmin, clkmax$). The largest delay amongst all the functional units is $clkmax$. Design libraries often specify the maximum clock frequency at which the clock input of a bistable circuit may be driven such that stable transitions of logic levels are maintained. This frequency is used to determine the value of $clkmin$. In case such a maximum clock frequency is not specified, then $clkmin$ is approximated as the smallest value of $delay(t_i)$.

The function *FindOccurrences* examines the specification of behavior B and returns the number of occurrences of operations of type t_i in it. The delay associated with the functional units that implement an operation of type t_i is denoted by $delay(t_i)$.

For each clock cycle clk in the range ($clkmin, clkmax$), using Equation 7.8, the slack-minimization algorithm computes the slack associated with each functional unit that will implement an operation in the behavior. The average slack is then computed using Equation 7.9. Finally, the utilization corresponding to the current clock cycle clk is computed using Equation 7.10. The maximum clock utilization value computed by Algorithm 7.3.1 is maintained in *max_utilization*, and the corresponding clock cycle in *max_utilization_clk*. The value of the clock cycle that maximizes the clock utilization is returned as the slack minimal clock.

We shall illustrate the algorithm by applying it to the second-order differential equation example [PKG86]. The occurrences of each operation and the delays of the functional units that will be used to imple-

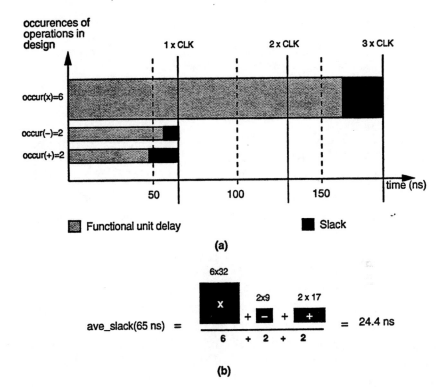

Figure 7.10: Computing (a) slack, (b) average slack for a clock cycle of 65 ns.

ment them are shown in Figure 7.9. The components used are from the VDP100 datapath library [VTI88].

In Figure 7.10(a), the delays of the functional units are represented graphically as the length of the lightly shaded regions along the X-axis. The number of occurrences of the operations in the behavior is represented by the height of the shaded regions along the Y-axis.

Since the VDP100 library specifies that the maximum frequency for clocking registers is 75 MHz, $clkmin = 1/75$ Mhz $= 14$ ns. The largest functional-unit delay is $clkmax = delay(\times) = 163$ ns.

We will compute the clock utilization for a clock cycle of 65 ns. Using Equation 7.8, we obtain the following:

$$slack(65, \times) = (3 \times 65) - 163 = 32 \text{ ns},$$
$$slack(65, -) = (1 \times 65) - 56 \;\; = 9 \text{ ns},$$
$$slack(65, +) = (1 \times 65) - 48 \;\; = 17 \text{ ns}.$$

The dark shaded regions represent the slack for each operation type in Figure 7.10(a). The average slack for a clock cycle of 65 ns is calculated using Equation 7.9 and is shown graphically in Figure 7.10(b). The average slack is 24.4 ns.

Finally, the clock utilization for a 65 ns clock cycle is obtained using Equation 7.10:

$$utilization(65 \; ns) = 1 - \frac{24.4}{65} = 0.62 \; or \; 62\%$$

The clock utilization calculation is repeated for all values of the clock cycle from 14 ns to 163 ns. The maximum value of clock utilization of 92% was achieved at a clock period of 56 ns, as shown in Figure 7.11(a). This value is selected as the slack minimal clock, $clk(SM)$. It is interesting to note that a clock period of 163 ns selected using the maximum operator delay method has a utilization of only 73%.

To demonstrate that the clock cycle with the highest utilization did indeed result in a fast execution time, for each clock cycle in the range $clkmin$ and $clkmax$, the actual execution times can be determined by scheduling the behavioral description and multiplying the number of control steps in the description by the clock period. The execution times for the differential equation example are plotted against the clock utilization, as shown in Figure 7.11(b). The figure shows that an execution time of 560 ns was obtained by the slack minimal clock of 56 ns, which had a utilization of 92%. Only one clock cycle (15 ns), corresponding to a utilization of 71%, resulted in a marginally faster design, with an execution time of 555 ns.

Experiments have shown that designs implemented with the clock estimated with the slack minimization method had 32% better performance than designs implemented with the maximum operator delay clock [NG92]. Shorter execution times were obtained regardless of the resource allocation used during design implementation.

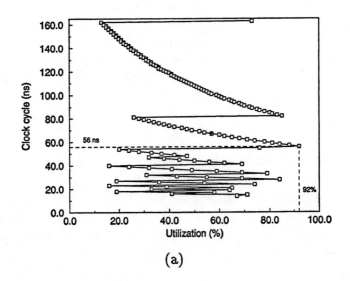

(a)

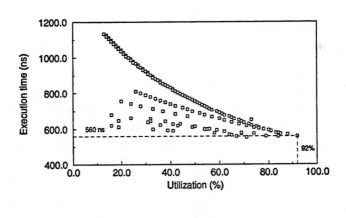

(b)

Figure 7.11: Differential equation example: (a) clock cycle vs. utilization, and (b) execution time vs. utilization.

Two modifications to the Slack-minimization algorithm were proposed in [GSV92]. First, the intermediate clock cycles of a multi-cycle operation were incorporated in the clock utilization calculation, leading to a better correlation between the execution time and the inverse of clock utilization than the utilization computed by Equation 7.10. Second, instead of examining the entire range of clock cycles from *clkmin* to *clkmax*, only those clock cycles were examined that were factors of the functional-unit delays, thus significantly reducing the computation time required by the algorithm.

7.3.3   Control step estimation

The number of control steps needed for a behavior's execution can be estimated in several ways. In this section, we first describe two techniques — operator-use method and scheduling algorithms — for estimating the number of control steps in a behavior specified as straight-line code. We then present a technique for estimating the number of control steps for a behavior that contains control constructs such as branching and iteration.

Operator-use method

The operator-use method estimates the number of control steps required to execute a behavior, given the resources for its implementation. The method partitions all statements in the behavior into a set of nodes in such a way that all statements in a node could be executed concurrently.

Let T represent the number of distinct types of operations in a behavior B. Let $num(t_i)$ and $clocks(t_i)$ represent the number and delay (in clock cycles) of functional units available to implement operations of type t_i. Then, if there are $occur(t_i)$ occurrences (or uses) of an operation type t_i in any node, then at least $\lceil \frac{occur(t_i)}{num(t_i)} \times clocks(t_i) \rceil$ control steps are needed to execute operations of type t_i. The number of control steps needed for any node n_j, $csteps(n_j)$, is equal to the maximum number of control steps needed to perform operations of any type in the node; that is,

$$csteps(n_j) = \max_{t_i \in T} [\ \lceil \frac{occur(t_i)}{num(t_i)} \rceil \times clocks(t_i)\ ] \qquad (7.11)$$

Once the control steps for each node have been determined, the total number of control steps required by the behavior B is determined as follows

$$csteps(B) = \sum_{n_j \in N} csteps(n_j) \qquad (7.12)$$

where N is the number of nodes in B.

Algorithm 7.3.2 : Operator-use method
 CreateNodes(B, N)
 $csteps(B) = 0$
 for each node $n_j \in N$ **loop**
 $csteps(n_j) = 0$
  /* for all operation types T in current node */
  for each operation type $t_i \in T$ **loop**
   /* compute control steps for operation type t_i in a node */
   $csteps(n_j, t_i) = [\ \lceil \frac{occur(t_i)}{num(t_i)} \rceil \times clocks(t_i)\ ]$
   /* compute maximum number of control steps in a node */
   if $csteps(n_j, t_i) > csteps(n_j)$ **then**
    $csteps(n_j) = csteps(n_j, t_i)$
   end if
  end loop
  $csteps(B) = csteps(B) + csteps(n_j)$
 end loop
 return $csteps(B)$

Algorithm 7.3.2 shows the operator-use method to determine the total number of control steps for behavior B. The procedure *CreateNodes* partitions the statements in behavior B into a set of N nodes. The statements in the behavior are merged into nodes in such a way that dependencies between the statements are maintained and the total number of nodes is minimal. If statement S_2 is dependent upon statement S_1, then

S_2 is assigned to a node that succeeds the node to which S_1 is assigned. The operator-use method groups the statements together into nodes independent of the clock cycle and of the amount of resources allocated to the design.

For each node, Algorithm 7.3.2 computes the number of control steps required to carry out operations of each of the T different operation types. The variable $csteps(n_j, t_i)$ represents the number of control steps needed in node n_j for computing operations of type t_i. The variable $csteps(n_j)$, computed by Equation 7.11, represents the number of control steps required to execute all the operations in node n_j. The number of control steps determined for each node are then summed, as in Equation 7.12, to determine the total number of control steps for the entire behavior.

The operator-use method is illustrated on the differential-equation example. Figure 7.12(a) shows the resource allocation and the delays in clock cycles for the adder, subtractor and the multiplier. The main body of the behavior is shown in Figure 7.12(b). The dependencies between the individual statements are denoted by arrows in Figure 7.12(c). In Figure 7.12(d), the statements are merged into the four nodes n_1, n_2, n_3 and n_4. Note that none of the dependencies in the original behavior have been violated during the merging of statements into nodes. In other words, if two statements are dependent on each other, then they will be assigned to two different nodes in order to preserve the dependency.

Figure 7.12(d) shows the computation of the number of control steps for each node using Equation 7.11. For example, consider the node n_1, which has one addition and four multiplication operations, that is, $occur(+) = 1$ and $occur(\times) = 4$. Since only two multipliers are allocated, and each multiplication requires four clock cycles, the four multiplication operations will require at least eight control steps. Similarly, the single add operation in the node requires one control step to execute. From Equation 7.11, we estimate that node n_1 requires at least eight control steps to perform its operations. Summing the number of control steps over all the nodes in the behavior, by using Equation 7.12, we estimate that 14 control steps are required to implement the differential-equation behavior.

The operator-use method can be extended to incorporate pipelined functional units and include memory accesses. For example, consider a

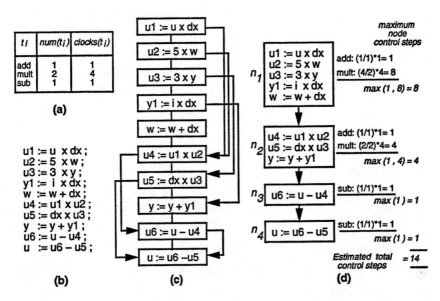

Figure 7.12: Operator-use method applied to the differential-equation example: (a) functional-unit allocation and delays, (b) loop body in the example, (c) dependencies between statements, (d) nodes with control step estimates.

multiport memory which has a fixed access time associated with it. If we treat a memory as a functional unit, the number of accesses to the memory in a node corresponds to the "occurrences" of an operation, the number of ports available for accessing the memory are equivalent to the number of functional units allocated for each operation, and the memory access time is equivalent to the delay of the functional unit. Therefore, Equation 7.11 can now be directly used to determine the number of control steps for a node in the presence of memory accesses.

The operator-use method can provide fairly rapid estimates of the number of control steps required by a behavior. If there are n operations in the behavior, the method has a computational complexity of $O(n)$. However, there is potential for error, since the method operates at a statement-level granularity and ignores the dependencies between the operations within a statement. For example, if two adders with a delay of one clock cycle are available, the method will conclude that the statement A := B + C + D can be executed in one control step. However, two control steps are needed in reality – one to compute the partial sum "$B + C$", and another to add D to the partial sum. In conclusion, the operator-use method will generate more accurate estimates if each statement in the specification is restricted to one operation.

Scheduling

A scheduling technique may be applied to the behavior in order to determine the number of control steps. Given resource constraints, the operations in the behavior are scheduled with a view to minimizing the total number of control steps. We will describe one such resource-constrained scheduling algorithm, list scheduling, in this section. A more complete discussion on scheduling algorithms can be found in [GDWL91].

For each type of operation in the behavior, the list scheduling algorithm maintains a priority list from which operations are assigned to control steps. At any stage, the priority list for an operation type t_i contains the set of operations that have all their predecessors already scheduled. A "predecessor" of an operation is any operation whose results are required for the execution of that operation. Thus, all predecessors of an operation must be executed before that operation itself is executed.

The list scheduling algorithm is described in Algorithm 7.3.3. As before, T is the number of distinct types of operations in the behavior, and $cstep$ represents the current control step for which operations are being scheduled. The priority list for operation type t_i is denoted by $plist(t_i)$. Given a list, the function $First$ returns the first element of the list, while the function $Tail$ returns the same list after deleting its first element. The procedure $CreatePriorityList$ initializes the priority list of each operation type to contain those operations that have no predecessor operations whereas the procedure $UpdatePriorityList$ scans the set of unscheduled operations, selects the operations with all their predecessors already scheduled, and adds the selected operations to the appropriate priority list. The procedure $UpdateSchedule$ modifies the schedule S by assigning the specified operation to the current control step.

Each iteration of the algorithm corresponds to selecting the set of operations to be assigned to the current control step. If $num(t_i)$ functional units have been allocated for operations of type t_i, then, at each control step, the algorithm assigns the first $num(t_i)$ operations from the corresponding priority list to the current control step. Each operation assigned to the current control step is deleted from the priority list and the schedule is updated to reflect this assignment. After all possible operations have been assigned to the current control step, the priority lists are updated. The algorithm iterates until all operations in the given behavior have been scheduled. The number of control steps required by the behavior will be the value of $cstep$ upon termination of the algorithm.

Algorithm 7.3.3 List Scheduling

   CreatePriorityList(V, $plist(t_1)$, $plist(t_2)$, ...)
   $cstep = 0$
   while(($plist(t_1) \neq \phi$) **or** ($plist(t_2) \neq \phi$) **or** ...) **loop**
      $cstep = cstep + 1$
      for i **in** 1 **to** T **loop**
         for j **in** 1 **to** $num(t_i)$ **loop**
            if $plist(t_i) \neq \phi$ **then**
               UpdateSchedule(S, First($plist(t_i)$), cstep)
               $plist(t_i) = $ Tail($plist(t_i)$)
            end if
         end loop
      end loop
      UpdatePriorityList(V, $plist(t_1)$, $plist(t_2)$, ...)
   end loop

An important issue in list scheduling is the selection of an appropriate priority function that is used to order the operations in the priority list. One such priority function is the **mobility** of an operation, defined as the number of potential control steps to which the operation can be assigned, without delaying the completion time required by the behavior as a whole. The lower the mobility of an operation, the higher its priority for scheduling, since the schedule can be expected to run out of alternative control steps sooner.

While scheduling algorithms allow the designer to obtain the exact number of control steps required to execute a behavior, it is computationally very expensive. List scheduling, for example, has a complexity of $O(n^2)$, where n is the number of operations in the behavior.

Design example	Operator–use method	List scheduling
Elliptical filter	22	19
Linear phase B–spline interpolated filter	6	6
Differential equation	14	13
AR lattice filter	14	11

Figure 7.13: Comparing control steps estimated by the Operator-use method and by List scheduling.

Figure 7.13 compares the estimates produced by the operator-use method with the actual number of control steps obtained by using a mobility-based list scheduler [Lis92] on a number of high-level synthesis benchmarks such as the *Elliptical filter* [KWK85], the *Linear phase B-spline interpolated filter* [PF89], the *Differential equation* [PKG86], and the *AR lattice filter* [JMP88]. The average error involved with the operator-use method is only 13%.

Behaviors with iteration and branching constructs

Both the operator-use method and scheduling can be used to estimate the number of control steps required by a behavior described using straight-line code. If a behavior has branching and iteration constructs, it is first converted into a set of basic blocks. A **basic block** [ASU88] is a sequence of consecutive HDL statements in which the flow of control enters at the beginning and leaves at the end without halting or the possibility of branching, except at the end. Each basic block consists of a set of sequential assignment statements which are sometimes called straight-line-code.

The number of control steps in each basic block can be determined using any of the above methods. The total number of control steps for the entire behavior depends on whether operations in mutually exclusive branches share the same control step or not.

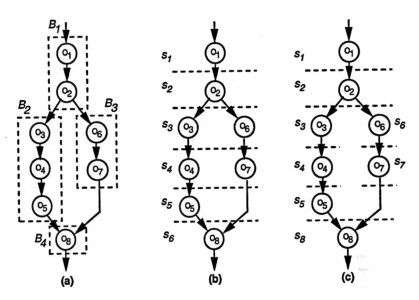

Figure 7.14: Estimating control steps: (a) behavior with branching, (b) schedule with shared control steps, (c) schedule with separate control steps.

Shared control steps: If the control steps are shared across the branches in the behavior, then the total number of control steps for the behavior is equal to the number of control steps along the longest path through the control flow graph. Sharing control steps for mutually exclusive operations results in fewer states in the control unit. However, such an implementation will require status registers whose value determines which one of the mutually exclusive operations is to be executed in any given state.

Separate control steps: If the operations in different branches of the behavior are assigned unique control steps, then the total number of control steps in the behavior is equal to the sum of the control steps required for each basic block. Such an implementation will have more states in the control unit. No status registers will be required, since each control step uniquely identifies the operations that are to be executed in that step.

As an example, consider the **control flow** representation of a behavior B that contains operations o_1 through o_8, shown in Figure 7.14(a).

The operations in the behavior are divided into four basic blocks, B_1 through B_4, indicated with the dashed boxes. Assume that the operations in the conditional branches represented by basic blocks B_2 and B_3 are mutually exclusive. A schedule with shared control steps is shown in Figure 7.14(b). In this schedule, operations o_3 and o_6, although in two different branches, are assigned the same control step, s_3. In this case, a total of six control steps are required for the whole behavior. On the other hand, a schedule with separate control steps, as shown in Figure 7.14(c), requires eight control steps to implement the behavior.

7.3.4 Execution time estimation

Given a complete functional specification, we now describe methods for estimating the execution time for a behavior.

If a behavior is described by straight-line code, the start-to-finish execution time for the behavior depends on the number of control steps into which the behavior is scheduled. Let $csteps(B)$ be the number of control steps estimated for the schedule for behavior B, and let clk be the clock cycle selected for the design implementation. Then the execution time, $exectime(B)$, for the behavior is computed as follows:

$$exectime(B) = csteps(B) \times clk \qquad (7.13)$$

In the general case, a behavior may consist of sequential statements that have branching and iteration constructs (such as loops, if and case statements). Since branching may be dependent upon input data, Equation 7.13 cannot be directly applied to determine the execution time for such behaviors. A probability-based flow analysis technique can be used in such cases.

We first determine the set of basic blocks for the behavior. Since each basic block consists of a set of sequential assignment statements, we can determine the execution time for each basic block by first determining the number of control steps it requires, as described in Section 7.3.3, and then applying Equation 7.13.

To determine the execution time for the entire behavior, the execution time $exectime(b_i)$ for each basic block b_i needs to be weighed by the **execution frequency** of the basic block. The execution frequency, $freq(b_i)$, for a basic block b_i is defined as the number of times that the basic block will be executed on the average, during a single execution of the behavior to which it belongs. Once the execution frequencies have been determined for each basic block, the total execution time for the behavior $exectime(B)$ is estimated as follows

$$exectime(B) = \sum_{b_i \in B} exectime(b_i) \times freq(b_i) \qquad (7.14)$$

We now present a method to determine the execution frequency of each basic block in the behavior.

Probability-based flow analysis

In order to calculate the execution frequency for each basic block, we must first create an equivalent **control flow** graph model for the basic blocks in the behavior. Let $G = (V, E)$ be a graph, where V is the set of vertices v_i, and E is the set of directed edges e_{ij} connecting vertex v_i to v_j.

For each basic block b_i in the behavioral description, there exists a corresponding vertex v_i in the graph G. The target block of a conditional statement (if, case or loop) is any basic block to which control could possibly be transferred on evaluating the condition. For any basic block b_j that is the target of a conditional statement following basic block b_i, there is a directed edge e_{ij} from vertex v_i to vertex v_j in G.

Having obtained a graph which represents the control flow for the behavior, we can determine the execution frequencies of each of its nodes using flow analysis based on the branching probabilities.

The **branch probability** is a measure of how often a branch is executed after evaluating the condition associated with a branching statement. Branch probabilities may be determined in several ways. First, probabilities may be computed statically. In the case of loop statements where the number of iterations, n, is known, a probability of $\frac{n-1}{n}$ is assigned to the loop edge and $\frac{1}{n}$ to the exit edge in the control flow graph. For other branching statements such as if or case, equal probabilities may be assigned to each branch. Second, the designer may directly associate probabilities with the branching constructs in the behavior using annotations in the specification or interactively at runtime. Finally, the probabilities may be obtained dynamically by simulating the behavior on several sets of sample data, recording how often the various branches were executed and consequently, deriving the probabilities for the individual branches.

We can now analyze the edge probabilities in the control flow graph to determine the execution frequencies of the individual nodes. The procedure is outlined below:

1. Add a start node, S, preceding the first node in the given control flow graph. Its execution frequency, $freq(S)$ is set to 1 since this node is executed exactly once whenever the control flow graph is executed.

2. The execution frequency for any node v_j depends on the weighted execution frequency of all its immediate predecessor nodes. The execution frequency for each predecessor node v_i is multiplied by the branch probability of the edge between v_i and v_j, $prob(e_{ij})$. We first formulate the equation for the execution frequency of each node in the graph. For any node n_j in the control flow graph,

$$freq(n_j) = \sum_{all\ predecessor\ nodes\ n_i} freq(n_i) \times prob(e_{ij}) \qquad (7.15)$$

3. The system of linear equations formulated in the previous step can be solved using techniques like Gaussian Elimination or LU Factorization to obtain individual node execution frequencies. These are also the execution frequencies of the corresponding basic blocks in the behavior.

We will illustrate the probability-based flow analysis method with an example of the VHDL behavior in Figure 7.15(a). The basic blocks for the VHDL statements are shown in Figure 7.15(b). The control flow graph of Figure 7.15(c) has a vertex for each basic block in the behavior. An edge exists between two vertices if control could be transferred between the corresponding basic blocks. For example, if the condition $D > A$ is true, control can be transferred from basic block B_2 to B_3.

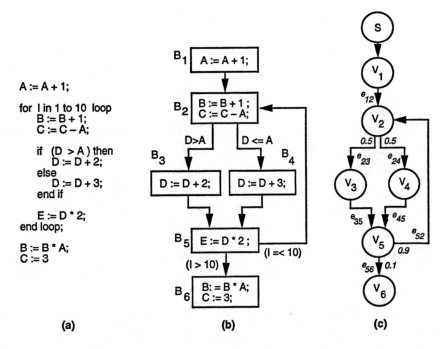

Figure 7.15: Constructing control flow graph for a behavior: (a) VHDL sequential statements, (b) basic blocks, and (c) equivalent control flow graph with probabilities.

Thus, there exists an edge e_{23} between the vertices v_2 and v_3. In addition, a dummy start node S has been added.

The probabilities of branching at nodes v_2 and v_5 are indicated in Figure 7.15(c). We can now formulate equations for the execution frequency of each node in the control flow graph. For example, consider node v_2, which has two predecessor nodes v_1 and v_5. Node v_2 will be executed once for every execution of node v_1, and 0.9 times for every execution of node v_5. Thus,

$$freq(v_2) = 1 \times freq(v_1) + 0.9 \times freq(v_5)$$

Continuing in a similar manner for other nodes in the graph of Figure 7.15(c), we obtain the following set of equations:

$$freq(S) = 1.0$$
$$freq(v_1) = 1.0 \times freq(S)$$

$$freq(v_2) = 1.0 \times freq(v_1) + 0.9 \times freq(v_5)$$
$$freq(v_3) = 0.5 \times freq(v_2)$$
$$freq(v_4) = 0.5 \times freq(v_2)$$
$$freq(v_5) = 1.0 \times freq(v_3) + 1.0 \times freq(v_4)$$
$$freq(v_6) = 0.1 \times freq(v_5)$$

Solving the system of linear equations thus obtained, we get the execution frequencies for all the nodes in the graph:

$$freq(v_1) = 1.0 \qquad freq(v_2) = 10.0$$
$$freq(v_3) = 5.0 \qquad freq(v_4) = 5.0$$
$$freq(v_5) = 10.0 \qquad freq(v_6) = 1.0$$

Once the execution frequency of each basic block is determined, we can apply Equation 7.14 to determine the execution time for the entire behavior.

In the above method, we obtained the execution time of the entire behavior by associating the execution time of the corresponding basic block with each node and performing flow analysis. Probability-based flow analysis can also be applied to determine other useful design characteristics by associating different types of information with each node in the control flow graph, For example, if each node in the control flow graph represents the number of memory accesses in the corresponding basic block, flow analysis will yield the average number of memory accesses during execution of the entire behavior. Similarly, if we associate the number of calls made to a certain procedure in the basic block with each node, we can determine the number of calls made by the entire behavior to that procedure. Finally, by associating the number of data transfers over a channel in the corresponding basic block with each node, flow analysis will yield the total number of channel accesses by the entire behavior.

7.3.5   Communication rate estimation

Communication channels may be either explicitly specified in the behavioral description or created when a variable being accessed by a portion of the behavior is assigned to a different chip during system partitioning.

The average and peak data transfer rates for communication between concurrent behaviors were defined in Section 7.2.3. The average number of accesses, $access(B, C)$, that a behavior B makes to a channel C can be computed by the flow analysis method presented in the previous section.

Let $bits(C)$ represent the number of bits received or sent over channel C in a single message. If a behavior is accessing an array variable over the channel, then the size of the address is also included in $bits(C)$. For example, if a behavior accesses a 16-bit scalar variables X and 32-word $\times$ 16-bit array variable Y over channels chX and chY, respectively, then $bits(chX)$ is 16 while $bits(chY)$ is 21 (5 bit address and 16 bit data).

The total number of bits sent over a channel C during the lifetime of behavior B is given by the following equation:

$$total\_bits(B, C) = access(B, C) \times bits(C) \qquad (7.16)$$

The total execution time for any behavior consists of two components: computation time and communication time.

Computation time, $comptime(B)$, is defined as the time required by the behavior B to perform its internal computations. These computations represent the execution of the statement such as assignments, loops, and conditional statements in the behavior.

Communication time is defined as the time spent by the behavior in accessing data external to the behavior. This communication could represent accesses over a channel to variables in other behaviors. The communication time required by a behavior B to transfer data over channel C is denoted by $commtime(B, C)$.

The computation time can be computed by the flow-analysis method described in the previous section. We will give formulas for communication rate estimates bellow. Let $protdelay(C)$ be the delay associated with the transfer of a single message over the channel C. For simplicity of explanation, assume that a behavior B has exactly one channel C over which it either receives or sends data. The communication time, $commtime(B, C)$, for such a behavior is computed as follows:

$$commtime(B, C) = access(B, C) \times protdelay(C) \qquad (7.17)$$

The average data transfer rate over channel C, $avgrate(C)$, can now be determined as follows:

$$avgrate(C) = \frac{total\_bits(B,C)}{comptime(B) + commtime(B,C)} \qquad (7.18)$$

The peak rate of the channel is computed as

$$peakrate(C) = \frac{bits(C)}{protdelay(C)} \qquad (7.19)$$

7.3.6   Area estimation

The primary task in estimating the size of any design is determining the number and type of components that will implement the given behavior. Once the required components have been determined, we can obtain size estimates for a variety of technologies. For an FPGA implementation, for example, an estimate of the total number of combination logic blocks (CLB) used in the design can be obtained by summing the number of CLBs used for each component in the design. For a gate array implementation, the design complexity can be measured by summing the number of equivalent gates needed for the components. For a full custom implementation, the design size may be approximated as the number of transistors in all the components or by the area of the bounding box obtained after performing component layout and component placement.

In this section, we will describe techniques for determining the number of components that will be required to implement a functional specification. As described in Section 7.3.1, the given behavior is assumed to be implemented as an FSMD with a control unit and a datapath – estimation of each of these will be discussed separately. We also describe a method for estimating the total layout area for a full custom implementation of a functional specification as an example. The same method can also be applied to other gate array and FPGA technologies.

Datapath

The datapath consists of three kinds of RT components: storage units (such as registers and latches), functional units (such as ALUs and comparators), and interconnect units (such as multiplexers and buses). Several methods for datapath synthesis have been discussed extensively in [GDWL91]. In this section, we will describe techniques for estimating the number, size and area of these components.

Storage units are required for holding data values represented by the constants, variables and arrays in the behavior. The simplest estimation strategy assumes that each variable in the behavior will be implemented as a separate register or memory. However, such an implementation may have an excessive number of storage units, since variable values are not needed during the entire execution of the behavior. It may be possible to minimize the number of storage units by mapping several variables that are not used concurrently to the same register or memory. To determine whether two variables are used concurrently, we must consider their corresponding lifetimes. The **lifetime** of a variable is defined as the time interval between its definition (i.e., writing into a variable) and its last use (i.e., reading a variable's value) before the next definition. The number of storage units that will be required in a design is equal to the maximum number of overlapping variable lifetimes. For example, consider the scheduled behavior of Figure 7.16(a), with variables v_1 through v_{11}. The lifetime of each variable is shown in Figure 7.16(b). Variable v_3 is computed in state s_1 as the sum of v_1 and v_2, and is last used in state s_3 by the addition operation that computes v_8. Consequently, the variable is "live" in states s_2 and s_3.

Once the variable lifetimes have been computed, several approaches may be used to determine the number of storage units required to implement the variables. A **clique partitioning** approach can be used to determine the set of variables that could be mapped to the same storage unit. A graph, $G = (V, E)$, is derived from the given behavior, in which every vertex $v_i \in V$ uniquely represents a variable v_i and there exists an edge $e_{i,j} \in E$ if and only if variables v_i and v_j can be stored in the same storage unit, that is, their lifetime intervals do not overlap. A complete subgraph or **clique** of G represents a storage unit for all the variables in the subgraph. To find the minimal number of storage units, we must partition graph G into a minimal number of cliques in

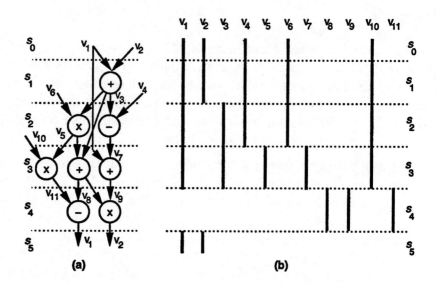

Figure 7.16: Variable lifetimes: (a) scheduled behavior (b) lifetime intervals.

such a way that each vertex belongs to exactly one clique. This problem is called clique-partitioning [CLR89].

We briefly describe a heuristic proposed in [CS86] to solve the clique partitioning problem. The approach consists of several iterations, in each of which the pair of nodes with the highest number of common neighbors is merged into a single node. Edges from other nodes in the graph to the two merged nodes are replaced by edges to the newly created merged node. Repeating the process of merging nodes until no edges remain in the graph will result in the creation of a set of cliques. Each clique corresponds to a storage unit that will implement the variables belonging to the clique.

We will demonstrate the clique-partitioning approach using a behavior whose variable lifetimes are given in Figure 7.16(b). Figure 7.17(a) shows the graph model obtained for the set of variables. Appropriate edges are added between the vertices. For example, there exists an edge between the vertices representing variables v_8 and v_{10}, since their lifetime intervals do not overlap. Vertices v_1 and v_{10} do not have an edge between them, since their lifetimes overlap. By applying clique-partitioning heuristic described above, we create five cliques shown in Figure 7.17(b) and assign them to registers R_1 through R_5.

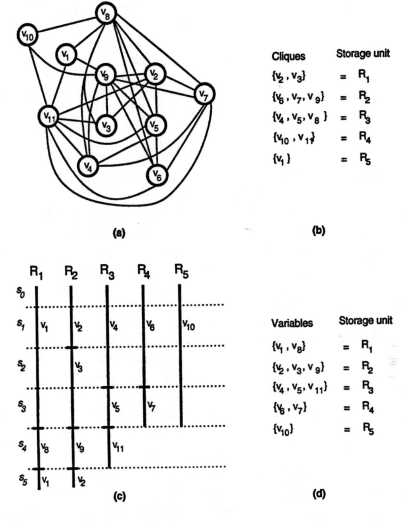

Cliques		Storage unit
$\{v_2, v_3\}$	=	R_1
$\{v_6, v_7, v_9\}$	=	R_2
$\{v_4, v_5, v_8\}$	=	R_3
$\{v_{10}, v_{11}\}$	=	R_4
$\{v_1\}$	=	R_5

(a)   (b)

Variables		Storage unit
$\{v_1, v_8\}$	=	R_1
$\{v_2, v_3, v_9\}$	=	R_2
$\{v_4, v_5, v_{11}\}$	=	R_3
$\{v_6, v_7\}$	=	R_4
$\{v_{10}\}$	=	R_5

(c)   (d)

Figure 7.17: Register allocation: (a) clique partitioning, graph model, (b) clique-partitioning solution, (c) overlapped lifetimes after left-edge algorithm, (d) resulting variable-to-storage-unit mapping.

Another heuristic for clique partitioning based on the left-edge algorithm [HS71] was proposed for minimizing the number of registers in REAL [KP87]. Given a list of variables in the behavior and their associated lifetime intervals, the algorithm first sorts the list of variables in ascending order of the start times of their lifetime. The algorithm makes several passes over the sorted list, examining the lifetimes of the variables in the order in which they occur in the list. In each pass, the algorithm allocates a new register and assigns a new variable to the register if its lifetime does not overlap with the lifetimes of the already assigned variables to that register. These assigned variables are then deleted from the sorted list of variables. The process is repeated until all variables have been assigned to registers.

To illustrate the left edge algorithm, we apply it to the scheduled behavior of Figure 7.16. The set of variables is first sorted according to the lifetime intervals resulting in the list, $L = (v_1, v_2, v_4, v_6, v_{10}, v_3, v_5, v_7, v_8, v_9, v_{11})$. In the first pass, a storage unit R_1 is allocated and the variable v_1 is assigned to it. Scanning list L, we observe that variable v_8 is the next variable that can be assigned to the storage unit R_1, since its lifetime interval does not overlap with that of variable v_1, already assigned to R_1. No other variable has a non-overlapping lifetime that does not overlap with those of variables v_1 and v_8. Thus, storage unit R_1 consists of the variables v_1 and v_8, and these variables are deleted from list L. In the second pass, storage unit R_2 is allocated and v_2 is assigned to it. Scanning the list, we see that variables v_3 and v_9 can also be assigned to R_2. Continuing similarly, a total of five passes over list L are required before all variables have been assigned to a storage unit. Figure 7.17(c) shows the variable lifetimes after five iterations of the left-edge algorithm whereas Figure 7.17(d) shows the final assignment of variables to registers.

The above methods allow more accurate estimation of the number of storage units required in a behavior than just assuming one storage unit per variable. However, this more accurate estimate is obtained at the expense of the extra computation needed for both the methods presented above.

Functional units are needed to implement the operations in the behavior. The required number of functional units can be estimated in several ways.

First, the system designer may specify the functional unit allocation explicitly.

Second, in case the behavior has already been scheduled into control steps, a clique partitioning [CS86] approach may be used to determine the number of functional units required. The approach involves the construction of a graph model similar to the one presented for determining the number of storage units. Each node in the graph represents an operation in the behavior. An edge exists between two nodes in the graph if and only if the corresponding operations have been assigned to different control steps and there are functional units that can perform both the operations. The cliques in such a graph represent the set of operations that can be executed by the same functional unit. The heuristic described in the previous subsection will determine necessary number of functional units.

Finally, if a performance constraint (such as the maximum number of control steps) is specified for the behavior, the minimal number of functional units required to implement the behavior can be determined using the **force-directed algorithm** [PK89b]. The algorithm attempts to distribute operations of the same type uniformly into all the available control steps. This uniform distribution ensures that functional units allocated to perform operations in one control step are used efficiently in all other control steps, leading to a high functional-unit utilization. In each iteration, the algorithm assigns exactly one unscheduled operation into a control step, so as to minimize the expected number of functional units needed in the design. After algorithm terminates, the maximum number of operations of a specific type assigned to any control step is the number of needed functional units of that type. Unlike clique-partitioning, the force-directed approach requires **functional-unit binding**, i.e., the assignment of operations in the behavior to specific functional units. Such a mapping of operations to functional units is essential, since it will enable us to determine the number of interconnections needed between the storage and functional units.

After all the variables and operations in the behavior have been mapped to storage and functional units, we can estimate the number of **interconnect units**, such as buses and multiplexers, which are required for interconnecting the storage and functional units. A bus implementation has the advantage of easier routability, since each bus usually runs along the set of units that communicate over it. A storage or functional unit that uses the bus to read or write data requires only a short connection to tap into the bus. A multiplexer implementation, on the other hand, could result in congestion, since it requires all the inputs to be routed to a single component, the multiplexer.

The interconnection units can be estimated directly from the description of the behavior and the mapping of variables and operations to registers and functional units, respectively.

First, the set of connections between the storage and functional units in the design is determined. For example, if a behavior has the statement A := B + C, then there exists a connection from the storage units to which the variables B and C have been assigned to the functional unit implementing the addition operation, and another from the functional unit to the storage unit to which A is bound.

Once the connections have been determined, they need to be mapped to a multiplexer or a bus. A simple strategy would be to implement the set of connections that have a common sink with the same multiplexer or bus. Figure 7.18(a) shows the connection between a set of registers and the two inputs of a functional unit. Since each input of the functional unit has four inputs, two 4×1 multiplexers, $M1$ and $M2$, are required to implement the connections, as shown in Figure 7.18(b). A reduction in the multiplexer cost may be obtained by **factoring** common inputs to different multiplexers and inserting a separate multiplexer to select one of the common inputs. For example, the multiplexers $M1$ and $M2$ in Figure 7.18(b) both have inputs from registers $R2$, $R3$ and $R4$. Connections from these registers to the two functional unit inputs can be "factored" out and implemented with multiplexer $M3$, as shown in Figure 7.18(c). Factoring the multiplexer inputs reduces the total number of multiplexer inputs in the design, and hence the multiplexer cost. For example, the two multiplexers in Figure 7.18(b) have a total of 8 inputs, while the three multiplexers in Figure 7.18(c) have only 7 inputs.

Another approach of estimating the number of connection units uses clique-partitioning. A graph model similar to the ones presented for determining the number of storage and functional units is constructed. Each vertex in the graph represents a connection between two units. An edge exists between two vertices if and only if the corresponding connections are not used concurrently for data transfer in the same control

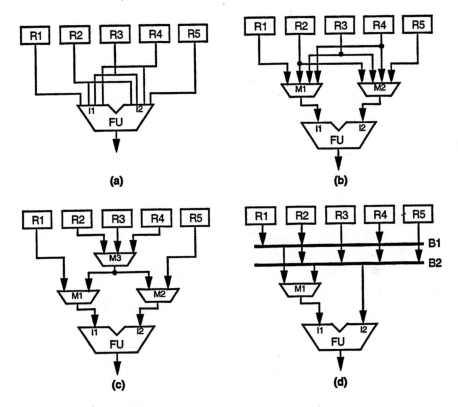

Figure 7.18: Determining interconnect units: (a) connections between storage and functional units, (b) multiplexer implementation, (c) reducing multiplexer inputs by factoring, (d) two-level interconnections after clique-partitioning.

step. Each of the cliques in such a graph represents an interconnect unit. All connections whose representative vertices are in a clique are assigned to the same multiplexer or bus.

Figure 7.18(d) shows the implementation of the connections in Figure 7.18(a) using two buses, after applying clique partitioning. Multiplexers may still be required in case two or more buses need to be connected to the same unit, resulting in a two-level interconnection structure. In Figure 7.18(d), both the buses, $B1$ and $B2$, are connected to input $I1$ of the functional unit by multiplexer $M1$. For any design, the interconnection between the set of storage and functional units may be implemented with multiple levels of interconnect units. A bus or multiplexer may be used to implement the interconnections at any level.

Having described methods to estimating the storage, functional and interconnect units in the datapath, we now show how the **total datapath area** may be determined for a custom ASIC implementation. The same formulas may easily be adjusted for gate array and FPGA implementations.

Datapath area estimation

The datapath layout is usually a bit-sliced stack [WCG91] in which the individual datapath components are placed in rows, one over the other, with the least-significant-bit (LSB) position of each unit aligned. This architecture is shown in Figure 7.19. A single routing channel is used to connect different units within the same bit-slice. Control lines run horizontally in second metal and power, and data lines run vertically in poly or first metal.

To determine the area of the datapath, we need to determine the total length L_{bit} and height H_{bit} of a bit-slice. We first determine the number of transistors in each bit-slice of the datapath, $tr(DP)$, under the assumption that L_{bit} is proportional to the number of transistors in each bit slice. Let R, F and M be the number of registers, functional units and multiplexers determined for the datapath. Let $tr(REG_i)$, $tr(FU_j)$ and $tr(MUX_k)$ be the number of transistors in each bit-slice of the ith register, jth functional unit and kth multiplexer. Then the number of transistors in each bit-slice is computed as follows:

$$tr(DP) \;=\; \sum_{i=1}^{R} tr(REG_i) \;+\; \sum_{j=1}^{F} tr(FU_j) \;+\; \sum_{k=1}^{M} tr(MUX_k) \quad (7.20)$$

Let α be the transistor pitch coefficient in $\mu m/$transistor. For a given library, α is obtained by averaging the ratio of cell width and the number of transistors in each cell in the library. The total length of each bit slice, denoted by L_{bit} in Figure 7.19, is determined as follows:

$$L_{bit} \;=\; \alpha \times tr(DP) \quad (7.21)$$

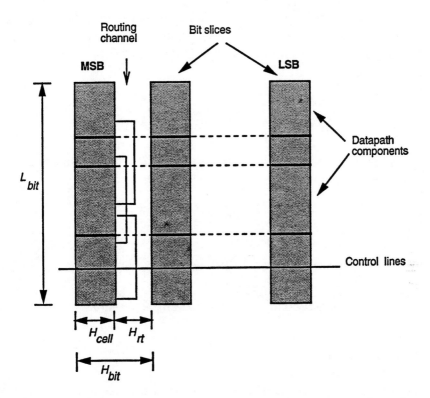

Figure 7.19: Datapath components arranged as bit-sliced stack.

The height, H_{cell}, of each cell in the bit slice is fixed and depends on the height of standard cells in the library. The height, H_{rt}, of the routing channel associated with each bit-slice depends on the number of routing tracks required to implement the nets between the datapath components. An estimate for the required number of tracks in each bit slice can be obtained only after the position of each unit in the bit slice is determined. A min-cut algorithm [FM82] can be used for this purpose. The required number of tracks is estimated as the maximum number of connections across any cut perpendicular to the channel. A better estimate can be obtained by using simple routing algorithms, such as the left-edge algorithm [HS71] which has $O(n\log n)$ complexity, n being the number of nets.

A simpler approach would require the average number of nets that can be implemented on the same track, *nets_per_track*, to be determined empirically. Let β be the wiring pitch, that is, the minimum separation between two metal lines. Let n represent the number of nets between the components in the datapath. The height of the routing channel, H_{rt}, can then be computed as

$$H_{rt} = \frac{nets}{nets\_per\_track} \times \beta \qquad (7.22)$$

The area of each bit-slice, $area(bit)$, can now be computed as

$$area(bit) = L_{bit} \times (H_{cell} + H_{rt}) \qquad (7.23)$$

Finally, if $bitwidth(DP)$ is the bitwidth of the datapath components, the total area of the datapath is calculated as follows:

$$area(DP) = bitwidth(DP) \times area(bit) \qquad (7.24)$$

Control unit area estimation

The control unit sequences a design through a series of control steps or states, each of which represents the set of datapath operations performed concurrently.

The control unit consists of a state register, the control logic and the next-state logic. The state register contains encoded states. The control logic defines the control signals for the datapath components as a function of the current state. The next-state logic defines the next state of the state machine as a function of the current state and the datapath status lines. The datapath status lines communicate results of comparison operations in the datapath to the control logic.

Methods for estimating the number of states required by a behavior were presented in Section 7.3.3. If a design has N control steps, then the state register bitwidth, $bitwidth(SR)$, will be $log_2 N$.

The control and next-state logic unit may be implemented as random logic, a read-only memory (ROM), or a programmable logic array (PLA). We will describe techniques for the estimation of random logic and ROM implementations in this section. Techniques for estimating the area of a PLA implementation of the control unit have been discussed in [GDWL91].

Figure 7.20 shows a **random logic** implementation of the control and next-state logic using a two-level network of AND and OR gates. In order to estimate the area of the control unit, we first need to determine the number and sizes of AND and OR gates and any drivers that will be required to implement the control unit.

The control unit is usually described as a state table that defines the control signals for the datapath components for each state. A set of Boolean equations can be generated for each control or next-state line and optimized in order to determine the total number of gates required in the control units. However, since the process of generating a state table, formulating the boolean equations and optimizing them is extremely time consuming, an alternative technique for estimating the control unit area is required. We now describe one such method to estimate the number and size of gates required for a random logic implementation of the control unit.

Consider the control unit shown in Figure 7.20. Since an OR-gate is required for each control and next-state line, the total number of OR-gates is equal to the number of control and next-state lines. The size (i.e., the number of inputs) of an OR-gate for a control line is identical to the number of control steps during which the corresponding control line is asserted. For example, a control line C_i that drives the load line of a register will be asserted whenever a data value is loaded in the register. The number of times that C_i will be asserted can be determined by examining the specification for the number of times any variable stored in that register is assigned a new value. Similarly, a control line that enables a functional unit is asserted whenever the functional unit performs an operation bound to it. If more than one functional unit of a given type is allocated for the design, then the number of control steps during which the individual control lines are asserted is estimated to be the number of operations of that type averaged over the number of functional units. To account for the binary encoding of select lines, each of the $log_2(n)$ select lines of an $n \times 1$ multiplexer can be assumed to be active for exactly half the number of states that the storage or functional unit for which the multiplexer selects data is active. To determine the size of an OR-gate for a next state line, we assume that each next-state line is "toggled" on the average during half of the control steps in the design. Thus, the size of each OR-gate driving a next-state line is assumed to be identical to half the number of control steps.

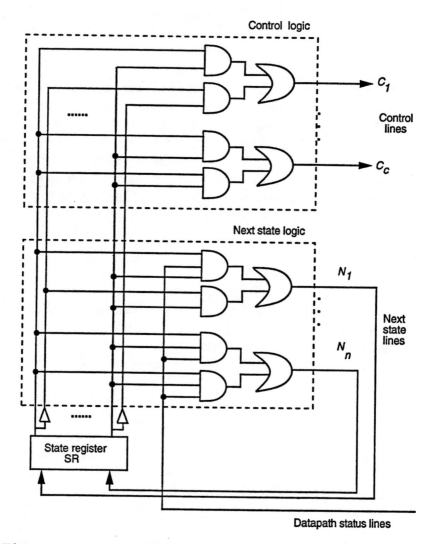

Figure 7.20: 2-level AND/OR implementation of the control unit.

AND-gates are required for decoding the current state represented by the value of the state register SR. The number of AND-gates in the control logic is the sum of the number of control steps during which any control or next-state line is asserted. The upper bound on the total number of AND-gates is the total number of control steps determined for the design. Assuming that at most one datapath status line affects a next-state line, the number of inputs to an AND gate is approximated as $bitwidth(SR) + 1$ i.e., one more than the bitwidth of the state register.

In addition, $bitwidth(SR)$ single-bit drivers are required to drive the non-inverted line for each bit of the state register, as shown in Figure 7.20.

Having determined the size and numbers of the OR gates, AND gates, drivers and state register, we can compute $tr(CL)$, the total number of transistors in the control unit. Let γ be the transistor area coefficient in μm^2/transistor. The coefficient γ can be determined experimentally for the given library of standard cells and the placement and routing tools used. The total area of the control logic is then approximated as follows:

$$area(CL) = \gamma \times tr(CL) \qquad (7.25)$$

The above equation does not consider the impact of logic minimization and technology mapping. The estimation of logic optimization for a specific logic library is still an open problem.

A **ROM implementation** of the control unit is shown in Figure 7.21. In a $W \times B$ ROM, W denotes the number of words in the ROM and B the number of bits in each word.

For each control step in the design, there exists a corresponding word in the ROM. Thus, the total number of words in the ROM, W, is the number of control steps determined for the behavior. Each word in the ROM contains a bit for each control and next-state line. Thus, the bitwidth B of the ROM is the sum of the number of control and next-state lines generated by the control unit.

The area of the control unit can then be computed as the sum of the areas of the state register SR and a $W \times B$ ROM.

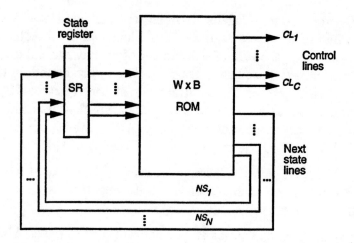

Figure 7.21: A ROM implementation of the control unit.

7.3.7 Pin estimation

A given behavior will often access data that is external to the behavior. Such communication will be implemented with a set of wires that connect the behavior to the data being accessed. If each behavior is synthesized into a separate chip, these wires will be the pins on the chip boundary.

The **communication width** or the number of wires at a behavior's boundary required for accessing external data depends on how the communication is specified in the functional specification:

1. **Port declarations:** The communication width of a port is estimated from the port's declaration in the behavior. For example, assuming that an integer is implemented as a 16-bit number in the design, the following port declarations will result in REQ being estimated as a single bit port, ADDR as a 16-bit wide port, and DATA as a 22-bit wide port at the behavior's boundary:

   ```
   port REQ : in bit;
   port ADDR : out integer;
   port DATA : in bit_vector(21 downto 0);
   ```

2. **Communication Channels:** Communication is often abstracted as a channel over which data is transferred. Channels can be de-

fined in HDLs like HardwareC [KD88, DK88], CSP (Communicating Sequential Processes) [Hoa78], and SpecCharts [NVG91a]. Channels will be synthesized into a bus consisting of a set of wires and a protocol defining data transfer operations over the wires. The communication width is the sum of all the data and control lines which constitute the bus. For example, if a channel over which integer data is transferred is implemented using a handshake protocol, then 18 bits are required to implement the communication (i.e., 16 bits to implement the data transfer and 2 control signals to implement the handshaking).

3. **Global Data:** Often a behavior in a specification will access variables that are visible to it but defined external to the behavior. For example, a VHDL process may communicate with another process by accessing a global signal. Accessing global data defines implicit ports at the behavior's boundary. As was the case with explicitly declared ports, the communication width depends on the type of global data declaration.

4. **Procedure calls:** The implementation of a procedure that is called from a behavior determines the communication width between the procedure and the behavior. If the procedure is inlined during synthesis, there is no external communication involved and thus no additional pins required at the behavior's boundary. However, if the procedure is implemented as a separate system component, then the required communication width is equal to the sum of the communication width required for each of the procedure parameters (determined from the parameter declaration type). In addition, handshaking signals might be needed to allow the main behavior to initiate/terminate the procedure appropriately.

For a given behavior B, let P represent the set of port declarations, C the set of communication channels, V the set of global variables accessed, and S the set of procedures called by the behavior. If $width(x)$ represents the number of wires required to access object x, the total interconnect at the behavior's boundary is determined as follows:

$$pins(B) = \sum_{p_i \in P} width(p_i) + \sum_{c_i \in C} width(c_i) + \sum_{v_i \in V} width(v_i) + \sum_{s_i \in S} width(s_i)$$

$$(7.26)$$

7.4   Software estimation

Software quality metrics were introduced in Section 7.2.2. Before we describe methods to estimate program size, data memory size and execution time, we will briefly discuss the underlying model for software estimation.

7.4.1   Software estimation model

For a software implementation, the behavior has to be compiled into the instruction set of the target processor. The variables in the behavior are assumed to be mapped to the memory associated with the processor. Consequently, all accesses to variables in the behavior are assumed to be implemented as memory read/write operations. Concurrent behaviors in a functional specification may be implemented on one or more processors. In the case of a single processor implementation, the execution of the concurrent behaviors may have to be interleaved in order to satisfy data dependencies or timing constraints. Communication between two or more behaviors mapped to the same processor is achieved through shared locations in the memory. In case two behaviors are mapped to two different processors, communication between them must be implemented either through a shared memory or through direct communication over joint physical connection.

Two models can be adopted for software estimation – the processor-specific model and the generic model. Each of these is examined separately.

Processor-specific estimation model

Under the processor-specific estimation model, shown in Figure 7.22(a), the exact value of a metric is computed by compiling each behavior into the instruction set of the desired processor using a compiler specific to that processor. From the **timing** information (such as the number of clock cycles needed to execute each instruction) and **size** information (such as the number of bytes required for each instruction) associated with each processor, we can determine the size and execution time for the compiled behavior. For example, if a behavior has to be implemented on an Intel 8086 microprocessor, it is first compiled into the 8086 instruction set. Having obtained the compiled behavior, we can use the timing and size information associated with the 8086 instruction set to determine the performance and size of the software implementation. Similarly, if the behavior is to be implemented on a Motorola 68000 processor, it needs to be compiled into the 68000 instruction set. Based on the 68000 instruction timing and size information, the estimator can obtain the software metrics for the behavior. Since the estimator is targeted to a specific processor, we call this a processor-specific model.

The main advantage of the processor-specific model is that the estimates obtained are very accurate, since the behavior is actually compiled for execution on the selected processor. However, such an estimation approach requires a dedicated compiler for each processor. Consequently, it is difficult to adapt an existing estimator for a new processor. In addition, compiling a behavior for the estimation purposes is computationally expensive.

Generic estimation model

Instead of using different compilers and estimators for different target processors in the processor-specific model, an alternative generic estimation model was proposed in [GGN94]. Under the generic estimation model shown in Figure 7.22(b), the behavior is first compiled into a set of generic three-address instructions. Processor-specific technology files are made available containing information about the number of clock cycles and bytes that each type of generic instruction requires. The estimator computes the software metrics for the behavior based on the generic instructions and the technology files for the target processors.

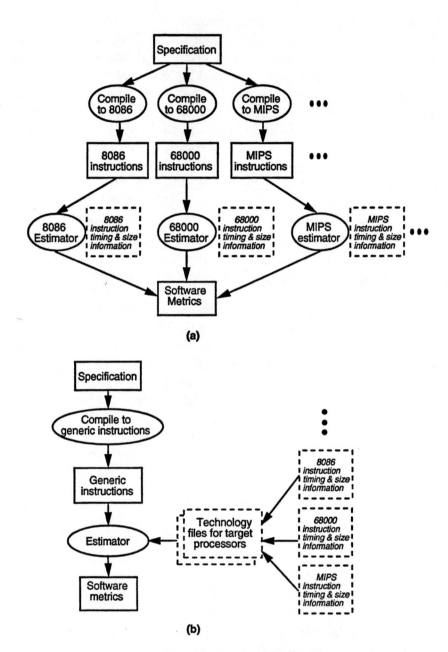

Figure 7.22: Approaches to software estimation: (a) processor-specific estimation model, (b) generic estimation model.

The proposed generic instruction set consists of the following five classes:

1. Arithmetic/logic/relational instructions: $\langle des \leftarrow src1 \; \mathbf{op} \; src2 \rangle$;
2. Move/load/store instructions: $\langle des \leftarrow src \; \rangle$;
3. Conditional jump instruction: $\langle \mathbf{if} \; cond \; \mathbf{goto} \; label \rangle$;
4. Unconditional jump instruction: $\langle \mathbf{goto} \; label \; e \rangle$;
5. Procedure call instruction: $\langle \mathbf{call} \; label \rangle$;

In the above instructions, *des* refers either to a register or to a memory location, while *src* and *cond* refer to constants, registers or memory locations. The term *label* refers to procedure names or instruction labels. In addition to the above, the generic three-address instruction set also includes the *return* and *null* instructions.

The technology file for each target processor can be derived from the timing and size information of the processor's instruction set. Figure 7.23 shows the computation of the number of clock cycles for a generic instruction of the type $\langle dmem3 \leftarrow dmem1 + dmem2 \rangle$. Here, *dmem* indicates a direct memory addressing mode. The generic instruction is first mapped to a sequence of target processor instructions. The total number of clock cycles of the generic instruction is obtained by summing the clock cycles of each individual instruction in the sequence. $EA1$ and $EA2$ in Figure 7.23 are the effective address calculation times used for displacement memory addressing mode, which are six and eight clock cycles on the 8086 and 68020 processors, respectively. Thus, the generic instruction will take 35 and 22 clock cycles on the 8086 and 68020 processors, respectively.

Using a similar approach we can derive the number of bytes that each type of generic instruction will require if it is compiled on the 8086 or 68020 processor. For example, the generic instruction given in Figure 7.23 is compiled into a sequence of three 8086 instructions. The total size of the three instructions is 10 bytes, which is entered in the technology file for the 8086 processor as the size of the generic instruction under consideration.

Compared with the processor-specific model, the generic estimation model has several advantages. First, the generic model does not require different compilers and estimators for different target processors.

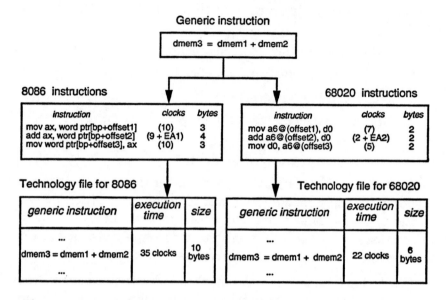

Figure 7.23: Deriving technology files for generic instructions.

Instead, only a single compiler, estimator and a set of technology files is required for software estimation. Second, the generic model makes retargeting the estimator to a new processor much easier. Retargeting consists of providing a technology file for the new processor. In the processor-specific model, we would require a compiler for the new processor in addition to the timing and size information of the processor's instruction set. Finally, the peculiarities of each type of processor can be reflected in the technology file for the processor. The generic three-address instructions are free of instruction idiosyncrasies. Thus, it is much easier and faster to compile the behavior into a generic instruction set than to compile the behavior into the complex instructions that may be part of a processor's instruction set. A disadvantage of the generic model is the lower accuracy of its estimates largely because the generic instruction set represents only a small portion of the processor's entire instruction set. A set of real processor instructions may be able to implement certain operations more efficiently than an equivalent set of generic instructions.

We will use the generic estimation model to introduce techniques for estimating program memory size, data memory size and performance for software implementations. The same techniques are also applicable to a processor-specific estimation model.

7.4.2 Program execution time

The software or program execution time of a behavior can be determined in one of two ways – **dynamic simulation** and **static estimation**. Given a set of input data, dynamic simulation executes the program and records the number of clock cycles required for each execution. Given different sets of input data, dynamic simulation may obtain a different number of clock cycles for that program due to the data-dependent conditional branches and loops. Static estimation, on the other hand, is insensitive to input data and can yield fairly accurate results if the number of loop iterations is known and the conditional branching probability can be predicted correctly. In addition, static estimation is faster and requires less space than dynamic simulation. In this section, we will describe a static estimation technique and its application to the performance estimation of software.

Software performance estimation is similar to the method described in Section 7.3.4 for estimating the hardware execution time. The functional specification is first divided into basic blocks. In each basic block, the set of statements is compiled into a set of generic three-address instructions. The execution time, $exectime(b_i)$, of a basic block b_i, can be determined by summing the execution time of each generic instruction in that basic block (i.e., the number of clock cycles associated with the generic instruction in the technology file for the target processor).

The basic block structure of the given behavior is then mapped to an equivalent control flow graph G. Each node in G has a weight equivalent to the software execution time of the corresponding basic block. By applying the probability-based flow analysis technique, we can obtain the execution frequencies of the basic blocks in the behavior. Finally, Equation 7.14 can be used to obtain the average-case software execution time for the entire behavior.

Generally, compilers optimize the object code by using optimization techniques such as register allocation, loop optimization and global optimization. The designer can invoke these optimizations directly by passing special flags to the compiler. The generic estimation model presented in this section does not employ any optimization heuristics; consequently, the estimates computed for software execution time are for non-optimized code. In order to estimate the performance corresponding to the optimized code, we need to know the optimization ratio of the compiler used by the designer to generate the machine instructions. The performance-optimization ratio, δ, is defined as the ratio of optimized code performance to the non-optimized code performance. By performing several experiments using well-known Livermore loop kernels, performance optimization ratios of 0.74, 0.68, 0.54 and 0.49 were reported in [GGN94] for the compilers from C to the 8086, 80286, 68000 and 68020 instruction sets, respectively. It must be emphasized that these coefficients are dependent on the data sets that were used. Therefore, the accuracy of the performance estimates will depend on how close the code and data sets are to the ones used for determining these ratios.

The performance estimate *exectime(B)* of a behavior B, obtained after flow analysis, is scaled by the performance optimization ratio δ, to account for compiler optimizations, i.e., if *optimized_exectime(B)* is the estimate of the software execution time for a compiled and optimized behavior, then

$$optimized\_exectime(B) \ = \ \delta \times exectime(B) \qquad (7.27)$$

The above estimation method works well for simple processors. The execution-time estimation for pipelined and parallel processors with instruction and data caches is still an open problem.

7.4.3   Program memory size

The first step in program size estimation also involves compiling the given behavior into a set of generic instructions. The size of each type of generic instruction is specified in the technology file for the target processor. Based on the size of each generic instruction, the program-memory size of a behavior is then computed as the sum of those generic instructions in the behavior. If a behavior B is compiled into a set of generic instructions G, and *instr_size(g)* represents the size of the generic instruction g, then the size of the program required for behavior B is computed as follows:

$$progsize(B) = \sum_{g \in G} instr\_size(g) \qquad (7.28)$$

As in the approach presented in Section 7.4.2, the average size optimization ratio, θ, can be computed to account for compiler optimizations. The program size obtained in Equation 7.28 can then be scaled by θ to obtain a more accurate estimate of the size of the compiled and optimized behavior.

7.4.4 Data memory size

The data memory size is determined by examining the data declarations in the functional specification. The data memory size, $datasize(d)$, of a declaration d is determined by the size of d's base type and the number of elements in d. The base type of any declaration is an indivisible type defined in the language. For example, consider the declarations

```
variable X: bit;
variable Y: array (9 downto 0, 15 downto 0) of integer;
```

The base type of variable X is bit and the number of its base type elements is 1. The base type of variable Y is integer and the number of its base type elements is 160.

The size required for the software implementation of a data item of each distinct base type provided in the description, is defined in a lookup table. Figure 7.24 shows the data memory sizes corresponding to some of the base types defined in VHDL. For a declaration d, $datasize(d)$ is computed as the size of d's base type multiplied by the number of base type elements in d. For example, declaration Y above has an integer base type which requires four bytes of storage, as determined from the lookup table of Figure 7.24. Since variable Y has 160 elements, the total size for declaration Y is 640 bytes.

Having obtained the data memory size of each declaration, the data memory size of a behavior B can be computed by summing that for each of its declarations. Let D denote the set of declarations in behavior B. The data memory size of behavior B is computed as follows:

Declaration base type	Data memory size (bytes)	
Bit, Boolean	1	
Bitvector	$\lceil n/8 \rceil$	*where n is the number of bits*
Character	1	
Integer, Natural, Positive	4	
Real	8	

Figure 7.24: Data size of a few VHDL base types.

$$datasize(B) \;=\; \sum_{d \in D} datasize(d) \tag{7.29}$$

The data memory size estimation described above is accurate under the assumption that all variables have lifetimes equal to the execution time of the behavior, which means we do not share memory locations for two variables. In case a behavior has a significant number of variables with short lifetimes, then data memory size estimation will have to incorporate lifetime analysis to overlay the variables that have non-overlapping lifetimes.

7.5 Estimation techniques in system-level tools

In this section, we will survey the quality metrics and estimation methods in several high-level synthesis and system design tools.

7.5.1 BUD

BUD (Bottom Up Design) [MK90] is a system which performs global analysis and scheduling as part of a high-level synthesis system. As explained in Section 6.5.2, BUD uses a hierarchical clustering algorithm for partitioning the operations of a single behavior into clusters, and uses detailed physical information to evaluate the area and performance of each cluster and the whole design.

The input to BUD is a value trace (VT) [EST78] representation of a behavior. In addition, a trace file of the behavior containing the number of times each operation was executed during simulation is provided. The execution probabilities of the operations in the behavior can be derived from the trace file when determining the average cycle time. BUD also has access to a database of units containing detailed information such as unit functions, delay, length, width, and power dissipation. The output of BUD estimators are the area and execution time required by an implementation of the behavior.

Given a set of clusters consisting of a set of operations, the **area** of each cluster is estimated first. A single functional-unit is allocated for each type of operation in the cluster. The clock cycle is initially specified by the system designer. Operations are assigned to control steps using a list scheduler. Lifetime analysis is used to determine the number and size of the registers in each cluster. The multiplexers are assigned to the clusters based on the number of ports in the cluster. The width and length of the cluster are determined from the width and length of the units selected to implement the registers, functional units and multiplexers.

Once the area of each cluster has been determined, BUD performs floorplanning to determine the placement and orientation of each cluster, using a technique proposed by Zimmerman [Zim88]. Basically, a behavior is partitioned recursively to create a tree representation of the design. The leaves of the tree are the individual clusters in the design. The tree representation is then traversed from the leaves towards the root to yield all possible arrangements of the clusters. A shape function is used to represent the relationship between the height and width for any combination of clusters. The arrangement of clusters for a specific aspect ratio can be computed from the shape function. The floorplan is finally adjusted to accommodate the wiring area required for connections between clusters.

Having determined the datapath, the clock cycle, clk, is recomputed as the largest delay through the datapath in any control step. From the trace files provided for the VT, the probability p_i that control step i, $1 \leq i \leq N$, will be executed can be determined. The average **execution time** for the behavior is then determined as

$$exectime(B) = clk \times (\sum_{i=1}^{N} p_i)$$

(7.30)

The main advantage of the estimator in BUD is that it incorporates detailed physical design information during estimation. For example, floorplanning is performed, wiring area is determined and wiring delays are taken into account during the computation of the clock cycle. Consequently, the estimates of the delays and area computed can be expected to be accurate. However, a consequence of the detailed estimation in BUD is that the time required for computing the estimates is likely to be high. For example, for the floorplanning step itself, an execution time of the order of seconds was reported in [MK90]. As the system size increases, design space exploration in BUD will become computationally expensive. In addition, BUD does not estimate the control unit area which can, in some designs, represent a significant portion of the total area.

7.5.2 Aparty   .

Aparty [LT91, Lag89, LT89] is an architectural partitioner which divides the behavior of a system into multiple partitions, each of which may represent a chip or a block on a chip. Given a VT representation of a behavior, Aparty employs a multi-stage clustering technique to generate a partitioning of the behavior.

The input to the estimators in Aparty is the set of clusters. Each cluster consists of several operations of the behavior. The estimator also has access to an area file that contains the area-per-bit required to implement each operation.

Aparty computes the **area** of a cluster as the sum of the areas of all functional units and multiplexers in the cluster. For each cluster, a single functional unit is allocated for each type of operation in the cluster. If there is more than one operation of a given type mapped to the same cluster, appropriate multiplexers are assigned for the functional unit implementing those operations.

Aparty estimates the **interconnect** (i.e., the number of wires) at each cluster boundary as the sum of the sizes of the connections between the cluster under consideration and other clusters.

Performance is estimated as the number of control steps produced by scheduling the functional specification using the CSTEP scheduler [Nes87].

Estimation in Aparty represents a tradeoff between speed and accuracy. By using a simple model for area estimation that consists only of functional units and multiplexers, rapid estimates of cluster area can be obtained. Consequently, the designer can afford to explore a larger design space. At the same time, the estimates are extremely coarse, since register, interconnect and control unit areas are not taken into account.

7.5.3 Vulcan

The Vulcan [GD90] partitioning tool represents the behavior as a graph with two types of edges: dependence edges and exclusion edges. Vertices represent the operations in the behavior. Dependence edges represent the dependencies between the operations, and exclusion edges between vertices represent the exclusivity of corresponding operations, which means that they can share the same functional unit during implementation. Associated with each vertex is an area cost and a delay representing the propagation delay (in whole number of clock cycles) through the corresponding operation. The clock period is specified as an input to Vulcan.

The **area** estimate of a graph is simply the sum of the area costs associated with all the vertices in the hypergraph. However, since the set of vertices linked by an exclusion edge represents operations that can share hardware, only one vertex from the set is counted toward the area estimate.

The **performance** of the graph is computed as the length of the longest start-to-finish path in the graph. The delay cost associated with each vertex in the longest path is summed up. If an edge connects two vertices assigned to different partitions, a unit delay is associated with the edge to reflect the communication cost involved.

The advantage of the estimators in Vulcan is that they can provide rapid estimates, because the area and performance estimates are constructed by simply summing up the costs and delays associated with the vertices in the graph. The accuracy of the area estimate is likely to be low, since routing, register areas, and sharing of functional units between vertices are ignored.

7.5.4 SpecSyn

SpecSyn [GVN94] is a system design framework which provides the designer with a set of system design tools to partition a system specification into a set of system components. The system components generated could represent a chip, a memory, software executing on a processor, or a bus.

The input to SpecSyn is an executable specification of the system. The VHDL [IEE88] and SpecCharts [NVG91a] languages are used for this purpose. To estimate hardware parameters such as behavior execution time, clock cycle and area, a design library is provided (containing information about the number, type, delay, area and RT components that will be used to implement the design). To estimate software metrics such as program execution time and size, processor technology files similar to the ones described in Section 7.4.1 are provided (containing information such as the instruction sizes and execution times for a target processor).

The **clock cycle** estimator selects a clock cycle using the slack minimization method presented in Section 7.3.2 SpecSyn also allows the designer to specify the clock cycle explicitly.

Area estimation in SpecSyn allows the designer to specify the functional unit allocation for implementing a behavior. If a functional unit allocation is not specified, a minimal allocation of one functional unit of each type is assumed. The number of control steps is estimated using the operator-use method described in Section 7.3.3. Registers are estimated using lifetime analysis. Since the estimator does not actually schedule the operations into control steps, the lifetimes of variables are defined at a statement-level granularity, i.e., statement numbers are used to determine the definitions and uses of a variable. This approach does not require the creation of a dataflow graph and is correspondingly much faster. The number and size of multiplexers for registers and functional units are then estimated. The control unit is assumed to be implemented using a state register and a two-level AND-OR gate network whereas the area of the control logic is estimated using the techniques similar to those presented in Section 7.3.6.

Given a behavior described using VHDL sequential statements, the SpecSyn **performance** estimator first determines the number of control steps required for each basic block, using the operator-use method presented Section 7.3.3. The estimates for each basic block are merged using probability-based flow analysis to obtain the execution time of the behavior.

If the SpecCharts language is used to specify a hierarchical behavior, performance estimation in SpecSyn is done in a bottom-up fashion. The execution time for each leaf behavior is determined in a manner similar to that described above for a set of VHDL sequential statements. The execution time of any behavior at any hierarchical level is then determined by combining the estimates computed for its sub-behaviors. If a behavior has concurrent sub-behaviors, the execution time of the behavior is the maximum of the execution times estimated for the sub-behaviors.

SpecSyn provides the designer with estimators for **pins** and the **number of accesses** made by a behavior to variables, procedures and communication channels. These can be used by the designer to decide the assignment of objects in the specification to different system components.

For a software implementation, SpecSyn provides estimators for **execution times, program size** and **data size** [GGN94]. The average and worst case errors reported for software execution times were 8% and 19%, respectively. The average and worst-case errors associated with program memory size estimation in SpecSyn were 5% and 8%, respectively.

Any system design decision usually makes only one or a few changes to the design. An example of such a decision may be relocating a variable from one system component to another during system partitioning. Re-estimating a metric afresh from the specification after each design decision will be time-consuming and wasteful, especially since only incremental changes have been made to the design itself. To avoid such re-estimation, SpecSyn estimators maintain design information in a manner which enables **incremental modification** of the estimate to account for any changes to the design. Given the executable specification of a system, the estimator initially undergoes a setup phase, during which a detailed internal structure containing the relevant design information is created. For any subsequent design decision, estimates can be obtained in a constant time by updating the internal structure to reflect the design decision and then recomputing the estimates. SpecSyn supports incremental estimation updates for the execution time, hardware area and pins, and software size. The main advantage of such an approach is that by reducing the time required to obtain an estimate, it allows the use of sophisticated partitioning algorithms that may evaluate thousands of partitions.

The main advantage of the SpecSyn estimators is the speed at which estimates are provided to the partitioner. SpecSyn uses approximations for most aspects of the design, such as estimating the design area as a function of the transistors without performing any floorplanning, or estimating the multiplexers without binding operations to specific functional units. Consequently, it enables the system partitioner to examine a large number of options in a relatively short time. However, the estimators in SpecSyn are description-dependent. For example, a single-state functional specification may contain conditional branching. The estimator for control steps will allocate a control step for testing each condition even though the entire design could be implemented in one control step. The estimator also does not perform any optimizations during the estimation of control logic area, and ignores wiring delays.

7.6   Conclusion and future directions

The need to explore large design spaces at the system level requires rapid estimates of quality metrics. In this chapter, we defined some of the quality metrics that are relevant at the system level for both hardware and software implementations: clock cycle, control steps, communication rates, hardware and software execution times, area, pins, and program and data memory sizes. We described techniques that can be used to estimate these system parameters. In addition, we defined three criteria which can be used to evaluate any estimation technique: accuracy, speed and fidelity. We discussed estimation approaches in some of the tools that have been developed for high-level synthesis and system design.

Further work in design quality estimation needs to address several issues, which can be classified into three broad areas:

(a) **Optimization:** Estimation techniques need to be enhanced to incorporate the effects of optimizations typically performed by synthesis and compilation tools. For example, logic minimization on control and datapath components may reduce the design area and

design point	E (D)	M (D)
W	112	109
X	128	137
Y	139	121
Z	205	132

Figure 7.25: Estimated and measured values of a metric.

delays significantly. Similarly, compilers perform several optimizations, such as dead-code elimination, register-file optimization, and common subexpresssion elimination. Absence of techniques to estimate the impact of these optimizations will likely result in overestimation of quality metrics like design area and software execution time.

(b) **New metrics**: As system designs grow more accurate, quality metrics and techniques for estimating them need to be defined. For example, metrics need to be defined and estimation techniques developed for design characteristics such as power dissipation, testability, hardware/software integration, maintainability and manufacturability.

(c) **New architectural features**: The effects of more complex architectural features on estimates need to be evaluated. For example, software estimation techniques need to be upgraded to incorporate architectural features such as VLIW, pipelined processing, instruction prefetching, vector processing and caching. Hardware estimation techniques need to be enhanced to incorporate features such as complex clocking schemes (e.g., multi-phase clocking).

7.7 Exercises

1. Figure 7.25 shows the estimated and actual measured values, $E(D)$ and $M(D)$, respectively, for a quality metric for four design implementations. Compute the fidelity of the estimator used.

operation	occur(t_i)	delay(t_i)
add	4	49
multiply	9	163

Figure 7.26: Operation occurrences and delays.

2. Devise two metrics for each of the following design characteristics:
   (a) power dissipation,
   (b) design for testability,
   (c) manufacturability.

3. Consider the hardware design model of Figure 7.7. Formulate an equation for the clock period in terms of the component delays involved in the presence of the control and status registers (ignore any net delays).

4. Figure 7.26 shows the occurrences of various operations in the description of a behavior. The delays of the functional units that implement the operations are also given. Estimate the clock cycle using the maximum operator delay method and the slack minimization method. For each of the two estimates, compute the clock utilizations.

5. How can the operator-use method be modified to determine the number of control steps if some operations are implemented with pipelined functional-units?

6. Apply the operator-use method to estimate the number of control steps that the set of VHDL statements below will be scheduled into. Assume that the clock cycle is 25 ns, and that 1 multiplier (delay 100 ns) and 2 adders (50 ns) will be used to implement the design.

```
A := B + (C * 3);
B := B + C + D;
E := A * A;
X := C + D + Y;
D := A + E;
```

7. Devise two priority functions that can be used to order the operations in the priority lists while applying the List scheduling algorithm. Using the new functions, schedule the behavior of Figure 7.12(b). Assume that one adder, one subtractor and two multipliers are available.

8. How can the List scheduling algorithm of Section 7.3.3 be modified to account for each of the following?

   (a) multi-cycle operations,
   (b) pipelined functional units,
   (b) accesses to a memory requiring a fixed delay.

9. For a behavior that will be implemented on a processor with a cache memory, let the hit ratio (i.e., the probability of finding the desired data in the cache) for cache accesses be 0.8. If the cache and main memory access times are 50 ns and 300 ns, respectively, what is average time required by the behavior for each memory access?

10. *Assume that for each operation in a behavior, the component library has several functional units with different delays and costs. How can the number of functional units be estimated in such cases?

11. **How will the method for estimating the software execution time presented in Section 7.4.2 have to be modified to account for instruction pipelining in RISC processors?

12. **Given the description of a behavior that will be implemented as software executing on a processor with a cache memory, devise a strategy to estimate the hit ratio for cache accesses (i.e., the probability of finding the desired data in the cache).

Chapter 8

Specification Refinement

In Chapters 2, 3, 4 and 5 we described several methods for obtaining a functional specification of a system. In Chapters 6 and 7, we described several techniques for partitioning this functionality among the various system components, and for estimating design quality of such partitions. In this chapter, we will turn our attention to the creation of a refined specification which reflects the chosen partition and the selected components, thus bringing us one step closer to the final implementation.

8.1 Introduction

A system specification consists of **functional objects** such as behaviors, variables and communication channels. During system design, we group these functional objects in the specification into a set of **system components** such as processors, ASICs, memories and buses. While functional objects are devoid of any structure, system components have a well-defined structure, such as the number of pins on a chip, the number and size of words in a memory, or the number of wires in a bus. Updating the specification to reflect the transformation of the functional objects into system components is called **specification refinement**.

Specification refinement is important in system design for several reasons. First, it makes the specification consistent in all respects by updating it to reflect grouping decisions made during system partitioning. For example, when variables are grouped to be assigned to a single memory, declarations and references to those variables must be updated. Specification refinement will replace the variable declarations with an array declaration for the memory, and references to the original variables will be updated to access array elements. Second, refinement makes the specification simulatable, allowing the designer to verify the system's functional correctness after a system design step. Finally, the refined specification that is generated serves as an input for verification, synthesis and compilation tools that may follow system design.

In this chapter we present the set of specification refinement tasks. First, we describe the refinement tasks associated with the implementation of variable and channel groups. Second, we introduce mechanisms for resolving access conflicts that may arise when several behaviors concurrently access variables or channels that have been grouped together into a memory or a bus. Third, we discuss the effect of binding behaviors in the specification to standard components with fixed interfaces in terms of the pin structure and the protocols used for communication. Methods for interfacing two standard components with incompatible protocols are also presented. Finally, we discuss issues related to the implementation of communication between behaviors that have been assigned to hardware and software system components.

8.2   Refining variable groupings

The memory to which a group of variables has been mapped is modeled in the refined specification as an array with the appropriate size and bitwidth. Two refinement tasks have to be performed for variable groupings – variable folding and memory address translation.

8.2.1   Variable folding

System partitioning maps a group of variables to an allocated memory with a fixed number of words and width. Different variables may have different sizes (i.e., number of bits). Variable folding refers to the assignment of the bits in a variable to the bits in each word of the memory.

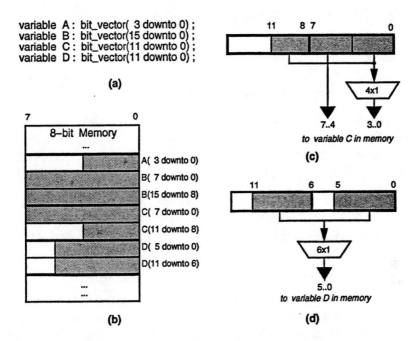

Figure 8.1: Memory-width mapping: (a) variable declarations, (b) mapping to an 8-bit wide memory, (c) writing a 12-bit value to C, (d) writing a 12-bit value to D.

Variable folding is simple if the variable bitwidth is smaller than the memory width or if it is an exact multiple of the memory width. Consider the variable declarations in Figure 8.1(a), which have to be mapped to an 8-bit memory, as shown in Figure 8.1(b). Variables A and B are assigned one and two memory words, respectively.

If the variable width is not an integral multiple of the memory width, it can be mapped in one of two ways. For the 12-bit variable C, the eight least significant bits are assigned to one address and the remaining four bits to the next address, as shown in Figure 8.1(b). Variable D is another 12-bit variable for which the six least significant bits are mapped to one address and the remaining six to the next address. The first approach requires a smaller multiplexer when writing to variable C in the memory, but requires eight bus drivers to be connected to the memory data bus, as shown in Figure 8.1(c). The latter approach requires a larger multiplexer, but requires only six bus drivers to be connected to the memory data bus, as shown in Figure 8.1(d).

8.2.2   Memory address translation

The assignment of addresses to variables mapped to a memory and the modification of all references to those variables in the specification is known as **memory address translation**.

To assign memory addresses, one can consider the variables in any order. The number of memory words required for each variable can be determined by variable folding. Elements of an array variable must be assigned contiguous addresses in the memory.

For scalar variables, memory address translation is relatively straightforward. Assume a scalar variable V belongs to a group of variables represented by the array MEM, and that V is assigned to address 30 within MEM. All references to variable V in the specification are simply replaced by references to $MEM(30)$.

For an array variable that has been grouped with other variables, the addresses that index the variable must be updated while refining references to that variable. For example, for an array variable $V(63\ downto\ 0)$ assigned to addresses 100 to 163 in MEM, we must consider several issues while updating references to V.

First, if array variable V is indexed entirely by numeric addresses, then references to it are simply replaced by corresponding references to memory MEM. Thus, reference $V(0)$ will be replaced by $MEM(100)$, and $V(36)$ by $MEM(136)$.

Second, if the array is indexed by an expression involving variables, then an offset, corresponding to the starting memory address of the array variable's first element, must be added to the expression. For example, consider array variable V, which is indexed by J or K in the code of Figure 8.2(a), Since V has been assigned addresses starting at 100 in MEM, a reference $V(J)$ will be replaced by $MEM(J + 100)$, and a reference $V(K)$ will be replaced by $MEM(K + 100)$, as in Figure 8.2(b).

Third, if a variable is used to index exactly one array, then the offset addition can be avoided by initializing the address variable appropriately. For example, in Figure 8.2(a), the variable J only indexes the array variable V. Figure 8.2(c) shows how updating all initializations of J (including the for-loop bounds) eliminates the need to add offsets. However, this may not always be possible if variable J indexes several

```
variable  J, K : integer := 0;
variable  V : IntArray (63 downto 0);
....
V(K) := 3;
X := V(36);
V(J) := X;

for  J in 0 to 63 loop
    SUM := SUM + V(J);
end loop;
....
                    (a)
```

```
variable  J, K : integer := 0;
variable  MEM : IntArray (255 downto 0);
....
MEM(K +100) := 3;
X := MEM(136);
MEM(J+100) := X;

for  J in 0 to 63 loop
    SUM := SUM + MEM(J +100);
end loop;
....
                    (b)
```

```
variable  J : integer := 100;
variable  K : integer := 0;
variable  MEM : IntArray (255 downto 0);
....
MEM(K + 100) := 3;
X := MEM(136);
MEM(J) := X;

for  J in 100 to 163 loop
    SUM := SUM + MEM(J);
end loop;
....
                (c)
```

Figure 8.2: Memory address translation: (a) original specification, (b) specification with offset to all index expressions for V, (c) specification with updated index variable J.

arrays. In this case, we can avoid offset addition for at least one array variable by assigning it memory addresses starting from 0.

8.3 Channel refinement

Concurrent behaviors in a specification communicate with one another by sending messages over abstract communication channels. To minimize interconnect cost, the channels in the system are grouped in such a way that each group of channels is implemented by a common physical medium called a bus. A bus consists of a set of wires over which the actual data transfer takes place under a bus protocol. The task of generating buses and their protocols for each group of channels is called **interface refinement**. In this section we describe methods for interface refinement. The term "behavior" in this section refers to one of a set of concurrent behaviors, usually referred to as a process.

8.3.1   Characterizing channels and buses

For any channel, exactly one **master** behavior initiates and controls the data transfer and one or more **slave** behaviors respond to communication initiated by the master behavior. If the master behavior sends (or receives) data over the channel, then the **direction** associated with the channel is write (or read). Channels are usually unidirectional, which implies that if a behavior both reads and writes to a variable in another behavior, distinct channels for each direction of data transfer are needed.

Channels are characterized by four parameters. Methods for estimating the value of these parameters were outlined in Chapter 7. Channel **data size**, $bits(C)$, represents the number of bits in a single message transferred over channel C. The data size includes any address bits that may be required to access array variables over the channel. The **number of accesses**, $access(P, C)$, represents the number of times that behavior P transfers data over channel C in its lifetime. The **channel average rate**, $avgrate(C)$, is the rate at which data is sent over channel C over the lifetime of the behaviors communicating over the channel. The **channel peak rate**, $peakrate(C)$, is the rate at which a single message is transferred over the channel C.

Any bus implementation of a channel or a group of channels can be characterized by four parameters. The **buswidth**, $buswidth(B)$, is the number of data lines in bus B over which the messages can be transferred between the behaviors. Associated with each bus is a protocol that defines the exact sequence of operations that implement the message transfer over the set of data lines. The **protocol delay**, $protdelay(B)$, is the total delay of the protocol employed for a single transfer of data over the bus. The **average bus rate**, $avgrate(B)$, is the rate at which data is sent over the bus during the entire lifetime of the system. The **peak bus rate**, $peakrate(B)$, is the maximum rate at which data can be transferred across the bus. The peak bus rate and the buswidth have the following relation with one another:

$$peakrate(B) \;=\; \frac{buswidth(B)}{protdelay(B)} \qquad (8.1)$$

8.3.2 Problem definition

Given a group of abstract communication channels, interface refinement determines the buswidth and the protocol for the bus that will implement the channels. Interface refinement is driven by two often conflicting goals. First, it attempts to minimize the interconnect cost between the system components that use a bus by reducing the buswidth, $buswidth(B)$. Second, it seeks to maximize the communication performance over the bus by increasing the peak rate of the bus, $peakrate(B)$, and consequently increasing the $buswidth(B)$.

Interface refinement consists of two tasks – bus generation and protocol generation. Given a set of constraints, **bus generation** determines the width of the bus that will implement the group of channels. After the desired buswidth has been selected, **protocol generation** selects and generates the communication protocol that will actually implement the data transfer over the bus. We will examine bus generation and protocol generation separately.

8.3.3 Bus generation

In this section, we describe techniques for determining the buswidth for implementing a group of channels.

A simple case of buswidth generation in which all the channels in a group have an identical message size is presented in [FKCD93]. In this case, channels are merged in such a way that all channels in any group are used exclusively over time to communicate between the same two behaviors. Consequently, each channel group is implemented with a buswidth identical to the size of any channel.

In a more general case, behaviors communicating over channels that have been grouped together may want to transfer data over the shared physical medium simultaneously. In addition, different channels may be transferring messages of different sizes between the behaviors. Such a scenario is shown in Figure 8.3. Behaviors P, Q, R and S communicate over channels X, Y and Z, which have been grouped by system partitioning to be implemented as a single bus, B. The three channels transfer data of different sizes — 8, 16 and 12 bits — respectively over the bus. In addition, behavior P may need to transfer data to behavior R at the

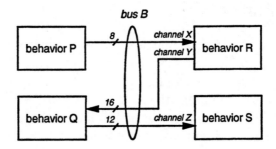

Figure 8.3: A typical bus formed by merging channels transferring data of different sizes between several behaviors.

same time that behavior Q needs to send data to behavior S. An approach to bus generation for such a general case is presented in [NG94]. We now describe this approach in detail.

Determining the bus rate

Consider two channels, X and Y, which transfer 8-bit and 16-bit messages respectively, as shown in Figure 8.4. The number of bits associated with each message transfer is indicated above the message. For the sake of simplicity, assume that the four second time interval shown in the figure represents the data transfer over the lifetimes of the behaviors that communicate over channels X and Y. Channels X and Y have average rates of 4 and 12 bits/second, respectively. If channels X and Y are merged into a single bus B, then the bus needs to send data at a rate of at least 16 bits/second to be able to satisfy the data transfer requirements of the two original channels. The individual messages transferred over the channels have been labeled in the figure to make it easier to associate them with the data transferred over the shared bus. Consider the message labeled $Y2$ transferred at the $t = 1$ second in the original channel Y, which is now transferred on bus B at $t = 1.5$ seconds. While individual message transfers may be delayed due to bus access conflicts, the total number of bits transferred over the individual channels before channel merging are still sent over the shared bus in the same amount of time.

In synthesizing the bus B in Figure 8.4, advantage is taken of the fact

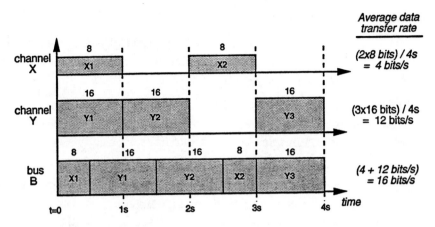

Figure 8.4: Merging channels X and Y into bus B.

that the individual channels will not always be transferring data. One channel's idle time slots are utilized for data transfers of other channels by synthesizing a bus over which data is always being transferred at a constant rate.

Before being merged into a bus, if a channel is transferring data at a certain average rate, it should be able to transfer the data over the bus at the same average rate. This can be achieved if the average rate, $avgrate(B)$, of bus B is greater than the sum of the individual channel average rates. Thus,

$$avgrate(B) \geq \sum_{C \in B} avgrate(C) \qquad (8.2)$$

The goal of bus generation should be to synthesize a bus with a minimum number of wires and an average rate given by Equation 8.2. The most efficient bus implementation will be achieved if the bus is never idle, and if it is constantly transferring data at a fixed rate. Under such ideal conditions, the bus peak and average rates will be identical:

$$peakrate(B) = avgrate(B) \qquad (8.3)$$

Constraints for bus generation

For a given set of channels that have been grouped together to be implemented as a single bus, constraints and relative weights can be specified for several bus and channel parameters.

A minimum/maximum **buswidth** constraint may be derived from the overall pin constraints specified for the modules or chips to which the behaviors communicating over the bus have been mapped.

Channel average rate may be constrained to ensure that the behaviors are not slowed down due to communication delays over the bus. Given constraints on the execution time of a behavior that communicates over several channels, the designer may allocate or budget the amount of time spent for communication over the various channels, from which a minimum channel average rate constraint can be derived. A maximum channel average rate may be specified in cases when one of the behaviors communicating over the channel represents a slow device that is incapable of sending or receiving data faster than a certain rate.

In certain cases, a minimum **channel peak rate** may be specified to ensure that a single message transfer over the channel does not take an excessive amount of time. For example, consider channel X in Figure 8.5(a), which transfers a 16-bit message in each of the first two time slots, $t = 0$ and $t = 1$. The other two time slots are used to perform internal computations by the behavior that communicates over channel X. If we were to implement the channel as a bus by itself, from Equation 8.2, the bus average rate would be 8 bits/second, resulting in the execution trace of Figure 8.5(b). However, the behavior now requires four time slots just for communicating over the bus. This is clearly unacceptable, since two additional time slots will still be required to perform the internal computations of the behavior (originally performed in time slots $t = 2$ and $t = 3$ in Figure 8.5(a)). If a minimum peak rate of 16 bits/second is specified for channel X, we will get the desired bus implementation of Figure 8.5(c), one that does not require any additional time slots. Thus, for all channels C that have a minimum peak rate constraint associated with them,

$$peakrate(B) > peakrate(C) \qquad (8.4)$$

In case a minimum channel peak rate constraint is specified, the resulting bus may be idle at times.

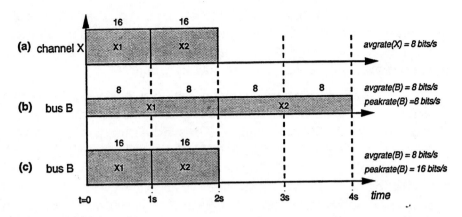

Figure 8.5: Channel peak rate constraints: (a) execution trace of channel X, (b) bus B synthesized without channel peak rate constraint, (c) bus B synthesized with channel peak rate constraint of 16 bits/second.

Algorithm for determining buswidth

Having introduced the constraints that may be specified for bus generation, we now present an algorithm for determining the width of a bus implementation [NG94]. The algorithm assumes that the data and control lines are disjoint. At any given instant, only one channel can transfer data over the bus. If the width of the bus is greater than the address and data bitwidths, then the address and data bits are sent simultaneously over the bus, otherwise, they are sent separately in two distinct transfers. In the latter case, the address bits have to be latched in the receiving behavior. If the buswidth is smaller than the size of the message being sent over it, the message is sent in multiple transfers.

All the behaviors which communicate over one of the channels in the bus are assumed to be have a synchronous implementation. Thus, transferring a message over the bus requires a whole number of clock cycles. A variable accessed over the bus is modeled by a separate behavior that sends and receives its value over the bus in response to requests from other behaviors. Thus, while computing the execution time of a master behavior that accesses a variable over the bus, the slave behavior which models that variable is assumed to be always ready for data transfer, i.e. no synchronization delays occur for variable accesses over the bus.

The input to the buswidth-generation algorithm consists of a set of channels to be implemented on a single bus and constraints on the channel rates and buswidth. The output of the algorithm is the width of the bus that will implement that channel group.

The buswidth-generation algorithm examines a range of potential buswidths. For each buswidth, the bus peak rate and the individual channel average rates are computed. In synthesizing a bus that constantly transfers data, Equations 8.2 and 8.3 require that the bus peak rate should be greater than the sum of the channel average rates. Each buswidth for which the above condition holds represents a feasible bus implementation. From the set of feasible bus implementations, each corresponding to a different buswidth, we select the one which has the least cost. In case no constraints are specified, a unit buswidth corresponding to a serial data transfer is selected.

The buswidth-generation algorithm is summarized in Algorithm 8.3.1. First, the range of buswidths examined by the algorithm is determined. The largest buswidth, *maxwidth*, is the size of the largest message transferred by any channel. The lowest buswidth, *minwidth*, is 1.

The variable *currwidth* represents the current buswidth being evaluated by the algorithm. For each value of *currwidth* in the range (*minwidth*, *maxwidth*), the bus peak rate is computed using Equation 8.1.

The estimation of channel average rates was presented in Chapter 7. In the interest of simplicity, assume that a behavior P has exactly one channel C over which messages are transferred. In case the current buswidth is less than the number of bits in the message, several transfers ($\lceil \frac{bits(C)}{currwidth} \rceil$) may be required to implement a single message transfer. The communication time for the behavior P is then calculated as follows:

$$commtime(P) = access(P, C) \times (\lceil \frac{bits(C)}{currwidth} \rceil \times protdelay(B)) (8.5)$$

Using the value of *commtime(P)* computed above, Equation 7.18 can now be used to estimate the average rate for each channel mapped to the bus. The sum of the channel average rates for a specific value of *currwidth* is stored in *avgratesum*.

Algorithm 8.3.1 : Buswidth generation
    if no constraints specified **then**
        return (1)
    end if

    /* compute range of buswidths */
    $minwidth = 1$
    $maxwidth = \text{Max}(bits(C))$

    $mincost = \infty$
    $mincostwidth = \infty$
    for $currwidth$ in $minwidth$ to $maxwidth$ **loop**

        /* compute bus peak rate */
        $peakrate(B) = currwidth \div protdelay(B)$

        /* compute sum of channel average rates for $currwidth$ */
        $avgratesum = 0;$
        for all channels $C \in B$ **loop**
            $avgrate(C) = \dfrac{access(P, C) \times bits(C)}{comptime(P) + commtime(P)}$
            $avgratesum = avgratesum + avgrate(C);$
        end loop

        if $(peakrate(B) > avgratesum)$ **then**
            /* feasible solution, determine minimal cost */
            $currcost = \text{ComputeCost}(currwidth)$
            if $(currcost < mincost)$ **then**
                $mincost = currcost$
                $mincostwidth = currwidth$
            end if
        end if
    end loop

    if $(mincost = \infty)$
        then return($failure$)
        else return($mincostwidth$)
    end if

If the bus peak rate, represented by $peakrate(B)$, is lower than the sum of the average rates of all the channels, then *currwidth* represents an infeasible implementation for the bus. We repeat the computation of the bus peak rate and sum of the channel rates with the next higher buswidth in the range ($minwidth, maxwidth$).

If the bus peak rate is greater than the sum of the individual channel rates, then *currwidth* represents a feasible implementation of the bus. For any of the constraints on buswidth, channel average and peak rates specified for the bus, the procedure *ComputeCost* calculates the cost of a feasible bus implementation as the sum of the squares of any constraint violations weighted by the relative weights specified for that constraint. For example, assume that the only constraint specified was a maximum buswidth constraint represented by *maxwires*. Let k represent the relative weight specified for this constraint. For any value of the buswidth, *currwidth*, the cost function for the bus would be defined as follows:

$$cost = \begin{cases} (k \times (currwidth - maxwires))^2 & currwidth > maxwires \\ 0 & \text{otherwise} \end{cases}$$

$$(8.6)$$

Other cost functions may also be defined to evaluate the cost associated with a specific buswidth. For example, if we desire a bus implementation with the least number of wires, the cost can be computed to be simply the value of *currwidth*.

If more than one feasible solution exists for the group of channels, the buswidth with the lowest cost is selected for implementing the bus. Variable *mincost* in Algorithm 8.3.1 represents the minimum cost computed for all feasible implementations, while variable *mincostwidth* represents buswidth, which corresponds to the minimum cost.

If there were no feasible solutions for all the buswidths examined, then an implementation for the group of channels would not be possible. Any implementation for such a group of channels would progressively delay the behaviors communicating over the bus. Such a situation can arise when several channels with very high average rates are grouped together to be implemented as a single bus. One solution would be to split the group of channels to be implemented further by more than one bus. Alternatively, the lowest cost infeasible buswidth may be selected.

Channel C	Behavior P	Variable accessed	bits(C)	access(P,C)	comptime(P) (clocks)
ch1	P1	V1	16 data + 7 addr = 23 bits	128	515
ch2	P2	V2	16 data + 7 addr = 23 bits	128	129

Figure 8.6: Message size, number of channel accesses and computation times for two channels of Temperature Controller.

An example of buswidth generation

We illustrate the buswidth-generation algorithm by considering a Temperature Controller. The controller consists of two inputs that sense the temperature and humidity in a room, and it evaluates a set of four rules to control the operation of an air-conditioning system. System partitioning mapped the behaviors and the array variables to two different system components, thus creating several channels between them. Two behaviors $P1$ and $P2$, of the temperature controller access the array variables $V1$ and $V2$, respectively over communication channels $ch1$ and $ch2$, which were grouped together to be implemented as a single bus, B. Figure 8.6 lists the channel bits, computation times and number of channel accesses for these two channels of the temperature controller. For the sake of simplicity, all execution times and data transfer rates have been expressed in terms of control steps. The buswidth-generation algorithm can now be used to determine the buswidth of a bus formed by merging these two channels. Assume that the only constraint specified for the bus implementation is a minimum peak rate constraint of 10 bits/clock for channel $ch2$ with a relative weight of 10.

First we determine the range of buswidth that will be examined. Both $ch1$ and $ch2$ are used to access array variables with 128 words (7 address bits) of 16 bits each. Thus, the largest number of bits involved with any transfer over either channel is 23. The range of buswidths that will be examined are:

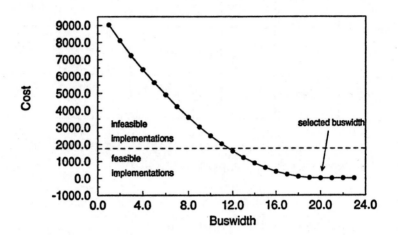

Figure 8.7: Temperature controller: cost vs. buswidth.

$minwidth = 1$ and $maxwidth = 23$.

We will compute bus and channel rates for $currwidth = 18$. Assume that a full-handshake protocol will be used to implement the bus, and that the associated protocol delay is 2 clock cycles, i.e., $protdelay(B) = 2\ clocks$. According to Equation 8.1:

$$peakrate(B) = 18 \div (2) = 9\ bits/clock$$

Also for $currwidth = 18$ bits, the average rates for channels $ch1$ and $ch2$ are calculated from Equation 7.18:

$$avgrate(ch1) = (128 \times 23) \div [515 + (128 \times \lceil \tfrac{23}{18} \rceil \times 2)] = 2.86\ bits/clock$$

$$avgrate(ch2) = (128 \times 23) \div [129 + (128 \times \lceil \tfrac{23}{18} \rceil \times 2)] = 4.59\ bits/clock$$

Since the the sum of the two channel average rates is less than $peakrate(B)$ computed above, a buswidth of 18 represents a feasible implementation of the bus.

We can now calculate the cost associated with this buswidth. The channel peak rate had a minimum constraint of 10 bits/clock with a weight of 10. Since the bus peak rate was determined to be 9 bits/clock,

$$cost = (10 \times (10 - 9))^2 = 100$$

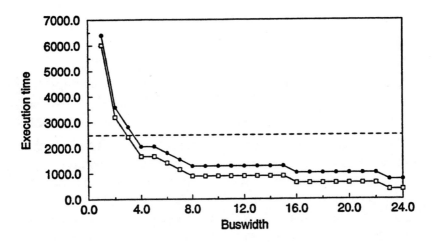

Figure 8.8: Temperature controller: execution time vs. buswidth.

Repeating the above computations for other values of the buswidth in the range < 1, 23 >, will produce a graph of cost vs. buswidth, as shown in Figure 8.7. According to the graph, the minimum cost is 0 which occurs at a buswidth of 20. This buswidth is selected for implementing the bus consisting of channels $ch1$ and $ch2$.

Figure 8.8 shows how the performance of the two behaviors, $P1$ and $P2$, transferring data over bus B is affected by the various buswidths that can be used to implement the bus. For each buswidth, a performance estimator was used to obtain the execution times of the behaviors. Clearly, as the buswidth increases, the execution time for the behaviors decreases. Given certain performance constraints for these behaviors, the designer can select an appropriate width for implementing the bus. For example, assume that behavior $P2$ has a maximum execution time constraint of 2500 clocks, shown as the dashed line in Figure 8.8. From the point where this line cuts the graphs for $P2$, we can conclude that only buswidths greater than four bits need to be considered for implementing the bus.

8.3.4   Protocol generation

Once an appropriate buswidth has been selected to implement the channel group, protocol generation defines the exact mechanism of data transfer over the bus. A bus consists of three sets of wires.

Data lines are used to send data over the bus. The number of data lines (i.e., the buswidth) required can be determined by the buswidth-generation algorithm, or it can be specified by the system designer.

Control lines are required to synchronize the behaviors that communicate over the bus. The number of control lines required depends on the type of protocol selected to implement the data transfers. For example, a standard handshake protocol requires two control signals, *START* and *DONE*. The signal *START* is set/reset by the master behavior and, *DONE* is set/reset by the slave behavior associated with a channel. The set of control lines are shared by all the channels mapped to the same bus.

Identification or mode lines are required to identify the particular channel that is transferring data over the bus at any point in time. Since the bus control signals are shared by all channels, such identification (ID) lines are essential to enable behaviors to recognize when the control signals over the bus are meant for them. Each channel in the bus is assigned a unique ID, which serves as its address. Every time a master behavior initiates transfer of data over the bus, it places the corresponding ID of the relevant channel on the bus ID lines so that only the corresponding slave behavior will respond to the control signals. The ID lines can also be directly encoded into the addresses of data accessed over the bus. In such cases, the slave behaviors must have an address detection mechanism which examines each address placed on the bus, to determine whether they should respond to the control signals set by the master behavior.

We shall illustrate protocol generation through a simple example, shown in Figure 8.9. Variables X and MEM are accessed by behaviors P and Q. The dashed lines indicate the assignment of the behaviors and variables to system components. Channels *CH0, CH1, CH2* and *CH3* are grouped into a single bus B, whose width has been determined to be eight bits. Protocol generation consists of several steps:

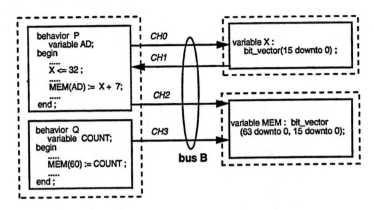

Figure 8.9: Behaviors accessing variables over channels grouped into a bus.

1. **Protocol selection:** Various communication protocols may be selected for a bus implementation, such as a full-handshake, half-handshake, and even hardwired ports. Each protocol requires a different number of control lines. For bus B in Figure 8.9, a full handshake protocol is selected. Two control signals, $START$ and $DONE$, are used to implement the handshaking.

2. **ID assignment:** If N channels are implemented on the same bus, $log_2(N)$ lines will be required to encode the channel ID. A unique ID is assigned to each channel. The four channels in Figure 8.9 require two ID lines. Channel $CH0$ is assigned the ID "00", $CH1$ is assigned "01" and so on.

3. **Bus structure and procedure definition:** The structure determined for the bus (i.e. the data, control and ID lines) is defined in the specification. For each channel mapped to the bus, appropriate send and receive procedures are generated; encapsulating the sequence of assignments to the bus control, data and ID lines to execute the data transfer. Figure 8.10 shows the declaration of an eight bit bus, with two control lines and two ID lines. The bus B is declared to be a global variable (a signal in the case of VHDL) so that all behaviors can access it. Behavior P writes to the 16-bit variable X over channel $CH0$. Since the buswidth is only eight bits, procedures $SendCH0$ and $ReceiveCH0$ in Figure 8.10(b) transfer

```
type  HandShakeBus is record
      START, DONE : bit ;
      ID : bit_vector(1 downto 0) ;
      DATA  : bit_vector(7 downto 0) ;
end record ;

signal  B : HandShakeBus ;

procedure  ReceiveCH0( rxdata : out bit_vector)  is
begin
      for J in 1 to 2 loop
          wait until  (B.START = '1') and (B.ID = "00") ;
          rxdata (8*J-1  downto 8*(J-1)) <= B.DATA ;
          B.DONE <= '1' ;
          wait until  (B.START = '0') ;
          B.DONE <= '0' ;
      end loop;
end ReceiveCH0;

procedure  SendCH0( txdata : in bit_vector)  is
      bus B.ID <= "00" ;
      for J in 1 to 2 loop
          B.DATA <= txdata(8*J-1  downto  8*(J-1)) ;
          B.START <= '1' ;
          wait until  (B.DONE = '1') ;
          B.START <= '0' ;
          wait until  (B.DONE = '0') ;
      end loop;
end SendCH0;
```

Figure 8.10: Defining bus B and the send and receive protocols for channel $CH0$.

the 16-bit message associated with channel $CH0$ over the bus, in two transfers of eight bits each.

4. **Update variable-references:** References to a variable that has been assigned to another system component by system partitioning must be updated in behaviors that were originally referencing it directly. Accesses to variables are replaced by the send and receive procedure calls corresponding to the channel over which the variable is accessed. For example, in Figure 8.9, behavior P writes the value "32" directly to variable X. Channel $CH0$ represents the write to variable X. The statement ''X <= 32'' is replaced by the send procedure call ''sendCH0(32)'' as shown in Figure 8.11. The statement ''MEM(60) := COUNT'' in behavior Q is updated to ''sendCH3(60, COUNT)'', indicating that the value in $COUNT$ is to be written to address 60 of array MEM.

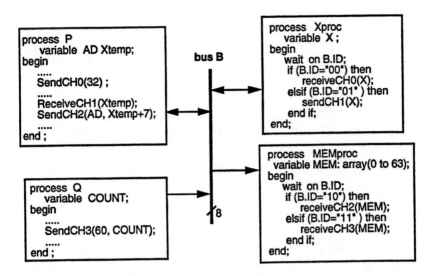

Figure 8.11: Refined specification after protocol generation.

5. **Generate processes for variables:** In order to obtain a simulatable system specification, a separate behavior is created for each group of variables accessed over a channel. Appropriate send and receive procedure calls are included in the behavior to respond to access requests to the variable over the bus. In Figure 8.9, the variables X and MEM were assigned to different system components, as shown by the dashed lines. In Figure 8.11, behaviors $Xproc$ and $MEMproc$ have been created for these two variables.

The protocol generation presented in this section has several advantages. First, the refined specification is simulatable, and the design functionality, after insertion of buses and communication protocols, can be verified. Second, by encapsulating data transfer over the bus in terms of send and receive procedures, the description of the behavior remains less cluttered than it would be if we were to insert the assignments for the control and data lines at each communication point in the behavior. Finally, if at a later stage another communication protocol were selected for communication over the bus, only the bus declaration and send and receive procedures need be changed. The system's behavior descriptions, including the send and receive procedure calls, remain unchanged.

8.4   Resolving access conflicts

Access conflicts occur in systems when two or more behaviors attempt to access the same resource simultaneously. Such conflicts may arise, for example, due to variable and channel groupings during system partitioning. Variables grouped together may be accessed by different behaviors simultaneously. Access conflicts will result if the memory that will implement the variable group has fewer ports than concurrent accesses to it. Similarly, communication channels may be grouped together to be implemented as a single bus. Behaviors communicating over these channels may attempt data transfer simultaneously, leading to contention for the bus.

Arbitration resolves access conflicts between behaviors that concurrently access a shared resource. **Arbiter generation** is a refinement task that inserts an arbitration mechanism in the specification whenever there is a resource contention in the system.

8.4.1   Arbitration models

Resources often have multiple access ports supporting a limited number of concurrent accesses. Examples of such resources may be a multiport memory with a fixed number of ports. If the number of behaviors that simultaneously access such a resource exceeds the number of access ports, we need to be able to resolve the conflict of simultaneous accesses. Two arbitration models are commonly used for this purpose – static arbitration and dynamic arbitration. These models are illustrated with the example of behaviors accessing a two-port memory in Figure 8.12.

In a **static arbitration** model, accesses by a behavior are assigned to a specific port of the memory. In Figure 8.12(a), behavior P accesses the memory Mem through $port2$, while behaviors Q and R access the memory through $port1$. The mapping of accesses to specific ports is static; i.e., a behavior will access data through the port assigned to it throughout the lifetime of the system. In such a model, only concurrent accesses over a single port are arbitrated. Thus, the arbiter $MemArbiter$, is required to resolve access conflicts for $port1$ between behaviors Q and R. While the static arbitration model is simple to implement, it may result in poor performance; since port assignments are made statically,

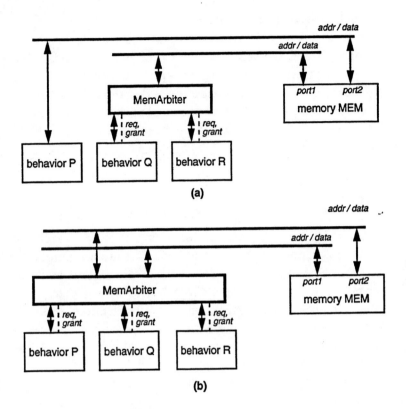

Figure 8.12: Arbitration models: (a) static, and (b) dynamic.

a behavior may be required to wait for the port statically assigned to it to become available, even though another port is unused.

In a **dynamic arbitration** model, behaviors may access the memory through different ports at different times, depending on their availability. In Figure 8.12(b), all the three behaviors are routed to each of the two memory ports by using a switching network. The arbiter, *MemArbiter*, limits accesses to *MEM* to two behaviors at any time. The main advantage of such an arbitration model is the higher utilization of the two ports, which in turn leads to faster execution times for the behaviors accessing the memory. However, dynamic arbitration requires a more complex implementation, since *MemArbiter* has to route the data from each of the three behaviors to both the memory ports, in addition to selecting which behaviors are allowed to access the memory.

8.4.2   Arbitration schemes

As mentioned above, the accesses by a set of behaviors to the shared resource must be prioritized. Given a group of behaviors needing to access a given resource, an **arbitration scheme** determines their relative priority in order to resolve potential access conflicts. Arbitration schemes may be classified as fixed priority and dynamic priority. We will describe each of these schemes next.

Fixed-priority

A **fixed-priority** scheme statically assigns a priority to each behavior. The relative priorities assigned to the behaviors are unchanged throughout the lifetime of the system. If two behaviors request an access to a common resource simultaneously, the behavior with higher priority will be granted the access. However, fixed-priority schemes may also be **preemptive** if a behavior accessing a shared resource has to relinquish its access privileges to another behavior with a higher priority. An example of preemptive priority can be found in the Intel 8237 DMA controller, which allows peripheral devices with higher priority to preempt lower priority devices.

Determining the fixed priority for various behaviors depends on some metric which has to be optimized. One such metric, **mean waiting time,** represents the average time spent by any behavior waiting to gain access to a shared resource. A lower mean waiting time will result in faster execution of the behaviors accessing the resource.

Thus, behaviors should be assigned priorities in a manner that minimizes the mean waiting time. For a specific assignment of priorities to behaviors, the resulting mean waiting time can only be determined dynamically by simulating the specification. To determine priorities of the behaviors statically, the mean waiting time is usually approximated by metrics that can be evaluated relatively easily. One such metric is the **size of the data** associated with accesses made by a behavior. For example, if a behavior transfers large amounts of data in a single transfer over a channel, then that behavior is assigned a lower priority, to prevent other behaviors from being denied access to the bus for a significant period of time while the data is being transferred. Another metric that can be expected to lower the mean waiting time is the **frequency of accesses** made by the behavior to the shared resource. The greater the access frequency, the higher the priority assigned to that behavior.

In determining the priority of the behaviors, the system designer may use either a single criterion or a weighted combination of several criteria.

Dynamic-priority

A **dynamic-priority** scheme determines the priority of a behavior according to the state of the system at run-time. For example, a **round-robin** scheme assigns the lowest priority to the behavior that most recently accessed the shared resource. A **first-come-first-served** scheme will grant access privileges to behaviors in the order they requested the access. Such schemes are characterized by the absence of any absolute order in which behaviors are granted access to a resource. Consequently, dynamic arbitration schemes can be expected to be fair, or in other words, a behavior will not have to wait indefinitely to gain access to the shared resource.

8.4.3 Arbiter generation

Once an arbitration scheme has been selected, accesses by different behaviors to the shared resources are prioritized on the basis of the arbitration scheme. An arbiter behavior is then generated and incorporated in the specification to arbitrate between concurrent accesses. In this section, arbiter generation is illustrated for a case in which concurrent accesses by behaviors are prioritized on the basis of a fixed-priority arbitration scheme.

The arbitration mechanism for each shared resource is represented by a separate behavior concurrent with all the behaviors accessing the resource. Each access to a shared resource in a behavior is modified to incorporate a handshake mechanism between the behavior and the arbiter. A behavior desiring access to the resource will request the arbiter for permission by asserting the request signal *Req*. The arbiter examines access requests from several behaviors, and grants access to the highest priority behavior by asserting the appropriate *Grant* signal.

Algorithm 8.4.1 Generate Arbiter
/* Introduce request and grant signals in behaviors */
for each behavior B_i which accesses resource R **loop**
   Precede all accesses of R in B_i by the following:
      `Req_i <= '1' ;`
      `wait until (Grant_i = '1') ;`
   Append the following after all accesses of R in B_i:
      `Req_i <= '0';`
end loop
/* Generate arbiter behavior */
Add the following to head of the arbiter behavior:
   `wait until Req_1 or Req_2 or ..  or Req_N ;`
while *priority_list* $\neq \phi$ **loop**
   $B_k = \text{First}(priority\_list)$
   $priority\_list = \text{Tail}(priority\_list)$
   Append the following to the arbiter process:
      `if (Req_k = '1') then`
         `Grant_k <= '1';`
         `wait until (Req_k = '0');`
         `Grant_k <= '0';`
      `end if;`
end for

Algorithm 8.4.1 [RVNG92] generates the VHDL description of the arbiter behavior for a given resource R. B_i represents the $i'th$ behavior that accesses resource R. The priorities assigned to the behaviors are assumed to be stored in *priority_list* in decreasing order. Procedure First(L) returns the first item of list L, and procedure Tail(L) returns a list identical to list L except that the first element of the list is deleted.

Arbiter generation is illustrated for behaviors P and Q in Figure 8.11, which transfer data over bus B, whose width and protocol have been determined in Section 8.3. Assume that behavior P has been assigned a higher priority than behavior Q for data transfers over bus B. The arbiter behavior $B\_arbiter$ generated for bus B is shown in Figure 8.13. Appropriate handshake signal assignments (shown in bold) for request-

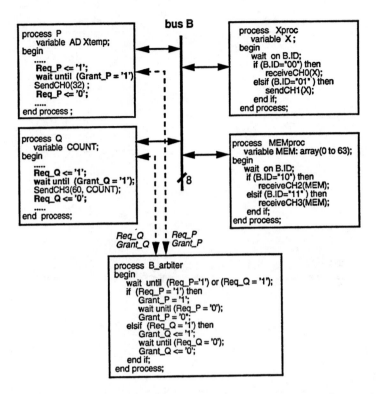

Figure 8.13: Refined specification after generation of an arbiter behavior for bus B.

ing access to the bus have been inserted in the master behaviors, P and Q. When behaviors P and Q need to transfer data over the bus, they each request access to the bus by asserting Req_P and Req_Q, respectively. Behavior $B\_arbiter$ assigns bus access rights to P by asserting $Grant\_P$. Q is granted access to the bus only when P is not simultaneously requesting access.

8.5   Refining incompatible interfaces

The system designer may bind single functional objects or groups of them to off-the-shelf components. Variable groups may be bound to standard memories, behaviors may be bound to standard chips or processors, and

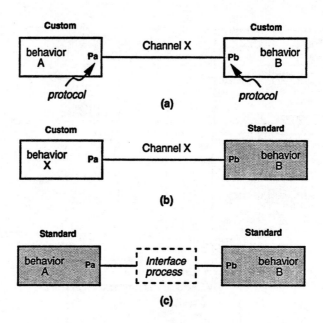

Figure 8.14: Effect of binding behaviors to custom or standard components.

the channel groups may be bound to standard bus protocols. The pin structure and the communication protocols of these standard components are fixed and cannot be changed. Consequently, communication among system components with different communication protocols is possible if proper interfaces are introduced.

In order to examine the effect of binding functional objects in the system to standard components, consider channel X in Figure 8.14(a), over which two behaviors A and B transfer data. Let P_a and P_b be the protocols that will implement the communication for behaviors A and B, respectively. One of the following three situations may arise, depending upon which of the behaviors have been bound to standard components:

1. **Neither behavior is bound to a standard component**, as shown in Figure 8.14(a). The communication between them can be implemented by generating the bus and inserting a protocol into behaviors A and B, as explained in Section 8.3.

2. **One behavior is bound to a standard component**, as behav-

ior B is in Figure 8.14(b). The protocol P_b associated with that standard component is fixed. Since the other behavior, A, will be custom designed, its protocol is modified to be the exact **dual** (i.e. compatible with) of the protocol P_b, thus ensuring that behaviors A and B are still able to communicate with each other. Modifications made to P_a are incorporated into the specification of behavior A.

3. **Both behaviors are bound to standard components**, as behaviors A and B are in Figure 8.14(c). In such a case, the corresponding protocols P_a and P_b are both fixed. If the two protocols are compatible with each other, we simply need to connect the appropriate ports on both the standard components to ensure that they are able to communicate with each other. However, if the protocols P_a and P_b are incompatible, an **interface process** needs to be inserted between the two standard components. The interface process, shown with dashed lines in the figure, is a behavior which facilitates data transfer between two standard components by interfacing their two incompatible protocols.

Apart from situations where behaviors are bound to standard components, interface processes may be required in certain other circumstances. For example, pin constraints on two system components may cause the number of data pins in each of the system components to be different. Unequal number of data pins will lead to incompatible communication protocols between the two system components. An interface process will thus be required to interface the two protocols in this case.

8.5.1 Problem definition

Interface process generation is the refinement task that defines an interface process between two communicating behaviors with fixed but incompatible protocols. The goal of interface process generation is to create an interface process that responds appropriately to the control signals of both protocols and sequences the data transfers between them. In other words, the interface process translates one protocol into another. For example, the protocol in one component may transfer 16 bits of data at a time, while the other component can receive data only in 8-bit bytes.

The interface process would then receive the 16-bit data from the first component and send it to the second component in two transfers of 8-bits each. A second goal of interface process generation is to obtain a simulatable refined specification.

8.5.2   Specifying communication protocols

Before we describe techniques for generating interface processes, we briefly examine methods for specifying communication protocols.

A protocol consists of a set of **atomic** operations. There are five types of atomic operations: (1) waiting for an event on an input control line, (2) assigning a value to an output control line, (3) reading value from input data lines, (4) assigning a value to an output data line, and (5) waiting for a fixed time interval. Any protocol can be specified using a combination of the above atomic operations.

Communication protocols are usually specified in three ways: state machines, timing diagrams, and hardware description languages. We shall illustrate each of them with the example in Figure 8.15.

In Figure 8.15(a), two behaviors A and B have been mapped to standard components. Behavior A reads a 64K×16 memory, modeled by variable $MemVar$ in behavior B. The two behaviors have fixed protocols, P_a and P_b. Protocol P_a has 8 address, 16 data and 4 control lines, while protocol P_b has 16 address, 16 data and 1 control line. The variables $AddrVar$ and $DataVar$ used in protocol P_a and $MemVar$ in protocol P_b are local to the corresponding behaviors and provide (receive) the relevant data values assigned to (read from) the data lines. For example, variable $AddrVar$ in protocol P_a provides a 16-bit address that refers to a location in the memory being accessed by master behavior A. For ease of identification, all port names have a "p" suffix.

Figure 8.15(b) shows the **state machine** representation of the fixed protocols P_a and P_b, associated with behaviors A and B, respectively. Transitions between the states are triggered by the occurrence of an event on an input signal. For example, in the state machine for P_a, a rising event on $ARCVp$ to '1' causes a transition from state a_2 to a_3. Values can be assigned to and read from ports in each state. In Figure 8.15(b), state $a1$ assigns values to the address port $ADDRp$ and control port

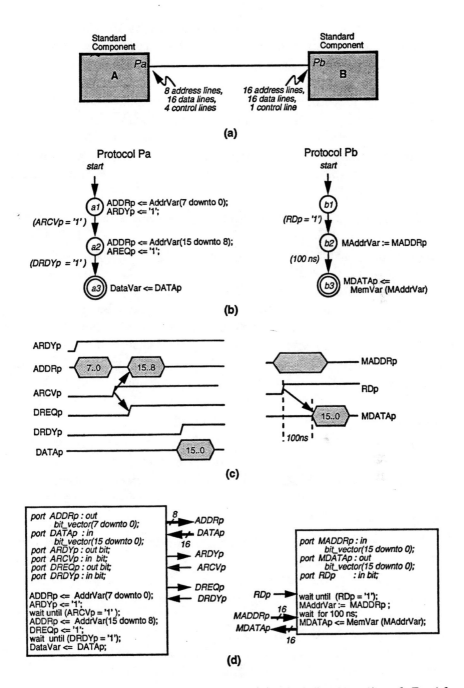

Figure 8.15: Representing protocols: (a) two behaviors A and B with fixed protocols P_a and P_b, (b) state-machine representation, (c) timing diagram representation, (d) HDL representation.

ARDYp. Delays between successive events may be specified directly as a condition on a transition, as is the 100 ns delay between states *b2* and *b3* in the state machine for P_b. Other approaches have used special timing arcs to capture inter-event timing constraints between any two events in the protocol. State machine specification of protocols suffer from shortcomings similar to those outlined during our discussion of conceptual model features in Chapter 3 – branching and iteration – have to be implemented explicitly using extra states and transitions. However, since most protocols consist of only a few operations, this limitation may not be serious.

Timing diagram protocol descriptions are commonly found in semiconductor product databooks. The timing diagram description of the protocols of behaviors *A* and *B* is shown in Figure 8.15(c). Each port of the protocol has a corresponding waveform in the timing diagram. The ordering of events can be inferred from the relative position of the transitions in the timing diagram. Explicit ordering can be specified using arrows between input events and output assignments. For example, in the timing diagram for protocol P_a, an arrow ensures that *DREQp* is asserted only after the input line *ARCVp* attains a value of '1'. Delays between events can be specified as shown in the timing diagram for protocol P_b, where a 100 ns delay is specified between the rising transition on *RDp* and the output of data on *DATAp*.

The main advantage of timing diagrams is the ease with which the protocol can be comprehended in terms of the relative occurrence of protocol operations. In addition, they allow a direct representation of timing constraints between pairs of events. However, timing diagrams suffer from several drawbacks.

First, they lack an "action" language to represent the protocol operations associated with the data lines. In other words, the exact source and destination of the data being transferred by the protocol cannot be specified. In Figure 8.15(b), for example, the state machine representation of protocol P_b reads an element of array variable *MemVar*. In the timing diagram, the only information that can be represented is that the data read from the array variable is valid on the data lines at certain times. Consequently, timing diagrams cannot be simulated with the rest of the system specification.

Second, specification of repetitive event sequences is not representable without actually unrolling the loop and repeating the event sequence in the timing diagram, leading to a large timing diagram. Finally, representation of conditional event sequences using timing diagrams requires multiple diagrams for each condition or mode in the protocol. Some of the above issues were addressed in [Bor88], where a timing diagram was divided into a set of labeled segments. A regular-expression syntax was applied to the alphabet of segment labels to allow specification of repetitive and conditional event sequences. Extended Timing Diagrams (ETD), proposed in [MAP93], allow decomposition of a timing diagram into hierarchical and concurrent sub-diagrams. Actions can be associated with events and conditions in a timing diagram at any hierarchical level. The protocol behavior is made simulatable by generating a VHDL description from the corresponding ETD.

Figure 8.15(d) shows a **hardware description language (HDL)** description of the two protocols. The variables that represent the actual data items transferred can be specified in the protocol description, allowing specification of details such as which bit slices of the variables are assigned to or read from the data ports at any time. For example, the two assignments to $ADDRp$ in protocol P_a specify that the least and most significant bytes of the address $AddrVar$ are transferred by the protocol in two separate transfers. Delays between operations can be specified using delay statements (such as the $wait$ statement in VHDL).

The main advantage of an HDL-based protocol description is that it is complete – all port information (names, number, and type), repetitive and conditional protocol operations can be represented easily using the constructs of the host HDL. No extra language or annotations are necessary. Second, the protocol can be simulated with the system specification to verify functional correctness not only of the data transfers, but that of the system as a whole. The main drawback of an HDL-based protocol representation is that specification of inter-event timing constraints can be cumbersome. In the ISYN system [Nes87], labels were attached to statements of an ISPS [Bar81] description of the interface. These labels were then used to specify pairwise timing constraints between the corresponding operations in the interface protocol.

8.5.3   Interface process generation

We now describe a technique for generating interface processes. The inputs for interface process generation are the HDL descriptions of the two fixed protocols detailing the number of control and data lines and the sequence of data transfers over those lines. The output is an HDL description of the interface process and information related to the connection of ports of the two protocols.

We will illustrate interface process generation with the example of the two behaviors, A and B, in Figure 8.15(a) that have been mapped to standard components. The two behaviors have fixed protocols, P_a and P_b, the HDL descriptions of which are given in Figure 8.15(d).

Representing protocols as ordered relations

The first step in interface process generation is representing each of the two protocols as an ordered set of relations. A **relation** defines a set of assignments to output control and data lines and the reading of values from input data lines, upon the occurrence of a certain condition. The condition could be an event on an input control line or a fixed delay with respect to some previous event.

Figure 8.16(a) shows how the set of relations can be derived from the HDL description of protocol P_a. The first two assignment statements are not preceded by any condition. Hence, the first relation, labeled A_1, consists of a default "true" condition and the assignments to ports $ADDRp$ and $ARDYp$. The next statement wait until (ARCVp = '1') represents a condition which must be true before the protocol can perform any other operation. The second relation, labeled A_2, thus consists of the condition $(ARCVp = \text{'1'})$ and the subsequent assignments to the data port $ADDRp$ and control port $DREQp$. Finally, the third relation, labeled A_3, consists of the condition $(DRDYp = \text{'1'})$ and the assignment of the value read from the data port $DATAp$ to the variable $DataVar$.

Similarly, two relations are constructed for protocol P_b, as shown in Figure 8.16(b). The first relation, B_1, consists of condition $(RDp = \text{'1'})$ and the assignment to the internal variable $MAddrVar$, which stores the value of the address read from port $MADDRp$. The delay of 100 ns

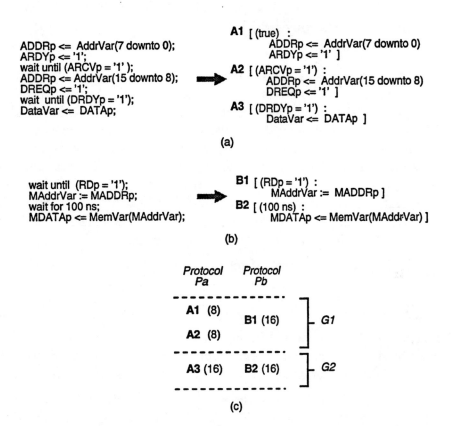

(a)

(b)

(c)

Figure 8.16: Deriving and partitioning of relations: (a) deriving relations for protocol P_a, (b) deriving relations for protocol P_b, (c) partitioning relations of two protocols into relation groups.

specified by the wait statement represents a condition for the subsequent operations. Hence, the relation B_2 consists of a delay condition (100 ns) followed by the assignment to the port $MDATAp$.

The advantage of a relational representation for a protocol is that it provides an easy way to capture the I/O relationships between events in a protocol, regardless of how the protocol is specified. In Figures 8.16(a) and (b), the protocols were specified using an HDL. But the protocols could have been specified initially as a finite-state machine or a timing diagram and represented just as easily by a set of relations.

Partitioning relations into blocks

An interface process can be generated if and only if a **datum** (i.e., a data item) of a certain size is sent by one behavior while the other behavior is expecting a datum of an identical size. For example, behavior A in Figure 8.15(a) sends a 16-bit address while behavior B expects a 16-bit address. As long as the total size of the address sent by behavior A is identical to the that expected by behavior B, it is irrelevant that behavior A actually sends the address in two transfers of 8 bits each and that behavior B receives it as a single block of 16 bits. Similarly, behavior B sends a 16-bit data item fetched from the memory, which is identical to the data size expected by behavior A.

Having derived the set of relations for the two protocols, we now need to group the relations in the two protocols into a set of relation groups. A **relation group** is an ordered subset of the set of relations that represents a unit of data transfer between the two behaviors. The relation groups are created in such a manner that the size of the data generated by the relations in the group from one protocol is identical to that expected by the relations in the group from the other protocol.

Figure 8.16(c) shows how the relations of the two protocols are partitioned into relation groups. The relations of both protocols are listed with the number of bits transferred by the operations in each relation enclosed within parentheses. Relation B_1 of protocol P_b reads 16 bits of data from $MADDRp$. Scanning the list of relations for P_a, we see that both relations A_1 and A_2 together output 16 bits of data. Thus, the first relation group, G_1, consists of the relations A_1, A_2 and B_1. The ordering of relations belonging to two protocols within a relation group is determined by the data dependencies between the relations. B_1 can read the 16-bit address only when A_1 and A_2 have generated it. Therefore, A_1 and A_2 precede B_1 in relation group G_1:

$$G_1 = (A_1 \ A_2 \ B_1)$$

The notation for a relation group that consists of a set of relations specifies a sequential execution of the operations in A_1, A_2 and B_1, taken from left to right.

Continuing in a similar manner, we create another relation group, G_2, by merging relations A_3 and B_2. Since the 16-bit data is generated

Atomic operation	HDL equivalent	Dual operation
waiting for event	wait until (Cp = '1')	Cp <= '1'
assign control line	Cp <= '1'	wait until (Cp = '1')
read data line	var <= Dp	Dp <= TempVar
assign data line	Dp <= var	TempVar := Dp
fixed delay	wait for 100 ns	wait for 100 ns

Figure 8.17: Duals of atomic protocol operations.

by the operations in relation B_2 and read by the operations in A_3, B_2 precedes A_3 in relation group G_2, i.e.:

$$G_2 = (B_2 \ A_3)$$

Generating the interface process

Having combined the relations into a set of relation groups, we now generate the interface process to make the two protocols compatible. The set of operations in the relation groups taken in order represents the sequence of atomic operations across the two protocols. The interface process can be obtained by simply inverting each operation in the relation group. "Inverting" an atomic operation means replacing it with its exact **dual** or complementary operation.

Figure 8.17 shows the corresponding dual operation for each of the five atomic protocol operations. For example, waiting for an event on an input control port, Cp is represented in the interface process by its dual, i.e., an assignment to the control signal Cp. The atomic operation which assigns a value to a control line Cp has, as its dual in the interface process, an operation that waits for the same control line to attain that value. Assignments to a data port by a protocol are represented as reading the value from the data port into a local variable, internal to the interface process. Reading the value from a data port by a protocol is represented in the interface process by an assignment to the data port from an internal variable.

The delay operation is its own dual. To see when a delay operation is included in the interface process, consider operation o_1, which represents a delay in one protocol and operation o_2, which waits for an event on an input control line in the other protocol. If o_1 is followed by o_2 in the same relation group, then the dual of the delay operation o_1 is included in the interface process. This ensures that operation o_2 in the other protocol does not execute prematurely. For example, relation group G_2 consists of relations B_2 and A_3. According to the definition of the relations in Figure 8.16, we can observe that the condition (100 ns) in relation B_2 is followed by a wait for condition ($DRDY_P = $ '1') in relation A_3. To make sure that protocol P_a does not read the data lines $DATAp$ before P_b can output the data on the lines, the delay operation must be included in the interface process.

The interface process, IP, is obtained by inverting the operations in the relation groups determined in the previous step:

$$IP = (G_1')\,(G_2')$$
$$= (A_1'\,A_2'\,B_1')\,(B_2'\,A_3')$$

Replacing each operation in the above relations by the corresponding duals, we obtain the interface process of Figure 8.18(a). For example, consider relation A_1, which consists of the operations representing the first two statements of protocol P_a in Figure 8.16(a):

```
ADDRp <= AddrVar(7 downto 0);
ARDYp <= '1';
```

A_1' is the dual of these two operations, resulting in the following statements:

```
TempVar1(7 downto 0) := ADDRp;
wait until (ARDYp = '1');
```

These statements are the first two of the interface process, shown in Figure 8.18(a).

Any internal variables required by the interface process are declared within the process. Port declarations for each control and data line of both protocols are added to the interface process with the direction reversed (i.e., an "in" port of a protocol is declared as an "out" port in the interface process, and vice versa). Finally, the control and data ports on each of the two behaviors are connected with the corresponding ports on the interface process.

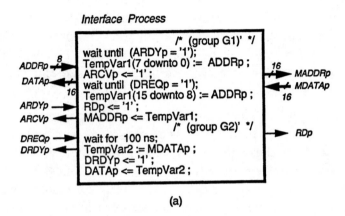

(a)

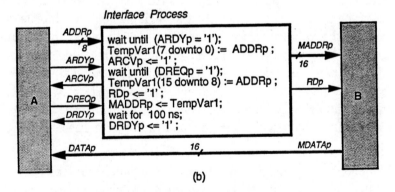

(b)

Figure 8.18: Generating interface process: (a) interface process with dual of operations in blocks G_1 and G_2, (b) interface process after interconnect optimization.

Interconnect optimization

The interface process generated in the previous step requires that all data and control lines of both protocols be connected to it, as shown in Figure 8.18(a). In some cases, it may be possible to connect some of the control and data ports of the two communicating behaviors directly, effectively bypassing the interface process entirely. This has two advantages. First, it simplifies the interconnect in the system by reducing the number of nets in the system. Second, operations related to these ports in the interface process can be deleted altogether. This will result in a more efficient interface process, both in terms of size and performance, when logic is synthesized.

The first type of interconnect optimization attempts to reduce the data lines connected to the interface process. Assume that two data ports, D_1 and D_2, belonging to the two protocols have the same size. If the interface process writes to port D_1 every time it reads a value from port D_2, and there is no delay (i.e., "wait" statement) between the operations, then the data ports on the two protocols can be connected directly. All writes to port D_1 and reads from D_2 can be eliminated from the interface process. Consequently, the variable generated for temporarily holding the value transferred between the ports can be eliminated. In Figure 8.18(a), the ports $MDATAp$ and $DATAp$ have an identical size of 16 bits, with no delay between reading of a value from $MDATAp$ and writing it to $DATAp$; consequently, these ports can be connected directly. In addition, the temporary variable $TempVar2$ and statements in the interface process for reading and writing to these ports can be eliminated.

The second type of optimization examines the control ports of the two protocols. Consider two control ports, C_1 and C_2, from each of the two protocols. If, every time the interface process waits for a particular value on C_1, it updates C_2 with the same value, then the ports C_1 and C_2 can be connected directly. For example, in Figure 8.18(a) control ports $DREQp$ and RDp of protocols P_a and P_b, respectively, can be connected to each other directly. The corresponding wait and assignment statements can be deleted from the interface process.

The optimized interface process generated for protocols P_a and P_b is shown in Figure 8.18(b). The data ports $MDATAp$ and $DATAp$, and the control ports $DREQp$ and RDp are connected directly.

Algorithm 8.5.1 : Generate Interface Process
  /* generate relations for each protocol */
  R_a = CreateRelations(P_a)
  R_b = CreateRelations(P_b)

  /* partition relations into a set G of relation groups
  G = GroupRelations(R_a, R_b)

  /* add dual statement for each operation in G to interface process
  for each relation group $G_i \in G$ **loop**
    for each relation $R_j \in G_i$ **loop**
      for each atomic operation $o_k \in R_j$ **loop**
        AddDualStatement(IP, o_k)
      end loop
    end loop
  end loop

  CreateAndOptimizePorts(IP, P_a, P_b)

Evaluating interface process generation

Algorithm 8.5.1 summarizes the steps involved in interface process generation. Given the HDL description of a protocol, *CreateRelations* generates the set of relations that represent the protocol. The procedure *GroupRelations* partitions the set of relations R_a and R_b into a relation groups represented by the set of G. For each atomic operation of a relation in a relation group taken in order, the procedure *AddDualStatement* adds the corresponding dual statement, as determined from Figure 8.17, to the interface process IP. Once the statements for the interface process have been generated, *CreateAndOptimizePorts* generates the set of ports between the two protocols and the interface process, and optimizes them if possible.

    The main advantage of the technique presented in this section is that it can interface any two protocols that can be represented using sequential HDL statements. The interface process that is generated can be simulated with the rest of the system specification to verify system functionality after binding a group of functional objects to a standard component. The method is general in that it supports the interfacing of two protocols with different data port widths. Timing information supported by the method takes the form of non-overlapping delays between protocol operations. However, since only an HDL description of the interface is generated, minimum and maximum timing constraints between events are not supported. These constraints can be passed on to the synthesis tool that will synthesize the hardware for the interface process.

8.5.4   Other approaches for protocol compatibility

We will now describe three other approaches that have addressed the issue of protocol compatibility between standard components.

Transducer synthesis

Synthesis of interface transducers between custom chips and system buses was presented in [BK87, Bor88]. A **transducer** is defined as the glue logic that connects two circuit blocks. Timing diagrams of the two incompatible interfaces are specified as input. The output is a logic specification of the transducer circuit.

We will illustrate synthesis of a logic circuit from timing diagrams with the example of a FIFO stack control cell [Bor88] in Figure 8.19. The cell has two inputs and three outputs, as shown in Figure 8.19(a). The stack control cell operates asynchronously, i.e., there is no external clock to synchronize the operations within the cell.

Figure 8.19(b) shows the timing diagram relating the cell inputs and outputs. The dashed arrows denote ordering constraints between the various events in the cell. The first step generates an **event graph** from the timing diagram. For every event in the timing diagram, such as a rise or fall transition, there is a node in the event graph. The arcs between nodes in the event graph represent ordering or minimum and maximum timing constraints between the corresponding events in the timing diagram. Figure 8.19(c) shows the event graph constructed for

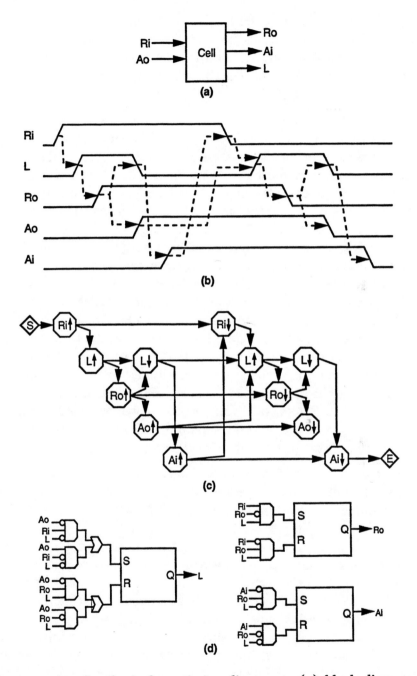

Figure 8.19: Synthesis from timing diagrams: (a) block diagram of FIFO stack control cell, (b) timing diagram, (c) event graph, (d) skeletal circuit.

the timing diagram of Figure 8.19(b). For example, for each of the two rising and falling transitions for output L in the timing diagram, there are nodes in the event graph, labeled as $L \uparrow$ and $L \downarrow$, respectively. Since the first rising transition on L is triggered by the rising transition on Ri, there is an arc added in the event graph from the node $Ri \uparrow$ to the node $L \uparrow$.

Once the event graph has been generated, a template matching strategy is used to generate a skeletal circuit for each output produced by the cell. Each node in the event graph is implemented with a circuit template that will generate the appropriate transition on the output. Three different types of templates are employed by the synthesis method to reflect the various events that have to be generated – one for generating asynchronous events, one for generating synchronous events from other synchronous events, and one for generating synchronous events from asynchronous events. Each template consists of an SR latch. Rise and fall transitions are achieved by appropriately setting or resetting the SR latch. Figure 8.19(d) shows how the skeletal circuit is constructed from the event graph of Figure 8.19(c) for each of the three outputs L, Ro and Ai. As an example, consider the cell output L. The first rising transition on L is triggered by three conditions: input Ao is low, input Ri has a rising transition, and L is low. Hence, the SR latch for L is set whenever $\overline{Ao}Ri\overline{L}$ is true. This is implemented as an AND gate driving the S input of the latch for output L. The final step applies logic optimization techniques to minimize the skeletal circuit generated.

In the example of Figure 8.19, a logic circuit was obtained from a single timing diagram. To synthesize transducers, separate event graphs are generated from the timing diagrams of the two interfaces first. Next, the two event graphs are combined into a single graph by either explicitly specifying merge labels that connect nodes in the two event graphs or by examining the data dependencies between the two interfaces. The template matching strategy explained above is then applied to the combined event graph to generate the skeletal circuit. Latches for different output signals are then interconnected by a breadth-first traversal of the event graph. Any timing constraint violations and race conditions in the circuit are corrected by adding appropriate logic circuitry. For example, minimum timing constraints may be satisfied by inserting delay elements in the circuit. Finally, the resulting circuitry is optimized.

The main advantage of the transducer synthesis method is that it incorporates detailed timing constraints between events in the two interfaces. Second, unlike the interface process generation method of the previous section, the output of transducer synthesis is a logic circuit – no further synthesis is required. One of the limitations of the approach is the fact that the datawidth mismatches on the two interfaces are not allowed. In addition, the resulting transducer circuit is not simulatable with the timing diagrams of the protocols it connects.

Protocol converters

A **protocol converter** is a behavior that matches the control signals on each of the two protocols to enable data transfers between them. An approach to the synthesis of protocol converters was presented in [AM91, Ake91]. The protocols being interfaced were specified using Verilog-based finite-state machines. A cross product of the two state machines was obtained and optimized to obtain the state-machine description of the transducer. This approach can potentially lead to a very large number of states in the protocol converter. Protocol conversion assumes that the datapath of the converter is given, consequently, this approach, like that of the transducer synthesis above, does not support any data width mismatches.

System interface modules

A method for the design of system interface modules was proposed for the SIERA design environment in [SB92]. SIERA [SSB91] seeks to minimize the system design effort by providing a library of modules containing detailed I/O structure and protocols (specified as event graphs). Details of protocols are represented in the form of event graphs in the library and are kept hidden from the system designer. Inter-module communication is abstracted to a level where the designer need only instantiate the appropriate system modules from the library and specify their interactions in terms of the interconnection of the source and destination ports using high-level primitives in a special-purpose language, IDL.

An interface module consists of a protocol controller and an interface controller. The protocol controller interfaces the control signals of the two protocols within a single transfer. The interface controller configures the interconnections between the two sets of data lines and instructs the protocol controller to interface the handshaking events between the protocols.

First, a control flow graph is constructed from the user specification of the interconnection of the modules. Scheduling and allocation are applied to the control flow graph to generate the interface controller, and a datapath to implement the data transfers between the data lines of the two protocols. Next, the event graphs for the two protocols are obtained from the module library and interconnected based on data dependencies between the operations in the two protocols. From this event graph, a protocol controller is synthesized to respond to the control signals of the two module protocols.

The main advantage of this approach is that it frees the designer from the burden of considering any low-level details, such as I/O control signals and timing constraints since such information is stored in the module library. The designer need only specify the high-level data transfers using the IDL language. While two protocols with differing data widths can be interfaced, the designer needs to specify the interconnection and multiplexing explicitly between the two sets of data lines that need to be implemented in the interface module. Another limitation of the approach is that the synthesized interface module is not simulatable with the original protocols.

8.6   Refining hardware/software interfaces

Any behavioral description can be implemented either as software or as hardware. If we choose to implement it as **software**, the behavioral description will be compiled into the instruction set of the chosen processor. If, on the other hand, we decide to implement the behavioral description as custom **hardware**, it will have to be synthesized into a structure of components drawn from a given library. In some cases, these components could be off-the-shelf, whereas others can be generated by component generators. The important point, though, is that any system comprising software and hardware components will need a hardware-software interface to accommodate the communications between its various parts.

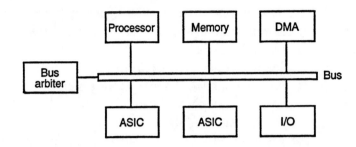

Figure 8.20: A hardware-software system architecture.

Consider the system in Figure 8.20. In this system, the *Processor* with the *Memory* is considered a **software component**, while the other items are regarded as **hardware components**. These hardware and software components are connected by a bus, which means that each component could be either a bus master or a bus slave. A **bus master** is any component that can control the bus and initiate data transfers, such as processors, disk controllers, and DMA controllers. In contrast, a **bus slave** is any component that can respond to the commands issued by the bus master, but not initiate the bus transactions. Typical bus slaves would be memories and I/O components. In the case of ASICs, we could make them either as bus masters or bus slaves, depending on the particular functions they perform. For example, a floating-point co-processor would generally be implemented as a bus slave, with input and output buffers in the co-processor to store the operands and the result. On the other hand, an ASIC that captures video-frames would generally be implemented as a bus master, since this is the best way to achieve high-speed data transfer to and from the memory. Note that when two or more bus masters are connected to a single bus, we would require a **bus arbiter** to ensure that only one master controls the bus at any one time. Most buses, such as the VMEbus or the Multibus, are designed with bus arbitration schemes incorporated in their protocols. On the other hand, in some processor-dependent buses such as the PC/XT/AT variety, it is the processor that arbitrates between concurrent requests for bus control.

The **bus** itself, as an interconnect component, can be designed for a specific application, as described in Section 8.3.3, or it could be chosen from a set of predefined buses, including the Multibus, VMEbus, NuBus,

PC/XT/AT bus, STD bus, and so on. Since each of these buses has its own communication protocol, any component connected to it must follow the protocol of the bus. Sometimes, however, we may run into a problem when the communication protocol of an off-the-shelf component does not match the protocol of the bus we has chosen, in which case the designer will need to include an interface component between these elements to ensure correct communication, as discussed in Section 8.5. Note that, if an ASIC has not yet been implemented, the protocol of the chosen bus could be incorporated into the functionality of the ASIC, and this could resolve the interface problem.

In the following sections, we will discuss several tasks that are related to the interfacing of hardware and software components. The process of **variable distribution**, for example, can be used to assign variables to either software or hardware in order to satisfy the data transfer rate at a minimal cost. The task of **interface generation** adds an interface process that will enable components to communicate correctly with incompatible buses. Finally, **data and control access refinement** tasks insert into software and hardware description the communication protocols needed for data or control transfer.

8.6.1   Target architecture

In order to explain hardware-software interfacing, we will use as an example the architecture shown in Figure 8.20. This architecture is very simple, consisting of one processor and several ASICs. The reason we have restricted ourselves to only one processor is that this makes the refinement of the hardware-software interface easier to explain. A more complex architecture would require us to consider the synchronization of inter-processor communication and the problem of memory protection, which are beyond the scope of this book.

Typically, we start the refinement of hardware-software interfaces from a partitioned specification, like the one shown in Figure 8.21. In this specification, $v1$ to $v6$ represent variables, $B1$ to $B4$ are behaviors, and $p1$ to $p3$ are ports. The edges in the figure represent data accesses by the behaviors to the variables or ports. A behavior that is mapped to the software partition is called a **software behavior**, and similarly, the one mapped to the hardware partition is called a **hardware behav-**

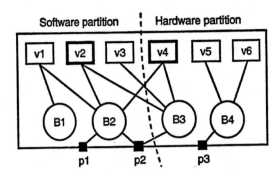

Figure 8.21: A partitioned specification.

ior. In this example, $B1$ and $B2$ are software behaviors, while $B3$ and $B4$ are hardware behaviors. **Software variables** or **software ports** are defined as those variables or ports that are accessed exclusively by software behaviors. For example, $v1$ is a software variable and $p1$ is a software port. Similarly, those variables or ports that are accessed only by hardware behaviors are called **hardware variables** or **hardware ports**. In this example, $v3$, $v5$, and $v6$ are hardware variables, and $p3$ is a hardware port. Finally, those variables or ports accessed by both software and hardware behaviors are called **shared variables** or **ports** respectively, as is the case with $v2$ and $v4$, which are shared variables, and $p2$, which is a shared port.

8.6.2 Variable distribution

The process of variable distribution refers to the assignment of the variables in the specification to software or hardware – in other words, to memory or ASICs. Typically, all the software variables would be assigned to the memory, since the memory is usually large enough to accommodate them. We could, alternatively, assign the software variables to the ASIC's storage, but this would have no advantages, and would only increase the cost of the ASIC due to the extra silicon it would require. For the hardware variables, we would probably be inclined to assign them to the memory, to accommodate the limited size of ASIC chips, but we must realize that this kind of assignment will tend to increase bus traffic and slow down the ASIC, since the ASIC might encounter memory-access

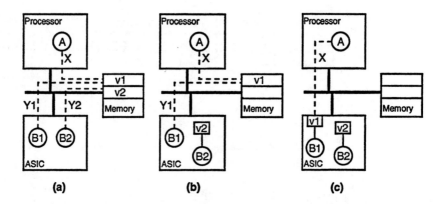

Figure 8.22: Variable distribution: (a) both hardware and shared variables reside in memory, (b) hardware variable resides in ASIC while shared variable resides in memory, (c) both hardware and shared variables reside in ASIC.

contention with the processor. This consideration is especially critical when ASIC accesses these variables frequently. We should also be aware that there are similar tradeoffs between performance and cost for any shared variables that might be assigned to either the memory or the ASIC's storage.

Figure 8.22 shows three different alternatives for variable distribution. In this example, behavior A is executed on a processor and behaviors $B1$ and $B2$ are synthesized into an ASIC. Note that variable $v1$ is a shared variable accessed by both A and $B1$, and that the corresponding communication channels for variable accesses are X and $Y1$, respectively. Also, note that variable $v2$ is accessed only by $B2$, through channel $Y2$. The difference among these three variable distributions is that Figure 8.22(a) has both the hardware and the shared variables assigned to the memory, Figure 8.22(b) has only the shared variable assigned to memory with the hardware variable assigned to ASIC, and Figure 8.22(c) has both the variables assigned to ASIC.

If we assume the average rates of channels X, $Y1$, and $Y2$ are $avgrate(X)$, $avgrate(Y1)$, and $avgrate(Y2)$ respectively, then the bus transfer rate required for the cases in Figure 8.22(a), (b), and (c) will be $avgrate(X) + avgrate(Y1) + avgrate(Y2)$, $avgrate(X) + avgrate(Y1)$, and $avgrate(X)$, respectively. From these different variable distributions, we can also determine the relative costs: Figure 8.22(b) would be calculated as $cost(v2)$, and Figure 8.22(c) would be $cost(v1) + cost(v2)$, where $cost(v)$ denotes the cost of the silicon required for implementing variable v on the ASIC. And note that $cost(v1)$ is greater than $cost(v2)$, since $v1$ needs dual ports.

We can see from this example that the best way to reduce the bus transfer rate would be to assign all hardware and shared variables to ASICs. On the other hand, such a variable assignment would be expensive, since the cost of ASICs is much higher than the cost of standard components. Figure 8.22 shows that the required bus transfer rate decreases from case (a) to (c) at the cost of extra silicon. Let's call this extra silicon cost the **variable-access cost**.

As mentioned above, to interface software and hardware we must select a bus that will allow communication between disparate software and hardware components. To select a bus, we have to consider both the required bus transfer rate and the **bus cost**, which includes the cost of the bus itself as well as the cost of its interfacing components. At the bottom end of the scale, we know that the interface cost will be zero if the component's protocol matches the bus's protocol. Alternatively, if we can use an off-the-shelf interface circuit to connect an incompatible component to a bus, the interface cost will be equal to the cost of the interface circuit. Finally, if such an interface circuit is not available, the interface cost will be high, since we will need to synthesize a custom ASIC for the interface.

We should be aware that bus selection and variable distribution are interrelated. For a given bus, for example, the goal of variable distribution would be to find the distribution that will satisfy the bus transfer rates while minimizing variable-access cost. Similarly, for a given variable distribution, the process of bus selection will involve choosing a bus that satisfies the required transfer rates as well as minimizing the bus cost. In most cases, since we need a solution that satisfies data transfer rates at a minimum system cost, we would consider bus selection and variable distribution together.

In Algorithm 8.6.1, we show an algorithm that can be used for concurrent bus selection and variable distribution. Intuitively, the algorithm examines a set of potential buses, S_b, which can be provided by the designer or stored in a library containing all available buses. For each bus B belonging to S_b, we would then consider each possible variable distribution D for a set of variables, S_v, which contains either all the hardware and shared variables given in the partitioned specification or just a subset of these selected by the designer. Note that S_v does not contain any software variables, because all of the software variables should automatically be assigned to memory.

Algorithm 8.6.1 : Variable distribution
 Determine S_b /* set of buses */
 Determine S_v /* set of variables */

 $mincost = \infty$
 $mincost\_bus = unknown$
 $mincost\_var\_dist = unknown$

 for each $B \in S_b$ **loop**
  for each D of S_v **loop**
   $datarate(D, B) = \sum_{C \ mapped \ to \ B} avgrate(C)$
   if $(datarate(D, B) \leq rate(B))$ **then**
    $currcost = Cost(B) + Cost(D)$
    if $(currcost < mincost)$ **then**
     $mincost = currcost$
     $mincost\_bus = B$
     $mincost\_var\_dist = D$
    end if
   end if
  end loop
 end loop

 if $(mincost = \infty)$
  then return($failure$)
  else return(mincost_bus, mincost_var_dist)
 end if

For each variable distribution D, then, we can determine the required data transfer rate on a selected bus B, expressed as $datarate(D, B)$, by computing the sum of the channel average rate ($avgrate(C)$) of all channels C that are mapped to bus B. (The definition of $avgrate(C)$ was given in Section 7.2.3.) In this way, we can determine whether the given transfer rate of the bus, $rate(B)$, can satisfy the data transfer rate required by a particular configuration. This algorithm will then return the configuration in which the bus satisfies the required data transfer rate and the total cost is minimal. The cost includes both $Cost(B)$ and $Cost(D)$, which are the bus cost and the variable-access cost respectively. Note that the temporary variables $mincost$, $mincost\_bus$, and $mincost\_var\_dist$ are used to record the best configuration found so far.

The complexity of the algorithm is $O(N \times M)$, where N is the number of buses and M is the number of variable distributions to be examined. It is important to note that, since the $rate(B)$ is often given as the peak rate of the bus B, the algorithm should compute $datarate(D, B)$ as the sum of the peak rates, $peakrate(C)$, of all the channels C mapped to bus B. (The definition of $peakrate(C)$ is given in Section 7.2.3.) However, in many cases, using the channel peak rate would be too conservative and may lead to an inefficient use of the bus, since most of time the channels may not transfer data at the peak rate. Selection of $peakrate(C)$ versus $avgrate(C)$ in computing $datarate(D, B)$ requires an analysis of the data transfer profile.

8.6.3 Interface generation

As mentioned above, a designer will sometimes encounter a situation where the communication protocols of the selected bus and the selected component are incompatible, and there are no off-the-shelf components available to be used for the interface. In these cases, we need to generate an interface that will convert one protocol into the other, using a process similar to one discussed in Section 8.5. In that section, we presented a technique for generating an interface between two incompatible components, which consists of the following steps: (1) represent the protocols of the components to be interfaced as ordered relations; (2) partition relations into relation-groups; (3) generate an interface description by inverting each operation in the relation-group, that is, replacing each

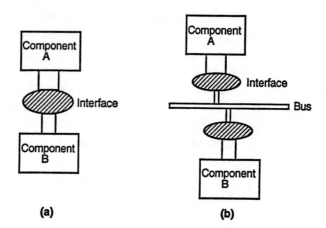

Figure 8.23: Interfacing between: (a) two components, (b) a component and a bus.

operation in the relation-group with its dual operation.

The technique used to generate an interface between a component and a bus is similar to the method just mentioned for interfacing two components, except for one slight difference. Let us use the example in Figure 8.23 to illustrate this difference. Assume that component A in Figure 8.23(a) sends data using its protocol to component B, which receives the data using its own protocol. The *interface* between them accommodates these two incompatible protocols of A and B, by receiving the data from A using a protocol **matched with** A's, and then sending the data to B using a protocol **matched with** B's. These matching protocols in the interface will be composed of operations dual to those of A and B, as shown in Section 8.5.3. In Figure 8.23(b), however, what we need is an interface between component A and the bus, which has to receive the data from A using a protocol **matched with** A's and then send the data on to the bus using a protocol **same as** the bus's protocol. Similarly, we need an interface between the bus and component B, which will receive the data using the bus's protocol and then send it to component B with the protocol that is matched to B's. Note that if an interface is required to use a protocol **matched with** a component's protocol, it will contain the operations **dual** to those of the component's protocol. On the other hand, if a interface is required to use a protocol **same as** a component's, it will contain the **same** operations as those in the component's protocol. Therefore, the interface between a component and a bus will consist of operations dual to those of the component's protocol, but same as those of the bus's protocol.

Figure 8.24 shows an example of interface generated for a *read* operation of a component connected to a bus which is a simplified version of the VMEbus. We can see that the resulting interface, presented in Figure 8.24(d), consists of operations that are dual to those of the component's protocol, and the same as those of the bus's protocol, with the operations same as those of the bus's protocol highlighted. Note that the star associated with signal AS indicates that AS is active low. The details of protocol generation have been described in Section 8.5.3.

8.6.4 Data access refinement

When we assign a behavior and the variable it accesses to different partitions, we need to refine the variable access in the description since the definition of the variable has been moved away from the behavior. Returning to the specification shown in Figure 8.21, let's assume that after variable distribution, the shared variable $v2$ and the hardware variable $v5$ have been assigned to memory, while the shared variable $v4$ has been assigned to the ASIC's dual-port buffer, as shown in Figure 8.25. The data accesses within the same partition are not a problem, since they will be taken care of either by software compilation, as is the case with $v1$ in Figure 8.25, or by a hardware synthesis tool, as is the case with $v3$ and $v6$. Therefore, the task of data access refinement is to refine data accesses across partitions, as is the case with $v2$, $v4$, and $v5$.

In Figure 8.25, each location in the memory or in the ASIC's buffer has a unique address in the global address space which is visible to any bus master. Since a processor usually has a fixed number of pins, with no extra pins for ports, the ports accessed by the software behaviors would have to be mapped to locations in the global address space, and accessed through the processor's bus. Therefore, port accesses in software behaviors will also require refinement. Note that port accesses in hardware behaviors would not need refinement, since ASIC can have pins for ports. All data-access channels that would need to be refined for the example are indicated in Figure 8.25 by the dashed lines.

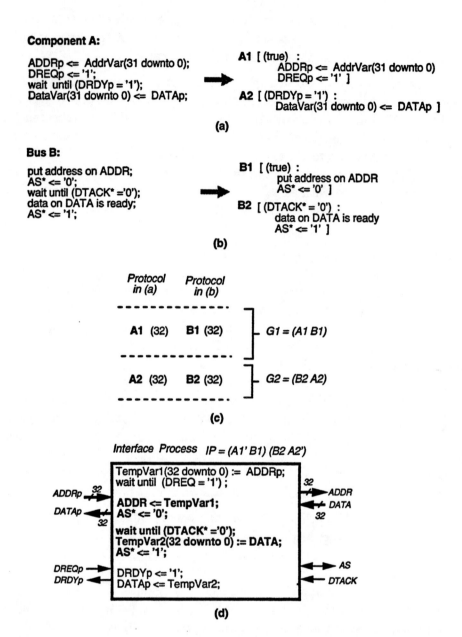

Figure 8.24: Component-bus interface: (a) relations for the component's protocol, (b) relations for the bus's protocol, (c) relation-groups, (d) generated interface.

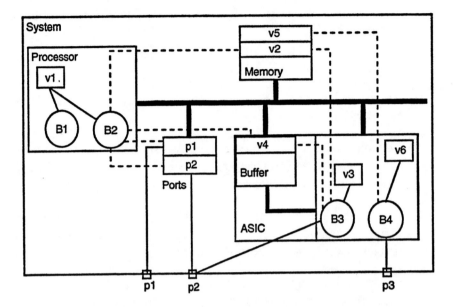

Figure 8.25: A specification mapping to target architecture.

There are four basic types of data access:

1. **Software behaviors access memory locations:** This type of data access is carried out through the processor's **load/store** instructions. In Figure 8.25, $B2$'s access of $v2$ belongs to this type.

2. **Hardware behaviors access memory locations:** Since this type of data access is carried out by ASIC through a direct-memory access (DMA) mechanism, we call them **DMA** operations. They are similar to load and store operations, except that ASIC first has to gain control of the bus. In Figure 8.25, $B3$'s access of $v2$ and $B4$'s access of $v5$ belong to this type.

3. **Software behaviors access ports or the ASIC's buffer:** This type of data access is carried out through the processor's **in/out** or **move** instructions. In Figure 8.25, $B2$'s access of $p1$, $p2$, and $v4$ belongs to this type.

4. **Hardware behaviors access the ASIC's buffer:** Since this type of data access is carried out by ASIC's access to its buffer locations, we call them **buffer** operations. These operations use a

separate bus in the ASIC. In Figure 8.25, $B3$'s access of $v4$ belongs to this type.

The tasks of data access refinement are then specified as follows:

1. Assign addresses to the variables or ports that have been mapped to the global address space.

2. Replace the software accesses to those variables assigned to memory by load and store operations. Similarly, replace hardware accesses to those variables with DMA operations.

3. Use in and out operations to replace software accesses to those variables that are mapped to ASICs. Use buffer operations to replace their accesses from hardware behaviors.

4. Use in and out operations to replace any software accesses to the ports that are mapped to the global address space.

8.6.5   Control access refinement

Unlike data access channel which exists between behavior and variable, control channel exists between two behaviors to indicate the starting or completion of behavior. Figure 8.26(a) shows an example in which behaviors $B1$, $B2$ and $B3$ are scheduled sequentially, that is, $B2$ starts after $B1$ finishes, and $B3$ starts after $B2$ finishes. Therefore, control channels exist between $B1$ and $B2$, and between $B2$ and $B3$. If, however, behavior $B2$ is assigned to a hardware implementation, then the control channels connected to $B2$ would have to be refined to conform to the hardware-software interface.

One solution to this problem would be to introduce hand-shaking protocols, using two shared variables: *start* and *done*. In this case, the protocol statements will be inserted in place of $B2$, while $B2$ itself will be enhanced with matching protocol statements, as shown in Figure 8.26(b). If we then mapped the variables *start* and *done* to a dual-port buffer, the specification in Figure 8.26(b) could be mapped to the target architecture shown in Figure 8.26(c). The control refinement will be completed after the data access refinement for shared variables *start* and *done* is performed.

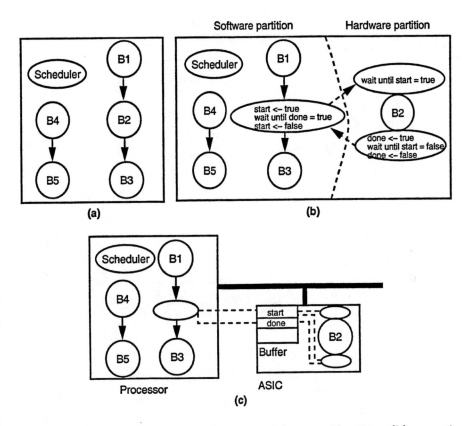

Figure 8.26: Control access refinement: (a) a specification, (b) a partitioned specification with hand-shaking protocols for the control channels, (c) a specification mapping to the target architecture.

This control refinement scheme is a simple one since the rest of software parts will not be affected by *B*2's being moved to hardware. We should be aware however, that this scheme would require the processor to **poll** the location that stores the value of the variable *done*, and this may waste processor's clock cycles.

Since commercial processors usually provide an interrupt mechanism, a more efficient method of control access refinement is possible. In Figure 8.27(a), for example, we show a scheme that uses the **interrupt** mechanism to indicate the completion of the hardware behavior. In this case, *B*2 has been replaced by a new behavior, which consists of a pro-

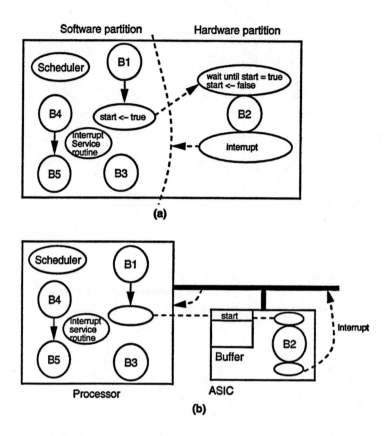

Figure 8.27: Control access refinement: (a) a partitioned specification with an interrupt indicating completion of the hardware behavior, (b) a specification mapping to the target architecture.

tocol statement that starts $B2$. In addition, the behavior $B2$ has been extended to include protocol statements in the front and interrupt statements at the end. For each interrupt, we insert a corresponding service routine in the software partition. When the interrupt occurs, the control will be turned over to the service routine. By using interrupt mechanism, the processor can start $B3$ without waiting for $B2$ to finish, as long as there is no data dependences between $B2$ and $B3$, or alternatively, the processor can start other software behavior, such as $B4$.

The tasks of control access refinement can be summarized as follows.

1. Choose a control scheme, such as polling or interrupt. Then, insert the corresponding communication protocols in the software and the hardware behaviors.

2. Insert any necessary software behaviors, such as interrupt service routines.

3. Refine the accesses to any shared variables that have been introduced by the insertion of the protocols.

8.7 Conclusion and future directions

In this chapter we presented the set of tasks that have to be performed to refine the system specification after system partitioning. We first demonstrated the importance of specification refinement in system design. We discussed issues relating to the implementation of variable and channel groups. A method for bus generation was introduced, and the tradeoffs between buswidths and system performance were evaluated. For a selected buswidth, we showed how communication protocols can be generated. Methods for resolving access conflicts to a shared resource in a system were discussed. We examined the effects on communication of binding functional objects to off-the-shelf components. We described techniques for interfacing two fixed incompatible protocols. Finally, we presented methods for refining the communication between behaviors that have been mapped to hardware and software implementations.

The work presented in this chapter can be extended in several directions. First, during protocol generation we need to develop metrics to evaluate several candidate protocols that may be selected for implementing transfers over the bus. Second, during our discussion of bus generation, arbitration delays were assumed to be negligible, which may not always be the case. We need to incorporate the effect of arbitration delays on the behavior execution times and channel average rates. Third, the effect of different bus arbitration schemes on the performance of the behaviors communicating over a bus needs to be investigated.

Optimizations that can be applied to interface processes generated to make two protocols compatible need to studied. An example of such an optimization might be the minimization of the number and size of variables used by the interface process to reduce the size of the hardware that will implement the interface process. Finally, while the HDL descriptions of arbiter and interface processes allow the designer to simulate them along with the system specification, synthesizing these processes using traditional HDL-based synthesis methods would result in inefficient design. For example, synthesis tasks such as scheduling applied to the arbiter process would result in multi-state implementation of the arbiter. However, arbiters typically consist of only combinational logic. Thus, methods need to be developed for the efficient synthesis of interface and arbiter processes from their HDL descriptions.

8.8 Exercises

1. A variable group is implemented with a memory with 16 bits in each word. Discuss the advantages and disadvantages of mapping two variables with a size of 8 bits each to the least significant and and most significant bytes of the same address in the memory.

2. If an array A containing 100 elements is assigned addresses from 201 through 300 in a memory MEM to which it is mapped, update the references to A in the following set of statements:

```
X := A(30);
for I in 30 to 60 loop
   Y := A(I+20) * A(I −20) + Y;
end for;
A(X+A(10)) := 3;
```

3. Assume that a behavior B communicates with other behaviors over a set of channels. How would Equation 7.18 for computing the average rate of a specific channel C need to be modified to incorporate the communication time required by the other channels?

4. In Figure 8.10 send and receive procedures were generated for a scalar variable accessed over the 8-bit bus. Generate the send and receive procedures for access to an array variable, A, over the bus. Assume that A has 256 elements, each of which is 16 bits wide.

5. Assume that there are N concurrent accesses to a shared resource. Generate an arbiter process that implements a rotating priority arbitration scheme.

6. For the dynamic arbitration model presented in Figure 8.12(b), sketch the schematic of the interconnection logic in *MemArbiter*. Clearly show how address/data lines from the behaviors A, B and C are connected to those of the two memory ports. Assume that each behavior may read or write to either port of the memory.

7. N channels are merged into a bus. Arbitration for access to such a bus will require two signals, *request* and *grant*, for each channel, i.e., a total of $2N$ signals. Develop an algorithm to minimize the number of arbitration signals by sharing them between different channels used exclusively over time.

8. Assume a set of behaviors that access a shared resource have constraints specified for their execution times. If a fixed priority scheme is used to resolve access conflicts, how would the relative priorities of the behaviors be determined?

9. Develop heuristics to trim the search space for variable distributions in Algorithm 8.6.1.

10. Use the technique presented in Section 8.6.3 to generate an interface connecting Intel 8086's data transfer operations to the VME-bus.

11. Give an example that demonstrates how the order in which behaviors are executed will affect I/O data rates. Devise some techniques for rescheduling software behaviors or operations so that they will satisfy the I/O data rate constraints.

12. **A set of behaviors communicates over a group of channels is to be implemented as a single bus. Devise a strategy that would predict the effect of arbitration delays on the behavior execution times.

Chapter 9

System-Design
Methodology

In the previous chapters of this book, we have described a number of the issues and techniques that are central to system specification and design. If we are to make the most of these techniques, however, we would need to incorporate them within a coherent and comprehensive methodology that can easily be applied to real systems. In this chapter, then, we will present such a system-design methodology, in addition to outlining the tools that would best support it, and describing how these tools and this methodology relate to existing design practice.

9.1 Introduction

Every product goes from conceptualization to manufacturing through many design phases or tasks. This process is called **design process**, and the sequence of design tasks and associated CAD tools is called **design methodology**. At the lower levels of abstraction, the methodologies are well defined and supported by many commercial CAD tools. However, at the system level the methodologies are not well defined, and very few CAD tools are available. Furthermore, the system methodologies vary with the organization, design team and product. In this chapter we will present a coherent system-level methodology intended to facilitate the paradigm shift of research and commercial efforts from the logic and architectural levels to the system level.

In the previous chapters we defined system-level design, discussed models and languages for system specification, and presented issues and algorithms for partitioning, estimation and refinement. In this chapter we tie those concepts together into a system-level methodology. First, we illustrate the methodology with an example. We then describe a hypothetical design process and corresponding synthesis system that incorporates the proposed methodology. We briefly describe design tools at all levels of abstraction. Finally, we discuss an environment for supporting system-level tools.

9.2   Basic concepts

We first define the meaning of a design methodology before presenting our system-level approach. A design methodology must clearly specify the following:

(a) the syntax and semantics of the input and output descriptions,

(b) the set of techniques for transforming input into output descriptions,

(c) the set of components to be used in the design implementation,

(d) the definition and ranges of design constraints,

(e) the mechanism for selecting components and architectural styles, and

(f) design exploration strategies (usually called scenarios or scripts) that define synthesis tasks, their parameters, and the order in which they are executed.

Usually, requirements (a) and (b) are defined by the choice of a description language and a set of synthesis tools, while requirements (c) and (d) are determined by the chosen technology and system architecture. Requirements (e) and (f) are usually not defined at all and are assumed to be the designer's responsibility. We will explain requirements (a) through (f) by means of one example and derive a synthesis system to satisfy those requirements.

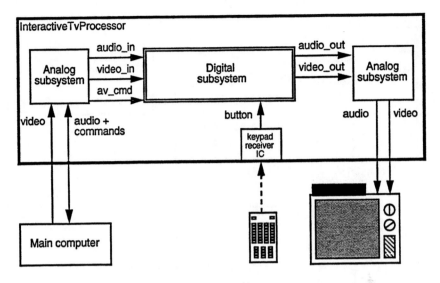

Figure 9.1: The ITVP's environment

9.3 An example design methodology

Let us consider as a design example an interactive television processor (ITVP). The system stores video frames and displays them as still pictures while audio is played. A user can interact by using a keypad, remote control or touchscreen to select a menu item, resulting in a new video frame being displayed with accompanying audio. Such systems are common in hotels, stores, and post offices, with possible future uses for interactive TV multimedia environments. They can be used to take a video tour of a hotel, shop through a video catalog, play video games, perform banking transactions or make airline reservations. The system resides in a box adjacent to a monitor or television set, similar to a box for cable TV. A diagram of the overall system is presented in Figure 9.1, which shows only certain data flows. An analog subsystem converts analog signals to digital ones and also extracts various synchronization signals from the video input. Another analog subsystem converts digital signals to analog ones, performing various other tasks as well. The core of the ITVP is a digital subsystem that we must design.

The main behaviors, data objects, and flows of data for the digital subsystem of Figure 9.1 are shown in Figure 9.2. The actual system

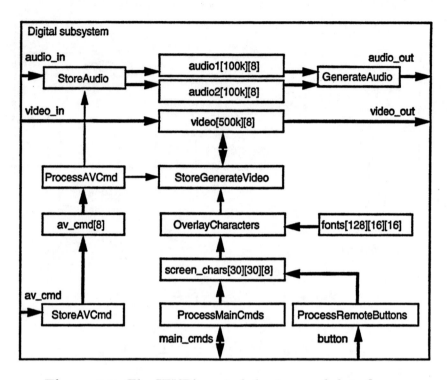

Figure 9.2: The ITVP's main behaviors and data flows

consists of 32 behaviors and 69 data objects, but, to keep the diagram simple, only the large or important items are shown. The system contains a behavior called *StoreAudio* that stores several thousand successive audio bytes from the audio input received through a modem, and another behavior called *GenerateAudio* that generates those audio bytes on command. Two arrays, *audio1* and *audio2*, are used to specify the stored audio bytes. Two arrays are required, rather than just one, because the system may be generating audio while storing another set of audio bytes. Another behavior, *StoreGenerateVideo*, stores and generates video frames along with an array, *video*, that specifies the stored video bytes. An array called *fonts* indicates which of the 16x16 pixels should be illuminated for each of the 128 ASCII characters supported by the system. Another array called *screen_chars* indicates which ASCII character, if any, should be displayed in each of the 30x30 screen positions. A behavior, *OverlayCharacters*, reads the screen-character and font arrays and then indicates to the video generator when to override a video pixel with a white pixel so that a white character will appear on the screen. The behavior *StoreAVCmd* and variable *av_cmd* capture an encoded command that specifies in which audio array to store incoming audio bytes, and from which array to generate output. This command also specifies the type of data to be accepted on the video input, so that the system can be expanded to capture software encoded in the video. The software will be executed on the processor to handle more time-constrained interactive programs such as video games. The behavior *ProcessRemoteButtons* responds to buttons pressed on the keypad or remote control. The behavior *ProcessMainCmds* responds to commands issued by the main computer, and the behavior *ProcessAVCmd* handles the encoded video command.

The system is transformed into a physical implementation in three major steps [GVN94]:

1. **Functionality specification:** The entire system's desired functionality is defined and described with a language. The functional description consists of computations and possibly of timing relations, but does not contain any details related to physical implementation.

2. **System design:** Standard system components, such as processors and memories, together with custom components such as gate arrays, FPGAs and ASICs, are allocated to the design. The system's functionality is partitioned among those components, resulting in a functional description for each component.

3. **Component implementation:** Each component's functionality is implemented as hardware or software, depending on the component type.

After the first two steps, the system components are defined, and the system may be summarized in "block-diagram" form, a form familiar to most designers. A block-diagram for our example is provided in Figure 9.3. The system is implemented with six components: three memories, two ASICs and a processor. Each of the behaviors and variables from Figure 9.2 is assigned to exactly one of these components. The *Memory1* component stores both the *audio1* and *audio2* arrays, while

Memory2 stores the *video* array. *Memory3* stores both the *fonts* array and the *screen_chars* array. *ASIC1* implements the *StoreAudio* and *GenerateAudio* behaviors. *ASIC2* implements the *StoreGenerateVideo* behavior as well as the *StoreAVCmd* behavior and the *av_cmd* variable. *Processor* implements the *ProcessAVCmd*, *ProcessMainCmds*, *ProcessRemoteButtons* and *OverlayCharacters* behaviors.

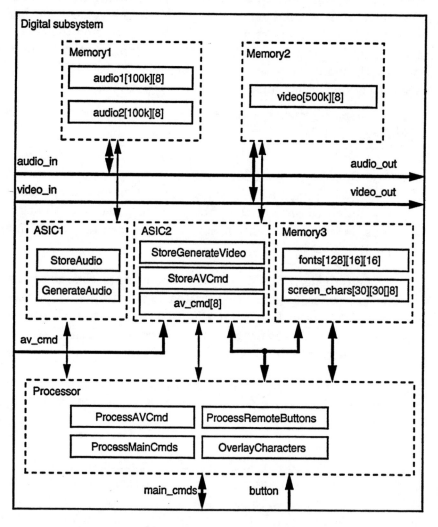

Figure 9.3: One possible design for the ITVP

Let us consider the decisions which were made in the ITVP example design. The audio and video arrays were stored in separate memories because the values in these arrays must be output simultaneously. Storing them in the same memory would have required multiplexing memory accesses, which, in turn would have violated minimum audio/video output-rate constraints. The *StoreAudio, GenerateAudio* and *StoreGenerateVideo* behaviors were implemented on ASICs because software implementations would not have met input and output rate constraints. The audio and video behaviors appear on different ASICs because they would not both fit on a single 20,000-gate ASIC. The *StoreAVCmd* behavior and *av_cmd* variable were also implemented on an ASIC because the audio/video command must be captured immediately, making them difficult to implement on the processor. The *fonts* and *screen_chars* arrays are not accessed concurrently, so they were mapped to a single memory without loss of performance. The behaviors assigned to the processor do not have tight performance constraints, so they are executed sequentially in software without violating any constraints, even though the behaviors are specified as executing concurrently.

The block diagram in Figure 9.3 represents just one of many possible ITVP implementations. For example, the two ASIC components could be replaced with a single, larger gate array. Or we could use an ASIC technology with different cost and performance characteristics. We can even use a microcontroller rather than a processor to lower costs. Numerous alternative assignments of behaviors and variables to a given set of components are possible. System design, in general, consists of enumerating and exploring those alternatives for different component sets, architectures and technologies.

The remainder of this chapter will address the following questions: "What is a good system design methodology?" and "What tools are necessary to support such a methodology?"

9.3.1 Current practice

We now describe the current practice for performing the three design steps introduced above. It is summarized pictorially in Figure 9.4.

Functionality specification: A system's functionality is described informally in a natural language such as English. Sometimes the descrip-

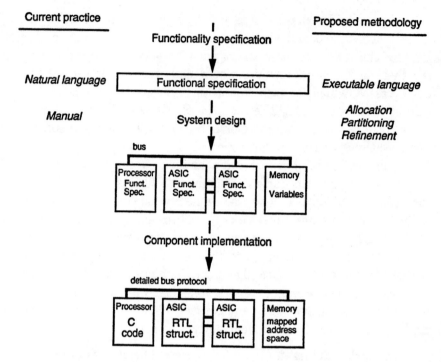

Figure 9.4: System design: current practice and proposed methodology.

tion is accompanied by dataflow diagrams, flowcharts, timing diagrams and tables. We saw in Chapter 4 the difficulty of creating a natural-language description that is both precise and readable. Thus, most natural-language descriptions are written imprecisely in order to maintain readability.

System design: System design is performed manually, often in an ad-hoc fashion, with design decisions based on previous experience or on hand-calculated quality estimations. A manual design methodology has several disadvantages. First, considering all possible design alternatives manually is too time-consuming, as demonstrated in Chapter 6. Second, obtaining an accurate mental estimation is difficult because of the large numbers of details that must be considered, as discussed in Chapter 7. Third, documenting the system-design decisions is tedious and time-consuming, and therefore omitted in most cases.

Component implementation: After the system block diagram is obtained, each component's functionality is specified in a natural language. This description is used to design RT or logic-level structure for each component. In some cases, each component's functionality is specified in an executable language so that functional verification can be performed. In rare cases, high-level synthesis tools are used to design the RT-level structure from the component's functional description.

In conclusion, current design practice puts very little effort into functionality specification and system design while overemphasizing component implementation. The lack of design effort at the system level can be attributed to a lack of proven design methodologies and a lack of tools to support the design tasks at this level.

9.3.2 System-level methodology

We shall now discuss the methodology described in this book. It is also summarized pictorially in Figure 9.4.

Functionality specification: The system's functionality is described in an executable language rather than a natural language. Verification or simulation is performed to ensure correct functionality, before any system design has taken place. These two steps result in a very precise description of functionality.

System design: System design consists of three well-defined tasks performed on three classes of functional objects, summarized in Figure 9.5. The three classes of functional objects contained in every functional specification are **variables**, **behaviors**, and **channels**. Variables store data, behaviors transform data, and channels transfer data between behaviors. The three tasks performed on each class of objects are allocation, partitioning, and refinement.

Allocation defines system components for the given functional specification. One class of system components consists of memories, ROMs, register-files, and registers. They are used to store scalar and array variables. The second class of components consists of processing elements such as standard processors, microcontrollers, and ASIC chips. These standard and custom processors are used to implement behaviors. The third class consists of physical buses, used to implement channels.

System–design tasks

	Allocation	Partitioning	Refinement
Variables	Memories	Variables to memories	Address assignment
Behaviors	Processors	Behaviors to processors	Interfacing
Channels	Buses	Channels to buses	Arbitration/protocols

Functional objects

Figure 9.5: System-design tasks

Partitioning assigns functional objects to allocated components. Variables are assigned to memories, behaviors are assigned to standard and custom processors, and channels are assigned to buses, as discussed in Chapter 6.

Refinement upgrades the original specification to reflect the impact of a given allocation and partition. Variables that are partitioned among memories require memory address translation. Behaviors that are separated among components must be modified to maintain correct communication among them. Channels that are assigned to buses require interface synthesis to determine communication protocols, and require arbiter synthesis to resolve simultaneous requests to a bus. Refinement was the subject of Chapter 8.

The above three tasks convert a functional specification, which is void of any implementation detail, into a new specification, which contains some structural information. The structural information describes the system-level architecture.

There is no fixed order in which one must apply these three tasks. One ordering of the tasks which may lead to good results is shown in Figure 9.6. After the functionality is specified, large variables are mapped to memories, with "close" variables sharing the same memory (see Chapter 6 for definitions of variable closeness). Channels are mapped to buses in a similar manner. Then processor or ASIC components are allocated and behaviors (as well as those variables that are not mapped to a memory) are partitioned among those components, in such a way that the overall software and hardware cost is minimized. Variable or channel repartitioning may follow these tasks to reduce the cost further.

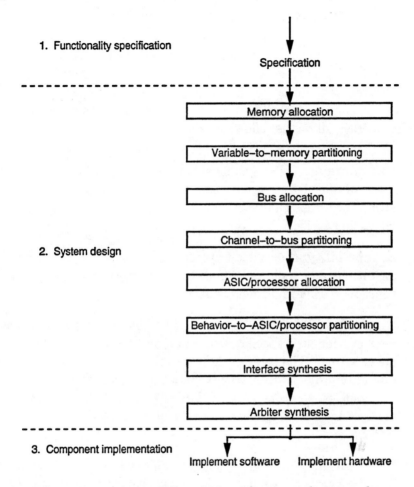

Figure 9.6: A possible ordering of system-design tasks

Interface synthesis and arbiter synthesis are then performed, in order to obtain a complete functional specification for each of the system components.

Component implementation: Software components are implemented by compiling the component's functional description into machine code. ASIC components are manually designed or synthesized with CAD tools. However, since the components are defined formally, synthesis follows naturally.

9.4   A generic synthesis system

In this section we describe a hypothetical generic synthesis system for designing embedded systems from concepts to manufacturing. It is generic because it brings together all the main concepts discussed in the previous chapters. It is hypothetical because no research or commercial synthesis system satisfies all of the following criteria:

(a) **Completeness:** The system should provide synthesis tools for all levels of the design process from specification to manufacturing documentation. The tools should accommodate a variety of implementation styles.

(b) **Extensibility:** The system should be flexible enough to allow new algorithms and tools to be added. The system should support the addition of new implementation styles.

(c) **Controllability:** A designer should be able to control the types of tools applied to a specific description and the order in which they are executed. The same designer should be able to control design exploration by selecting components, topologies, architectures and technologies. In order to assist the designer in the selection process, the system should provide a variety of design-quality metrics and tradeoff hints.

(d) **Interactivity:** A designer should be able to interact with synthesis tools by partially specifying the design structure or by modifying the design after synthesis.

(e) **Upgradability:** The synthesis system should allow evolutionary upgrade from a capture-and-simulate to a describe-and-synthesize methodology, and it should allow both strategies to be mixed at each level of abstraction.

The global diagram of a generic synthesis system, based on a similar one described in [GDWL91], is shown in Figure 9.7. It is complete, since it supports synthesis on the system, chip, logic and physical levels, including software-hardware codesign. It has a system synthesis tool to partition an executable specification into a set of specifications, one for

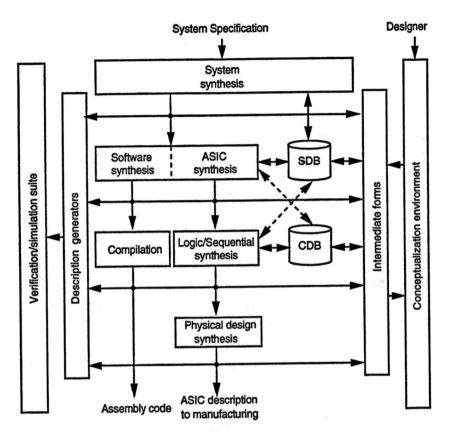

Figure 9.7: A generic synthesis system.

each custom, semicustom, or standard component used to implement the system's functionality. A software synthesis tool converts a specification for a processor to standard code, which can then be compiled into the processor's instruction set. An ASIC synthesis tool converts the specification of a chip into a set of RT components. A sequential and logic synthesis tool converts FSM and logic descriptions into a network of gates. Each synthesis tool is described in more detail below.

The generic system has a *Conceptualization environment* to support interactivity and controllability. Extensibility is supported through two databases. The *Component database (CDB)* supports the addition of new components for ASIC synthesis, while the *System database (SDB)* supports design engineering and management.

The system also supports both the capture-and-simulate and describe-and-synthesize methodologies. The first methodology is supported by capturing the schematic through the *Conceptualization environment* and its simulation through one of the simulators in the *Simulation suite*. The second methodology is supported by capturing design descriptions in one or more capture languages available in the conceptualization environment and synthesizing them with appropriate synthesis tools.

Different *Intermediate forms* are used for different design aspects and design phases in the conceptualization environment. The captured design description is translated into one of many standard intermediate forms for a particular type of synthesis and simulation. Instead of many intermediate forms, we could define one universal language for all levels and design styles. However, such a language would be too cumbersome and inefficient. It would take many years to reach an agreement on a standard and probably many more years to teach designers how to use it. On the other hand, we could use a standard simulation language such as VHDL. However, such a language is burdened by the constructs necessary for simulation, and is difficult to use for capturing other design aspects. It is thus convenient to use specific intermediate forms, each of which is close to a designer's view of the problem, to capture specific design information, as long as we provide a simulation code generator to translate the intermediate form into a simulatable description. The *Description generators* shown in Figure 9.7 are used for this purpose.

The concept of code generators also fits the capture-and-simulate methodology. For example, we can think of a schematic as an intermediate form translated by a netlist generator into a simulatable description. Similarly, intermediate forms on the logic, sequential, register-transfer and system levels can be translated into VHDL or some other simulation language. This approach enables the captured description to be close to a designer's way of thinking and to be simulatable by any standard simulator for which a description generator is available. Furthermore, the intermediate forms can be used for interactive synthesis to support manual allocation, partitioning, interfacing, arbitration, transformation and verification of specifications and designs, as well as for design-quality assessment and for estimating the effect of design changes on quality.

In the sections that follow, we will explain briefly each of the parts of the generic synthesis system.

9.4.1 System synthesis

System synthesis takes an executable specification of the complete system and partitions it into a set of executable specifications, one for each custom, semicustom or standard system-component used in the system implementation. Each of the component specifications satisfies all the component constraints. For example, if a component is a 50,000-gate array in a 100-pin package, the component specification must be implementable with fewer than 50,000 gates and use fewer than 100 pins for data communication and power. At the same time, if a component is a standard memory, then the component specification must include the memory protocol for accessing data stored in this memory. Similarly, if the component is a standard processor, then the component specification, when compiled into machine code, must execute in the time required by the given constraints.

A system-synthesis environment (Figure 9.8) consists of a compiler with a corresponding system representation (SR) and a set of system-design tools. An *Allocator* selects the types and numbers of system components in the design. A *Partitioner* assigns each portion of the SR to a component. Both the allocator and partitioner annotate the SR with the new information they create, as described in Chapter 6. *Estimators* quickly provide the allocator and partitioner with estimated values of various quality metrics, as described in Chapter 7. An *Interface synthesis* tool adds descriptions of protocols for buses used for communication between system components. An *Arbiter synthesis* tool adds new descriptions for arbitrating concurrent bus accesses. These last two tools are essential for transforming the original system specification into component specifications. They were described in Chapter 8.

The *Transformer* tool is the only one that was not discussed in earlier chapters. It performs a set of SR transformations that will improve certain quality metrics in the final design. The SR may need to be transformed because it has been derived from a specification written with readability in mind and is not easily partitionable. For example, a procedure P may be used to encapsulate a complex computation performed in many places in the specification. Implementing P as a single FSMD may lead to an excessive number of pins or poor performance if P is called by several other FSMDs. In this case, it may be better to replicate P, and add it to each calling FSMD. It may even be best to inline

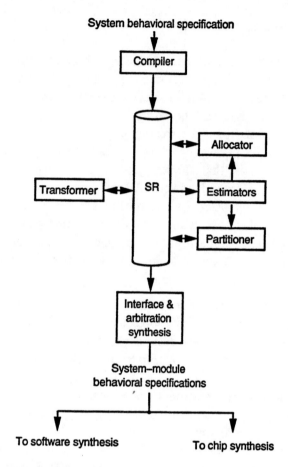

Figure 9.8: A generic system-synthesis environment.

P, which would result in redundant hardware but may improve performance and decrease interconnect cost. Other possible transformations include: (a) unrolling a loop to expose more concurrency, (b) splitting an array variable into a set of scalar variables or splitting a behavior into a set of finer-grained behaviors in order to provide for more partitioning options, (c) sequentializing concurrent behaviors to reduce the number of FSMDs required, and (d) parallelizing sequential behaviors to improve performance. Such transformations are highly interrelated, since a particular transformation may enable or restrict one or more of the other transformations.

The role of transformations in system design is not fully understood, although research in the area of system-level transformations has shown very promising results [TAS93, HT93, WT89, IOJ94]. Specification transformations should be included as the fourth major task in system-design in the future.

9.4.2 ASIC synthesis

System synthesis defines a set of system components with fixed interfaces, and an executable specification for each component. Chip synthesis, often called high-level synthesis (HLS), transforms a component's specification into a structure of register-transfer components (RTC) such as registers, multiplexors, and ALU's. Such a structure usually consists of two parts: a controller implementing a finite-state machine, and a datapath executing arithmetic operations. We refer to such a structure as a finite-state machine with datapath, or FSMD [GDWL91]. The controller controls register transfers in the datapath and generates signals for communication with the external world. A generic chip-synthesis environment based on ideas from [BM89, BCD+88, CR89, TLW+90, CST91, Gaj91, KD91, LND+91, NON91] is shown in Figure 9.9.

The synthesis environment consists of a compiler with a corresponding representation scheme, a set of HLS tools, an RTC database, a technology mapper and an optimizer. The input executable specification is first compiled into a design representation called a control/dataflow graph (CDFG), which exposes control and data dependencies between basic operations such as additions and comparisons. For example, Figure 9.10 shows a simple behavior and its equivalent CDFG. Note that the addition operation $a + b$ and the comparison operation $a = b$ can potentially be executed in parallel, even though they are written sequentially in the specification. Also note that the subtraction operation $x - y$ must occur *after* $a + b$, since x depends upon the result of $a + b$.

Several HLS tools annotate this representation as they build an RT-level structure. A *Component selector* selects, from an RTC database, the storage, function and bus units to be used in the design. A *Scheduler* maps operations to control steps, each of which usually represents one clock period or clock phase. Scheduling is necessary since all operations usually cannot be executed at once due to data dependencies or due to

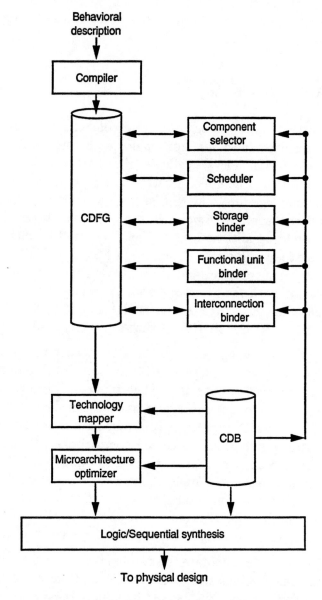

Figure 9.9: A generic chip-synthesis environment.

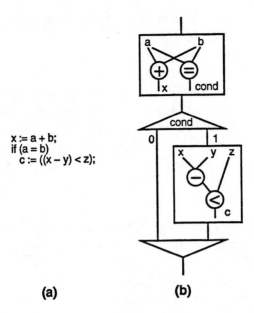

$x := a + b;$
$if (a = b)$
$\quad c := ((x - y) < z);$

(a)   (b)

Figure 9.10: CDFG example: (a) input behavior, (b) CDFG.

a limited number of units capable of executing particular operations. In the example, the + and = operations can be performed in a single control step if they use different ALU's. The condition $a = b$ can be checked in a second control step, the − operation can be performed in a third control step, and the < operation in a fourth. Note that the − and < operations cannot be performed in the same step because of a data dependency between them. Scheduling is one of the central subjects in ASIC synthesis research, for which many different algorithms exist [GDWL91]. *Storage, Functional,* and *Interconnect unit binders* map scalar and array variables to registers and memories, operations to function units, and connections to buses. In the above example, we may select two ALUs, and bind the + and − operations to one ALU and the = and < operations to the other. While most research has assumed a very basic set of RT components, recent attempts have focused on more realistic component libraries.

It should be obvious that there is no unique selection, scheduling or binding for any particular description. For example, we could use only one ALU in the example, in which case the + and = operations would require a total of two control steps instead of one. We could also schedule the − operation in the same control step as the condition evaluation $a = b$ and discard the result of the − operation if the condition evaluated to false. These were just two of examples of different selection, binding and scheduling. Different selection, binding and scheduling decisions yield designs that differ primarily in size and performance. At times, size constraints take high precedence over performance. In these cases, the design goal would be to achieve the best performance for a selected set of components satisfying the size constraint. At other times, performance constraints take precedence. In these cases, the design goal would be to select the smallest set of components for which the required performance could still be satisfied.

It should also be clear that the tasks of selection, binding and scheduling are heavily interrelated. If we select and bind first, then we limit the possible schedules. For example, two operations bound to a single component cannot be scheduled in the same control step. On the other hand, if we schedule operations first, then we limit the possible selections and bindings. For example, two operations scheduled for the same control step cannot share a single component. Some attempts have been made to merge selection, binding and scheduling into a single algorithm [CT90, BM89, Geb92a] in order to consider these interdependencies among the three tasks. Each of the tasks of selection, binding, and scheduling is an NP-complete problem.

The *Component Database* (*CDB*) stores RT components to be used during synthesis and answers queries about their characteristics. The *Technology mapper* maps generic components from the synthesized design description into component instances from the *CDB*. Since the estimated critical paths through the design and delays along those paths may change after mapping to real components, the *Microarchitecture optimizer* reduces delays on critical paths by redistributing components, inserting faster components on critical paths and slower components on non-critical paths.

Some of the components in the *CDB*, such as memories and multipliers, are implemented as standard macrocells. The others, such as FSMDs, are synthesized from the behavioral description. They are combined into an ASIC during the physical design.

9.4.3 Logic and sequential synthesis

Chip synthesis generates a set of controllers and datapaths. Each controller is modeled as a finite-state machine (FSM). A controller-synthesis tool must convert an FSM to a hardware structure consisting of a state register and a combinational circuit, which generates the next state as well as the controller's outputs. The tasks involved in creating such a structure include state minimization, state encoding, logic minimization and technology mapping. A generic logic-synthesis system based on ideas from [DSVA87, BRSVW87, DMNSV88] is shown in Figure 9.11.

State minimization reduces the number of states in an FSM by replacing equivalent states with a single state. Two states are equivalent if the sequence of outputs for any sequence of inputs does not depend on which of the two states we start in. State minimization is important since the number of states determines the size of the state register and control logic.

State encoding assigns binary codes to symbolic states. The goal is to obtain a binary code that minimizes the controller's combinational logic. *Logic minimization* is used after encoding to reduce the size or delay of the combinational logic.

While two-level combinational logic is usually implemented with a PLA, multi-level logic can be implemented with standard logic libraries. *Technology mapping* transforms a technology-independent logic network produced by the logic minimizer into a net-list of standard gates from a particular library.

Since we assume that every design can be described with a set of communicating processes and implemented with a set of communicating FSMDs, designing communication logic is a necessary part of synthesis. The interface circuitry can be implemented as an integral part of each FSMD or as a stand-alone FSMD. If a communication protocol is part of the FSMD description, then each response to a protocol signal takes an integral number of states or clock cycles since output signals change only on state boundaries. For example, we can implement the request-acknowledge protocol using a wait state and an acknowledge state. The assertion of the request signal forces the FSMD to leave the wait state and enter the acknowledge state in which the acknowledge signal is asserted. When the request is removed, the FSMD will leave the acknowledge

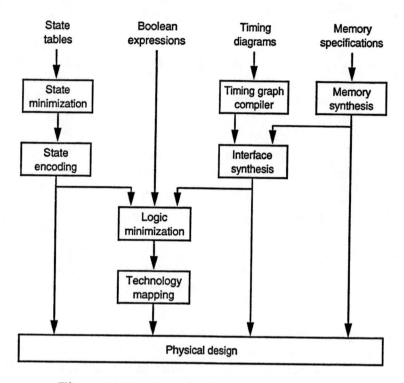

Figure 9.11: A generic logic-synthesis tool.

state. On the other hand, when two standard FSMDs with different protocols must be interfaced, then a third FSMD must be synthesized to convert one protocol into another [Bor91, NT86].

Interface synthesis is difficult because of the lack of interface description languages and synthesis methods for mixed synchronous and asynchronous sequential logic. The communication protocols are usually described with timing diagrams that have imposed timing constraints, as shown in the description of memory read-write cycles in commercial memory and microprocessor databooks. Interface synthesis consists of mapping the timing graph into a minimum number of latches and flip-flops and reducing the logic for setting and resetting them. Depending on the protocol supported by the standard components, the interface logic may be synchronous or asynchronous.

Memory synthesis generates a memory structure for given memory requirements such as the number of words, number of bits per word, number of ports, port types (e.g., read, write, or read/write), access rates, access protocol, and timing constraints. Synthesizing memories may be complex for certain requirements. For example, designing a four-port memory using only single-port memory chips may be simple if the data can be partitioned into four groups, with each group accessed only over one port. However, if the same data is accessed over two different ports, or two ports access the data in the same single port memory chip, then conflict-resolution logic needs to be added, increasing the memory's access time.

9.4.4 Physical design

After the above synthesis steps have been performed, the hardware part of the design is described as a net-list of logic and RT-level components. Numerous technologies, each with its own design methodology, are available for physical implementation of such a net-list. For example, the net-list can be implemented as a custom layout. Design issues for such an implementation include placement and orientation of transistors, transistor sizing, and routing. Regular structures such as an 8-bit ALU may be implemented using module generators, which exploit the regularity to achieve very compact layouts. If standard cells are used instead of custom layout, cell placement and routing are the key issues. Module generators can again be used.

One popular technology uses field-programmable gate arrays which consist of hundreds of interleaved blocks of routing switches and combinational/sequential logic [Xil89]. Logic blocks have n inputs and m outputs where n and m are small integers between 2 and 10. The blocks and switches can be programmed by a designer in the field, eliminating the slow turnaround time of standard cell and custom approaches. The design issues include decomposition of logic expressions into n-input expressions, and assignment of the n-input expressions to logic blocks in such a way that the gate arrays are routable.

9.4.5 Software synthesis

An executable specification usually possesses special features not found in traditional programming languages such as the C language. A typical compiler cannot usually compile these features. We define *software synthesis* as the task of converting a complex executable specification into a traditional software program that can be compiled by traditional compilers.

One such common feature of executable specifications is the definition of concurrent tasks. If two concurrent tasks are mapped to a single processor, then the tasks must be scheduled to execute sequentially. Such scheduling is often called multiprogramming [HB85]. In such scheduling, it is important to ensure that every task has a chance to execute, or in other words, that no task is "starved." Another issue is minimizing the amount of "busy-waiting": the time the processor spends waiting for some external event. A third issue is ensuring that timing constraints for each task are satisfied. For example, data may be arriving at a specific rate and must be captured and processed by a given task, or a task may have to output data at a certain rate to ensure satisfactory system performance. Such tasks must be guaranteed a minimal rate of execution.

Several techniques exist for performing such scheduling [HB85, GD93, AS83]. One uses a global task scheduler, which activates each task (or portion thereof) by calling each as a subroutine. This technique may require overhead to maintain the state of each task as it switches from one to the other. Another technique reduces this overhead by maintaining data locally within each task, and modifying each task to relinquish control of the processor whenever it must wait for an event or an interrupt occurs. Choosing a technique usually involves a tradeoff between performance and program size.

At times we may wish to map a set of concurrent tasks to multiple processors. In such cases, several issues related to multiprocessing must be dealt with [HB85].

Another feature common in specifications that must be converted to a compilable form is the use of special time-related statements, such as the *wait* statement in VHDL or the concurrent statements in HardwareC. Such statements can usually be transformed into an equivalent set of traditional program statements, often with the addition of some extra variables, as discussed in Chapter 5.

9.4.6 System database

Traditionally, synthesis systems start as a loose collection of stand-alone design tools. Such systems suffer from mismatch as in data representations and in input and output formats. The second generation of such a synthesis system can be developed as a tightly or loosely integrated system. A tightly integrated system uses a common data representation, with all tools using the same procedures to access it. Such a system is very efficient but extremely rigid, since a change in format influences all the tools. A loosely integrated system separates design data from the tools. The data is stored in a database and each tool accesses only the information that it needs, using its own representation to process the retrieved information [CT89, LGP+91, LND+91, RG91].

Databases can also support many different versions of the same design during design exploration. Such support relieves the designer from the chore of managing the design revisions and configurations. With a system database, each version of the system is stored along with a list of differences from previous versions. Any version can be retrieved at any time, to allow backtracking. Differences among versions can be output to serve as documentation of design decisions. Various quality metrics of alternative designs can be output in order to assist with tradeoff decisions between the designs. Different portions of a design can be modified by different persons simultaneously, with the database managing the data consistency.

9.5 Conceptualization environment for system design

The complete automation of the design process from a specification is an important, although not immediately practical goal. Even if all system and chip-level tools were available today, designers would have to gain familiarity and confidence in using them. It will also take time for synthesis tools to achieve uniform quality over different design styles. Therefore, it is necessary to provide an environment in which designers can control the design decisions and manually override automatic synthesis and optimizations. Even when synthesis algorithms become perfect, designers should still be allowed to make high-level decisions

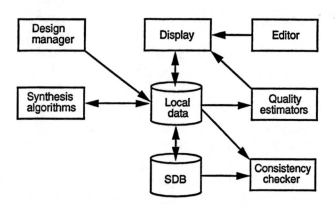

Figure 9.12: A conceptualization environment for system design.

such as selection of system components, implementation styles, and constraints. Thus, a conceptualization environment must allow control of design decisions and design strategy through every stage of the design process, which in turn requires the environment to provide rapid feedback of usable quality metrics to every level of abstraction and allow the designer to select components, topologies, implementation styles, optimization goals, cost functions, design constraints, technology mappings, and partitions [BE89, CPTR89, YH90, HG91]. The conceptualization environment works in tandem with system and component databases. These databases store all versions of the design data over long periods of time, whereas the conceptualization environment accesses only small parts of the data for modification or refinement over short periods of time. The conceptualization environment can be thought of as short-time storage (scratch pad) used by designers during design refinement. The conceptualization environment (Figure 9.12) consists of several parts: design manager, quality estimators, synthesis algorithms, design-consistency checkers, displays and editors.

The *Design manager* maintains local design data, such as the current allocation of components and partition of objects. The *Quality estimators* provide rapid feedback of design metrics, as described in Chapter 7. *Synthesis algorithms* make the actual changes to the design. They can be applied to the total design or just to some of its parts. A designer should be able to divide synthesis into small steps and apply algorithms for each step separately. We may think of synthesis tools as providing hints to the designer during manual design. For example, in the partitioning process, a designer may assign behaviors to system components one at a time; the partitioning algorithm may suggest the best mapping for each behavior, which a designer may accept or reject. The *Design consistency checker* ensures that manual design changes do not alter the desired system functionality. For example, when a designer takes two concurrent behaviors and sequentializes them in order to map them to a sequential processor, the consistency checker must ensure that the sequentialized behaviors generate the same result as the original concurrent ones.

The *Displays and editors* allow design data and constraints to be viewed and edited. These two items comprise what is usually referred to as the *user interface*, or UI. The UI is a crucial part of the environment, because a designer can use the tool effectively only with an understandable and useful display and editor of data. Without a good UI, even the best synthesis algorithms are of no use, since the designer cannot decide when to apply those algorithms. For the system-design tasks we have described, a good UI must summarize the overall design status in a form that is quickly comprehensible, that can serve as documentation, and that highlights portions of the design that need special attention (such as constraint violations). The overall design status consists of an executable specification, the current allocation of components and their connectivity, the current mapping of functional objects onto those components, and estimations and constraints for the selected quality metrics.

The designer can explore many avenues given the overall design status. She may examine details concerning the manner in which the various estimations were made. If it appears that an estimator is making an assumption she does not agree with, she may override that estimation. She may modify constraints. She may modify the display of the design status to concentrate on a portion of the design, or on certain metrics. She may manually perform some design tasks such as allocation or partitioning. She may request hints as to the best possible single object placement, scheduling, binding, etc.

A possible example of a system-design tool's user interface is shown in Figure 9.13. The information displayed corresponds with the partition shown in the block diagram of Figure 9.3. The *Mappings* column shows the mapping of functional objects to allocated system components. For example, the *ASIC1* component contains the behaviors *StoreAudio* and

Mappings	Comp. type	Cost	Execution time	Area	Pins	Instr
System		105/100*				
ASIC1	X100	30		16k/20k	46/60	
StoreAudio			100/110			
GenerateAudio			100/110			
ASIC2	X100	30		18k/20k	48/60	
StoreGenerateVideo			100/110			
StoreAVCmd			100/110			
Memory1	V1000	10				
audio_array1						
audio_array2						
Memory2	V1000	10				
video_array						
Processor1	Y900	25				6k/5k*
ProcessRemoteButtons						
ProcessMiscCmds						

Cost: 5.43 | View options | | Partition/Allocate | | Refine |

Figure 9.13: System-synthesis tool user interface

GenerateAudio. The *Component type* column indicates the type of each system component, in other words, the library item which the system component represents; all the information about this component can be found in the component library under this type. For example, the system component *Processor* is bound to a processor of type *Y900*. The remaining columns represent selected quality metrics. Each entry in a column provides estimated and required values for the corresponding quality metric. The *Cost* column denotes the monetary cost of each allocated component. The *Execution time* column shows the execution-time estimation. The *Area* and *Pins* columns provide the area and number of pins for each ASIC component. The *Instr* column gives the estimated number of machine instructions for the processor. Constraint violations are flagged by an asterisk. The buses and channels have been omitted from the figure in the interest of clarity. Other quality metrics (see Chapter 7) can be added to the display.

Quality metric	Estimate/Constraint	Violation?
$(System)	105/100	
Execution–time(StoreAudio)	100/110	
Execution–time(GenerateAudio)	100/110	
Execution–time(StoreGenerateVideo)	100/110	
Execution–time(StoreAVCmd)	100/110	
Area(ASIC1)	16000/20000	
Area(ASIC2)	18000/20000	
Pins(ASIC1)	56/60	
Pins(ASIC2)	58/60	
Instr(Processor1)	6000/5000	
		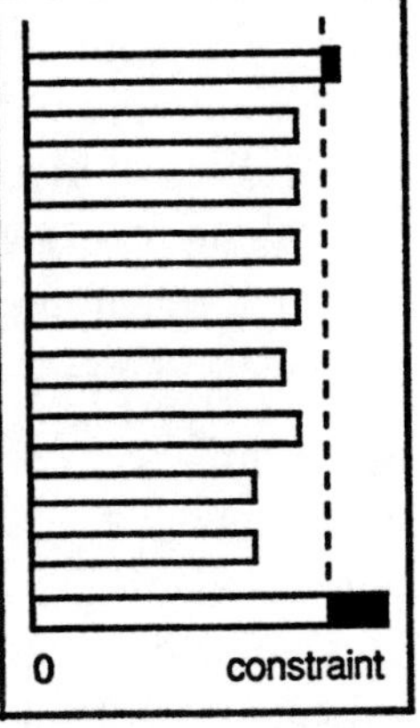 0 constraint

Figure 9.14: An optional view showing only estimates vs. constraints.

To improve designer comprehension, alternative views of the design can be requested. Some such views may involve selecting only some quality metrics for display, displaying the details of the cost function expression, or seeing detailed information about the way a particular quality metric value is obtained. Any view can be saved to a file to serve as design documentation. For example, Figure 9.14 illustrates a view that graphically displays estimates and constraints for all constrained quality metrics from Figure 9.13. The designer may use this information to determine which aspect of the design to focus on next. For example, the most significant violation is that of the number of program instructions for the processor. Noting that the area for both ASICs is nearly at capacity, the designer may choose to use a larger program memory rather than move a behavior from the processor to an ASIC.

There are also buttons in Figure 9.13 to activate a partitioning and allocation tool or a refinement tool. The partitioning and allocation tool allows browsing and selection of library components, allocation of those components, application of automated partitioners, and manual movement of a functional object from one component to another. It may also provide hints such as a list of closeness values of every functional object to a selected object, based on any of the various closeness criteria discussed in Chapter 6. The refinement tool allows communication protocols and arbitration schemes to be selected.

The conceptualization environment allows many different methodologies to be used. A designer should be able to iterate through the same task as many times as necessary to satisfy the requirements. It is reasonable to expect that a designer will make most of the high-level decisions but manually synthesize only a small portion of the design. The rest of the design will be generated by automatic synthesis tools that are not expected to affect drastically high-level decisions made by the designer.

In summary, a conceptualization environment allows designers to perform manually the same tasks that all designers do when working at higher levels of abstraction. However, it also allows designers to complete those tasks partially with automatic synthesis tools. As algorithms improve, more of the design work will be shifted to automation.

9.6   Conclusion and future directions

In this chapter, we introduced a three-step design methodology consisting of specification capture, system design, and component implementation. The first two steps are the focus areas of CAD research as well as of this book. We defined the major tasks in the system design step, and discussed design and tool issues at the system, chip, logic, and physical levels. We also briefly described a support environment for system design consisting of a system database and a conceptualization environment for interactive and automated synthesis. Areas for future research include the following:

(a) Estimation methods must be developed for new hardware technologies, implementation styles, and architectures. New estimation algorithms must be developed for predicting the results of hardware and software optimization techniques.

(b) Formal verification techniques can be incorporated to improve the design correctness and to reduce the tremendous amount of time currently spent simulating each phase of the design.

(c) Design for testability must be introduced early in the design process, and testability metrics evaluated at each design phase.

(d) Frameworks and databases must be developed to manage system-level tools and data.

(e) System-level transformations must be researched and added to the current design tasks.

(f) Quality metrics must be fed back from design implementations to higher levels of the design process to support design iteration.

(g) Techniques for interactive synthesis, which allows manual control of the synthesis process, can be developed further.

(h) The automation of design exploration can be greatly aided by the definition of design-quality metrics and an understanding of the influence of styles, architecture topologies and design methodology on the design quality. Thus, work on the comparative analysis of design quality at all levels of design would be very useful.

In summary, serious work is needed not just in algorithm development, but also in the development of the infrastructure for system and ASIC synthesis. We hope that this book will make an initial step in that direction.

9.7 Exercises

1. Describe the limitations of the design methodology that uses a natural language for functionality specification. List the advantages and disadvantages of using an executable specification language and its effects on methodology.

2. Define an ordering of system-design tasks in Figure 9.6 that produces a system with a minimum number of wires between components.

3. Define a design process for synthesizing systems from specifications in which only a processor chip and a memory chip are used as components.

4. Develop an algorithm for selecting a minimal-cost component set from a functional description, given fixed total execution time of the functional specification.

5. Extend the algorithm developed in Problem 5 to generate shape functions which allocate minimal-cost component sets for a range of performance constraints.

6. List three cost functions for partitioning channels into buses.

7. Develop an algorithm to schedule concurrent behaviors on two processors.

8. *Develop a technique for sequentializing concurrent behaviors under timing constraints.

9. *Develop requirements for the transformation tool of Figure 9.8.

10. *List all the design phases during system design that require designer interaction. Define the metrics to be displayed to designers and design parameters to be entered by designers.

11. *Develop a scheme for consistency checking in the system database shown in Figure 9.7.

12. *Define several useful system-level transformations other than those listed in the chapter.

13. *Define the information model for the component database in Figure 9.7. Define the type of information the database supplies in different design process phases and the type of queries the database answers.

14. *Describe and illustrate a graphical display for interactive partitioning, as opposed to the textual display shown in Figure 9.13. How is the current partition displayed? How are estimations and constraints shown? How does the designer allocate components or move objects?

15. **Devise a technique for using real implementation metrics in system or ASIC synthesis, in order to support design iteration between synthesis and implementation.

16. **Develop a method for incorporating detailed timing information into system synthesis.

Appendix A

Answering machine in English

This section contains an English description of the functionality for the telephone answering-machine controller introduced in Chapter 4. The SpecCharts specification of the controller was derived directly from this English description. We have numbered each sentence in the description for ease of reference. The controller's environment and interface were already introduced in Section 4.2 and in Figure 4.1.

Responding to external buttons and switches

1. When the "power" switch is in the "off" position, the machine ignores the phone line and all buttons.

2. When "on", the display shows the current number of messages, initially 0.

3. Pressing the "play-messages" button will play all messages.

4. Regular tape-player buttons also exist: play, forward, rewind, and stop; pressing any of these will make the current number of messages zero.

5. Pressing the "record-announcement" button causes a beep to sound, followed by another beep several seconds later.

6. Anything spoken into the microphone between these two beeps becomes the prerecorded announcement.

7. The announcement can be heard by pressing the "play-announceme⟩ button.

8. Pressing and holding the "memo" button allows one to record a⟩ message by speaking into the external microphone.

9. The message is terminated when the button is released.

10. The "memo" function is thus useful for leaving messages to other household members.

Responding to the phone line

A. Monitoring the line for rings

11. The "on/off" button is used to toggle the machine state from "on" to "off", and vice-versa. (When the machine is "off", the controller should not respond to calls, whereas when "power" is "off", the controller should not respond to *any* inputs).

12. When "on", the light-emitting diode below the number of messages display is illuminated.

13. When "on", the machine usually answers after *four* rings.

14. However, if "tollsaver" is "on" and there is at least one message recorded, the machine answers after *two* rings.

15. Tollsaver allows the machine owner to determine over the phone whether messages have been recorded.

16. If the phone rings three times, then there are no messages and the owner can hang up, thus avoiding any long-distance charges.

17. Sometimes the owner will forget to turn on the machine before leaving the household.

18. Therefore, even when "off" the machine answers after *fifteen* rings.

19. The owner can then remotely turn the machine on, as described below.

B. Normal answering activity

20. Once the machine has answered the phone, it plays the announcement.

21. When the announcement is complete, a beep is produced and the message on the phone line is recorded until a hangup is detected, or until a maximum message time expires.

22. The machine hangs up and again monitors for rings.

23. If a hangup is detected while playing the announcement, the machine immediately hangs up, and does not proceed to record a message.

24. If button-tone 1 is detected either while playing the announcement or while recording a message, the machine immediately enters remote-operation mode.

C. Remote-operation answering activity

25. The first step in the remote-operation mode is to check a user-identification number.

26. The next four button-tone numbers that are pushed are compared to four numbers stored internally.

27. If they do not match, the machine hangs up the phone.

28. If they do match, the machine enters the *basic-commands mode*, in which it can be instructed to perform any of several basic commands.

29. Button-tone 2 plays all messages.

30. Button-tones 3 through 6 correspond to standard tape-player buttons play, forward, rewind, and stop.

31. Button-tone 7 causes the number of messages to be indicated by a number of beeps.

32. Button-tone 8 instructs the machine to leave the *basic-commands mode* and enter the *miscellaneous-commands mode.*

33. In this mode, button-tone 3 "erases" all messages, i.e., rewinds to the beginning of the tape, sets the message counter to zero.

34. Button-tone 4 plays the announcement.

35. Button-tone 5 is identical to pressing the "record-announcement" button.

36. Button-tone 6 causes the machine-on state to toggle upon hangup from "off" to "on" or vice-versa.

37. Button-tone 2 returns the machine to the basic-commands mode.

38. If a hangup occurs in either of these command modes, the tape is reset to the end of the last message, i.e., any existing messages are saved.

39. This reset also occurs if button-tone 9 is pressed in basic command mode.

40. The machine hangs up after this reset, or if a hangup occurs while checking the user-identification number.

Miscellaneous requirements

41. If "on/off" is pressed after the machine has answered, any current activity is terminated and the machine monitors the phone line, as above.

42. Such functionality is useful for screening calls, since one can listen to a message and then pick up the phone and press "on/off" to turn the machine "off" and begin speaking with the caller.

43. Machine buttons have priority over the machine answering the phone; hence, pressing any external button will also terminate any current activity.

Appendix B

Answering machine in SpecCharts

```
--*************************************************
--Answering machine controller
--*************************************************

entity ansE is
  port (
    --Interface to line circuitry
    hangup_p          :  in  bit; --hangup detected
    offhook_p         :  out bit; --answers
    produce_beep_p    :  out bit; --produces a beep
    ring_p            :  in  bit; --ring detected
    tone_p            :  in  bit_vector (3 downto 0); --binary tone
    --Interface to display
    num_msgs_p        :  out integer range 0 to 31; --msgs display
    on_light_p        :  out bit; --turns on led
    --Touch--sensitive buttons
    but_fwd_p         :  in  bit; --forward tape
    but_hear_ann_p    :  in  bit; --play pre--recorded announcement
    but_on_off_p      :  in  bit; --toggle machine--on state
    but_memo_p        :  in  bit; --record message via microphone
    but_play_msgs_p   :  in  bit; --play all messages
    but_play_p        :  in  bit; --play tape from curr position
    but_rec_ann_p     :  in  bit; --record a new announcement
    but_rew_p         :  in  bit; --rewind tape
```

```
      but_stop_p        :  in  bit; --stop tape
      --Switches
      power_p           :  in  bit; --power switch
      tollsaver_p       :  in  bit; --answer after 2 rings if msg
      --Interface to announcement player
      ann_done_p        :  in  bit; --end of announcement reached
      ann_play_p        :  out bit; --plays announcement
      ann_rec_p         :  out bit; --records announcement
      --Interface to tape player
      tape_fwd_p        :  out bit; --forwards tape
      tape_play_p       :  out bit; --plays tape
      tape_rew_p        :  out bit; --rewinds tape
      tape_rec_p        :  out bit; --records on tape
      tape_count_p      :  in  integer --tape position, start is 0
   );
end;

architecture ansA of ansE is
begin

behavior ans type concurrent substates is

   --Global declarations
   type four_buttons_type is array (1 to 4) of bit_vector(3 downto 0
   signal user_code        :  four_buttons_type;      --user id num
   signal machine_on       :  bit;  --current state of machine
   signal machine_on_toggle :  bit;  --toggle on hangup
   signal num_msgs         :  integer range 0 to 31; --num of mess
   signal any_button_pushed :  bit;  --1 if machine button pushed

begin

   Main :  ;
   MachineOnToggler :   ;
   ConcAsgns1 :   ;
   ConcAsgns2 :   ;


   --*****************************************
   behavior Main type sequential substates is
   --*****************************************
   --main control behavior of the answering machine controller
```

```
--Terminates any tape player, announcement player, or beep
--activity.    Useful after exceptions such as hangup.
--
procedure TerminateAnyActivity is
begin
   produce_beep_p  <= '0';
   ann_rec_p       <= '0';
   ann_play_p      <= '0';
   tape_fwd_p      <= '0';
   tape_play_p     <= '0';
   tape_rew_p      <= '0';
   tape_rec_p      <= '0';
end;


--Produces a beep with the indicated length
--
procedure Beep (len :  in time) is
begin
   produce_beep_p <= '1';
   wait for len;
   produce_beep_p <= '0';
end;

begin
   SystemOff :  (TI,  power_p = '1', SystemOn);
   SystemOn  :  (TI,  power_p = '0', SystemOff);

   behavior SystemOff type code is
   begin
      TerminateAnyActivity;
      on_light_p <= '0'; --turn off led
   end SystemOff;

   behavior SystemOn type sequential substates is

      signal terminal_tape_count:  integer; --end of last message
      signal toggle_on_hangup :  bit; --toggle machine--on state

      --Plays all messages by saving tape count of end of last
      --message, rewinding to start of tape, and playing until
      --end tape count.
      procedure PlayAllMsgs
              (signal terminal_tape_count :  inout integer ;
```

```
            signal tape_count :  in integer ;
            signal tape_rew :  out bit ;
            signal tape_play :  out bit ) is
begin
   --Save tape count of end of last message
   terminal_tape_count <=  tape_count_p;
   --Rewind to start of tape
   tape_rew <=  '1';
   if not (tape_count = 0)  then
      wait until tape_count = 0;
   end if;
   tape_rew <=  '0';
   --Play until end of last message
   tape_play <=  '1';
   if (tape_count < terminal_tape_count) then
      wait until tape_count = terminal_tape_count;
   end if;
   tape_play <=  '0';
   --Beep to indicate that all messages have been played
   Beep(1 s);
end; --PlayAllMsgs


begin

   InitializeSystem :
      (TOC, true, RespondToLine);
   RespondToLine :
      (TI, any_button_pushed = '1'
      and any_button_pushed'event,
      RespondToMachineButton);
   RespondToMachineButton :
      (TOC, true, RespondToLine),
      (TI, any_button_pushed = '1'
      and any_button_pushed'event,
      RespondToMachineButton);


   --Rewinds to beginning of tape, sets message number to 0
   --
   behavior InitializeSystem type code is
   begin
      num_msgs <=  0;
      tape_rew_p <=  '1';
```

```
    if (tape_count_p /= 0) then
        wait until tape_count_p = 0;
    end if;
    tape_rew_p <=  '0';
    toggle_on_hangup <=  '0';
end InitializeSystem;
```

--Monitor and answer line as opposed to handling
--machine buttons
--
behavior RespondToLine type sequential substates is
begin

```
    Monitor :
        (TOC, true, Answer),
        (TI, hangup_p = '1' and hangup_p'event, Monitor);
    Answer :
        (TOC, true, Monitor),
        (TI, machine_on = '0' and machine_on'event, Monitor);
```

--Monitors line for required number of rings
--If the machine is off, it answers after 15 rings
--(just in case the owner forgot to turn the machine
--on before leaving home).
--If the machine is on, it answers after 4 rings,
--UNLESS tollsaver is on and there is a message, in
--which case it answers after 2 rings.
--
behavior Monitor type code is

```
    variable rings_to_wait:  integer range 1 to 20;
    variable i:  integer range 0 to 20;

    --Computes the number of rings to wait for
    function DetermineRingsToWait return integer is
    begin
        if ((num_msgs > 0) and (tollsaver_p = '1') and
            (machine_on = '1')) then
            return(2);
        elsif (machine_on = '1') then
            return(4);
        else
```

```
                        return(15);
                    end if;
                end;

            begin
                TerminateAnyActivity;
                --Turn on led if machine is on
                if (machine_on='1') then
                    on_light_p <= '1';
                else
                    on_light_p <= '0';
                end if;

                rings_to_wait := DetermineRingsToWait;
                i := 0;
                --Loop until required rings have been detected
                while (i < rings_to_wait) loop
                    wait on tollsaver_p,machine_on,ring_p;
                    if ring_p = '1' and ring_p'event then
                        i := i + 1;
                    end if;
                    --If machine_on or tollsaver has changed, the
                    --number of rings to wait may also change,
                    --so let's recompute
                    if (machine_on'event or tollsaver_p'event) then
                        rings_to_wait := DetermineRingsToWait;
                    end if;
                end loop ;
                offhook_p <=  '1'; --answer the line
            end Monitor;

            --Answers the line.
            --Normal sequence:  PlayAnnouncement, RecordMsg, Hangup
            --If a hangup is detected while playing or recording,
            --machine hangs up.
            --If tone 1 is detected, enters remote operation mode.
            --
            behavior Answer type sequential substates is
            begin

                PlayAnnouncement :
                    (TI, tone_p = "0001", RemoteOperation),
                    (TI, hangup_p = '1' and hangup_p'event, HANGUP),
```

```
          (TOC, true, RecordMsg);
RecordMsg :
          (TI, tone_p = "0001", RemoteOperation),
          (TOC, true, Hangup);
Hangup :
          (TOC, true, stop);
RemoteOperation :
          (TOC, true, HANGUP);
```

```
--Plays announcement until end of announcement
--
behavior PlayAnnouncement type code is
begin
    ann_play_p <=  '1';
    wait until ann_done_p = '1';
    ann_play_p <=  '0';
end PlayAnnouncement;
```

```
--Produces a beep, then records line until hangup or
--until a maximum time is reached.
--Places a beep at the end of the recorded message.
--
behavior RecordMsg type code is
begin
    Beep(1 s);
    tape_rec_p <=  '1';
    if not (hangup_p = '1')  then
        wait until hangup_p = '1' for 1000 s;
        Beep(1 s);
        num_msgs <=  num_msgs + 1;
    end if;
    tape_rec_p <=  '0';
end RecordMsg;
```

```
--Hangs up.   Toggles machine--on state if necessary
--
behavior Hangup type code is
begin
    offhook_p <=  '0';
    ann_play_p <=  '0';
    if (toggle_on_hangup = '1') then
        toggle_on_hangup <=  '0';
        machine_on_toggle <=  '1';
```

```
            wait for 1 s;
            machine_on_toggle <=  '0';
        end if;
end Hangup;


--Processes remote commands given by machine owner
--correct user identification number is entered
--
behavior RemoteOperation type sequential substates
    signal code_ok :  bit; --true if correct id
begin

    CheckUserId :
        (TOC, code_ok = '1', RespondToCmds),
        (TOC, code_ok = '0', stop),
        (TI, hangup_p = '1', stop);
    RespondToCmds :
        (TOC, true, stop);


--Checks next four button--tones against user i
--sets code_ok to true if all four match
behavior CheckUserId type code is
    variable entered_code:  four_buttons_type;
    variable i:  integer range 1 to 5;
begin
    TerminateAnyActivity;
    code_ok <= '1';
    i := 1;
    while i <= 4 loop
        wait until tone_p /= "1111" and tone_p'even
        if (tone_p /= user_code(i)) then  --wrong
            code_ok <= '0';
        end if;
        i := i + 1;
    end loop ;
end CheckUserId;


--Processes user commands.   When done with
--commands, resets tape to end of last message,
--unless of course the user has erased all
--messages.   HearMsgsCmds is the initial mode
--which allows commands related simply to hearin
--messages.   If tone="0010" is detected, enter
```

```
--MiscCmds, in which miscellaneous, more advanced
--commands related to machine maintenance
--can be applied.
--
behavior RespondToCmds type sequential substates
is begin

   HearMsgsCmds :
      (TOC, true, MiscCmds),
      (TI, hangup_p = '1', ResetTape);
   MiscCmds :
      (TOC, tone_p = "0010", HearMsgsCmds),
      (TOC, other, ResetTape),
      (TI, hangup_p = '1', ResetTape);
   ResetTape :
      (TOC, true, stop);

   --Normal command processing mode.    All comman
   --related to hearing messages can be applied.
   --
   behavior HearMsgsCmds type code is
      variable i :  integer;
   begin

      if (tone_p = "1111") then
         wait until tone_p /= "1111";
      end if;

      tape_play_p <=  '0';
      tape_fwd_p <=  '0';
      tape_rew_p <=  '0';
      --"1000" enters MiscCmds
      if (tone_p /= "1000") then
         case (tone_p) is
            when "0010" => --play all messages
               PlayAllMsgs(terminal_tape_count,
                           tape_count_p,
                           tape_rew_p,tape_play_p);
            when "0011" => --play tape
               tape_play_p <=  '1';
            when "0100" => --forward tape
               tape_fwd_p <=  '1';
            when "0101" => --rewind tape to start
```

```
                    tape_rew_p <=  '1';
                    if (tape_count_p /= 0) then
                        wait until tape_count_p = 0;
                    end if;
                    tape_rew_p <=  '0';
                when "0110" => --stop tape
                    tape_play_p <=  '0';
                    tape_fwd_p <=  '0';
                    tape_rew_p <=  '0';
                when "0111" => --beep number messag
                    wait for 5 s;
                    i := 0;
                    --one beep / msg
                    while (i < num_msgs) loop
                        Beep(1 s);
                        wait for 1 s;
                        i := i + 1;
                    end loop ;
                when others =>
            end case;
        end if;
end HearMsgsCmds;


--In this mode the user can perform less
--common commands related to machine
--maintenance.
--
behavior MiscCmds type code is
begin
    --Indicate new mode with a beep
    Beep(1 s);
    loop
        wait until tone_p /= "1111"
                    and tone_p'event;
        case (tone_p) is
            when "0010" => --exit MiscCmds mode
                exit; --exit loop
            when "0011" => --rewind tape
                tape_rew_p <=  '1';
                if not (tape_count_p = 0)  then
                    wait until tape_count_p = 0;
                end if;
```

```
                        tape_rew_p <=  '0';
                        terminal_tape_count <=  0;
                    when "0100" => --hear announcement
                        ann_play_p <=  '1';
                        wait until ann_done_p = '1';
                        ann_play_p <=  '0';
                    when "0101" => --record announcement
                        --preparation time
                        wait for 50 s;
                        --beep indicates start
                        Beep(1 s);
                        wait for 0 s;
                        --record for full length
                        ann_rec_p <=  '1';
                        wait until ann_done_p = '1';
                        ann_rec_p <=  '0';
                        --beep indicates end
                        Beep(1 s);
                    when "0110" => --toggle mach--on state
                        toggle_on_hangup <=  '1';
                    when others =>
                end case;
            end loop;
        end MiscCmds;


    --Reset tape to end of last message.
    --Rewinds if past end, forwards if before end.
    behavior ResetTape type code is
        variable tape_count:  integer;
    begin
        if (tape_count_p > terminal_tape_count) then
            tape_rew_p <=  '1';
            wait until
                (tape_count_p<=terminal_tape_count);
            tape_rew_p <=  '0';
        elsif (tape_count_p<terminal_tape_count) then
            tape_fwd_p <=  '1';
            wait until
                (tape_count_p>=terminal_tape_count);
            tape_fwd_p <=  '0';
        end if;
    end ResetTape;
end RespondToCmds;
```

```
        end RemoteOperation;
      end Answer;
  end RespondToLine;

--Processes command indicated by a button being pressed
--on the machine.
behavior RespondToMachineButton type code is

    procedure HandlePlayPushed is
    begin
       tape_play_p <=  '1';
       num_msgs <=  0;
    end ;

    procedure HandleFwdPushed is
    begin
       tape_fwd_p <=  '1';
       num_msgs <=  0;
    end ;

    procedure HandleRewPushed is
    begin
       num_msgs <=  0;
       tape_rew_p <=  '1';
       if (tape_count_p /= 0) then
          wait until tape_count_p = 0;
       end if;
       tape_rew_p <=  '0';
    end ;

    procedure HandleMemoPushed is --record message via mic.
    begin
       Beep(1 s);
       tape_rec_p <=  '1';
       wait until but_memo_p = '0' for 1000 s;
       Beep(1 s);
       num_msgs <=  num_msgs + 1;
       tape_rec_p <=  '0';
    end ;

    procedure HandleStopPushed is
    begin
       num_msgs <=  0;
```

```
        tape_play_p <=  '0';
        tape_fwd_p <=  '0';
        tape_rew_p <=  '0';
        tape_rec_p <=  '0';
    end ;

    procedure HandleHearAnnPushed is --play announcement
    begin
        ann_play_p <=  '1';
        wait until ann_done_p = '1';
        ann_play_p <=  '0';
    end ;

    procedure HandleRecAnnPushed is --record announcement
    begin
        wait for 50 s;
        Beep(1 s);
        wait for 0 s;
        ann_rec_p <=  '1';
        wait until ann_done_p = '1';
        ann_rec_p <=  '0';
        Beep(1 s);
    end ;

    procedure HandlePlayMsgsPushed is --play all msgs
    begin
        terminal_tape_count <=  tape_count_p;
        tape_rew_p <=  '1';
        if not (tape_count_p = 0)  then
           wait until tape_count_p = 0;
        end if;
        tape_rew_p <=  '0';
        tape_play_p <=  '1';
        if (tape_count_p < terminal_tape_count) then
           wait until tape_count_p = terminal_tape_count;
        end if;
        tape_play_p <=  '0';
    end ;

begin --RespondToMachineButton

    if (but_play_p='1') then
       HandlePlayPushed;
```

```
                    elsif (but_fwd_p='1') then
                       HandleFwdPushed;
                    elsif (but_rew_p='1') then
                       HandleRewPushed;
                    elsif (but_memo_p='1') then
                       HandleMemoPushed;
                    elsif (but_stop_p='1') then
                       HandleStopPushed;
                    elsif (but_hear_ann_p='1') then
                       HandleHearAnnPushed;
                    elsif (but_rec_ann_p='1') then
                       HandleRecAnnPushed;
                    elsif (but_play_msgs_p='1') then
                       HandlePlayMsgsPushed;
                    end if;

           end RespondToMachineButton;
      end SystemOn;

end Main;

behavior MachineOnToggler type code is
begin
   machine_on <=  '0';
   loop
      wait until but_on_off_p = '1' or machine_on_toggle = '1';
      if machine_on = '0' then
         machine_on <=  '1';
      else
         machine_on <=  '0';
      end if;
   end loop ;
end MachineOnToggler;

--Sets any_button_pushed to 1 if any machine button is pushed.
--
behavior ConcAsgns1 type code is
begin
   loop
      wait on but_play_p,but_fwd_p,but_rew_p,but_memo_p,but_stop_p
            but_hear_ann_p,but_rec_ann_p,but_play_msgs_p;
      if (but_play_p = '1' and but_play_p'event) or
         (but_fwd_p = '1' and but_fwd_p'event) or
```

```
            (but_rew_p = '1' and but_rew_p'event) or
            (but_memo_p = '1' and but_memo_p'event) or
            (but_stop_p = '1' and but_stop_p'event) or
            (but_hear_ann_p = '1' and but_hear_ann_p'event) or
            (but_rec_ann_p = '1' and but_rec_ann_p'event) or
            (but_play_msgs_p = '1' and but_play_msgs_p'event) then
            any_button_pushed <= '1';
        else
            any_button_pushed <= '0';
        end if;
    end loop ;
end ConcAsgns1;


--Updates num_msgs_p port with current value of internal signal
--num_msgs so that numerical display shows number of messages.
--
behavior ConcAsgns2 type code is
begin
    loop
        wait on num_msgs;
        if (num_msgs'event) then
            num_msgs_p <= num_msgs;
        end if;
    end loop ;
end ConcAsgns2;


end ans;
end ansA;
```

Bibliography

[AB91]   T. Amon and G. Borriello. "Sizing synchronization queues:
           A case study in higher level synthesis". In *Proceedings of
           the Design Automation Conference*, 1991.

[Ake91]   J. Akella. *Input/Output Performance Modeling and In-
           terface Synthesis in Concurrently Communicating Systems*.
           PhD thesis, Carnegie Mellon Unversity., November 1991.

[AM91]   J. Akella and K. McMillan. "Synthesizing converters be-
           tween finite state protocols". In *Proceedings of the Inter-
           national Conference on Computer Design*, 1991.

[AS83]   G.R. Andrews and F. Schneider. "Concepts and notations
           for concurrent programming". *ACM Computing Surveys*,
           15(1): 3–44, March 1983.

[ASU88]   A. Aho, R. Sethi, and J.D. Ullman. *Compilers: Principles,
           Techniques, and Tools*. Addison Wesley, 1988.

[Aul91]   R.J. Auletta. "CSP specified digital repeater and transla-
           tion to synchronous logic". Technical Report, Dept. ECE,
           George Mason University, 1991.

[AWC90]   A. Arsenault, J.J. Wong, and M. Cohen. "VHDL transition
           from system to detailed design". In *VHDL Users' Group*,
           April 1990.

[Bar81]   M.R. Barbacci. "Instruction set processor specifications
           (ISPS): The notation and its applications". In *IEEE Trans-
           actions on Computers*, January, 1981.

425

[BCD⁺88]   R.K. Brayton, R. Camposano, G. DeMicheli, R.H. Otten, and J.T.J. van Eijndhoven. "The Yorktown silicon compiler system". in D.D. Gajski, Editor, *Silicon Compilation*, Addison-Wesley, 1988.

[BE89]   O.A. Buset and M.I. Elmasry. "ACE: A hierarchical graphical interface for architectural synthesis". In *Proceedings of the Design Automation Conference*, pages 537–542, 1989.

[Ber91]   G. Berry. "A hardware implementation of pure Esterel". Digital Equipment Paris Research Laboratory, July, 1991.

[BHS91]   F. Belina, D. Hogrefe, and A. Sarma. *SDL with Applications from Protocol Specifications*. Prentice Hall, 1991.

[BK87]   G. Borriello and R.H. Katz. "Synthesis and optimization of interface transducer logic". In *Proceedings of the International Conference on Computer-Aided Design*, 1987.

[BM89]   M. Balakrishnan and P. Marwedel. "Integrated scheduling and binding: A synthesis approach for design space exploration". In *Proceedings of the Design Automation Conference*, 1989.

[Boo91]   G. Booch. *Object-oriented Design with Applications*. Benjamin/Cummings, Redwood City, California, 1991.

[Bor88]   G. Borriello. *A New Interface Specification Methodology and its Applications to Transducer Synthesis*. PhD thesis, University of California, Berkeley, May 1988.

[Bor91]   G. Borriello. "Specification and synthesis of interface logic". In R. Camposano and W. Wolf, Editors, *High-Level VLSI Synthesis*, Kluwer Academic Publishers, Boston, 1991.

[BRSVW87]   R.K. Brayton, R. Rudell, A. Sangiovanni-Vincentelli, and A.R. Wang. "MIS: A multiple-level logic optimization system". *IEEE Transactions on Computer-Aided Design*, 6(6): 1062–1080, November 1987.

[CB87]   R. Camposano and R.K. Brayton. "Partitioning before logic synthesis". In *Proceedings of the International Conference on Computer-Aided Design*, 1987.

[CG93]   V. Chaiyakul and D.D. Gajski. "High-level transformations for minimizing syntactic variances". In *Proceedings of the Design Automation Conference*, 1993.

[Che77]   P. S. Chen. *The Entity-Relationship Approach to Logical Data Base Design*. Q.E.D. Information Sciences, Wellesley, Massachusetts, 1977.

[CLR89]   T.H. Cormen, C.E. Leiserson, and R.L. Rivest. *Introduction to Algorithms*. MIT Press, Cambridge, MA, 1989.

[CPTR89]   C.M. Chu, M. Potkonjak, M. Thaler, and J. Rabaey. "HYPER: An interactive synthesis environment for high performance real time applications". In *Proceedings of the International Conference on Computer Design*, pages 432–435, 1989.

[CR89]   R. Camposano and W. Rosenstiel. "Synthesizing circuits from behavioral descriptions". *IEEE Transactions on Computer-Aided Design*, 8(2): 171–180, February 1989.

[CS86]   C.Tseng and D.P. Siewiorek. "Automated synthesis of datapaths in digital systems". *IEEE Transactions on Computer-Aided Design*, pages 379–395, July 1986.

[CST91]   R. Camposano, L.F. Saunders, and R.M. Tabet. "High-level synthesis from VHDL". In *IEEE Design & Test of Computers*, 1991.

[CT89]   R. Camposano and R.M. Tabet. "Design representation for the synthesis of behavioral VHDL models". In *Proceedings of the International Symposium on Computer Hardware Description Languages and their Applications*, 1989.

[CT90]   R. Cloutier and D.E. Thomas. "The combination of scheduling, allocation and mapping in a single algorithm". In *Proceedings of the Design Automation Conference*, June 1990.

[CvE87]   R. Camposano and J.T. van Eijndhoven. "Partitioning a design in structural synthesis". In *Proceedings of the International Conference on Computer Design*, 1987.

[Dav83]   W. S. Davis. *Tools and Techniques for Structured Systems Analysis and Design*. Addison-Wesley, Reading, Massachusetts, 1983.

[DCH91]   N. Dutt, J. Cho, and T. Hadley. "A user interface for VHDL behavioral modeling". In *Proceedings of the International Symposium on Computer Hardware Description Languages and their Applications*, 1991.

[DeM79]   T. DeMarco. *Structured Analysis and System Specification*. Yourdon Press, New York, 1979.

[DH89]   D. Drusinsky and D. Harel. "Using Statecharts for hardware description and synthesis". In *IEEE Transactions on Computer-Aided Design*, 1989.

[DK88]   G. DeMicheli and D.C. Ku. "HERCULES - a system for high-level synthesis". In *Proceedings of the Design Automation Conference*, 1988.

[DMNSV88] S. Devadas, H.K.T. Ma, A.R. Newton, and A. Sangiovanni-Vincentelli. "MUSTANG: State assignment of finite state machines targeting multilevel logic implementations". *IEEE Transactions on Computer-Aided Design*, 7(12): 1290–1299, 1988.

[DSVA87]   G. DeMicheli, A. Sangiovanni-Vincentelli, and P. Antognetti. *Design Systems for VLSI Circuits: Logic Synthesis and Silicon Compilation*. Martinus Nijhoff Publishers, 1987.

[EHB94]   R. Ernst, J. Henkel, and T. Benner. "Hardware-software cosynthesis for microcontrollers". In *IEEE Design & Test of Computers*, pages 64–75, December 1994.

[EST78]   D.P. Siewiorek E.A. Snow and D.E. Thomas. "A technology-relative computer-aided design system: Abstract representation, transformations and design tradeoffs". In *Proceedings of the Design Automation Conference*, 1978.

[FKCD93]   D. Filo, D. Ku, C.N. Coelho, and G. DeMicheli. "Interface optimization for concurrent systems under timing constraints". In *IEEE Transactions on Very Large Scale Integration Systems*, pages 268–281, September 1993.

[FM82]   C.M. Fiduccia and R.M. Mattheyses. "A linear-time heuristic for improving network partitions". In *Proceedings of the Design Automation Conference*, 1982.

[Gaj91]   D.D. Gajski. "Essential issues and possible solutions in high-level synthesis". in R. Camposano and W. Wolf, Editors, *High-Level VLSI Synthesis*, Kluwer Academic Publishers, Boston, 1991.

[GD90]   R. Gupta and G. DeMicheli. "Partitioning of functional models of synchronous digital systems". In *Proceedings of the International Conference on Computer-Aided Design*, pages 216–219, 1990.

[GD92]   R. Gupta and G. DeMicheli. "System-level synthesis using re-programmable components". In *Proceedings of the European Conference on Design Automation (EDAC)*, pages 2–7, 1992.

[GD93]   R. Gupta and G. DeMicheli. "Hardware-software cosynthesis for digital systems". In *IEEE Design & Test of Computers*, pages 29–41, October 1993.

[GDWL91]   D.D. Gajski, N.D. Dutt, C.H. Wu, and Y.L. Lin. *High-Level Synthesis: Introduction to Chip and System Design*. Kluwer Academic Publishers, Boston, Massachusetts, 1991.

[Geb92a]   C.H. Gebotys. "Optimal scheduling and allocation of embedded VLSI chips". In *Proceedings of the Design Automation Conference*, pages 116–119, 1992.

[Geb92b]   C.H. Gebotys. "Optimal synthesis of multichip architectures". In *Proceedings of the International Conference on Computer-Aided Design*, pages 238–241, 1992.

[GGN94] J. Gong, D.D. Gajski, and S. Narayan. "Software estimation from executable specifications". In *Journal of Computer and Software Engineering*, 1994.

[Gif78] W. Giffin. *Queueing: Basic Theory and Applications*. Grid Inc., Columbus, Ohio, 1978.

[GJ79] M.R. Garey and D.S. Johnson. *Computers and Intractability: A Guide to the Theory of NP-Completeness*. Freeman, San Francisco, CA, 1979.

[GSV92] A. Gutierrez, P. Sanchez, and E. Villar. "VHDL high-level silicon compilation: Synthesis methodology and teaching experience". In *Proceedings of the Third Eurochip Workshop on VLSI Design Training*, 1992.

[GVN93] D.D. Gajski, F. Vahid, and S. Narayan. "SpecCharts: A VHDL front-end for embedded systems". UC Irvine, Dept. of ICS, Technical Report 93-31,1993.

[GVN94] D.D. Gajski, F. Vahid, and S. Narayan. "A system-design methodology: Executable-specification refinement". In *Proceedings of the European Conference on Design Automation (EDAC)*, 1994.

[Hal93] Nicolas Halbwachs. *Synchronous Programming of Reactive Systems*. Kluwer Academic Publishers, 1993.

[Har87] D. Harel. "Statecharts: A visual formalism for complex systems". *Science of Computer Programming 8*, 1987.

[HAWW88] F.T. Hady, J.H. Aylor, R.D. Williams, and R. Waxman. "Uninterpreted modeling using the VHSIC hardware description language (VHDL)". In *Proceedings of the International Conference on Computer-Aided Design*, pages 172–175, 1988.

[HB85] K. Hwang and F. Briggs. *Computer Architecture and Parallel Processing*. McGraw-Hill, 1985.

[HG91] T. Hadley and D.D. Gajski. "A decision support environment for behavioral synthesis". UC Irvine, Dept. of ICS, Technical Report 91-17,1991.

[Hil85]   P. Hilfinger. "A high-level language and silicon compiler for digital signal processing". In *Proceedings of the Custom Integrated Circuits Conference*, 1985.

[HLN+88]   D. Harel, H. Lachover, A. Naamad, A. Pnueli, M. Politi, R. Sherman, and A. Shtul-Trauring. "STATEMATE: A working environment for the development of complex reactive systems". In *Proceedings of the International Conference on Software Engineering*, 1988.

[Hoa78]   C.A.R. Hoare. "Communicating sequential processes". *Communications of the ACM*, 21(8): 666–677, 1978.

[Hoa85]   C.A.R. Hoare. *Communicating Sequential Processes*. Prentice-Hall International, Englewood Cliffs, New Jersey, 1985.

[HP90]   J.L. Hennessy and D.A. Patterson. *Computer Architecture: A Quatitative Approach*. Morgan Kaufmann Publishers Inc., San Mateo, CA, 1990.

[HR92]   P. Hilfinger and J. Rabey. *Anatomy of a Silicon Compiler*. Kluwer Academic Publishers, 1992.

[HRSV86]   M.D. Hung, F. Romeo, and A. Sangiovanni-Vincentelli. "An efficient general cooling schedule for simulated annealing". In *Proceedings of the International Conference on Computer-Aided Design*, pages 381–384, 1986.

[HS71]   A. Hashimoto and J. Stevens. "Wire routing by optimizing channel assignments within large apertures". In *Proceedings of the Design Automation Conference*, 1971.

[HT93]   J.W. Hagerman and D.E. Thomas. "Process transformation for system level synthesis". Technical Report CMUCAD-93-08, 1993.

[IEE88]   IEEE Inc., N.Y. *IEEE Standard VHDL Language Reference Manual*, 1988.

[IOJ94]   T.B. Ismail, K O'Brien, and A.A. Jerraya. "Interactive system-level partitioning with Partif". In *Proceedings of* the European Conference on Design Automation (EDAC), 1994.

[JMP88]   R. Jain, M. Mlinar, and A. Parker. "Area-time model for synthesis of non-pipelined designs". In *Proceedings of the International Conference on Computer-Aided Design*, 1988.

[Joh67]   S.C. Johnson. "Hierarchical clustering schemes". *Psychometrika*, pages 241–254, September 1967.

[JPA91]   A. Jerraya, P. Paulin, and D. Agnew. "Facilities for controllers modeling and synthesis in VHDL". In *VHDL Users' Group*, April 1991.

[KC91]   Y.C. Kirkpatrick and C.K. Cheng. "Ratio cut partitioning for hierarchical designs". *IEEE Transactions on Computer-Aided Design*, 10(7): 911–921, 1991.

[KD88]   D.C. Ku and G. DeMicheli. "HardwareC - a language for hardware design". Stanford University, Technical Report CSL-TR-90-419, 1988.

[KD91]   D. Ku and G. DeMicheli. "Synthesis of ASICs with Hercules and Hebe". in R. Camposano and W. Wolf, Editors, *High-Level VLSI Synthesis*, Kluwer Academic Publishers, Boston, 1991.

[KGRC93] F.J. Kurdahi, D.D. Gajski, C. Ramachandran, and V. Chaiyakul. "Linking register-transfer in physical levels of design". In *IEICE Transactions on Information and Systems, Vol E76-D, No 9*, September 1993.

[KGV83]   S. Kirkpatrick, C.D. Gelatt, and M. P. Vecchi. "Optimization by simulated annealing". *Science*, 220(4598): 671–680, 1983.

[KL70]   B.W. Kernighan and S. Lin. "An efficient heuristic procedure for partitioning graphs". *Bell System Technical Journal*, February 1970.

[KL93]   A. Kalavade and E.A. Lee. "A hardware/software codesign methodology for DSP applications". In *IEEE Design & Test of Computers*, 1993.

[KP87]   F.J. Kurdahi and A.C. Parker. "Real: A program for register allocation". In *Proceedings of the Design Automation Conference*, 1987.

[KP91]   K. Kucukcakar and A. Parker. "CHOP: A constraint-driven system-level partitioner". In *Proceedings of the Design Automation Conference*, 1991.

[KR78]   B. Kernighan and D. Ritchie. *The C Programming Language*. Prentice-Hall, Englewood Cliffs, NJ, 1978.

[Kri84]   B. Krishnamurthy. "An improved min-cut algorithm for partitioning VLSI networks". *IEEE Transactions on Computers*, May 1984.

[KV93]   N. Kumar and R. Vemuri. "Partitioning for multicomponent synthesis from VHDL specifications". In *VHDL International Users' Forum*, pages 19–28, 1993.

[KWK85]   S. Kung, H. Whitehouse, and T. Kailath. *VLSI and Modern Signal Processing*. Prentice-Hall, 1985.

[Lag89]   E.D. Lagnese. *Architectural Partitioning for System Level Design of Integrated Circuits*. PhD thesis, Carnegie Mellon Unversity., March 1989.

[Laz84]   E. D. Lazowska. *Quantitative System Performance: Computer System Analysis Using Queueing Network Models*. Prentice-Hall, Englewood Cliffs, New Jersey, 1984.

[Len90]   T. Lengauer. *Combinatorial Algorithms for Integrated Circuit Layout*. John Wiley and Sons, England, 1990.

[LG88]   J. Lis and D.D. Gajski. "Synthesis from VHDL". In *Proceedings of the International Conference on Computer Design*, 1988.

[LGP+91]   D. Lanneer, G. Goossens, M. Pauwels, J. Van Meerbergen, and H. De Man. "An object-oriented framework supporting the full high-level synthesis trajectory". In *Proceedings of the International Symposium on Computer Hardware Description Languages and their Applications*, pages 281–300, 1991.

[LGR92]   B. Lutter, W. Glunz, and F.J. Rammig. "Using VHDL
           for simulation of SDL specifications". In *Proceedings of
           the European Design Automation Conference (EuroDAC)*,
           pages 630–635, 1992.

[LHHR92]   N. Leveson, M. Heimdahl, H. Hildreth, and J. Reese. "Re-
           quirements specification for process-control systems". UC
           Irvine, Dept. of ICS, Technical Report 92-106,1992.

[Lis92]   J. Lis. *Behavioral Synthesis from VHDL Using Structured
           Modeling*. PhD thesis, University of California, Irvine, Jan-
           uary 1992.

[LND+91]   D. Lanneer, S. Note, F. Depuydt, M. Pauwels, F. Catthoor,
           G. Goosens, and H. De Man. "Architectural synthesis for
           medium and high throughput signal processing with the
           new CATHEDRAL environment". In R. Camposano and
           W. Wolf, Editors, *High-Level VLSI Synthesis*, Kluwer Aca-
           demic Publishers, Boston, 1991.

[LT89]   E.D. Lagnese and D.E. Thomas. "Architectural partition-
           ing for system level design". In *Proceedings of the Design
           Automation Conference*, 1989.

[LT91]   E.D. Lagnese and D.E. Thomas. "Architectural partition-
           ing for system level synthesis of integrated circuits". *IEEE
           Transactions on Computer-Aided Design*, July 1991.

[MAP93]   P. Moeschler, H.P. Amann, and F. Pellandini. "High-level
           modeling using extended timing diagrams". In *Proceed-
           ings of the European Design Automation Conference (Eu-
           roDAC)*, 1993.

[Mar91]   F. Maraninchi. "Argos: A graphical synchronous language
           for the description of reactive systems". Report RT-C29,
           Univeriste Joseph Fourier, 1991.

[McF86]   M.C. McFarland. "Using bottom-up design techniques in
           the synthesis of digital hardware from abstract behavioral
           descriptions". In *Proceedings of the Design Automation
           Conference*, 1986.

[MK90]   M.C. McFarland and T.J. Kowalski. "Incorporating bottom-up design into hardware synthesis" *IEEE Transactions on Computer-Aided Design*, September 1990.

[MW90]   R. MacDonald and R. Waxman. "Operational specification of the SINCGARS radio in VHDL". In *AFCEA-IEEE Tactical Communications Conference*, pages 1–17, 1990.

[Nes87]   J.A. Nestor. *Specification and Synthesis of Digital System with Interfaces*. PhD thesis, Carnegie Mellon Unversity., April 1987.

[NG92]   S. Narayan and D.D. Gajski. "System clock estimation based on clock slack minimization". In *Proceedings of the European Design Automation Conference (EuroDAC)*, 1992.

[NG93]   S. Narayan and D.D. Gajski. "Features supporting system specification in HDLs". In *Proceedings of the European Design Automation Conference (EuroDAC)*, 1993.

[NG94]   S. Narayan and D.D. Gajski. "Synthesis of system-level bus interfaces". In *Proceedings of the European Conference on Design Automation (EDAC)*, 1994.

[NON91]   Y. Nakamura, K. Oguri, and A. Nagoya. "Synthesis from pure behavioral descriptions". In R. Camposano and W. Wolf, Editors, *High-Level VLSI Synthesis*, Kluwer Academic Publishers, Boston, 1991.

[NT86]   J. Nestor and D. Thomas. "Behavioral synthesis with interfaces". In *Proceedings of the International Conference on Computer-Aided Design*, pages 112–115, 1986.

[NVG91a]   S. Narayan, F. Vahid, and D.D. Gajski. "System specification and synthesis with the SpecCharts language". In *Proceedings of the International Conference on Computer-Aided Design*, 1991.

[NVG91b]   S. Narayan, F. Vahid, and D.D. Gajski. "Translating system specifications to VHDL". In *Proceedings of the European Conference on Design Automation (EDAC)*, 1991.

[NVG92]   S. Narayan, F. Vahid, and D.D. Gajski. "System specification with the SpecCharts language". In *IEEE Design & Test of Computers*, Dec. 1992.

[OG86]   A. Orailoglu and D.D. Gajski. "Flow graph representation". In *Proceedings of the Design Automation Conference*, 1986.

[OvG84]   R. Otten and L. van Ginneken. "Floorplan design using simulated annealing". In *Proceedings of the International Conference on Computer-Aided Design*, pages 96–98, 1984.

[Pet81]   J. L. Peterson. *Petri Net Theory and the Modeling of Systems*. Prentice-Hall, Englewood Cliffs, New Jersey, 1981.

[PF89]   D. Pang and L. Ferrari. "Unified approach to general IFIR filter design using the B-spline function". In *Proceedings of Asilomar Conference on Signals, Systems & Computers*, 1989.

[PK89a]   P.G. Paulin and J.P. Knight. "Algorithms for high-level synthesis". In *IEEE Design & Test of Computers*, Dec. 1989.

[PK89b]   P.G. Paulin and J.P. Knight. "Force-directed scheduling for the behavioral synthesis of ASICs". *IEEE Transactions on Computer-Aided Design*, June 1989.

[PKG86]   P.G. Paulin, J.P. Knight, and E.F. Girzyc. "HAL: A multiparadigm approach to datapath synthesis". In *Proceedings of the Design Automation Conference*, 1986.

[PP85]   N. Park and A.C. Parker. "Synthesis of optimal clocking schemes". In *Proceedings of the Design Automation Conference*, 1985.

[PPM86]   A.C. Parker, T. Pizzaro, and M. Mlinar. "MAHA: A program for datapath synthesis". In *Proceedings of the Design Automation Conference*, 1986.

[Rei92]   W. Reisig. *A Primer in Petri Net Design*. Springer-Verlag, New York, 1992.

[RG91]   E.A. Rundensteiner and D.D. Gajski. "A design data base for behavioral synthesis". In *Proceedings of the International Workshop on High-Level Synthesis*, 1991.

[RG93]   L. Ramachandran and D.D. Gajski. "Architectural trade-offs in synthesis of pipelined controls". Proceedings of the European Design Automation Conference (EuroDAC), 1993.

[RSV85]   F. Romeo and A. Sangiovanni-Vincentelli. "Probabilistic hill climbing algorithms: Properties and applications". In *Proceedings of the 1985 Chapel Hill Conference on VLSI*, pages 393–417, 1985.

[RVNG92]   L. Ramachandran, F. Vahid, S. Narayan, and D.D. Gajski. "Semantics and synthesis of signals in behavioral VHDL". In *Proceedings of the European Design Automation Conference (EuroDAC)*, 1992.

[SB92]   J.S. Sun and R.W. Brodersen. "Design of system interface modules". In *Proceedings of the International Conference on Computer-Aided Design*, pages 478–481, 1992.

[Sod90]   Jag Sodhi. *Computer Systems Techniques: Development, Implementation and Software Maintenance*. TAB Professional and Reference Books, Blue Ridge Summit, Pennsylvania, 1990.

[SP91]   S.Prakash and A.C. Parker. "Synthesis of application-specific multiprocessor architectures". In *Proceedings of the Design Automation Conference*, pages 8–13, 1991.

[SSB91]   J.S. Sun, M.B. Srivastava, and R.W. Brodersen. "SIERA: A CAD environment for real-time systems". In *3rd Physical Design Workshop*, May 1991.

[SST90]   E. Sternheim, R. Singh, and Y. Trivedi. *Hardware Modeling with Verilog HDL*. Automata Publishing Company, Cupertino, CA, 1990.

[Sut88]   A. Sutcliffe. *Jackson System Development*. Prentice-Hall, New York, 1988.

[TAS93]   D.E. Thomas, J.K. Adams, and H. Schmit. "A model and methodology for hardware/software codesign". In *IEEE Design & Test of Computers*, pages 6–15, 1993.

[Teo90]   T. J. Teorey. *Database Modeling and Design: The Entity-relationship Approach*. Morgan Kaufman Publishers, San Mateo, California, 1990.

[TLK90]   T. Tikanen, T. Leppanen, and J. Kivela. "Structured analysis and VHDL in embedded ASIC design and verification". In *Proceedings of the European Conference on Design Automation (EDAC)*, pages 107–111, 1990.

[TLW+90]   D.E. Thomas, E.D. Langese, R.A. Walker, J.A. Nestor, J.V. Rajan, and R.L. Blackburn. *Algorithmic and Register-Transfer Level Synthesis: The System Architect's Workbench*. Kluwer Academic Publishers, 1990.

[TM91]   D.E. Thomas and P. Moorby. *The Verilog Hardware Description Language*. Kluwer Academic Publishers, 1991.

[VG91]   F. Vahid and D.D. Gajski. "Obtaining functionally equivalent simulations using VHDL and a time-shift transformation". In *Proceedings of the International Conference on Computer-Aided Design*, 1991.

[VG92]   F. Vahid and D.D. Gajski. "Specification partitioning for system design". In *Proceedings of the Design Automation Conference*, 1992.

[VNG91]   F. Vahid, S. Narayan, and D.D. Gajski. "SpecCharts: A language for system level synthesis". In *Proceedings of the International Symposium on Computer Hardware Description Languages and their Applications*, 1991.

[VTI88]   *VDP100 1.5 Micron CMOS Datapath Cell Library*, 1988.

[WC91]   R. Walker and R. Camposano. *A Survey of High-Level Synthesis Systems*. Kluwer Academic Publishers, 1991.

[WCG91]   C.H. Wu, V. Chaiyakul, and D.D. Gajski. "Layout-area models for high-level synthesis". In *Proceedings of the International Conference on Computer-Aided Design*, 1991.

[WM85]   P. T. Ward and S. J. Mellor. *Structured Development for Real-Time Systems.* Yourdon Press, New York, 1985.

[WT89]   R.A. Walker and D.E. Thomas. "Behavioral transformation for algorithmic level IC design". *IEEE Transactions on Computer-Aided Design*, October 1989.

[Xil89]   Xilinx Corporation. *The Programmable Gate Array Data Book*, 1989.

[YC78]   E. Yourdon and L. L. Constantine. *Structured Design: Fundamentals of a Discipline of Computer Program and Systems Design.* Yourdon Press, New York, 1978.

[YEBH93]   W. Ye, R. Ernst, T. Benner, and J. Henkel. "Fast timing analysis for hardware-software co-synthesis". In *Proceedings of the International Conference on Computer Design*, pages 452–457, 1993.

[YH90]   H.S. Yoo and A. Hsu. "Debbie: A configurable user interface for CAD frameworks". In *Proceedings of the International Conference on Computer Design*, pages 135–140, 1990.

[Zim88]   G. Zimmerman. "A new area and shape function estimation technique for VLSI layouts". In *Proceedings of the Design Automation Conference*, 1988.

Glossary

Abstraction level A measure of the implementation detail existing in a conceptual model or system specification. The more detail, the lower the abstraction level.

Allocation (v) The act of adding a new system component, such as an ASIC, to a design. (n) The set of system components in a design. (The term "allocation" is also popular in the high-level synthesis community to indicate the addition of an RT component to a design).

ASIC (Application-specific integrated circuit) A chip which can be custom designed to implement a digital function.

Behavior A piece of system functionality, more complex than an arithmetic operation.

Capture-and-simulate A design approach in which a system is first implemented and then captured as an RT or gate netlist, and then simulated to verify correct functionality.

Channel An abstract communication medium between two concurrent behaviors over which data is transferred.

Closeness A number representing the desirability of grouping two objects during partitioning, based on one or more metrics.

Component A physical object that implements functionality.

Constraint The maximum or minimum value allowed for a given metric.

Cost The value returned by an objective function, indicating the desirability of a given design. Also see "monetary cost."

Describe-and-synthesize A design approach in which a system's functionality is first described as an executable specification, simulated to verify correct functionality, and then converted, either manually or through synthesis, to an implementation.

Description See Specification.

Design (n) The structure that implements part or all of a system's functionality. (v) The act of adding structure to a system.

Designer The person whose task it is to perform system design.

Estimation Computing metric values without a complete implementation, but instead from functionality and perhaps a partial implementation.

Executable language A machine-readable and simulatable language.

Functional object A variable, behavior, or channel derived from an executable specification.

Functional partitioning The act of partitioning functional objects among system components.

Implement The act of creating a structure that executes a given functionality. Also, the act of a structure executing a given functionality, e.g. an ALU implements arithmetic operations.

Implementation The structure that completely implements a system's functionality, at a level of detail suitable for manufacturing.

Interface process A behavior which accomplishes data transfer between incompatible protocols of communicating behaviors.

High-level synthesis The act of converting an ASIC's executable specification to an RT-level structure, by performing the tasks of scheduling, allocation, and binding. The tasks may be fully or partially automated.

Metric A parameter used to evaluate an implementation's quality or desirability.

Modeler The person whose task it is to write an executable specification.

Monetary cost The price of an implementation.

Natural language A spoken language.

Objective function A function which evaluates the desirability of a design based on quality metrics and constraints.

Partition (n) An assignment of objects to groups.

Partitioning (v) The act of assigning each object from a set of objects to groups.

Process A behavior which is concurrent with other behaviors.

Processor A system component which implements functionality by sequencing through a set of states, where in each state it sets control line values to move data through a datapath, such that a particular computation is achieved. The component may be a standard, off-the-shelf processor such as an Intel 8086, or it may be custom designed.

Protocol Communication details specifying the sequence of data transfers and control signaling over a fixed set of wires.

RT component A physical object that implements register-transfer (RT) level functionality, such as an ALU, counter, or register.

Selection The addition of a new RT component, such as an ALU, to a design.

Specification A written description of desired system functionality. A *natural-language* specification is described using a language spoken by humans. An *executable specification* is described using a formal, machine-readable language which can be simulated in order to verify the functionality.

Standard component A previously designed off-the-shelf component with a fixed functionality and interface.

Standard language An executable language with a large base of users and supporting tools.

Structural partitioning The act of partitioning structural components among system components.

Structure An interconnection of components.

System A set of inputs and outputs, a functionality, and possibly a set of components that implements the functionality. The functionality is more complex than arithmetic operations, consisting instead is one or more algorithms.

System component A physical object that implements system-level functionality, such as an ASIC, processor, or memory.

System design The act of allocating system components, partitioning system functionality among those components, and defining the functionality of each component, in order to implement a system's functionality.

System functionality The complete actions of a system, defining the system's outputs as a function of its inputs and of time.

Index